THE
NATURAL
GARDEN

THE
NATURAL
GARDEN

KEN DRUSE

DESIGN BY
BARBARA PECK

Clarkson N. Potter, Inc./Publishers
DISTRIBUTED BY CROWN PUBLISHERS, INC., NEW YORK

To mentors, teachers, visionaries, and friends.
Elvin McDonald
Marilyn Bethany
Lois Molinari
and
Victor Nelson

Principal photography by Ken Druse

Published by Clarkson N. Potter, Inc.
201 East 50th Street, New York, New York 10022.
Member of the Crown Publishing Group.

Random House, Inc. New York, Toronto, London, Sydney, Auckland

CLARKSON N. POTTER, POTTER, and colophon are trade-
marks of Clarkson N. Potter, Inc.

Manufactured in China

Designed by Barbara Peck

Library of Congress Cataloging-in-Publication Data

Druse, Ken.
The natural garden.

Bibliography: p.
Includes index.
1. Natural gardens, American.   2. Natural gardens,
American—Pictorial works.   I. Title.
SB457.53.D78   1988   712'.6   87-22443
ISBN 0-517-55046-6

10   9   8   7   6

ACKNOWLEDGMENTS

*W*hen you've worked on a project for several years, a quandary arises—not whom to thank, but how many wonderful and supportive people can be mentioned in the allotted space.

Elvin McDonald, one of the great garden writers, has always been a model to me—for his work, of course, but mostly because he manages to remain true and honest. Marilyn Bethany, Design Editor of New York magazine and an extraordinary writer, has taught me a great deal.

Many people have influenced and inspired me. Mark Hulla and Wayne Harrison taught me to "see." Ron Borus and Victoria Borus showed me the gracious life. My dear friend Petie Buck has shared her ideas and friendship for more years than we'd like to count. And Judith Bromley has always been there to help.

I'd like to thank Linda Yang for commiserating with me, fellow photographer Felice Frankel for her understanding and support, and author Deirdre Colby.

I'm very grateful to JoAnn Barwick, Peggy Kennedy, Merv Kaufman, and all the other members of the House Beautiful staff for their patience during the time it took to create this book.

I must acknowledge Carol Southern, the guiding light at Potter; my editor, Gretchen Salisbury, who understood and shared my vision from the first; and Martina D'Alton, without whose help, I can honestly say, there would not be The Natural Garden.

I want also to thank the designer of this book, Barbara Peck, who was able to please my greatest critic (me); Creative Director, Gael Towey; Production Supervisor, Teresa Nicholas; Executive Managing Editor of Crown, Laurie Stark; Maria Bottino, our Production Editor; and Amy Schuler, Assistant Editor.

Thanks also to Jack Keely; to my close friend, Jim Doyle; to my parents, Helen and Harold Druse; and to my sister, Bobbi Druse Fischer, and her wonderful family.

My deepest gratitude to Lois Molinari for her confidence and hard work, and to Victor Nelson for always standing by. And a special blessing to Peter, the dog, who shared half my life with me and will always be in my heart.

And lastly, I'd like to thank all the wonderful home owners who shared their knowledge and their gardens with me and with you.

C O N T

E   N   T   S

PLANNING AND PLANTING
A NATURAL GARDEN

THE
NEW AMERICAN
LANDSCAPE

INTRODUCTION TO THE NATURAL GARDEN

Until recently the standard approach to the home landscape included a large expanse of grass lawn, disciplined beds of annuals, and brutally pruned shrubs. In most cases, the wisdom of such a landscape went unquestioned, even though home owners were actually battling nature instead of working with it to maintain their homesites. The same theme was repeated over and over throughout rural and suburban America even where inappropriate or environmentally unsound—in parts of the Southwest, for example, where water,

needed in abundance for a verdant lawn, is at a premium. No matter where it is located, keeping such a landscape "perfect" also requires the extensive use of chemical fertilizers, pesticides, and herbicides. Many of these substances are petroleum based, expensive, and ultimately hazardous to the environment. Sensitive gardeners are beginning to look for alternatives.

The overriding drawback of the traditional American homesite, however, is the tremendous amount of time and energy needed to maintain the typical lawn-and-annual-bed landscape. I shudder when I think of the hours spent in mowing grass lawns, deadheading annuals, shearing hedges, feeding, spraying, and so on. In this cycle of perpetual care, you quickly become a slave to your environment rather than a participant in its beautification.

WORKING WITH NATURE

The approach in *The Natural Garden* changes this system dramatically. Essentially, the Natural Garden is a garden planted with species that are natural to their envi-

ronments, species that would grow wild. Plants are chosen with an entire year, or years, in mind—they are not expected to work for just one season—and the garden design makes use of long-lasting natural materials. Thus the garden is beautiful year-round as well as being easy to maintain. Lawn is reduced to the minimum needed for recreation, shrubs bloom throughout and are seldom pruned, color comes from dependable perennials and easy-care hybrids, and spaces for entertaining are paved with permanent materials that match the resources in the landscape and require little care. Your garden is the product of a close collaboration between you and nature, in which what you want from the garden is met by the character of your particular location. Instead of fighting the elements to create that perfect lawn and formal garden, you work in partnership with nature to discover and enhance the best features of the land. The results look relaxed and spontaneous, and the entire homesite is more self-reliant than in the past.

This does not mean simply letting the landscape go. Nor does it mean that the garden is completely maintenance-free. Its care, however, is greatly reduced; you will decide how much time you wish to devote to work in the garden.

In the Natural Garden, massive changes are rarely undertaken. A respect for the character of your landscape is nurtured, with room for careful adjustment. Through sensitive planning and observation of what grows well in the wild places in your area, you design a garden that is appropriate to your own climate and terrain. In a heavily wooded place, you may wish to thin some trees to create a sunny clearing, or in a seaside garden, you may need to improve the soil in selected pockets with humus. Otherwise, you will be working to bring out the personality of your homesite. If its essential character is sunny and dry, a meadow of sun-loving grasses and perennials might

be appropriate; if there is a large rock outcropping, it may become the garden's focal point—host to ferns and mosses and all manner of rock-garden plants; if wetland predominates, moisture-loving plants and perhaps a water garden can be created; and if it's a shaded woodland, a wildflower garden, including such desirable natives as lady's slipper orchids, will flourish. A steep

embankment can support ground-hugging covers, some of which bloom from spring to fall. In shade too dense for lawn, a sea of ferns looks cool even on the hottest days. All these results are easier to achieve, maintain, and, in the long run, afford than a weed-free lawn.

In the Natural Garden plants perform many functions. Besides being lovely, they can frame your property, enhance desirable views, or hide unsightly ones; they provide shade to cool a recreation area and color and texture to enrich the landscape. No matter how plants are used, they will make your landscape more livable and inviting and, as a bonus, will increase its value.

INSPIRATION FROM NATURE

Although there is a growing body of literature on naturalistic garden design, nature is still the primary source of inspiration. Unfortunately, true native American wilderness has almost disappeared. Even protected areas—state and national parks—can become endangered, especially when commercially valuable resources are discovered there. Think of wilderness simply as those places where plants grow untended: California coastal highway meadows, Rocky Mountain glens of

aspen, New England woodlands, southwestern deserts, perhaps even the vacant lot at the end of your street. The list of such places is long and the inspiration to be gleaned from them is boundless.

The first step for any natural gardener should be to take a walk in the wild places in your area, carefully noting and identifying what grows there. You may find an appealing spot that resembles your property. Perhaps this will be a forest with its treetop canopy, understory of flowering shrubs, and floor of mosses, ferns, and wildflowers. Such a sight might inspire you to create, in miniature, a woodland retreat, resplendent with botanical wonders seen in the wild. Observe

how nature softens the edges of the forest; these transitional, staged, and layered plantings belong in your garden. Watch the ribbon of water, the woodland stream, and consider adding a water element to your garden. If water is out of the question, mimic the rush and flow of the stream with a cascade of flowering perennials or a meandering path of smooth-washed gravel.

Inspiration is all around you.

Even in teeming cities there are parks, and within their borders you can usually find an attractive wooded area where plants whose seeds may have been borne on the wind now grow wild. Most large parks also have a water element, a lake or stream, along whose banks are water plants. A small garden in the heart of the city can capture the mood of these places. Throughout the country is another source of inspiration, and an unlikely one at that—many of the country's highways are lined with beautiful, thriving wildings—California's Highway 1, New York's award-winning Taconic Parkway, or, in Virginia and North Carolina, the Blue Ridge Parkway that winds through some of America's botanical wonders.

Part of the credit for the ongoing beautification of America's highways belongs to Lady Bird Johnson, who promoted Operation Wildflower, a Texas project conceived in the 1930s but barely implemented until recently. Under her direction, land flanking Texan highways was partially seeded with wildflowers and encouraged to evolve naturally. Mrs. Johnson helped convince the highway maintenance department that this would be feasible and beneficial as well as beautiful. Her success can be seen today in the oceans of blue bonnets and drifts of yellow evening primrose or orange Indian paintbrush. Several other states have followed suit—notably Maryland, Georgia, and Oklahoma—helping to reeducate Americans to the beauty of wild plants growing free.

Places set aside for the promotion and conservation of wild plants are another good source of inspiration. One of the best known of these is the Garden in the Woods in Framingham, Massachusetts. Operated by the New England Wild Flower Society, the garden is staffed by experts who provide information and advice to visitors about their own gardens. There are similar organizations, including arboretums, botanical gardens, and nature preserves, in other parts of the country (see Source Guide, pages 287–92). In planning your Natural Garden do not neglect such ready sources of information about the plants that will do well in your area.

In your search for inspiration, visit your neighbors as well. Talk to them about their experiences, trade expertise, find out which plants have thrived in their gardens.

LOOKING BACK

No one knows when the first orna-

mental plants were nurtured, but most likely the earliest designed gardens were linked to wealth. It was a luxury to set aside land for plants that were valued primarily for their beauty.

Many centuries ago in China, the nobility created massive game preserves where they hunted and rode. Later, they created gardens, which, like the game parks, emulated nature. The craggy mountains of China were represented by rock constructions called *Jia shan,* and lakes, streams, and waterfalls were created, diverted, or otherwise controlled. China's gardens inspired Japan's meticulous, carefully controlled garden spaces.

In the West, garden styles were based on security and availability of water, in addition to wealth. In Egypt, for example, irrigation dictated that gardens would be based on formal, symmetrical plans, with walls surrounding the water source. Islamic and, later, Italian designs also followed this style. In the monastery garden, square planting beds radiated from the water source and all was enclosed by a wall to keep out animals and human intruders.

Cloistered gardens were also preferred by royalty and nobility. In England, Henry VIII's garden further developed this theme with elaborate, meticulously trimmed hedges, resembling interwoven rope knots, that ornamented the borders of the beds. Knot gardens became the fashion among the upper classes in England and, eventually, in France.

While the upper classes were competing with their elaborate formal gardens, the English peasants, prompted perhaps by necessity, developed the hodgepodge gardening

style we know as the cottage garden. Most plants in these gardens were utilitarian, a mélange of herbs and ornamentals. The haphazard arrangement was easy to maintain and filled the front yards of peasant homes throughout rural Britain.

A century later, England's upper classes also loosened their grip on formalism. When wealthy Britons began to travel beyond their tiny isle, they were enthralled by what they found, from the picturesque ruins of Italy to the asymmetrical, naturalistic gardens of exotic China. Returning to England, they began to echo foreign gardening styles and pastoral ideals. Ultimately, English gardeners abandoned both formalism and topiary in favor of what came to be called the "landskip" style. Pursued by such "place makers" as Lancelot "Capability" Brown, perhaps the foremost landscape designer, and planned on a massive scale, these huge gardens had no defined beginnings and no confined limits; they were just one endless verdant paradise of grass and ponds and woods, dotted with laboriously constructed "instant ruins"—follies and temples. Beautiful to behold, these enormous romantic creations were extremely costly and remained strictly the creations of the very rich. They were supposed to appear "natural" and, while they succeeded in doing so, they actually depended on acres of lawn to achieve their visual coherence and required massive restructuring of the landscape into hills, valleys, and lakes. Armies of gardeners were employed to maintain them.

With the nineteenth century, formalism returned. Victorian gardeners created great parterre beds planted with annuals. These annuals were tropical plants collected from the corners of the Empire and raised in abundance from seed. Ill-suited to harsh northern winters, they lasted only a single season. Later in the nineteenth century, huge glass greenhouses, a product of the technical advances of the Industrial Revolution, were perfected. Their development meant that the seeds of tender tropicals could be started indoors. The well-formed seedlings would then be transplanted outside once they were strong and winter's frost had passed. It was an elaborate scheme. Greenhouses, and the gardens surrounding them, became status symbols for the emerging class of wealthy industrialists.

The next influential departure from formalism was in direct reaction against the "carpet bedding" of annuals, as it was known. In the 1870s, William Robinson, an Irish garden-writer, published *The Wild Garden* and started the *Garden* magazine. In his writings, Robinson attacked formalism and presented a "new" way of gardening that took its inspiration from nature. In *The Wild Garden,* he found fault with the practice of growing annuals, which often meant "a general rooting out of all the old favourites . . . to such an extent that it was not uncommon . . . to find the largest gardens in the country without a single hardy flower."

Robinson did choose plant materials collected from distant lands, but he chose only plants from those temperate regions that were similar in climate to the British Isles. This meant plants that "might be naturalized, with a very slight amount of trouble, in many situations in our plantations, fields, and woods—a world of delightful plant beauty that we might in these ways make happy around us"—or, the right plant for the right place. While Robinson's views are most appealing, in general his creations were still on a large scale and demanded special attention. One garden writer of the time commented in all seriousness, "At last there is a landscape that can be maintained by only four people."

Perhaps Robinson's most lasting contribution to horticulture was his influence on one of the leading landscape designers of all time—Gertrude Jekyll. A native of Surrey, Jekyll popularized the herbaceous border, that long row of staged flowering perennials that we associate with the English garden. A prolific writer, in 1899 she published the influential *Wood and Garden* and in it credited much of her success to

the little cottage gardens that help to make our English waysides the prettiest in the temperate world. One can hardly go into the smallest cottage garden without learning or observing something new. . . . But the lesson I have thoroughly learnt, and wish to pass on to others, is to know the enduring happiness that the love of a garden gives. For the love of gardening is a seed that once sown never dies, but always grows to an enduring and ever increasing source of happiness.

Many of Gertrude Jekyll's practices are not suitable to the Natural Garden, as they too require staffs of gardeners to keep the plantings staked and well groomed. Jekyll's love for the garden, however, ex-

pressed so eloquently in her recently reissued books, is inspirational.

Developments in England were keenly felt on this side of the Atlantic. In the seventeenth century, this meant the colonists were striving for formalism. Recently, at Bacon's Castle, a small town in Virginia, a formal, English-style Renaissance garden dating to the 1680s was excavated. Its carefully laid out plan of rectangular beds and borders directly parallels formal gardens in England from the same period. Soil analysis will probably indicate similar plant materials as well.

In the mid-nineteenth century,

American Andrew Jackson Downing avidly promoted the landscape style he had seen in England. His 1841 book, *A Treatise on the Theory and Practice of Gardening Applied to North America,* became the bible of America's new generation of landscape architects, notably Frederick Law Olmsted, who designed parks across America. Many New Yorkers believe that when Manhattan was planned a central area was simply left as wilderness and named Central Park. This is far from the truth. Olmsted transformed former pastures into the park, creating hills, lakes, streams, lawns, woodland, rocky glens, and other "natural" features. He estimated that if all the soil he had brought in from other places were spread evenly over the surface of the park, it would be more than four feet deep. Olmsted's creations, many of which have reached the century mark intact, are found in cities across America, from Boston, Massachusetts, to Berkeley, California.

America's unique contribution to the history of domestic landscape design truly begins in the twentieth century with the concept of the garden as "outdoor living space." The late landscape architect Thomas Church, in his widely read book *Gardens Are for People* (1955, reissued in 1983), presented the home landscape as an extension of the house, a convenient space for recreation and entertainment. His landscapes, mostly situated in the western United States, included swimming pools, cooking and eating areas, and paved spaces, and many of his innovations have been adopted by gardeners all over the United States and in Europe. His designs, however, still required heavy maintenance, featuring, among other things, large plots of lawn, pots of annuals, and pruned shrubs. Designed for carefree living, these gardens often required more time for maintenance than they allowed for simple relaxation.

In this century, several influential American landscape architects have promoted a natural style of gardening. The late Jens Jensen of Chicago, who has been called the

"Frank Lloyd Wright" of landscape architecture, pursued the great potential in the inherent flora of a site by integrating additions as subtle parts of the landscape. A necessity such as a drainage ditch might be disguised as a woodland stream with a bridge cunningly made to mimic a fallen tree. In New England, A. E. Bye, the elder statesman of naturalism, has created many natural gardens. He "edits" the environment, removing some plants to reveal exceptional features, such as a rock outcropping, and adding to the beautiful plants already thriving in their native home —from ferns and wildflowers to shrubs and trees.

There are other firms, such as Oehme, Van Sweden & Associates in Washington, D.C., or Ron Lutsko Jr. & Associates in San Francisco, who pursue similar courses. Their work is found in many of the photographs in this book.

In the best Natural Gardens of today, the traditions of the past are represented, but with an important difference—the most demanding aspects of these past garden styles have been eliminated. The casual arrangements of the cottage garden and the romantic schemes of the English landskip are so attractive, however, that their styles are welcome in your garden. Just limit your plant selection to those that will grow best for you. Even a formal design is appropriate to a Natural Garden if paving is substituted for grass, and beautiful hardy perennials, ornamental grasses, and other plants replace the annuals and delicate plants of the past that needed pruning and deadheading. You can create a sentimental feeling, incorporate the naturalness of William Robinson's creations, or integrate into your design the humanizing influences of Thomas Church. By picking and choosing, analyzing and synthesizing, you will carry forward the great traditions of the past, adjusted to suit the modern world.

THE NATURAL GARDEN DEFINED

Like people, no two plots of earth are exactly the same. Each has its own personality, complete with strengths and weaknesses, and each will suggest its own garden design. Even so, all Natural Gardens have some things in common. Not only are they inspired by nature, especially by the character of the region in which they are situated, but they are also based on certain principles of design. The garden is organized into three distinct areas; these are planted with carefully selected, easy-care plants; and a variety of permanent elements, from paved

terraces and paths to sturdy outdoor furniture, are chosen for their low maintenance requirements. (The actual design process is covered in greater detail in the planning guide, pp. 234–37.)

NATURAL GARDEN AREAS

The division of the Natural Garden into three areas gives it an essential cohesiveness and adds to its manageability. These areas need not be sharply delineated—in fact, they often flow into each other—nor are there hard and fast rules about their relative size, character, or position on the site. Instead they are planned in response to the character of the land, but within the garden, each area does have its own purpose. I call them the Inner, In-Between, and Outer Areas.

The Inner Area is the most formal. It is the private space, screened from neighbors and sometimes sheltered from the elements. Here you entertain friends, sunbathe, read, eat, or congregate with the family. It is the inner sanctum of the Natural Garden, where elements from paint to plants are chosen for near-permanence and durability. Because it is the most heavily used part of the garden it should ideally be paved with a hard-surfaced material—brick or flagstone or the like

—which will be both easy to care for and aesthetically pleasing. If you have small children, however, you will probably prefer a small expanse of soft lawn for their play area; later when the children are grown, you may decide to pave over this space.

The In-Between Area is the "view" from your core space, from inside the house or from the inner area. Here you can let your imagination run free, creating great sweeps of color with masses of flowering plants. In fact, season-long color is the most frequent theme of the In-Between Area, whether in a meadow planting or in free-flowing flower beds. The plantings here are the most ambitious in the Natural Garden; they require forethought, design, preparation, and most of the maintenance of your low-maintenance garden.

The Outer Area is the wildest part of the Natural Garden. In many cases it will be woodland with a canopy of trees, an understory of flowering shrubs, and a floor of evergreen ground cover, ferns, and shade-tolerant wildflowers; it is the last place on earth to grow lawn. There is almost no garden too small for such a woodland setting. Even a strip 6 feet deep by 20 feet wide, perhaps at the rear of a small city garden, is enough to support such growth. Set along the fringe of your property, the informal plantings of the Outer Area form a backdrop for the elaborate

plantings of the In-Between Area. They may also serve several practical functions—ensuring privacy, cutting off the world by hiding it from view, acting as a buffer for noise, and providing wind protection for the Inner Area.

Occasionally you will want to venture into the Outer Area. You should therefore include a path of some kind in its design. This can be a simple dirt path, which will eventually wear smooth, or a more elaborate fieldstone, pebble, or stepping-stone path. As you walk it, pick wildflowers or edible berries

if you have them, or simply wander into your own bit of wilderness for a moment of restorative peace.

PERMANENT ELEMENTS

The woodland path in the Outer Area and the paved surface of the Inner Area are just two of the permanent elements in your Natural Garden. Other such elements include outdoor furniture, a lighting system, fencing, perhaps a gazebo or a bridge over a stream, and even decorative touches such as sculpture or garden urns. All these items will be chosen for their low maintenance as well as their aesthetic appeal.

PLANT SELECTION

The three areas of the Natural Garden organize your space, and the permanent elements reduce maintenance, but only careful plant selection will make the Natural Garden succeed. The idea is to use the right plant in the right place; by choosing plants that are perfectly suited to your location, you will at the same time be choosing those that require the least care.

Several years ago, I found myself

facing a challenge: I had acquired enough space for a new garden. The site was a very unusual one. There were great views: to the south the twin towers of the World Trade Center, to the north the dramatic silhouette of the Empire State Building. Where, you may wonder, in such an urban setting can there be room for a private garden? The answer is that the patch of "ground" I called my garden was actually a tar-covered rooftop seven stories above lower Manhattan's SoHo streets. Not only was I determined to turn this space into a garden, but it was to be a Natural Garden, a counterpoint to the formality and discipline of the vast urban landscape surrounding it.

The garden that finally evolved surpassed even my wildest dreams. In it I tested some of the basics of

the Natural Garden: by seeking inspiration from nature and carefully choosing the right plant for the right place, it is possible to create a garden that is low on maintenance and high on the rewards of beauty and relaxation. In my case, this meant planting in containers of varying sizes and shapes and handling the difficulties that such plantings entail. Because the containers were subjected to driving winds and exposed to intense radiant heat in the summer, working with nature meant that I had to seek out hardy, drought-tolerant meadow flowers and other plants—the same plants that thrive in the neglect of wild spaces. My garden finally bloomed with hundreds of daylilies, purple cone flowers, Queen Anne's lace, black-eyed Susans, and iris, and it looked beautiful throughout the seasons.

In your garden, too, nature is your partner and companion; nature will see to it that a carefully selected and sited plant thrives with little attention from you. Finicky, fussy plants—those that need frequent dividing, staking, or coddling of any kind—are out. Shrubs that are susceptible to insect infestations, or trees that host infectious diseases, are not welcome.

You do need variety—primarily to create visual richness and beauty,

but also for the sake of your garden's health. By planting a mix of species, you reduce the chance of being devastated by a host-specific disease (as when, several years ago, the elm trees that shaded so many of America's streets fell victim to Dutch elm disease). Therefore, you will want to choose a variety of vigorous plants with few bad habits, adaptable to the widest range of conditions, whose needs and requirements closely match the intended environment. They should also be long-living plants that will need replacement only infrequently.

Once these requirements are met, the range of choices from nature's catalogue is vast; it includes any plant that suits the climate and location, is easy-care (does not require extensive watering, for example), and can do battle with weeds for garden supremacy. Some of these plants are wild American natives, others are naturalized citizens that have been introduced over the last two hundred years. You need not exclude the latter on the grounds of purity. Many of them arrived as seeds clinging to the clothing of immigrants or tucked into packing crates, botanical stowaways aboard ships bound for the New World; others were imported deliberately for economic reasons or ornamental uses. Eventually most of these

plants escaped from warehouses or railroad cars and settled into their new land. These naturalized aliens are more than welcome in the Natural Garden. Among their numbers are some of the most beloved wildflowers. The sunny daisy (*Chrysanthemum leucanthemum*), sky blue chicory (*Cichorium intybus*), and Queen Anne's lace (*Daucus carota* var. *carota*), actually a wild carrot, are just a few of the hundreds of aliens that came from every corner of Europe or Canada. The tawny daylily (*Hemerocallis fulva*) and the familiar beach rose (*Rosa rugosa*), which blooms with white or deep pink flowers and bears edible fruits called hips, traveled from Asia. Other plants came from India, Africa, and other parts of the globe.

While you will want to include as many of these wild plants—both native and alien—as possible, that does not mean excluding hybrids. The breeders' purpose in developing new plants is improvement, and most of their achievements have benefited mankind greatly. Plants have been bred for higher yields, longer blooming periods, sturdier growth, or greater resistance to disease or insects than their wild ancestors. Some hybrids can thrive in very specific conditions, during a drought or under a burning sun, for

example. Hybridists also develop new forms of old varieties. From the handful of ancestral species of plants there are now many thousands of dependable garden hybrids in every corner of the plant kingdom. For the natural gardener, including hybrids is simply a matter of pick and choose, and there are such rewarding ones, sturdy and subtly colored, that it would be folly to ignore them.

Unfortunately, not all hybridization has been for the better. In producing larger, more vividly colored ornamental plants, the hybridist has also sometimes bred out desirable qualities such as the sweet fragrances of yesteryear. Old gardening books sing the praises of the lovely aroma of evening nicotiana, but sadly, today's 'Nicki' hybrid is nearly devoid of scent. And in many cases, the huge size of the modern hybrid seems freakish and the enhanced color garish, reversing the old adage: bigger—and brighter—is not always better. Many gardeners are now seeking seeds and stock from firms that carry nonhybrids and older varieties, often referred to as heirlooms, antiques, or traditionals.

For the Natural Garden you will probably want to choose hybrids with subtle colors that blend compatibly with their wild cousins. Daylilies, for example, offer an extraordinary range of choice. From a few simple wildings, hybridists have produced over ten thousand registered, named varieties. I cannot imagine my garden without 'Catherine Woodbury', an exquisite cream and lavender flower dusted with pink, or 'Prairie Blue-eyes', a lilac-colored bloom. These natives, aliens, and hybrids are the plants

you choose to set out in your Natural Garden. There are also those inevitable plants that choose you—the volunteers—plants that grow from seeds accidentally introduced, borne on the wind, attached to clothing, or brought to the garden by birds and wild animals. These can be very happy accidents and should be watched for and welcomed.

This chapter has been a broad introduction to the Natural Garden—its character, components, and origins. In subsequent chapters you will see these principles at work and come away with a whole "wish list" for your own garden. The practical advice and lists of sources will help you make your wishes come true. The plants that are included in each chapter of this book are highlighted in lists within the chapters. Detailed descriptions and growing information can be found in the Plant Selection (page 242–83).

We Americans are, by and large, an outdoor people, pursuing sport and recreation, peace and pleasure, health and happiness in the great outdoors of our spectacular homeland. Often, the wild places can only be found by leaving home; it is my hope to change this, to help you bring the flavor of the wilderness close to home—to just a few steps beyond the garden door.

A PORTFOLIO OF

*The fresh, independent style of the Natural Garden
has been honed and developed by an inspired group of
pioneers. These gardeners are eager to get the word
out: ease of culture and beauty can be realized by
working with nature, not against it. Some of them are
dedicated, revolutionary landscape architects; others are
simply adventurous homeowners imbued with a love of*

NATURAL GARDENS

nature and sensitive to the integrity of their land. This chapter features seven Natural Gardens, some created by professionals, some by gifted amateurs. They reflect the range of possibilities and present inventive solutions to a variety of landscapes and locations. That the Natural Garden style is appropriate to so many situations is a measure of its strength and resilience.

A GARDEN FOR COLOR

On a single acre of sloping Connecticut woodland, Ruth and Jim Levitan have created a garden of intense season-long color. The original site was a fairly typical tangle of thorny underbrush and root-clogged, rocky New England soil. Into this landscape had been wedged an equally typical developer's house, which Ruth's mother humorously called "the shoe box in the woods." When the Levitans purchased the property in the early 1960s, both had

law careers. After a few years, they also had three daughters to raise. They had little time to devote to the garden. Gradually, however, as the family settled down, the children grew, and they came to know their woodland acre better, the Levitans became intrigued with the idea of creating a garden that would be both a private retreat and a natural outgrowth of the landscape. Even at this early stage, Ruth recognized her own inexperience as a liability. She began an intensive series of courses at the New York Botanical Garden, sharing her newly acquired expertise with Jim, and the two of them began to plan and plant the garden.

In the best traditions of the Natural Garden, they let the design come from the land's own structure and faced its personality with admirable realism. First, they analyzed the patterns of use that they had already traced on their land over the years. The children, for example, had forged trails through the thickets to such favored sites as a picnic rock, a neighbor's house, and a small pond. The Levitans used these as their starting points, the skeleton on which to arrange their plantings. They widened the trails, covering them with a carpet of grass. "Land is like a person you marry thinking you can change him," says Ruth, "and of course you can't." And so, although they both wielded crowbars to remove or reposition ornery New England boulders, they left many such immutables in place, simply incorporating them into

ABOVE: *The In-Between Area, looking toward Outer Area woodland. White dogwood and brilliant red azaleas* (A. indicum) *form woodland understory and transitional growth.* **RIGHT:** *Jack in the-pulpit* (Arisaema atrorubens).

their scheme. Finally, after careful consideration, discussion, and some admittedly heated arguments, they cleared some of the trees to let in more light, essential not only to the existing dogwoods but also to the flowering plants they planned to add.

The additions were made slowly; there was never a "master blue print" to follow. As they grew more knowledgeable and came to understand fully the soil composition, available light, and microclimate of their site, they matched plants to location. Today, what began as a spring-blooming garden, although it retains its peak period of bloom, also supplies a summer-long display of contrasting and complementary colors and textures, and daylilies become

the seasonal showstoppers. Tucked into the landscape are three carefully chosen pieces of sculpture: a whimsical rabbit, a fountain figure by the pond, and Roseanne George's sculpture of parents bathing their child, set in a sweeping planting of a bugleweed hybrid (*Ajuga reptans*).

Even though it has no walls or fences, the garden possesses a rare feeling of privacy, of a world apart, with quiet corners for contemplation by the still waters of the pond, or on a garden seat under a flowering dogwood. The "shoe box" house may be unchanged, but it now has an understated dignity, its straight lines acting almost as an Oriental element to break the flowing lines of the garden.

LEFT: *The small trees of the woodland understory include a magnolia, center, past flowering, as well as dogwood. A Japanese pieris* (Pieris japonica) *blooms, left center, beyond an azalea.*
ABOVE: *In the Outer Area the grass path narrows past a deciduous azalea in bloom, left.*

LEVITAN GARDEN: SELECTED PLANT LIST

Ground covers for color	*Ajuga reptans*, bugleweed
	Aurinia saxatilis (Alyssum saxatile), basket-of-gold
	Aquilegia canadensis, columbine
	Dicentra eximia, bleeding-heart
	Myosotis alpestris, forget-me-not
	Narcissus sp. and hybrids, daffodils
	Phlox divaricata, phlox
	P. subulata, moss pink
	Polemonium foliosissimum (*P. caeruleum*), Jacob's-ladder
	Trillium spp., wake robin
	Viola hybrids, violets
Trees	*Cornus florida*, dogwood
	Magnolia x *soulangiana*, saucer magnolia
	Asian and native rhododendrons are the most prevalent shrubs. They include evergreen and deciduous species and hybrids.

A plan for this garden appears on page 236.

A SMALL GARDEN IN A BIG CITY

The Georgetown area of Washington, D.C., is one of the most elegant residential communities in America. Along its quiet, tree-lined streets are carefully kept town houses and small, mostly formal gardens. Yet tucked into this rarefied world is a tiny piece of wilderness. It is the garden of Anne Sheffield's town house, and it is no accident that this little wilderness thrives, for in fact it has been carefully planned and planted.

PAGE 20:
An oversized ceramic urn, one of a pair by Curtis Ripley, provides a formal focal point beside the pool;
PAGE 21: *The Inner Area viewed from the upper level.*
PRECEDING PAGES: *The house, cloaked in Boston ivy (Parthenocissus tricuspidata) and viewed in summer,* **LEFT,** *when yellow coneflowers (Rudbeckia fulgida 'Goldsturm') are in bloom; and in fall,* **RIGHT,** *when the ivy, now rust colored, and maiden grass (Miscanthus sinensis 'Gracillimus') fill the foreground.*

The site is fairly typical of city gardens—a long sliver of space, in this case literally wedged between its neighbors, tapering from 18 feet wide at the house to a mere 14 feet at its farthest boundary. The original garden was unused and sadly neglected. It sloped away from the house at a sharp angle and was covered with weeds and a few scraggly raspberry shrubs.

Ms. Sheffield, who is deeply involved in Washington life, did not want a standard lawn-and-flower bed garden, even if one had been feasible in such an awkward tiny space. Living alone and not a do-it-yourselfer, she had neither time nor inclination to work in a garden. With this in mind, she hired the landscape architectural firm of Oehme, Van Sweden & Associates and gave them a simple directive: create a formal entertaining area, and a natural viewing garden that would serve as a backdrop to frequent social gatherings and would need very low maintenance. Their solution was to divide the 40-foot long space into a formal area, a lev-

eled and paved terrace just behind the house, and an informal area, the lower garden, planted with easy-care grasses and flowers, and connected to the terrace by a small staircase. Twelve carefully placed double outlets were installed throughout to allow for flexible lighting, and the garden fairly twinkles at night with spots and mushroom lamps. Because the Washington climate is relatively mild (zone 7), the outdoor space can be used roughly from April to October; during the few remaining months, it functions as a viewing garden and has been planted with appropriate species to assure year-round interest. Even in deep winter, when seen from within the house, the garden is a still life of dried grasses and flowers against a curtain of evergreens.

As for maintenance, the only regular chores are watering the container plants on the terrace and—hardly a chore—venturing into the lower garden from time to time to pick flowers or harvest raspberries from the pruned and restored shrubs.

ABOVE: *The dining area is on a separate level of the Inner Area, defined by an old balustrade, which, like the garden bench, was salvaged from a wrecking company. The redwood fence assures privacy.*

BELOW: *Boston ivy softens the short staircase connecting the Inner and Outer Areas. Coneflowers and maiden grass appear as a wild tangle, and pink, bobbing raspberries are just beginning to ripen, left.*

ABOVE: *A large, paned picture window at one end of the living room frames the garden, which is well lit at night. Canada hemlocks (Tsuga canadensis) in the Outer Area provide year-round color.*

SHEFFIELD GARDEN: SELECTED PLANT LIST

Trees and Shrubs	*Cornus kousa*, dogwood
	Ilex x *attenuata* 'Fosteri', holly
	Magnolia virginiana, magnolia
	Malus spp., crab apple
	Nandina domestica, heavenly bamboo
	Oxydendrum arboreum, sourwood
	Rubus idaeus cv., raspberry hybrid
	Tsuga canadensis, Canada hemlock
Perennials	*Ceratostigma plumbaginoides*, plumbago
	Hosta spp., hosta
	Lamium maculatum, lamium
	Ligularia dentata 'Desdemona', golden ray
	Liriope muscari, lilyturf
	Miscanthus sinensis 'Gracillimus', maiden grass
	Nymphaea spp., water lily
	Parthenocissus tricuspidata, Boston ivy
	Pennisetum alopecuroides, fountain grass
	Photinia x *fraseri*, redleaf photinia
	Rudbeckia fulgida 'Goldsturm', yellow coneflower
	Yucca filamentosa, Adam's needle yucca

A plan for this garden appears on page 236.

A ROMANTIC SEASIDE LANDSCAPE

On the eastern end of Long Island, the wide sky, flat windswept lowlands, and quality of light recall the work of seventeenth-century Dutch landscape painters. Today, many members of New York's art community—from artists to art dealers to collectors—seek refuge from the city in a place that soothes and inspires.

Alex and Carole Rosenberg, whose New York gallery is in the center of the midtown art

scene on Fifty-seventh Street, found their haven in the seaside community of Water Mill. On jewellike Mecox Bay, they purchased a parcel of land and a shingle-style beach house that would be their weekend retreat. As soon as they moved in they began trying to create a garden that would capture a spirit of "live and let live." After three summers and the dismissal of two professional landscapers, they were still fighting a losing battle against a bramble of honeysuckle and bayberry shrubs that completely blocked their view of the water. One weekend Lila Katzen, a sculptor and friend whose work they exhibited in their gallery, was their guest. The three of them had spent a long day tucking bulbs into the ground and doing other late fall chores, and they stepped back to

appraise their efforts. A keen visual sense and years in the art world forced them to be brutally honest; they were failing in their attempt to achieve an ideal landscape, one that was both natural and artful.

Lila, however, had recently collaborated on a sculpture installation with the landscape architectural firm of Oehme, Van Sweden & Associates, and had been impressed by their work. She urged Carole to meet them. "They knew exactly what we were trying to express," Carole says. The Rosenbergs hired them.

Under the guidance of Jim Van Sweden and Wolfgang Oehme, the tangled marshy underbrush was eventually transformed into a free-flowing tapestry of naturalized plantings, perfectly suited to their seaside location and beautiful all

year long. But before any planting could be done in earnest, some restructuring was called for. The area between the house and the water was cleared and leveled with 8,500 cubic feet of landfill, the sandy soil was improved with the addition of fish emulsion and Osmocote pellets (a slow release, long-lasting fertilizer), and a bulkhead and landing dock were built on the bay.

The property is just above sea level and basically square in outline, but because the house is situated almost exactly in the middle, the space is treated in a more circular fashion, thought of as radiating from or encircling the house. There are two Inner Areas, each with its own purpose. East of the house are vegetable and cutting gardens where the Rosenbergs spend peaceful hours doing the routine garden

chores that they enjoy. The Inner Area to the west of the house includes a pool and patio and is a place for relaxing and entertaining. The pool, created by Buffy Johnson, another artist friend, "is the only signed and numbered swimming pool in the history of art," jokes Alex. Surrounded by a slate patio and enveloped by sedum and grasses, it provides the mood of serenity and privacy that best suits an Inner Area. Here, as a formal touch, but very much in keeping with the spirit of their sculpted grasses, the Rosenbergs have positioned a much loved sculpture by Lila Katzen.

The Outer Area includes a three-quarters circle of evergreens that blends well with both the ornamental grasses of the garden and the native rushes growing beyond the property line. The fourth quarter is

OPPOSITE:
ABOVE, *Hybrid purple loosestrife* (Lythrum salicaria 'Beacon'); BELOW: *Lavender, a semievergreen subshrub, blooms for much of the growing season.*

taken up by a wide swath of lawn that hugs the water's edge. It keeps the view open from house to bay but is still small enough to make mowing a minor chore.

The In-Between Area sweeps in broad strokes of color around the house, with free-flowing beds of perennials and grasses. "This is not the usual gardener's garden . . . not fussy, not demanding," says Van Sweden, who planned the bands of rich seasonal color with plantings of easy-care, self-reliant species suitable to the Mid-Atlantic region. His partner Oehme also subscribes fully to the theory of the right plant for the right place. "You must know where a plant belongs, aesthetically and horticulturally; it should be happy growing there. Then just let it go and be itself. Our plants look like they're dug up from along the highway. That's what appeals to Americans about this democratic garden—its free spirit."

Each year, the boundaries of the Rosenbergs' beds of grasses and perennials are different as the plants "fight it out" for space, taking territory from or surrendering it to each other. The garden is a living sculpture that changes not only with the seasons but with the years.

The Rosenbergs' garden reflects the romantic ideal. In spring tender green grass and perennial shoots complement naturalized spring

bulbs. In summer spiky purple loosestrife (*Lythrum salicaria* 'Beacon') shoots up, as does yarrow (*Achillea filipendulina* 'Parker') and fountains of ornamental grasses. In fall the stocky sedum (*Sedum spectabile* 'Autumn Joy') that has been broccoli green all summer turns a blazing, show-stopping rusty red, and all the grasses come into full flower. In the winter golden and silver grasses arch and bend, murmuring in the winter winds.

All of the plants are allowed to be themselves; they are not shaped or pruned. This is the secret of easy-care, and keeps maintenance very low. Eventually the grasses will need thinning, though, and the Rosenbergs do replenish the supply of Osmocote from time to time. Each season, by choice, they tend their vegetable garden, which, although it is high on maintenance, they both enjoy for its culinary rewards. Paths of square slate flagstones set in pine bark mulch connect the Inner and Outer Areas. Pine bark mulch is also used around the grasses to conserve water and discourage weeds. To further keep maintenance to a minimum, the Rosenbergs installed an automated irrigation system. After all, this is primarily a weekend house, and the garden must look after itself during the week, an assignment it handles very well.

ABOVE: *Grasses arch over the pool, softening its edge.*

LEFT *and* ABOVE: *The sedum blooming in the fall, living up to its hybrid name, 'Autumn Joy.'*

ROSENBERG GARDEN: SELECTED PLANT LIST

Grasses

Festuca ovina var. *glauca,* blue fescue

Miscanthus floridulus, giant eulalia grass

M. sinensis 'Gracillimus', maiden grass

M. sinensis 'Stricta', eulalia grass

Molinia arundinacea 'Karl Foerster', molina grass

Pennisetum alopecuroides, fountain grass

Perennials

Achillea filipendulina 'Parker', fernleaf yarrow

Ceratostigma plumbaginoides, plumbago

Hibiscus moscheutos, common mallow rose

Hosta spp., plantain lilies, hostas

Lavandula angustifolia subsp. *angustifolia,* lavender

Ligularia dentata 'Desdemona', golden ray

Lythrum salicaria 'Beacon', loosestrife

Perovskia atriplicifolia, Russian sage

Sedum spectabile 'Autumn Joy', showy sedum

Styrax japonicus, Japanese snowbell

Trees and Shrubs

Amelanchier canadensis, shadbush, serviceberry

Cytisus x *praecox* 'Moon-light', moonlight broom

Hamamelis mollis, Chinese witchhazel

Juniperus horizontalis 'Wil-

tonii', ('Blue rug') juniper

Magnolia virginiana, sweet bay

Oxydendrum arboreum, sourwood tree

Pyrus calleryana 'Bradford', Bradford callery pear

A plan for this garden appears on page 237.

AN "ENGLISH" COTTAGE GARDEN

When you grow up in England, especially in rural Surrey, the gardens of childhood leave an indelible impression on your mental geography, and they become a bottomless well of inspiration for later life. In England, gardening is simply "in the blood," says Surrey-raised Sybil Ittmann. "We always had gardens, thanks to my mother who felt very close to our English gardening heritage and could always be found puttering outdoors."

PRECEDING PAGES: LEFT, *Beyond island beds of daylilies, foreground, and perennial thinleaf sunflower* (Helianthus decapetalus multiflorus), *the house nestles beneath a very old, fragrant mimosa* (Albizia julibrissin) *in bloom;* RIGHT, *Some of the more than 500 kinds of daylilies in Sybil Ittman's garden. White purple coneflower blooms, lower right.*

Those early gardens certainly instilled a love of green growing things in Sybil—today she is a botanical artist who lives and works on Long Island. Her studio is separated from her house by a one-half-acre sea of flowers, tumbling and arching and cascading in a riot of color and texture from early spring to late fall. Their exuberance belies the planning and selecting that went into the creation of the garden. Low maintenance combined with the atmosphere of English country gardens were absolute musts. "I love the flowing flower beds of the English country house," she says, "but in order to have elaborate expansive plantings, I had to limit myself to the easy-care perennials available to Americans. Luckily, many of these are my favorite flowers." For example, she included more than two hundred varieties of daylily, explaining that they "thrive on

neglect, are never bothered by pests, their roots choke out nearly all the weeds, and they bloom and bloom!" Tamed wildflowers add charm to the beds and, because they are matched to climate and location, are also easy-care. The succession of blooms begins in April with spring bulbs and flowering ornamental fruit trees; in June, the iris and poppies star, followed by the perennials of summer: black-eyed Susans, pink liatris, purple coneflowers, loosestrife, hostas, bee balm, phlox, and, of course, the early, midseason, and late-flowering daylilies.

As careful as the selection of plant material was, there was nothing timid about Sybil's approach to planning and planting. Although she describes her method as "slapdash and casual," it is based on a lifetime of gardening experience. "I didn't draw the plans on paper," she says, "I just arranged lengths of

Hybrid columbine (Aquilegia *cv.*)

Daylily hybrid (Hemerocallis *cv.*)

Poppy (Papaver orientale *'Helen Elizabeth'*)

Perennial thinleaf sunflower (Helianthus decapetalus multiflorus)

Tulip hybrid 'Apricot Beauty'

Rose-of-Sharon (Hibiscus syriacus *'Bluebird'*)

garden hose into outlines of the shapes I wanted and dug the beds." The result was three interlocking beds separated by a serpentine grass path of consistent width and without sharp corners, to make mowing less of a chore. The central beds are accented with smaller, isolated beds of her favorite flowers, but when seen from the house, the effect is one of a single mass of color.

To reduce maintenance further and to conserve moisture, Sybil uses a mulch of shredded pine bark throughout the beds; it is attractive, inexpensive, widely available, and easy to apply. She waters the garden late at night or very early in the morning to allow moisture to seep down to the roots before the hot summer sun evaporates it from leaves and topsoil.

In a sense these flower beds bind together Sybil Ittmann's past and present. They not only inspire fond memories of her Surrey childhood, but she has included in the beds some precious plants that accompanied her from one American house to another before she finally settled in a place that she will always know as *home.*

ITTMANN GARDEN: SELECTED PLANT LIST

Perennials	*Helianthus decapetalus multiflorus,* thin-leaf sunflower
	Hemerocallis hybrids, daylilies
	Iris Bearded German, bearded German iris
	I. kaempferi, Japanese iris
	Liatris spicata, gay-feather
	Lupinus 'Russell Hybrids', lupines
	Lythrum salicaria 'Morden's Pink', purple loosestrife
	Paeonia hybrids, peonies
	Papaver orientale, Oriental poppy
	Phlox paniculata hybrids, phlox
	Salvia splendens, sage
	Veronica spicata, veronica
Trees and Shrubs	*Albizia julibrissin,* mimosa
	Hibiscus syriacus 'Bluebird', rose-of-Sharon

GARDEN BY A STREAM

Whe Jean and Daniel Pope first surveyed their marshy landscape, they were dismayed to find in its midst an overturned car. Their property had once been used as a dumping ground. Determined to turn this soggy wetland into a tranquil garden, they began with cleanup and restoration. First they removed the junked car. Then they directed the waters of the swamp into a single stream, its bed lined with large creek rocks and its course

running down the middle of the property and under the driveway. With this accomplished, they drained the soil and brought in enough sod to cover what would be their Inner Area: small rounds of lawn on either side of the stream, connected by flat wooden bridges.

Jean Pope, a Cornell University graduate and major in Floriculture and Ornamental Horticulture, designed and planned the garden, while Daniel Pope provided most of the "earth-moving" power. "I love to wave my arms and create," says Jean, but part of the design process is also knowing when to leave well enough alone. For example, an existing stone spring house was untouched and is now the focal point for plantings of ferns and other woodland plants. A hillside "grotto" was covered with daffodils, early bulbs, and wildflowers, followed by daylilies and hostas. In fall and winter, this is a dramatic, rugged patch of stone and fern.

The garden slopes away from the house and can be seen from the covered porch and inner living spaces. The Outer Areas, thickets of dense trees and shrubs, shield the site from neighbors; In-Between Area plantings, masses of hostas and daylilies, soften the transitions. In all more than seventy-five plant varieties were introduced: hedges of privet, euonymus, and viburnum interplanted with ferns and wildflowers; berry shrubs—blueberries, currants, gooseberries, and elderberries; spring bulbs; and perennials. Although located in a populous suburban area, the Popes' garden is quiet and restful, the way they wanted it. The space is meant for relaxation, not entertainment, sport, or other pursuits.

PRECEDING PAGES: LEFT, *View from the Outer Area. An orange double-form daylily blooms with hostas and a collection of hybrid daylilies beside the reclaimed and redirected stream;* **RIGHT,** *Marsh marigold (Caltha palustris).*

OPPOSITE: *A branch of the stream, lined with cinnamon fern (Osmunda cinnamomea), daylilies, and hosta, winds through one of the islands of lawn.* **ABOVE:** *A bench reached by simple wood bridges provides a quiet spot.*

In keeping with the look of the stone-and-wood house, rustic wooden benches are used outdoors, path surfaces are laid with flagstones, and fencing is made of wood planks, treated but unpainted. Mulches, and the thick plantings of daylily, help keep weeds, and maintenance, down. The small circles of grass can be mowed in about five minutes; a few spring and autumn weekends are spent on typical cleanup chores. Otherwise the garden needs only a couple of hours of work each week during the season to look its best—a cool retreat in which to contemplate "a green thought in a green shade."

POPE GARDEN: SELECTED PLANT LIST

Caltha palustris, marsh marigold
Epimedium pinnatum, bishop's hat
Ferns, assorted
Hemerocallis hybrids, daylilies
Hosta hybrids, hostas
Macleaya cordata, plume poppy
Pachysandra terminalis, Japanese spurge
Primula x *polyantha,* polyanthus primrose
P. veris, cowslip
P. vulgaris, primrose
Rheum hybrid, rhubarb
Sambucus racemosa, elderberry
Symplocarpus foetidus, skunk cabbage

OPPOSITE: *Early spring in the Outer Area, where another bridge crosses a branch of the stream and the many plantings of the garden are evident.*

ABOVE: *The old pump house with white elderberry (Sambucus race-mosa) blooming above it and a mound of rhubarb far left, two of the edibles in this garden.* LEFT: *Cinnamon fern, just past the edible fiddlehead stage.*

CALIFORNIA CHAPARRAL

A combination of "blessings and drawbacks"—that is how landscape architect Ron Lutsko described the new home-site of Bill and Peggy Grier. Located in the San Francisco area, it had fine views of mountain and ridge and canyon, but they were often shrouded by a damp, ground-hugging winter fog. The generally mild, pleasant climate could become scorchingly hot in summer, with temperatures over 100° F. The soil was nutrient

rich, but it had more the consistency of adobe brick than garden loam. To make matters worse, "seeps magically appeared on hillsides during late winter and spring," says Lutsko. "One vein of thin decomposed sandstone cut a large swath through one of the most prominent views on the site." This drawback, however, was offset by one of California's true blessings, its "wonderful grasslands —Ireland-green from December to May and straw-blond from June to December. The changing colors offer a unique potential for using different color schemes at different times of the year to respond to the changing backdrop."

The surrounding growth included oak woodlands and chaparral, but close by the house there was virtually no vegetation, other than a single valley oak on the west side and, south of the driveway, a small grove of oaks and bays with undergrowth of poison oak and snowberry. The house itself is a modern geometric design, sided with horizontally installed planks of cedar that have bleached a silver gray. The developer had rough-graded the site, and as Lutsko investigated the work and tracked the drainage patterns, he began to suspect that the crowns of the oaks—where

bark meets roots—had been buried in a layer of soil. To test the theory, he personally undertook the excavation of one of the trees. "I dug down 18 inches," he remembers, "before hitting original grade, the whole time pulling roots that had been brought in with the fill. When I finished it was dark, but I had discovered the need for a retained pit with a sump pump to draw off any collected water and prevent further damage to the oaks. Two days later, I discovered that the roots in the fill soil were all poison oak roots." The rest of the excavation had to wait until Lutsko recovered. It then took two days of work to excavate and

redesign the area, creating a 5-foot-deep, dry stream bed with a small bridge crossing it. The oak trees were breathing free.

The Griers had recently moved from the Pacific Northwest to northern California, and they were captivated by the rich native flora of their new home state. When they commissioned Lutsko and his firm to design their garden, they gave a single strong directive: use as many of California's drought-tolerant and low-maintenance plants as would fit on the site. Lutsko admits that the request was "limiting from a design perspective, but it was certainly a challenge and one I rose to with en-

ABOVE, FROM LEFT: *The Outer Area bridge crosses a dry streambed. A thicket of purple and white California lilacs seen from the path in the Outer Area. Beyond the back of the house are several California live oaks saved in the process of landscaping.*

thusiasm. Although it is not often remembered, the famous old gardens of the Mediterranean were composed primarily of plants native to that arid region, which is not unlike our own, and the resulting sense of fit speaks for itself."

Lutsko set out to create a garden that would embody that same "sense of fit." This meant it should harmonize not only with the landscape but, as in the best Natural Gardens, with the architecture of the house as well. Angles and straight lines, therefore, dominate the garden's Inner Area, which centers around pool and patio. Paved surfaces are concrete mixed with gravel, in tune with the geometry of the house, but as you walk away from the house, into the Outer Areas of native grasses and chaparral, concrete gives way to gravel-only paths that meander over the landscape, following its contours.

The preliminary design for the

plantings in all three areas included nearly fifty species of plants, already over the limit of what Lutsko felt a garden on a single acre of land could accommodate while still maintaining its integrity. To his surprise, the Griers, who loved the overall proposal, were disappointed only in the number of plants—there weren't nearly enough. By the time they all agreed on a planting scheme it included over one hundred species. Lutsko worried that with such diversity the garden would fall apart as a design. "I was left hoping that I had repeated sufficient plants to give the garden enough backbone to develop a strong theme. By the repeated use of *Arctostaphylos, Ceanothus, Baccharis,* and *Quercus lobata* I think we accomplished it."

The species were chosen so carefully that Lutsko was able to install the plants with very little soil alteration or preparation. To maintain moisture levels, ground bark was added to the shade garden at

ABOVE:
RIGHT,
From the corner of the house, a view of the hillside and its evergreen ground cover of dwarf baccharis (Baccharis pilularis *'Twin Peaks');*
FAR RIGHT,
The linear pool is the centerpiece of the Inner Area. Exposed aggregate in concrete paving makes an easy transition from the adjacent screelike areas

the entry, and to increase drainage "sand and gravel were generously added to the rock gardens. Aside from this the plants are growing in the native clay or sandstone. With the possible exception of the entry, the garden gets watered an average of once a month during the summer."

For many gardeners this would be the end of the story—a perfectly sited garden that needs practically no care at all, and that is visited and studied by garden clubs, plant societies, and university classes. But for the Griers, who were intensely involved in its creation, the garden is an ongoing process. Like all living things, it is "becoming" rather than "there." In California fall is the rainy season and the optimum time to plant, as new plants will have time to develop their roots before the drier winter and very dry summer. Since the original installation in 1979, Ron Lutsko has answered a summons from the Griers almost every fall—"We bought a carful of

plants at the botanic garden sale, could you drop by and assist in the placement?" Today, only the Griers know how many more plants than the original hundred are at home on their California acre.

GRIER GARDEN: SELECTED PLANT LIST

Arctostaphylos densiflora, manzanita
Armeria maritima, common thrift
Artemisia stelleriana, dusty-miller
Baccharis pilularis 'Twin Peaks', Dwarf baccharis
Ceanothus arboreus 'Ray Hartman', California lilac
C. griseus 'Santa Ana', Casmel ceanothus
C. thyrsiflorus 'Snow Flurry'
Eriogonum crocatum, saffron buckwheat
Iris innominata, native iris
I. 'Pacific hybrids'
Quercus lobata, valley oak

A plan for this garden appears on page 237.

OUT OF A DREAM

Imagine a dream garden—
imagine the landscape you could create if there
were no constraints or boundaries. In the Mid-
West, one landowner was able to make that
dream come true. He turned his acres of essentially
undistinguished land into the quintessential
Natural Garden, a true reflection of an idealized
Great Lakes region woodland. To assure the
accuracy of his creation, he investigated many
sources, searching out arboretums and plant

associations, questioning their staffs, seeking advice. He explored the wild places, studying rock outcroppings, stream banks, shady glens, and the plants that grew nearby, drawing inspiration from nature. After massive land moving and years of work, this landscape boasts meadows and wooded retreats, streams and lakes, waterfalls and cascades—all man-made.

The gardens are entered through a gate and down a drive that passes meadows of sunny daisies. At the end of the drive a generous turn-around circles an island of small-scale shrubs and trees. Flanking the parking area are small plantings of naturalized, self-sowing annuals such as cosmos. It is inside the garden proper, however, that the magic really begins. One thousand water lilies bloom in an immense lake. The smooth surface of the sylvan lake reflects the perfectly selected and sited native trees such as birch, swamp maple, ash,

dogwood, and impressive rhododendrons that grow along its banks. Water, pumped from the lake to the top of a waterfall on the highest part of the property, cascades from level to level, skipping over stones and under bridges on its return to the lake. The scene is one of constantly evolving color, of natural serendipity combined with man-made touches that surprise and delight. Foxglove and hosta naturalize along the streambed; beside a woodland path there are smaller scale plantings, and a gem of a rhododendron glen. Farther on, a tiny waterfall peeks out beyond a turn in the path.

Hammocks hang invitingly from the trees, benches beckon from the lake's edge, and a delicate moon bridge leads from the path to a tiny island in the lake. All the elements —from plantings to permanent and personal touches—conspire to make one drift and dream. The garden is truly out of this world.

ABOVE, FROM LEFT: *View of the lake from the rhododendron glen. A simple wood-slatted bench creates a peaceful viewing perch in a meadow seeded with a mix that includes black-eyed Susans and wildings—the perfect spot to gaze upon the lake and watch dragonflies dart among the water lilies. The still water area where the stream feeds into the lake.*

"DREAM" GARDEN: SELECTED PLANT LIST

Hardwood trees	*Acer saccharum*, sugar maple
	Betula papyrifera, paper birch
	B. pendula, European white birch
	Pinus strobus, white pine
	Quercus palustris, pin oak
	Q. rubra, red oak
	Ulmus americana, American elm
Shrubs and perennials	*Cotoneaster* varieties, cotoneaster
	Rhododendron species and varieties
	Taxus baccata 'Repandens', spreading yew
	Chrysanthemum maximum, daisy
	Digitalis purpurea, foxglove
	Nymphaea odorata, water lily
	Rudbeckia hirta, black-eyed Susan

ELEMENTS

The elements used in landscape design are similar to those used by artists—line and plane, structure and form, color and shadow. Paving, steps, and walls are made of the same permanent, hard-surface materials of the artist, architect, and sculptor. But to these ingredients we add life. Plants grow, flower, twine, tower, spread, and sometimes die. In this section,

OF DESIGN

you'll discover the right materials for a given situation.
Ground-hugging plants for the base and foundation,
shrubs and trees for the middle story and canopies of the
plantings, wildflowers and grasses for color and
texture are all elements of design in the Natural Garden.
And then there is time—the unseen factor.
For garden art is art in the fourth dimension.

GROUND COVERS

Although I strongly advocate alternative ground covers, I think it only fair to begin with the most famous ground cover of all—grass lawn. When first introduced in seventeenth-century England, grass was meant to be an easy-care landscape plant; in fact, it was kept well shorn and fertilized not by a staff of gardeners but, for the most part, by grazing sheep and other animals. Many estate owners, however, came to dislike the intrusion

ABOVE, *Moss, though sometimes difficult to establish, makes a lush ground cover in shady places once it takes over.*

of animals in their landscapes. Eventually, lawn maintenance became the sole responsibility of man and machine, and the lawn mower became a permanent fixture in every household. In the Natural Garden, we are trying to break free of this tyrannical system, but even so, in some places the grass lawn may be the best solution in spite of its high maintenance requirements.

The Inner Area, usually close by the house, is the most visible and most visited part of the Natural Garden. Every aspect of its design is of the greatest importance, beginning with the ground cover. It is here that gardeners may want to plant grass, so soft, so inviting, so demanding. If you do opt for lawn in the Inner Area, there are ways to minimize its demands. Design the space to be no bigger than its purpose: if it is used for entertaining guests or for family meals and gatherings, it can be smallish and intimate; if, on the other hand, touch football, badminton, or croquet are part of the family tradition, you will need a fairly large expanse. If you want only to walk barefoot

on a cool grassy surface, you might consider creating a grass path that meanders through the In-Between Area plantings, or leads into a meadow, and choose handsome paving for the Inner Area instead.

Once you have settled on the size and location of the lawn, create a shape that will be easy to maintain —that is, one without sharp corners. Rounded shapes are easier to water by hand, easier to irrigate, and easier to mow. Include a mowing strip to facilitate trimming the borders where lawn meets plantings. The mower's tires ride on a permanent edging of brick or other material and the lawn edge is cut perfectly with one pass.

Although lawn seed companies and grass breeders are working to develop new varieties of short-growing, slow-growing grasses, the super lawn is still in the future. Until then, the best you can do is limit the amount of lawn, shape it thoughtfully, and choose the seeds carefully (perhaps with the advice of your local County Extension Service) so you will be growing the best variety for your area and situation.

LAWN ALTERNATIVES

If you decide to limit the size of your lawn (or to forego it altogether), you are about to overthrow the tyranny of lawn care. You can now choose from a wide range of attractive alternatives to lawn—living ground covers, nonliving mulches, or even paving materials (see Permanent Elements, pages 207–32). The choice depends upon what appeals to you, how you will use the space, and what the growing conditions are.

LIVING GROUND COVERS

Even if you are not yet ready to give up your lush green grass lawn, in spite of the many hours logged in its care, there are probably places on your property where grass simply will not grow—a hillside that cannot be mowed, an area of very damp or very dry ground, a corner of dense shade, a spot beneath trees and shrubs whose roots compete with grass or put the grass beyond the reach of the mower. Because nothing looks worse than a poor patch of lawn struggling to survive, here is where you might try something different.

Fortunately, there are many choices for grass substitutes among the living ground covers. By nature, ground covers are among the easiest plants to grow and maintain, but while I do call them "lawn alternatives," they are not completely maintenance free. No plant is. The process of gardening is an ongoing one; we deal with living things, impermanent and mutable—they are born, grow, change, and in some

FAR LEFT: On a sunny slope, bands of perennials have been chosen not only for floral color, but also for varying foliage. LEFT: In shade, periwinkle (Vinca minor) and wild ginger (Asarum europaeum) flank a narrow path and stairway, left and right.

Wild ginger (Asarum europaeum)

Woolly thyme (Thymus pseudolanuginosus)

Bugleweed (Ajuga reptans *'Burgundy Glow'*)

Barrenwort (Epimedium *x* veriscolor *'Sulphureum'*)

Periwinkle, vinca (Vinca minor)

Astilbe hybrid in spring

cases die. The goal in the Natural Garden is to seek out ground cover plants that will thrive, especially in difficult locations, with the least attention.

In the wild places, ground covers hug the mountain slopes and carpet the forest floor. They thrive in sun and in shade, in dry and wet areas. In the Natural Garden, they are just as versatile. On a steep embankment, they hold the soil and fight erosion. They bind the sandy soil of a seaside garden. Many, such as the familiar beach rose (*Rosa rugosa*), will even tolerate salt spray. In spaces where soil is poor, plant a tough ground cover such as crown vetch (*Coronilla varia*), which will grow almost anywhere. Some ground covers help ecologically in other ways—they are living mulches that moderate soil temperature, suppress weeds, and hold in moisture. In the forest they contribute their own leaves to the ground's rich humus and they trap leaf litter and plant debris, which are also added to the soil.

Ground covers are any plants— herbaceous perennials, shrubs, or vines—that grow horizontally as well as vertically, ultimately covering a given site. Heights vary: some are ground-hugging plants, maturing at under 6 inches; others can grow to knee-high or higher Plants, however, must spread horizontally to be considered ground covers. They spread by means of various growth habits.

Some ground covers, usually herbaceous perennials, creep along by enlarging their root systems; the daylily, for example, forms a clump that doubles in size each season. Initially planted a couple of feet apart, daylilies will form a mass of strappy foliage and flaring trumpet flowers within a few years. Thick clumps of daylilies can hold soil on a steep hill. Other ground covers spread along the surface by increasing their width every year. Shrubs such as prostrate juniper (*Juniperus horizontalis*) add to their long arching branches each season until eventually their patch of ground is solid with foliage. Vining ground covers such as ivy travel along the surface, rooting at their leaf nodes. Each rooted node can develop into a new plant that in turn sends out new growth. Other ground covers produce runners or *stolons*—stems that grow horizontally, seeking open soil in which to root new plants. The garden variety strawberry is a well-known stoloniferous plant. Another is the piggyback plant (*Tolmiea menziesii*), which is a popular ground cover in its native Pacific Northwest, and a house plant in colder climates. Still other plants reproduce vegetatively by means of *rhizomes*—horizontal stems that are either just underground or on the surface of the ground and from which new growth pushes up. Grass is such a plant. Lastly, many ground covers reproduce freely from self-sown seeds.

There are ample ground covers to solve any landscaping problem. In dry shade, the three most popular choices are evergreen ground covers: ivy (*Hedera* spp.), periwinkle (*Vinca* spp.), and pachysandra (*Pachysandra* spp.). These plants will do well in partial shade with as little as an hour of sun each day. In damp shade, a more common situation, varieties of flowering *Epimedium* will thrive as will the wild gingers (*Asarum* spp.), which form lovely mounds of leathery round leaves.

In dry sun, evergreen prostrate junipers or a perennial, such as moss pink (*Phlox subulata*), which creates a dense carpet of pink, red, or white flowers in spring, can be used. Many succulents will thrive in dry sun, from the ice plants, aloes, and agaves found in mild climates to the sedums and hardy cacti of the north.

Ground covers can also be used as strong design elements, for many have beautiful foliage, flowers, or both. *Picea* for example, the dwarf spruce, has unusual textured foliage; one variety, *Picea pungens* 'Glauca Pendula', spreads 12 feet or more and can be used to create an intricate layered cascade of silvery blue. The drought-tolerant ice plants are noted for their daisylike flowers, which bloom in solid carpets of pink or white. The beach rose (*Rosa rugosa*) has interesting foliage—crinkled and pleated apple-green leaves —as well as beautiful flowers—magenta or white single blossoms with sunny yellow centers—and produces fruits known as hips that are higher in vitamin C than the citrus fruits.

Most of these plants are for low-traffic areas, but some ground covers truly are lawn alternatives since they tolerate being walked on. Unlike grass, however, they do not require mowing. Of these, *thymus,* the herb, is one of my favorites for it also has a lovely aroma that perfumes the air as you walk through it. Corsican mint (*Mentha requienii*) can also tolerate traffic as can some of the ground-hugging bugleweeds (*Ajuga reptans* hybrids).

MAINTENANCE

Living ground covers are easy-care in the long run, but they must be planted and looked after conscien-

THIS PAGE: ABOVE, *Pachysandra or Japanese spurge* (Pachysandra terminalis) *provides year-round color and softens the look of brick or stone;* **BELOW,** *The stone of the house is complemented by a ground cover that combines a mulch of fist-sized rock with a feathery dwarf juniper* (Juniperus horizontalis), *foreground, and grasslike lilyturf* (Liriope muscari).

tiously in the early days. Installing ground cover plants is best done in the fall in the South (zones 7–10) and in the early spring in the North (zones 2–6). You should check the pH level of the soil before you choose the plants; you can make some adjustments, but it is better to select a plant that grows well in the existing pH level. Soil preparation is the same as for planting perennials or lawn: you need to turn over the ground with a garden fork or Roto-tiller to a depth of 6 to 8 inches and incorporate some organic material (compost, manure, and the like; see Plant Selection, pages 242–83). It is also a good idea to turn a 2-to-4-inch layer of peat moss under when you till.

The plants themselves can be obtained economically in flats of small young seedlings that will establish themselves quickly. They should be spaced far enough apart to produce healthy root systems and some good top growth but not so far that they will look like polka dots or take forever to grow together. The exact distance will depend on the plant; if you are in doubt, the supplier can advise you. Crowding the young plants for appearance's sake will only produce lanky, tangled, and unhealthy plants, but you can encourage the properly spaced plants to fill out by pinching back the terminal inch of new growth with your fingernails or shears. This will encourage bushiness—branching horizontal growth. You can also enhance the appearance of your planting by covering the bare spots temporarily with one of the degradable organic mulches discussed below. Once the plants have been set in the ground, keep them well-watered for the first several weeks,

THIS PAGE: ABOVE, *A bank of English ivy* (Hedera helix) *and pachysandra holds the steep hillside and looks trim and handsome year-round, setting off a shady, secluded, somewhat formal seating area;* BELOW, *Flowering alpine epimedium* (Epimedium alpinum), *a semi-evergreen ground cover, provides a delicate contrast to the flagstone path.*

LEFT: *Moss-covered steps create a dramatic, seemingly unbroken sweep from one level of lawn to another. Moss also softens the stone banisters, and foamflower* (Tiarella cordifolia) *blooms airily, left.* ABOVE: *Boston ivy* (Parthenocissus tricuspidata), *left, and English ivy* (Hedera helix), *right, nicely complement a more traditional set of steps at one entrance to a small enclosed lawn.* BELOW: *Informal steps of rough-hewn native stone are well matched by a cascade of trailing periwinkle* (Vinca minor) *in flower.*

Two varieties of bugleweed (Ajuga reptans): *White flower, 'Alba'; blue flower, 'Bronze Beauty'*

Ice plant (Lampranthus spectabilis)

Another bugleweed species (Ajuga pyramidalis)

Lily-of-the-valley (Convallaria majalis)

Crested iris (Iris cristata)

Wild Sweet William (Phlox divaricata) *and columbines* (Aquilegia canadensis)

Plumbago (Ceratostigma plumbaginoides)

Dead nettle (Lamium maculatum 'White Nancy')

Sweet woodruff (Galium [Asperula] odoratur

at least until new growth is clearly visible. The first season, pull out any weeds that appear in the mulch; this may be work now but it will mean less work later. Once they are established, the ground covers will need only an annual spring grooming to remove dead growth and eliminate weeds, and a yearly feeding, perhaps of a granular fertilizer such as Osmocote.

NONLIVING GROUND COVERS

Mulches, although heavily used in corporate parks, institutional grounds, and public spaces, are often overlooked as design elements in the home landscape. This is too bad, for they are not only great labor savers, but, carefully chosen, they can also make valuable aesthetic and ecological contributions to your property. They shade the soil, which, because many weed seeds need sunlight in order to grow, discourages weed growth. Their weight and density will also squelch and destroy many weed seedlings even after they begin to grow. They protect the earth from pelting rains, drying winds, and extremes of temperature. The soil underneath stays moist, does not wash out in a rainstorm or splash mud onto neighboring plants, paths, or buildings, and is not as susceptible to frost heaves in winter or overheating in summer as it would be otherwise.

Any substance that provides this protection can be used as a mulch. Mulches can be used around plants throughout the garden; they can also be used instead of plants as a ground cover. There are organic and inorganic mulches; they range from alkaline to acidic, from fine to coarse, and can be permanent or temporary (as when you mulched around the newly planted living ground cover seedlings). In late December, for instance, many gardeners in the coldest zones spread an extra layer of salt marsh hay or pine boughs from the Christmas tree over their herbaceous perennials to give them added protection once the ground has frozen. This mulch does not keep the soil warm; instead it keeps it cool, to prevent damage caused by early thawing. Several months later this mulch is removed.

Mulches are spread over the ground in 4-to-6-inch layers depending upon your choice of material. Fine mulches are not as thickly spread as coarse ones; if you remember that the idea is to shield the earth from the elements, you can probably determine the correct depth. If you are in doubt, however, consult your garden center or County Extension Service.

ORGANIC MULCHES. An organic mulch derives from some living material, usually the byproduct of another process—sawdust, woodchips, grass clippings, or leaves, for example. The type you select will depend on various factors, from the square footage of ground to be covered to the availability of different mulches in your area.

I chose tiny *buckwheat hulls* for the small protected places in my garden. This is a very attractive mulch, but because the seeds are lightweight and easily windblown, they work best in a small bed with an edging material such as brick.

If you have a lawn you can get

Salt marsh hay

Straw

the most from it, and from the mowing, by using the *grass clippings* to mulch flower beds, adding a new layer every time you mow, and keeping the layer about 2 inches deep. You must follow some precautions, however: never mulch with grass that has been treated with weed killer for it may be toxic to other plants; allow clippings to dry out if you plan a thick mulch or you will be inviting mold; and never put clippings in direct contact with perennial stems, for grass heats up as it decomposes. The last precaution also holds true for *leaves* used as mulch. When wet, leaves also pack down rather solidly, suffocating the earth. In most cases, it is best to chop dry leaves with the mower or to compost them into leaf mold before spreading. Some leaves, such as oak, curl before they drop, giving a layer of them good loft without chopping, but oak leaves are also quite acidic and best used only around plants that prefer a low pH level: azaleas, rhododendrons, or blueberry shrubs, for example. The same directive about acidity applies to *pine needles,* which are most attractive when spread under conifers. They break down eventually, but in the meantime they make a heavenly, soft, scented carpet for bare feet.

Aged, shredded fir bark

Leaf mold, or compost

Cocoa

Peat moss

Pine bark is a long-lasting acidic mulch, coarse textured, and comes in several sizes ranging from very small (pulverized) to large (shredded pieces). The smaller sizes, which are more compatible with the aesthetic aims of the Natural Garden, are used in a 2-to-4-inch layer. The larger sizes are used in layers as deep as 6 inches. Although relatively expensive as mulches go, pine bark will last a minimum of three years.

Grit

Gravel

Washed stones

Quarried gravel

Grass clippings

Pine cones

Finely chopped bark

Coarsely chopped fir bark

Licorice root

Buckwheat hulls

Quartz gravel
Large princeton stone

Small princeton stone
Oyster shells

It drains very well, does not steal water from the soil as peat moss does, and actually repels slugs and some rodents. Use the bark as is around plants that need an acidic soil; elsewhere, offset the acidity by raking in one pound of ground dolomite limestone to every square yard of soil surface before spreading the bark. The package label will supply instructions and advice about fertilizers. Pine bark requires nitrogen as it decomposes, so plant food with extra nitrogen should be used for adjacent plants.

Many people use hay as a mulch, mostly because of its low cost and easy availability, but this plant material can cause more problems than it solves: it mats down and can also introduce weed seeds into the garden. Two better choices are *salt marsh hay* and *straw*. Salt marsh hay grows wild in marshes and wetlands, mainly near the ocean but also wherever you find the marshy soil it requires for seed germination. This prerequisite means that the seed of salt marsh hay, unlike regular hay, will not sprout in your garden. Straw is similar in appearance to salt marsh hay, and being open-textured, it has less absorbancy and drains better than regular hay. Also, it generally looks more attractive than regular hay.

A terrific but hard-to-find organic mulch is *sugar cane,* the shredded stalks of which are called *bagasse.* It is coarse textured, has excellent moisture-holding ability, and breaks down slowly. Unfortunately, it is only infrequently available—ask your nursery for it.

Finally, I have recently learned of a new mulch, *chopped licorice root,* described by Jean Pope as the "Rolls-Royce of garden mulches."

The color of soil, licorice root comes in coarse or fine grades. Its only drawback is the cost, but used selectively, in highly visible places in the Inner Area, for instance, perhaps near the most-used entry to the house, it can be magnificent.

Peat moss is a slightly acidic mulch; add a sprinkling of ground limestone to correct the pH level for plants requiring an average soil. Use very coarse grade peat moss, which is sold semidry in plastic-wrapped bales of 4 or 6 cubic feet each. It must be thoroughly wetted before use. Prepare the bale by punching a few holes near the bottom, opening the top, and allowing water from a hose to trickle slowly into the bag until it runs out the bottom holes. Then shut the water off, allow the bag to stand a while, and test by squeezing a handful of peat. If a few drops of water appear, the peat is ready; if not, repeat the water trickling. Peat should be spread in a 2-to-4-inch layer; each spring, work the previous year's layer into the topsoil and apply a new layer of peat. One problem with peat moss is that it often blows around when it dries out and can be hard to re-moisten. It can also pull moisture from the soil. While these drawbacks make its use as a mulch question-able, it is an excellent additive that loosens and aerates the soil, qualities that offset its negative aspects.

INORGANIC MULCHES. A few inorganic mulches—derived from nonliving materials—can be used in the Natural Garden. *Mineral mulches,* for example, come in a range of sizes, shapes, and colors. Pebbles or stones—called loose aggregate—in a neutral tone will look best in the Natural

Garden. They can be spread on the soil in a 4-to-6-inch layer or used to camouflage a sheet of plastic mulch. In the first case, the only real chore will be occasional weeding. In the second case, they are almost completely permanent and mainte-nance free. You will have only to remove leaves and other debris each fall and to add a thin layer of fresh pebbles each spring to revitalize the appearance of the aggregate.

A very effective but absolutely hideous-looking mulch is *polyethyl-ene film*—either black, white, or clear plastic sheeting. This mulch guarantees warm, moist, weed-free soil, but in the Natural Garden it should be used sparingly if at all. It belongs only in areas where there are few plants, where low mainte-nance is essential, and where an-other mulch, such as pebbles, can be used to hide the plastic. Never use it in the Inner Area unless you are ab-solutely certain it will not be seen. Plastic film must be spread on the ground before seeds or seedlings are planted; then make holes in the plastic and plant, following the instructions on the package.

A well-chosen ground cover can create harmony and continuity in your garden. This may be almost literal; for example, an Inner Area of grass will be joined to the rest of the garden by a grass path leading into the Outer Area. The continu-ity, in another case, may be purely visual: using the same ground cover or mulch throughout acts as a com-mon thread. Ground covers com-bined with paving materials or other permanent elements provide a foundation for the garden as it evolves. When chosen carefully, they will be a handsome addition to the landscape.

GROUND COVERS:
A SELECTION

Achillea filipendulina 'Moonshine', yarrow

Aeonium spp., aconium

Ajuga pyramidalis, bugleweed

A. reptans, bugleweed

Artemisia absinthium, wormwood

Arundinaria variegata, dwarf bamboo, dwarf white stripe

Asarum europaeum, wild ginger

Ceratostigma plumbaginoides, plumbago

Convallaria majalis, lily-of-the-valley

Coronilla varia, crown vetch

Dennstaedtia punctilobula, hay-scented fern

Echeveria spp., echeveria

Epimedium spp., barrenwort

E. x *versicolor* 'Sulphureum', barrenwort or epimedium

Galium odoratum, sweet woodruff

Hedera helix, English ivy

Hosta spp. and hybrids, hosta, plantain lily, funkia

Iris cristata, crested iris

Juniperus horizontalis, dwarf, prostrate, or creeping juniper

Lamium maculatum 'White Nancy', dead nettle

Lampranthus spectabilis, ice plant

Lavandula angustifolia, lavender

Liriope muscari, lilyturf

Mentha requienii, Corsican mint

Ophiopogon planiscapus, Mondo grass

Oxalis oregana, redwood sorrel

Pachysandra spp., pachysandra

P. terminalis, pachysandra, Japanese spurge

Phlox subulata, moss pink

Picea spp. and hybrids, dwarf spruce

P. pungens 'Glauca Pendula', dwarf spruce

Rosa rugosa, beach rose

Sedum spp., stonecrop

Stachys lanata, lamb's-ears

Thymus pseudolanuginosus, woolly thyme

Thymus vulgaris, common thyme

Tolmiea menziesii, piggyback plant

Vinca minor, vinca, periwinkle

BULBS

Bulbs are the showy favorites of many gardeners. In the springtime they are truly the star attractions of the garden, especially in northern climes. Some, such as snowdrops (*Galanthus nivalis*), even push up through the snow well before any other flower could survive. But there are also many bulbs for the other seasons: some mature in the summer months, while others, less common, bloom in the fall. All bulbs need a period of

PRECEDING PAGES: LEFT, *Signs of spring— azalea shrubs in full flower and natural- ized daffodils (Nar- cissus spp.) in a gentle but effective planting at Magno- lia Plantations;* **RIGHT,** *Sprout- ing gladiolus bulbs.*

ripening after they flower, during which the foliage grows and feeds the bulb, plumping it out again. This period is followed by dor- mancy, which enables the bulb to set a flower for the next season. Some bulbs, such as daffodils, need a period of cold in order to bloom, making them unsuitable for south- ern gardens. But other tender bulbs thrive outdoors in the South and conversely must be grown indoors in the North—miniature amaryllis and sparaxis, for example.

Bulbs can be used in several ways in the Natural Garden, but natural- izing with bulbs is one of the most beautiful and least demanding practices. Naturalizing means estab- lishing a self-sustaining colony of plants, or "growing plants as they would grow in nature"—free to bloom, multiply, and spread at will. There is no rigid plan; happenstance

is the rule, with bulbs simply scat- tered in masses throughout the landscape. They can be naturalized in the lawn—daffodils are often planted this way—or they can ap- pear under trees in the Outer Area, or they can be underplanted in is- land beds or scattered in a meadow. Underplanting means that plants with different cycles can share the same ground; in this case, spring- blooming bulbs underplanted in the perennial bed will flower and ma- ture before the perennials push up through the soil.

Only bulbs that have the ability to spread and multiply can be naturalized; therefore, hybrid tulips, for example, cannot be naturalized. Naturalized plantings of bulbs, once established, are nearly maintenance- free, but planning and preparation must be carefully considered. After all, these plants are valuable perma-

ABOVE: A dense grouping of daffodils just outside the lawn demonstrates one way to naturalize.

nent contributors to the beauty of your landscape and they deserve special attention at the outset. Plant in quantity. Wordsworth never would have written "Daffodils" had he seen the paltry single row of daffodils that stands along many cement walks and at the edge of many lawns. Instead he was inspired by the sight of a sea of daffodils:

Continuous as the stars that shine
  And twinkle on the milky way,
They stretched in never-ending line
  Along the margin of a bay:
Ten thousand saw I at a glance
  Tossing their heads in sprightly
      dance.

This is the effect you are seeking, even if ten thousand is more than you can handle—or afford—at first. Many people naturalize several hundred to one thousand bulbs at a time; however, if even this seems

excessive, plant a concentrated drift of several dozen bulbs and add to it, increasing the area, each year. If your space is very limited, a small clump of bulbs will still put on a worthy show.

Planting of spring bulbs is done in the fall. The bulbs must be set in the ground at the correct depth in soil that is well drained and fertile. Sprinkle bonemeal into the hole before positioning the bulb; every spring you will sprinkle more bonemeal over the ground.

Once you have decided where you want to scatter the bulbs, there is a surefire way to make your planting naturalistic. Some people simply toss the bulbs over their shoulder and plant them where they land. Don't do it. The soft bulbs could be damaged. Instead substitute large pebbles or marbles. Wherever one lands, replace it with

ABOVE: *A free-form arrangement of daffodils naturalized directly in the lawn is another approach to bulb planting.*

**Grape hyacinth
(Muscari azureum)**

*A dainty species tulip
from Turkestan*

TOP: *The bulb fields of Holland.*
ABOVE: *A suburban garden showing its spring colors—yellow
from leopard's-bane* (Aronicum cordatum) *and daffodils; deep blue
from grape hyacinth* (Muscari armeniacum) *against a yellow screen
of forsythia.*

a bulb. Dig a hole with a spade, trowel, or special bulb planter, add bonemeal, position the bulb, then cover it with soil, and tamp it in place. If you have a huge number of bulbs to plant, it might be sensible to invest in a bulb planter. This device removes a perfectly cylindrical plug of earth, and can be purchased with a long handle that reduces the need for stooping.

Daffodils have long been favorites for naturalizing in lawns or fall-mown meadows. Almost all bulb companies sell mixes for this purpose with flowers that vary in form, color, and height. Some such mixtures are made up of "seconds" —bulbs that did not conform to the standard or were not produced in sufficient quantities to offer alone. These are good buys sometimes, but beware of those with prices too good to be true, for these bulbs will often need several years of growth before they flower. (One horticultural given is that there is no such thing as a bargain.) If the mixes do not appeal to you, create your own mix by buying the bulbs you like.

Spring-blooming daffodils naturalized in a lawn must not be mowed until their foliage ripens (six to eight weeks after the flowers fade) or, best of all, yellows. The leaves enable the bulbs to rebuild themselves, plumping out in readiness for next year's flowering. Mowing before they have ripened may mean losing next season's show, or losing the bulbs altogether, so wait at least six weeks after the final bulb has bloomed. In a high-traffic area this can pose a problem; it might be best to plant along the periphery unless your lawn has a path or walkway through it.

In addition to daffodils, there are other candidates for naturalizing, from some early spring crocuses to the dog-tooth violet (*Erythronium dens-canis*), and with proper planning you can have bulbs blooming from early spring on into the fall. Small bulbs can be planted near flowering shrubs; for example, grape hyacinths *(Muscari)* planted beneath low-growing *Forsythia* x *intermedia* 'Arnold Dwarf' make a wonderful color combination. A mixed planting of miniature daffodils and grape hyacinths beneath a flowering tree, such as magnolia or cherry, is enchanting. You can also underplant an island bed with long-lasting spring bulbs that will bloom and ripen before your perennials appear.

One of the few problems you may have with bulbs is overcrowding, but this will not happen for at least a decade or two. If flowering slows down even though you feed the bulbs regularly, overcrowding is probably the cause. The solution is simple. After the foliage yellows, dig the bulbs up, remove side bulbs and bulblets and replant them along with the original bulbs over a wider area. Discard any mushy, bruised, or dried up bulbs.

The only other potential problems are squirrels, woodchucks, moles, and other underground scroungers that have a taste for some bulbs. They can be discouraged by spreading dried blood (available from garden centers) over the newly planted ground, or by laying a piece of hardware cloth on top of the bulbs and covering it with soil. Some people even make complete wire cages for their bulbs. The easiest solution of all is to plant only daffodils in problem areas.

Daffodil and narcissus bulbs are poisonous, and wild creatures recognize them as such. You will rarely have an unwelcome dinner guest among your daffodils.

The value of bulbs was recognized in Europe some centuries ago when travelers to the East returned with exotic plants, including bulbs, especially tulips. In fact there was a time when tulip bulbs sold for the equivalent of $40,000 each and were traded on the stock exchanges of Europe. I saw some descendants of these prized bulbs recently when a photo assignment took me to the Netherlands. In a "bulb museum" far off the beaten track was the little 'lac van Rijn' tulip, which dates from 1620 and bears royal purple blossoms edged in white. Many rare, exquisite species of tulips, originally from Asia and the Middle East, are blooming there as well. The beauty and ease of culture of these species far surpass the souped up hybrids of the modern bulb industry and make the small extra effort in obtaining them well worthwhile. Many of today's commercially grown tulip bulbs must be dug up and discarded or replanted each year, while these dependable beauties of yesterday will bloom year after year. The species' simpler forms and subtler colors are also most compatible with the aesthetics of the Natural Garden. Search for them in late summer and early fall catalogues (see Source Guide, pages 287–92). They are sometimes described as "heirlooms" or "traditional" varieties.

Naturalizing is not the only way you can use bulbs, and not all bulbs can be naturalized, in any event. In corners of the garden, in the Inner Area in a miniature woodland setting, or in a rock garden, small bulbs can be positioned in groups near a focal point—a sculpture or a rock or other natural feature—to draw attention to their delicate beauty. If you want to set bulbs in a rock garden, be sure there is a good-sized pocket of soil, add a sprinkling of well-rotted manure, and then position the bulb. Select only dwarf and miniature varieties. In a wooded area, cluster bulbs in a clearing or beside a path. The nodding heads of many bulbs also belong beside a pool, wherever it may be in the garden. In the Inner Area, you might want to plant unusual species and hybrid bulbs.

Whatever the size of your garden, whether you have the space to naturalize a wide swath of lawn with daffodils or are limited to a miniature meadow of spring bulbs by a stone wall, you should find a way to use flowering bulbs. A modest number of bulbs, artfully placed, can make as strong a statement and as clear a contribution to your landscape as Wordsworth's "host of golden daffodils."

BULBS: A SELECTION

Allium giganteum, ornamental onion, giant allium

Anemone blanda, windflower

Clivia miniata, clivia, Lady Clive's lily, kaffir lily

Colchicum autumnale, autumn crocus

Crocus vernus, Dutch crocus

Endymion hispanicus (Scilla hispaniea), Spanish bluebell, wood hyacinth

E. non-scriptus (Scilla non-scriptus), harebell, English bluebell

Eranthis hyemalis, winter aconite, eranthis

Erythronium americanum, trout lily, dog-tooth violet

E. dens-canis, dog-tooth violet

Fritillaria meleagris, checkered lily, Guinea hen flower

Fritillaria persica, Persian fritillaria

Galanthus elwesii, snowdrop

Galanthus nivalis, snowdrop

Leucojum vernum, spring violet

Lilium canadense, Canada lily

Lilium superbum, Turk's-cap lily

Lilium tigrinum, tiger lily

Muscari armeniacum, grape hyacinth

Muscari azureum, grape hyacinth

Narcissus bulbocodium, hoop-petticoat daffodil, petticoat daffodil

Sparaxis tricolor, wand flower

Tulipa spp., species tulip

Zantedeschia aethiopica, calla lily

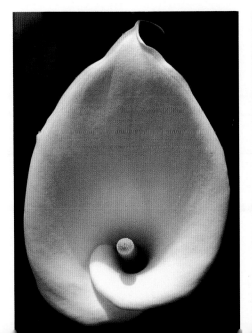

PERENNIALS

When we dream of old-fashioned gardens and the idealized flowers that bloom there, we imagine first the herbaceous perennials, those most beloved flowers of past and present—the black-eyed Susans, daisies, daylilies, iris, peonies, hosta, Queen Anne's lace, and myriad others, including many favorite wildflowers, native and alien. In any low-maintenance garden, beautiful and dependable flowering herbaceous perennials will be the

horticultural centerpiece. Remarkably varied as they are, all share certain characteristics: they die to the ground each fall and return in the spring, often larger and more vital. Once established, the varieties we use in the Natural Garden come up year after year with little care; they are long-living—like trees, some will outlive even the youngest gardener who plants them—and will thrive in the same location for many years without being divided, disturbed, or otherwise fussed over. There are perennials for every location—from full sun to shade to semishade; from dry conditions to wet. In short this is a vast group of plants with many qualities to recommend them.

In the Natural Garden, especially in the sunny summer garden, perennials are like broad strokes of color on a canvas, making the strongest statements. Many gardeners are a little afraid of color, seeing it as the ultimate test of their artistry. Color is mysterious and sometimes bewildering, but several approaches to it have proven true over time. Use them as guides but not strict rules, for gardening with color is highly subjective—whatever arrangements please you are arrangements that work.

The simplest approach to color in the garden is the all-of-a-color scheme such as the famous white garden at Sissinghurst, the creation of Vita Sackville-West and her husband Sir Harold Nicolson. They planted only all-white species—white-flowering roses, delphiniums, lilies, blackberry, lilac, iris, and others. The result is a subtle garden, based on the careful arrangement and blending of different shades, tones, and tints, from cool stark

PRECEDING PAGES: LEFT, A perennial planting in partial sun; RIGHT, From left, black-eyed Susan (Rudbeckia hirta), *gay-feather* (Liatris spicata 'Kobold'), *white purple coneflower* (Echinacea purpurea 'Alba'), *pink bee balm* (Monarda didyma), *a daylily* (Hemerocallis cv.), *purple coneflower* (E. purpurea), *Queen Anne's lace* (Daucus carota var. carota), *and blue speedwell* (Veronica spicata).
RIGHT: A "white" garden in late spring. White iris are framed by an ornamental blackberry (Rubus tridel), *left, and white lilac* (Syringa vulgaris).

TOP: *From the same side of the color wheel, the harmonious colors of purple loosestrife* (Lythrum virgatum 'Dropmore Purple') *and monarda* (Monarda didyma) *make a strong statement, accented by white garden phlox* (Phlox paniculata 'Mount Fuji').
ABOVE, LEFT: *Shasta daisies* (Chrysanthemum x superbum).
RIGHT: *Bleeding-heart* (Dicentra spectabilis) *and yellow leopard's-bane* (Doronicum plantagineum) *demonstrate complementary colors—from opposite sides of the color wheel.*

white to silver to warm off-white. The same idea has been tried with all-blue and all-yellow gardens While you may not want to commit your entire garden to a single color, it is an interesting and challenging theme to pursue in a small section, perhaps a single island bed.

Another way of dealing with color is to turn to the theories that have evolved since the nineteenth century when Chevreul, a French chemist working for the Gobelins Tapestry Works in Paris, first formulated the color wheel and introduced the ideas of primary and complementary colors. On the color wheel, red, yellow, and blue (more precisely, magenta, yellow, and cyan) lie at three points of an equilateral triangle. They are known as the primary colors because all other colors are mixed from them. Arrangements of two or all three primary colors "contrast" and are too jarring for the garden; instead, use primary colors in sweeping plantings by themselves (as in a field of daffodils) or mix them with other softer colors. They can also be used sparingly as accents in your plantings. Because red tends to overwhelm the other colors in the garden, I usually shy away from the brightest reds in my color arrangements. However, if you want an irresistible focal point, a red-flowering plant will provide it. There are also more subtle ways to incorporate red into the garden; for example, rhubarb has ruby red stems, not flowers, and other plants have reddish foliage that is not as arresting as a blazing red tulip or other flower.

Midway between each of the three primary colors are colors made of 50 percent of the two adja-cent primary colors on the wheel: violet, green, and orange. Arrangements of these colors and variations of them "harmonize" because they have colors in common. Violet and orange, for example, both contain red which lies between them. In the garden, therefore, a planting of purple loosestrife (*Lythrum salicaria* hybrid) and tawny daylily (*Hemerocallis fulva*) would harmonize well.

You can use this approach to color by dividing the color wheel into two halves and choosing any colors from one hemisphere to create a simple but effective color scheme. For example, if the wheel is divided between red and green, you can combine blue, violet, pink, mauve, and indigo set off by green foliage and accented with an occasional red highlight.

Complementary colors are those that lie directly opposite each other on the color wheel—red and green, blue and orange, violet and yellow—and these work well paired together as accents in a planting. Sweeps of bright yellow black-eyed Susan (*Rudbeckia hirta*) are perfectly highlighted by spikes of loosestrife, 'Morden's Gleam', in their midst.

While color is found throughout the Natural Garden, the In-Between Area is the canvas for your most carefully conceived color statements. In keeping with the changeable spirit of nature and the Natural Garden, these statements are best made in flowing plantings and large informal splashes of color. The Natural Garden is a celebration of nature rather than an homage to man's control of it. It has no room for carefully rendered arrangements such as rigid parterre beds.

The Natural Garden's island flower beds are freestanding, open

ABOVE: *A border includes yellow coreopsis* (Coreopsis lanceolata 'Sun Ray'), *white phlox* (Phlox carolina 'Miss Lingard'), *monarda* (Monarda didyma, 'Cambridge scarlet'), *blue balloon flower* (Platycodon grandiflorus), *tall snakeroot* (Cimicifuga racemosa), *white veronica* (Veronica spicata 'Icicle'), *and yellow yarrow* (Achillea filipendulina).

on all sides. Maintenance, when necessary, is easily accomplished because you can reach all sides of the bed. To keep such labor to a minimum, however, choose your plants with basic considerations in mind: suitability to location, ease of culture, sturdiness, duration of bloom, scale or size, and color. A plant that satisfies you on all these counts will certainly deliver what you desire.

Some gardeners prefer to develop a plan on paper, sketching approximate outlines of the islands and the position of plant masses. You can make tracing-paper overlays to show the succession of plantings, spring through winter. (For more on planning, see Adjustments and Improvements, pages 238–41.) Other gardeners (such as Sybil Ittman in An "English" Cottage Garden, pages 35–40) prefer the less-formal "hose method." This quite simply means using a length of garden hose to delineate the shape of the bed in situ and get a fairly accurate idea of how it will work in the landscape. Once you have a configuration you like, climb up on a ladder to double-check it from above, and go into the house for an inside out view. Make your adjustments, and then cut a line of sod or spread a thin line of ground limestone next to

the hose to mark the island while you work.

Preparing the soil is the next step. In *Through the Looking Glass,* Lewis Carroll's memorable Alice met a talkative tiger lily. When Alice commented on its ability to speak, the tiger lily, by way of explanation, had her feel the hard ground of its flower bed and said, "In most gardens . . . they make the beds too soft—so that the flowers are always asleep." Having talking flowers may not be your goal, but you do want wide-awake, healthy plants. For this properly prepared soil is essential because your long-living plants will remain in place for many years. The aim is to aerate the soil and enrich it with organic matter to make it loose, friable, and well drained—the perfect medium for perennials. There are various methods for preparing the soil of a large flower bed. If you do not mind heavy labor, you can use traditional double or single digging, which are well-documented in basic gardening books; or you can use a Rototiller to turn the earth, or better yet, you can use a new version of the "raised bed" method, especially tailored to the *laissez-faire* approach of the natural gardener.

Traditional raised beds are above-ground level planting areas contained by railroad ties, concrete blocks, large stones, or similar devices. I never find such beds attractive and prefer instead an alternative, a gently sloped "mountain" for planting. This new method is very straightforward: bring soil to the site and dump it directly on the spot, filling in the outline you have made. You can move soil from an out-of-the-way place on your property or have your

garden center truck in topsoil and dump it in place. My sister did not have to pay to have soil removed when her pool was dug—it simply became a large raised garden plot at the rear of her yard.

The covering of soil should be about 2 to 3 feet at its highest point and slope down to ground level on all sides. As you shape it, remove large stones and improve the soil with additives—peat moss, limestone, composted leaves, and so on, depending upon the composition of the soil and the needs of the plants you will be growing there. I advise obtaining a soil analysis from the state soil-testing laboratory (see Source Guide, pages 287–92); if you tell them what you plan to grow, they will also tell you how to adjust your soil to suit your plants. These additives should eventually equal about a third of the planting medium. Turn and mix the soil with a garden fork and tamp it down firmly with the back of a shovel.

Whether you use this easy method or a more traditional one, you should prepare the ground well in advance of planting to give the soil a chance to settle down and absorb the nutrients and organic amendments. In zones 7 to 10, this means the spring for fall planting; in zones 1 to 6, make preparations in fall for spring planting. While the soil is settling it will also kill off the grass underneath.

"Nature abhors a vacuum" the old saying goes and, unfortunately, at this stage the island is a perfect vacuum for weeds to fill. It is best to encourage them to grow by watering the mound; within a few weeks weed seeds will have germinated and sprouts appeared. It is then a simple matter to remove the

weeds with a loop-type hoe (known as a "hula hoe," swoe, or Dutch-hook). You can cover the mound with black plastic mulch over the winter. If not, most dormant weed seeds will germinate in early spring and can be easily removed by hoeing, saving you countless hours of work later. Weeds can be further reduced by mulching (see Ground Covers, pages 59–75).

If your island is very large, include a path of stepping stones through it. They may be almost hidden by the plantings during summer but will make access safe and easy. If the island runs from the In-Between Area into shrubs of the Outer Area or perimeter, leave a small path between the island and the shrubs. Make it paved or grassy and plant clumps or large groups of spring-blooming bulbs on either side. During the summer, this path too will be hidden by the flowering plants.

Now that location and size are determined and the soil is prepared, it's time to plant. At this point, it would be simple to create plantings of riotous color that would bloom for two to four weeks and then disappear for the rest of the year, a practice followed on some large estates. But in modern gardens, and especially in the Natural Garden,

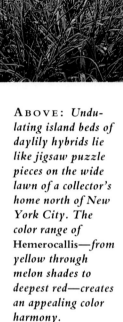

ABOVE: *Undulating island beds of daylily hybrids lie like jigsaw puzzle pieces on the wide lawn of a collector's home north of New York City. The color range of* Hemerocallis—*from yellow through melon shades to deepest red—creates an appealing color harmony.*

continuous color is very important. Not everything will bloom all season long, but you can plan your garden so that something will be colorfully in bloom from spring to fall. You are the artist in the Natural Garden, so the choice of colors is up to you. Paint your island pictures with as many living pigments as you like, but remember that masses of a single plant look better than small groups of many different plants. Study the Plant Selection lists beginning on page 242, look over the mail-order catalogues, and list your favorites by color, height, and time of bloom. This will help you arrange them to greatest effect for continuous color. You may want to cut photos out of the catalogues and key them to your plans.

The tallest plants should be positioned in the center of the island, the shortest along the perimeter. In general, your tallest plant should be no taller than one-half the island's width at its widest point. An island that is 10 feet across theoretically could have 5-foot plants in the center. This is a flexible rule of thumb and should be combined with your own good sense in making your choices; if you are planning a raised island bed, the center plants should

not be as tall as they would be in a flat bed, for example. Also keep in mind the ratio of the plant's width to its height, for this will determine how much space you will need for a mass of plants. In the broadest terms, the width of a plant is approximately one-half to two-thirds of its height. Therefore, if you have 3-foot plants, space them 2 feet apart to be sure they have enough elbow room. Many catalogues list heights and widths.

By now you may be somewhat daunted by the difficulty of creating a successful color garden. It is true that to make a large flower planting such as a series of island beds is a very ambitious project. You might prefer to start small, concentrating on a single bed. Then, when you have seen how that one works out, tackle another. No matter how much you learn from reading and research, there is no substitute for experience. The hands-on work you do in your garden does the most to develop that green thumb.

Herbaceous perennials were *the* plants of Gertrude Jekyll's borders, but her arrangements needed constant coddling by legions of gardeners. The Natural Garden may be inspired by her borders, with

OPPOSITE: *A single-blossom variety of peony* (**Paeonia lactiflora 'Krinkled White'**).

flowers arranged by height, color, and texture, but it will not demand the same heavy maintenance. This is because the plant selection is limited to easy-care plants such as those mentioned here and listed in the Plant Selection (pages 242–83). With few exceptions, these perennials can stay in place, without being divided, for at least five years. Peonies, for example, live contentedly in the same spot for a hundred years. When a plant does need dividing, think of it as a bonus, for you will gain new plants for other parts of the garden or to give to your gardener friends.

As for routine maintenance, perennial beds are traditionally cut to the ground after the first killing frost. This is done mostly as a precaution against plant disease, but I feel there are drawbacks to the wholesale clearing of perennials. For one thing, I like certain plants precisely because they are so beautiful when dried in the winter garden. If there is good air circulation, as there is bound to be in an island bed, you can safely leave just about anything in place. Also, some material that dries and falls over will act as a winter mulch. Therefore, clear selectively, leaving the grasses

ABOVE: *A herbaceous hedge of common peonies* (**Paeonia officinalis**). **BELOW:** *Anemoneform peony hybrid* (**Paeonia lactiflora 'Santa Fe'**).

and other winter ornamentals, such as black-eyed Susans. With a small rake remove any material that becomes mushy and falls flat against the ground. Then spread a winter mulch in the cleared spaces. In early spring, just before the first green shoots of the new season appear in the bed, cut the remains of last year's growth to the ground, remove the winter mulch, and toss it all on the compost heap. The cycle of life is about to recommence.

Perennials can also be used outside the island beds. In wooded areas, you may choose them for the wildflower garden of the forest floor (see Trees, Shrubs, and Woodland Areas, pages 145–67). There are also perennials that thrive in meadows—dry or wet (see Meadows, page 131)—and perennials for water gardens (see Water in the Garden, page 169) and rock gardens (see Rock Gardens, page 185). Many ornamental grasses are perennials (see Ornamental Grasses, page 113) and can be positioned in flower beds or in the Outer Area for season-long interest. Just remember that perennials will be with you a long time—many are almost permanent elements. In the enthusiasm a new garden engenders, it is often difficult to resist the temptation to buy many plants all at once. Even if you can afford massive impulse buying, it is far better to go slowly, to build your garden carefully and thoughtfully, and to get it right the first time. Otherwise you will find yourself pulling out plants that fail to thrive or that no longer fit your plans. Instead, the perennials in your garden should be planned and planted for the future as well as the present.

FAR LEFT: *Plants for a white garden include white bleeding-heart (Dicentra spectabilis), dusty-miller (Senecio cineraria 'Silver Dust'), and spirea (Spiraea x vanhouttii).* **LEFT:** *Columbine hybrids (Aquilegia 'McKana Hyrids') blooming in open shade.*

Sundrops or evening primrose (Oenothera fruticosa)

Phlox (Phlox paniculata) *and daylily*

Acanthus (Acanthus mollis 'Latifolius')

Yellow yarrow (Achillea filipendulina)

Golden marguerite (Anthemis tinctoria)

False indigo (Baptisia australis))

Lenten rose (Helleborus orientalis)

Siberian iris (Iris sibirica)

Narrowleaf plantain lily (Hosta lancifolia)

Acanthus mollis 'Latifolius', acanthus, bear's-breech

Achillea filipendulina, yarrow

Alchemilla vulgaris, lady's-mantle

Anthemis tinctoria, golden marguerite

Aquilegia hybrids, columbine

Aquilegia hybrida 'McKana Giants', columbine

Artemisia ludociviana, Silver King artemisia

Astilbe spp. and hybrids, astilbe

Astilbe x *arendsii,* astilbe

Baptisia australis, false indigo

Chrysanthemum x *superbum,* shasta daisy

Delphinium elatum, delphinium, larkspur

Dicentra spectabilis, bleeding-heart

Doronicum plantagineum, leopard's-bane

Echinacea purpurea, purple coneflower

Helenium autumnale, sneezewort

Helleborus orientalis, Lente rose

Hemerocallis, hybrids, 'Prairie Blue-eyes', daylily

Hemerocallis fulva, tawny daylily

Hosta spp., hosta

Hosta lancifolia, narrowleaf plantain lily

Iris pumila, dwarf bearded iris

I. sibirica, Siberian iris

Lavandula angustifolia, lavender

Liatris spicata 'Kobold', gay-feather

Ligularia x *przewalski* 'The Rocket', rocket ligularia

Lupinus 'Russell Hybrids', lupine

Lythrum salicaria hybrids, hybrid purple loosestrife

L. salicaria 'Morden's Gleam', purple loosestrife

L. virgatum 'Dropmore Purple', loosestrife

Macleaya cordata, plume poppy

Mimilus spp., monkey flower

Monarda didyma, monarda, bergamot, oswego tea, bee balm

Oenothera fruticosa, sundrops

O. missourensis evening primrose

Paeonia lactiflora, peony ('Krinkled White') ('Santa Fe')

P. officinalis, common peony

Phlox carolina 'Miss Lingard', thick-leaved phlox, Carolina's phlox

P. paniculata, garden phlox

Romneya coulteri, California tree poppy

Rudbeckia fulgida, coneflower

R. hirta, black-eyed Susan, gloriosa daisy

Stachys lanata, lamb's-ears

Sedum spectabile 'Autumn Joy', sedum live-forever

Veronica spicata, veronica, speedwell

Yucca filamentosa, yucca

EASY ANNUALS AND BIENNIALS

Unlike perennials, annuals and biennials, as a rule, do not usually come back year after year. Their life spans are shorter and so, in the easy-care Natural Garden, they are not used as frequently. They may, however, still have an important role to play.

Annuals are the larger of the two groups. They are plants that live, flower, form seed, and die in a single season—having fulfilled their reproductive cycle. They fall into three categories.

Forget-me-not (Myosotis alpestris)

Queen Anne's lace (Daucus carota *var.* carota)

Morning-glory (Ipomoea tricolor 'Heavenly Blue')

Most are "tender annuals" from the tropics, which are destroyed by the first touch of frost. Others are actually tender perennials from the subtropics, sometimes called "winter annuals." Then there are the "hardy annuals," plants that can tolerate cold and even survive the winter in some areas. Their seed can occasionally "overwinter." In the Natural Garden, we are interested in those plants that I call "easy-annuals" because their easy-care qualities allow them a place in the low-maintenance garden. They do not need to be deadheaded (that is, have their faded flowers removed to assure continuous bloom); they often self-sow in the garden (hardy annuals); they are easy to sow and to cultivate; and they attract few pests. Most require full sun, but there are some shade-loving exceptions such as *Impatiens.*

You will want to select annuals on the basis of color, height, and most of all suitability to location— from blue bachelor's buttons (*Centaurea cyanus*) to yellow coreopsis (*C. tinctoria*), from dainty Johnny-jump-ups (*Viola tricolor*) to towering sunflowers (*Helianthus*), from cool-growing calendula (*C. officinalis*) to heat-tolerant treasure flower (*Gazania rigens*). I have given you a head start on the selection process by compiling my list from annuals that tolerate a wide range of conditions (see Plant Selection, pages 242–83). New varieties are always being introduced and for the most part are improvements, although

California poppy (Eschscholzia californica), *closed on a gray day*

Sweet alyssum (Alyssum *hybrids*)

Mexican sunflower (Tithonia rotundifolia)

Impatiens, or patient Lucy
(Impatiens *hybrids*)

Sage (Salvia farinacea *'Victoria'*)

Vinca, or Madagascar periwinkle
(Catharanthus roseus)

the gaudy, double-flowered hydrids really do not belong in the Natural Garden. Annuals can be grown most inexpensively from seed, started indoors in February or March, or sown directly in the ground when all danger of frost has passed. Follow directions on the seed package. Many plants are also available as seedlings, sold in flats at the garden center. This is a bit more expensive, and supplies and selection will be limited, but purchasing just a few such flats will give you early color in the most visible parts of the garden, perhaps the Inner Area, while you wait for perennials to come up or for seeds to sprout and grow elsewhere.

One of the nicest things about easy-annuals is the way they extend the season. Like the ornamental grasses, many easy-annuals bloom late, after most of the summer perennials and before the fall flowers, and continue blooming into the fall. They are also perfect for temporary gardens in areas destined for change, perhaps where a pool or deck will eventually be built. They provide cover for a bare garden still being planned or for a new meadow planting. And, of course, they can be used in the old-fashioned style, as bedding and cutting plants in a more formal area of your Natural Garden. Despite these estimable qualities even easy-annuals are more demanding than well-established perennials or biennials. They do, however, have a place in the Natural Garden.

Johnny-jump-up (Viola tricolor *'Helen Mount'*)

Cosmos (Cosmos bipinnatus)

Sunflowers (Helianthus annuus)

ABOVE: *A bed of easy annuals, based on a red/white color scheme. Pink, red, and white globe amaranths* (Gomphrena globosa), *perfect for drying, dominate, with plumes of love-lies-bleeding* (Amaranthus *hybrids*) *at intervals.*

BIENNIALS

Biennials share some traits with both annuals and perennials. They must be sown from seed (or purchased as seedlings) but, like perennials, they will live through the winter. The main characteristic of biennials is that they are on a two-year cycle. The first year, planted from seed, they produce vegetative growth only, which in some cases is relatively insignificant. The second year, they flower and produce seed. If the conditions in your garden suit them, many biennials will self-sow, eventually blooming year after year.

Biennials may need a little extra patience and care in their siting, but they will be well worth it. There is only a handful of biennial plants, and these are usually listed in catalogues with the perennials because they are used much the way perennials are—in island beds or borders and in woodland wildflower gardens, for example. Some, such as foxglove (*Digitalis purpurea*), are true beauties; some bloom early, before most perennials, and will give you lovely color in the garden before the summer show really begins. Biennials are true naturals in the Natural Garden.

ABOVE: *Annuals in primary colors: red salvia* (Salvia splendens hyb.), *love-lies-bleeding* (Amaranthus tricolor cv.), *and China aster* (Aster hyb.); *yellow marigolds* (Tagetes hyb.); blue ageratum (Ageratum hyb.). Ornamental pepper, an edible annual, adds further interest to the front row. BELOW: *Meredith Sorensen displays the sunflower she grew.*

EASY-ANNUALS AND BIENNIALS: A SELECTION

Annuals

Ageratum hybrids, ageratum

Alyssum hybrids, sweet alyssum

Amaranthus caudatus, love-lies-bleeding

A. tricolor, Joseph's coat

Aster hybrids, annual aster, China aster

Calendula officinalis, calendula, pot marigold

Catharanthus roseus (Vinca rosea), vinca, periwinkle

Centaurea cyanus, blue batchelor's buttons, cornflower

Cleome spinosa 'Helen Campbell', cleome, spider flower

Coreopsis tinctoria, calliopsis

Cosmos bipinnatus, cosmos

Daucus carota, Queen Anne's lace (also biennial and perennial)

Eschscholzia californica, California poppy

Gazania rigens, treasure flower

Gomphrena globosa, globe amaranth, gomphrena

Helianthus annuus hybrids, sunflower

H. annuus 'Italian White', Italian white sunflower

Impatiens hybrids, impatiens, patient Lucy

Ipomoea alba, moon-flower

I. x nil, morning-glory

I. tricolor 'Heavenly Blue', heavenly blue morning-glory

Rudbeckia hirta 'Gloriosa Daisy', annual black-eyed Susan, gloriosa daisy

Salvia farinacea 'Victoria', sage

S. farinacea 'White Porcelain', sage (white flowered form)

S. splendens hybrids, salvia

Tithonia rotundifolia, Mexican sunflower

Viola tricolor 'Helen Mount', Johnny-jump-up

Biennials

Alcea rosea, single hollyhock, old farmhouse hollyhock

Digitalis purpurea, foxglove

Lychnis chalcedonica, Maltese-cross

L. coronaria, rose campion

Myosotis alpestris, forget-me-not

Verbascum bombyciferum, mullein

V. hybrids, hybrid mullein

FROM TOP: *Foxglove* (Digitalis purpurea). *Single, old-fashioned hollyhocks* (Alcea rosea cv.) *with annual sunflowers* (Helianthus annuus 'Italian White'). *Old farmhouse hollyhock* (Alcea rosea) *and yellow mulleins* (Verbascum bombyciferum).
BELOW: *A mullein hybrid* (V. bombyciferum 'Harkness Hybrid') *and pale orange Welsh poppy* (Meconopsis cambrica).

ORNAMENTAL GRASSES

Ornamental grasses have recently been gaining favor among home gardeners because of their undeniably "natural" look, their ease of culture, and their flowering dependability. Grasses are the oldest food plants under cultivation—the venerable wheat, rice, and corn are all members of this family— but even as ornamentals, grasses in the garden are not an altogether new phenomenon. In seventeenth-century Holland, for example, feather

grass (*Stipa pennata*) was considered a beauty and can be found in at least one engraving from the period. More recently, in the 1920s, dramatic plumes of pampas grass (*Cortaderia selloana*) were essential props in silent movies; they set the mood of ancient Egypt or graced an elegant salon. In the 1930s, when wildflower gardens became popular, ornamental grasses were the perfect backdrop. Older gardens, especially those ghostly gardens abandoned to time along with the deserted houses they surround, often harbor still-thriving plantings of ribbon grass (*Phalaris arundinacea* var. *picta*).

My own interest in ornamental grasses was born of necessity. I wanted something that would extend my garden's growing season, filling the late-summer lull between the summer and fall blooming periods of my herbaceous perennials. Easy-annuals did part of this job, but I wanted even more beautiful, less demanding plants. As an experiment, I selected a single variety—fountain grass (*Pennisetum alopecuroides*). In August its arching panicles of purple flowers gracefully fluttered and nodded in the breeze. I was hooked. I began to collect more grasses, realizing that they filled another gap in the growing season as well—their flower spikes persisted after frost and were actually lovelier

when standing, dry, against the winter snow. Winter color is the greatest challenge in any garden and grasses meet it, their dried flowers turning from beige to gleaming silver to feathery spun gold.

In spring the bright green, bronze, or even ruby red foliage of most grasses stands perfectly straight until the leaves grow tall enough to begin arching back to the earth, making near perfect half-spheres. Growth slows in summer, but starts up again in August, when most grasses prepare to bloom. The flowers are borne on vertical stems ranging from 12 inches to 12 feet tall, depending on the variety.

When selecting a grass, make certain that you plan for its eventual height and width. Along a property line a very tall grass or reed will make an impenetrable privacy screen, and will also act as a noise barrier, creating its own sweet sound even in the gentlest breeze. That same grass next to the house might look wonderful in the spring, but would soon take over—perhaps masking a treasured view or blocking the sun. Not all ornamental grasses are toweringly tall—some are only 6 inches high or even less— but as with your other plants, choose carefully and plan ahead.

Grasses are virtually pest-free and are vigorous growers that withstand

hot summer sun and driving rain equally well. Most require full sun, although some, such as striped orchard grass (*Dactylis glomerata* 'Variegata') will tolerate partial shade. Bottlebrush grass (*Hystrix patula*) actually prefers both shade and damp and would do well in a woodland wildflower garden resembling the northeastern woods in which it grows wild. Some grasses are grown not only for their beauty —those that spread have intricate, fibrous root systems that fight erosion and can break up poor soil and actually improve its texture. Grasses that will grow in clumps are good additions to a rock garden. Blue fescue (*Festuca ovina* var. *glauca*), for example, or red Japanese blood grass (*Imperata cyclindrica rubra*) are particularly good rock garden plants.

One of my favorite grasses is the very graceful maiden grass (*Miscanthus sinensis* 'Gracillimus'). This ornamental variety grows in a thick clump. Its light green leaves have a white midrib, it produces pinkish white flowers, and is beautifully golden in the winter. There is a zebra-striped maiden grass (*M. sinensis* 'Zebrinus') that likes a damp location and would add great natural beauty to an otherwise artificial swimming pool area. Another striking member of this family, eulalia

grass (*M. sacchariflorus*), grows to 12 feet, spreads by rhizomes, and has long been cultivated in Japan, where its stems are used to make brush handles and kitchen utensils.

If grasses do have a drawback it is that a few can become invasive, traveling either by airborne seeds or underground rhizomes. Most hybrids in cultivation, however, including the ornamentals listed here, do not spread and have sterile seeds. The one grasslike plant that has a truly bad reputation is bamboo.

Bamboos, which are not true grasses but very close relatives, are almost always considered troublesome. Although some form clumps, many of them, especially those that are suitable for northern gardens, "run" or actually race across the landscape if it is to their liking. I find them very beautiful and exotic, however, and if you are willing to do a little extra research and preparation they can find a place in the Natural Garden.

First, choose a species that clumps, such as *Bambusa oldhamii,* or that creeps at a very slow rate, such as green bamboo (*Phyllostachys viridis*). This species grows vertically very quickly while spreading horizontally rather slowly, and it is hardy to -8°F. Proof of its hardiness is the beautiful stand of 30-foot-tall green bamboo growing at Blithewold, an

ABOVE: LEFT, *Hardy golden bamboo* (Phyllostachys aurea); RIGHT, *A border of blue lily-turf* (Liriope muscari *'Variegata'*) *provides a transition from lawn grass to perennial bed.*

estate in Bristol, Rhode Island.

If you have selected a variety that travels, however, you must confine the growing area, before planting, by creating an underground barrier. This barrier must be made of a non-deteriorating material and must extend at least 18 inches, vertically, underground. Some people use slabs of slate or blue stone, or 2-foot wide sheets of expensive stainless steel. I know one gardener who sank an old bathtub into the ground for this purpose. If you choose a slow traveler, you can do without the barrier and can thwart the bamboo's escape simply by stepping on any new shoots that appear in undesirable places. Having carefully selected the species and taken these precautions, you should have no problems. Bamboo may require extra work at the outset, but its tantalizing beauty will repay your efforts many times over.

Perhaps you are intrigued by the idea of ornamental grasses, but are not ready to commit yourself and your garden to a perennial grass. Or perhaps you have a location that needs a quick and attractive planting until a perennial ground cover can take hold. In such cases, there are several varieties of annual grasses from which to choose. In Washington, D.C., huge raised planters at the new Pennsylvania Avenue Project were seeded with *Pennisetum setaceum,* as an annual, until the perennial pennisetum took hold. Another interesting annual grass is also one of the oldest ornamentals, Job's-tears (*Coix lacryma-jobi*), which has been in gardens since the fourteenth century. A year with this or any other of the annual grasses may convince you to include a perennial variety somewhere in your garden.

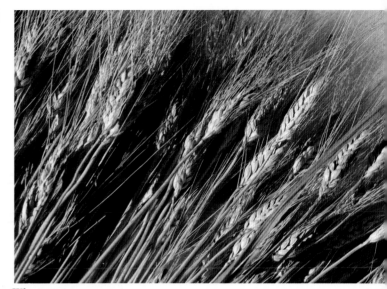
Wheat (Triticum *spp.*)

Fountain grass (Pennisetum alopecuroides)

Dwarf white stripe bamboo (Arundinaria variegata)

Switch grass (Panicum virgatum)

Feather reed grass (Calamagrostis *spp.*) *and miscanthus in winter*

Purple-leaf fountain grass (Pennisetum setaceum rubrum)

Zebra grass (Miscanthus sinensis '*Zebrinus*')

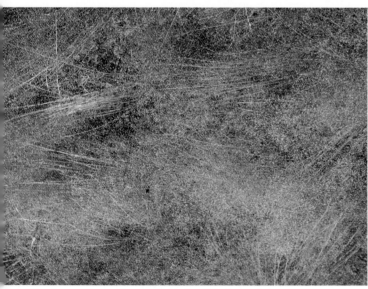

Cloud grass (agrostis nebulosa) *detail in late winter*

Foxtail (Alopecurus pratensis)

ABOVE: *A poolside planting of perennials against a screen of green bamboo* (Phyllostachys aurea viridis) *contained by stainless steel sheets.*

OPPOSITE: ABOVE, *Bands of colorful annuals and perennials are softened by feathery foxtail* (Alopecurus pratensis). *Tall green bamboo* (Phyllostacliys viridis) *provides a dark, dramatic backdrop at Blithewold in Rhode Island;* BELOW, *Plumes of pampas grass* (Cortaderia selloana) *beyond the spikes of century plants* (Agave americana).

ORNAMENTAL GRASSES: A SELECTION

Grasses

Arundo donax, giant reed

Calamagrostis acutiflora stricta, feather reed grass

C. arundinacea brachytricha, reed grass

Cortaderia selloana, pampas grass

Dactylis glomerata 'Variegata', striped orchard grass

Eragrostis spectabilis, purple love grass

Festuca ovina var. *glauca*, blue fescue

Hystrix patula, bottlebrush grass

Imperata cyclindrica rubra, red Japanese blood grass

Miscanthus floridulus (*M. sacchariflorus giganteus*) 'Floridus', giant Chinese silver grass

M. sacchariflorus, eulalia grass

M. sinensis condesatus, purple-blooming Japanese silver grass

M. sinensis 'Gracillimus', maiden grass

M. sinensis 'Gracillimus Variegatus', striped maiden grass

M. sinensis 'Variegatus', variegated maiden grass

M. sinensis 'Zebrinus', zebra grass

Molinia caerulea 'Variegata', purple moor grass

Panicum virgatum, switch grass

Pennisetum alopecuroides, fountain grass, pennisetum

P. setaceum, fountain grass

P. setaceum cv. *rubrum*, purple-leaved fountain grass

P. villosum, feathertop

Phalaris arundinacea var. *picta*, ribbon grass

Scirpus cernus, miniature bullrush

Setaria lutescens, foxtail grass (annual)

Stipa pennata, feather grass

Bamboos and Other Grasslike Plants

Arundinaria variegata, dwarf whitestripe bamboo

A. viridis-striata, variegated bamboo

Bambusa oldhamii, bamboo

Coix lacryma-jobi, Job's-tears

Liriope muscari, blue lily turf

L. muscari 'Variegata', blue lily turf

L. spicata, creeping lily turf

Phyllostachys aurea, golden bamboo

P. aureosulcata, yellow-groove bamboo

P. viridis, green bamboo

VINES

Vines are something extra,
a luxurious accessory. While ground covers, or
trees, or shrubs have practical uses, vines are
more purely ornamental. Like necklaces, lace,
icing, or gingerbread molding, they provide
the perfect finishing touch. Trained to climb
building facades, vines can soften hard-edged
architecture and dignify an otherwise plain and
monotonous wall. They frame doorways,
enhance barriers and gates, camouflage eyesores

such as chain link fencing, and shade a hot summer porch. If grown horizontally across the ground, they can even anchor the soil. Vines skip and tumble over rocks or cascade down a sloping bank.

The French novelist Colette, writing in her journal in 1925, exclaimed, "Vines, you shall rear yourselves into the sky, you shall breathe in the breeze that sometimes does not reach down to brush the earth, the rough undersides of your leaves shall taste the torrid mist that summer pumps up from the earth, and from your woody shoots, vines, I shall conjure myself a grove of trees!"

Colette's enthusiastic description closely reflects the true needs of these plants. In nature vines climb up a nearby host, usually a tree, compensating for weak stems that alone cannot support the vine's lush top growth and climbing to reach the sunlight and buoyant air of the forest canopy. The vine's roots grow deep into the cool, shaded forest floor where the soil is rich and moist. Knowing this, you can see that in the most general terms, you must provide rich, cool soil, a support for the plant to climb upon, and a place in the sun.

Vines grow vertically either by twining or clinging. Twiners grow in a spiral—some turning clockwise, others counterclockwise. Some twining vines have auxiliary tendrils that reach out and wind around anything handy, be it another plant, a branch, twig, wire, string, or pole. Clinging vines attach themselves to their support with tiny rootlike "holdfasts" that grip the surface. Some vines grow very quickly, soon covering an entire wall; others inch along year by year.

Habit and speed of growth are the two primary considerations in selecting an appropriate vine for your garden. A fast-growing clinger will do well against a brick or stone wall; a twiner would be appropriate for a trellis by the front door. Away from the house, in a wooded area, a vine will find a handy tree to climb, but in most cases it is better not to allow the vine to climb a prized living tree; eventually the vine's weight may damage if not actually kill the host plant. On the other hand, a vine trailing over an otherwise unsightly dead tree gives that tree a kind of second life. If you have such a tree, make certain it is well away from the house, presenting no danger should lightning strike, and that its limbs have been trimmed back, to lessen the chance of the tree coming down in high winds, before you

ABOVE: *Helen Stoddard collaborated with renowned landscape architect Fletcher Steel in the design of her garden, which includes an entry area softened by Virginia creeper (Parthenocissus quinquefolia).*

plant the vine at its base.

Of course you need not site a vine only in a wooded area. Vines are also wonderful accents in the Inner Area, growing against the side of the house or over the surface of a wall. Many people think that vines eventually damage any wall, but the consensus now is that a stone or brick wall in good condition will not be harmed. Still, however, I recommend that you give the vine an independent support system of wires, trellis, or latticework anchored to the ground some 4 inches away from the wall and attached at its top. The support may be detachable at the top and hinged at the bottom to allow you to swing it down and away from the wall for repainting or other maintenance on

the side of the house. This way you will not damage the plant and will have easy access to what lies beneath. Your major problem may be the soil—soil near the foundations of most houses is often the poorest on the property. In finishing off the foundation, the builder undoubtedly backfilled with whatever rubble was available. Before planting a vine near the house, therefore, you will need to prepare the ground even more carefully than you would elsewhere. Dig a hole about 2 feet in diameter and fill it with good garden loam and organic humus before positioning your plant. You must also consider the particular plant's needs—clematis, for example, needs alkaline soil.

Growing against the house, a

BELOW: *Ivy and wisteria turn an old tree trunk in Alice Barnhart's garden into a found sculpture. Goatweed (Aegopodium podograria 'Variegatum') is planted as a ground cover.*

vine's leaves will insulate the wall and protect it from the elements. Full cover from a deciduous vine, such as Boston ivy (*Parthenocissus tricuspidata*), will shade the house in summer and allow the sun to warm it in winter. An evergreen such as English ivy (*Hedera helix*) will give you year-round color. Evergreens do best in a sheltered location where they are unlikely to be burned by winter dehydration. You may not want to hide the architecture of your house, but only to cover a small area with a vine, to soften the lines of a chimney for example. Slow-growing, evergreen clinging vines, such as an ivy that does not need constant pruning, are best for this purpose. If the entry garden needs a touch of color or a bit of livening up, a vine trailing over a trellis around the doorway may add the right note. Choose one that has splashy flowers, such as a *Clematis,* or colorful fruits or berries, such as

porcelain berry, hops, or Virginia creeper. If shade from afternoon sun is the goal in a particular location, then choose a perennial with very dense foliage such as Dutchman's-pipe (*Aristolochia durior*), whose heart-shaped leaves overlap like shingles. Once found throughout New England, Dutchman's-pipe is also a favorite food of the pipe-vine swallowtail butterfly. If you want to experiment before making the commitment to a perennial, plant a fast-growing, easy-care annual such as cardinal climber, morning-glory, or moonflower.

Whether you decide on a clinging or twining, fast-growing or slow-growing vine, there are many beauties from which to choose. But make your selection carefully, a properly sited deciduous or evergreen perennial vine will be with you a long time. Planted in the Inner Area, it will be very much a part of your life.

ABOVE: *Persian ivy* (Hedera colchica 'Dentata Variegata')

LEFT: *Silver lace vine* (Polygonum aubertii) *creates a shade canopy above a garden bench*

ABOVE: *Fragrant, night-blooming moonflower* (Ipomoea alba)

BELOW: *Sweet autumn clematis* (Clematis paniculata)

Climbing hydrangea (Hydrangea anomala petiolaris) *masks a wall*

Boston ivy (Parthenocissus tricuspidata) *on a wall in autumn 1986,*

VINES: A SELECTION

Ampelopsis brevipedunculata,
porcelain vine

Aristolochia durior,
Dutchman's-pipe

Bougainvillea spectabilis,
bougainvillea, paper flower

Celastrus scandens,
American bittersweet

Clematis hybrids

Clematis armandii,
Armand clematis

C. x *jackmanii*

C. paniculata, (*C. maximow-icziana*) sweet autumn, evergreen clematis

C. virginiana, virgin's bower

Hedera canariensis
'Variegata',
variegated Algerian ivy

H. helix, English ivy

Hydrangea anomala petiolaris,
climbing hydrangca

Ipomoea alba,
moonflower (annual)

I. x *multifida,* cardinal
climber (annual)

I. tricolor 'Heavenly Blue',
morning-glory (annual)

Lonicera serotina florida,
Dutch honeysuckle

L. x *heckrottii,* goldflame
honeysuckle

Parthenocissus quinquefolia,
Virginia creeper

P. tricuspidata, Boston ivy

P. tricuspidata 'Veitchii',
small-leaved Boston ivy

Passiflora alatoce arulea,
passionflower

P. caerulea,
blue passionflower

P. incarnata,
hardy passionflower

P. vitifolia,
grape-leaf passionflower

Polygonum aubertii,
silver lace vine

Schisandra chinensis,
magnolia vine

Wisteria floribunda, Japanese
wisteria

W. sinensis, Chinese wisteria

Porcelain vine (Ampelopsis brevipedunculata)

Goldflame honeysuckle (Lonicera x heckrotii)

autumn 1987,

and autumn 1988

American bittersweet (Celastrus scandens), *beautiful but invasive*

Magnolia vine (Schisandra chinensis)

Grape-leaf passionflower (Passiflora vitifolia)

Passionflower (Passiflora incense)

MEADOWS

Ameadow of grasses and wildflowers is one of life's simple pleasures, a reminder of a time when we felt innocent and free and closer to nature. Whether that time ever actually existed does not matter—the feelings are real and there is restorative power in connecting with those feelings. A meadow, even a very small one, provides this connection. There is a tiny meadow of Queen Anne's lace and grasses nestled against a brownstone in

Brooklyn, and spending ten minutes beside it is a truly restful experience in a city bent on bustling.

The term *meadow* means grassland and applies equally well to a dry California slope covered with wildflowers as to a moist low-lying corner of Pennsylvania. A meadow's growth and composition depend on where it is, and what the prevailing conditions are. Meadows can be wet or dry (very dry meadows are known as prairies) and can have almost any soil type as long as it is not too nutritionally rich, but there is one requirement all meadows share. To thrive, they must have full sun at least six hours a day. If you cannot depend on that minimum in your space, you would do better to plan another kind of garden.

In the Natural Garden, large meadows work well as Outer Areas, on cleared land facing south and west, or at the often neglected outer edge of a large property. A meadow will also work in an In-Between Area, or could be planted instead of an island bed of perennials—it might be easier to maintain and will have an even less formal look, if that is your aim.

Once you have determined that a meadow will suit both your space and your dreams, you have to think about your neighbors. Intentionally establishing a meadow is a relatively new idea and has met with opposition, particularly in suburban areas where there are often so-called weed ordinances banning lawns over a certain height. These laws were enacted decades ago, well before the

ABOVE: LEFT,
A split-rail fence marks the boundary of a meadow;
RIGHT, *A picket fence contains meadow plants and defines the edge of an Inner Area.*

resurgence of appreciation of the principles behind the Natural Garden, to keep abandoned property from becoming an eyesore in residential areas. If you are going to create a meadow in view of neighbors, therefore, anticipate possible opposition and plan ahead.

The best thing to do is get permission in advance. Most city agencies are becoming familiar with lawn alternatives, and will probably be responsive to a well-presented case. Neighbors too can be convinced, especially if you show them examples of the kind of meadow you are planning, perhaps by letting them browse through this book.

Another approach is slowly to introduce the neighborhood to the idea of meadow in place of grass. Instead of plowing under your entire lawn all at once, let the meadow evolve gradually and give it a "planned" appearance to make it clear this is something you control and not just grass lawn run wild. Define a small area, perhaps a

BELOW: LEFT,
Tall-growing Joe-Pye weed (Eupatorium maculatum);
RIGHT, *Patti Hagan's vest-pocket meadow of Queen Anne's lace* (Daucus carota *var.* carota) *and sunflower* (Helianthus annuus) *thrives outside her Brooklyn brownstone.*

ABOVE: *Near the house, bands of yellow goldenrod* (Solidago *spp.*) *and violet New York ironweed* (Vernonia noveboracensis) *dominate a mature fall meadow.*

clearly delineated island, or a border that runs along a fence line and bulges slightly into the center. Outline this space with bricks, woodblocks, logs, a line of handsome stones, or a carefully mowed edge. In your first year's planting be sure to include seeds of fast-blooming annuals and, in prominent places, incorporate more expensive perennials from the nursery for fast results. Choose container-grown flowering perennials such as black-eyed Susans (*Rudbeckia hirta*), which are familiar and put on an honorable showing the first year, or plant a thick clump of graceful ornamental grass such as fountain grass (*Pennisetum alopecuroides*). Once a season of beautiful grasses and flowering

wildflowers has passed, the case will be made for you, and doubting neighbors may even be inspired to follow your lead.

Such a small "sample" meadow may be all some gardeners can manage, not because of neighbors' objections but because of space restrictions. Even a very small meadow area, however, can add a touch of the wild to an otherwise too-tame environment.

If you do have room for a large meadow, one of your joys will be to walk through it from time to time, perhaps to pick wildflowers or to reach a woodland area beyond. It is a good idea, therefore, to include in your initial plan the tracings of a path, which will not only look dec-

orative and inviting, but also protect the meadow plants and other wildlife from disturbance. It will also keep you from picking up barbed seeds or unwelcome insects. The path can be as simple as a meandering mowed strip—twice mower width to limit biweekly mowing to an out-and-back trip. It could also be made of stepping stones, log rounds, bricks, or some other permanent paving material (see Permanent Elements, pages 207–32). If your meadow is very large, it might be nice to include a small clearing in a spot that is shaded in the afternoon by a tree. Position a garden bench or rustic seat here and you will have a perfect retreat for morning coffee or afternoon tea. Along the path and around the clearing tuck in showy meadow plants in an irregular, free-form style, accessible for picking or easy viewing.

Whatever the size and style of your meadow, before selecting the plants, visit and study the wild places in your area to see what meadow plants are thriving. This is always my first suggestion, for regional differences in soil, rainfall, drainage, and climate determine the plants that grow well. Meadow plants fall into two categories—grasses and forbs (nongrass herbaceous plants such as daisies and Indian paintbrush). All meadows and prairies are comprised of these two plant materials.

ABOVE: *Late in the growing season, the meadow and its surroundings begin to change color. The mown grass path helps to define the space and make it easily accessible.*

LEFT: *Flanders poppies* (Papaver rhoeas) *with a sprinkling of blue bachelor's buttons, or cornflowers* (Centaurea cyanus).

Once you decide what meadow plants you want to grow, you can buy seeds by the pound, thereby customizing the mix. You will need from 5 to 20 pounds of seed per acre depending on the species, for seed weight varies greatly from plant to plant. For example, *Festuca ovina* var. *glauca,* a pretty blue ornamental grass, has 400,000 seeds to the ounce, while purple coneflower (*Echinacea* Rudbeckia *purpurea*) contains only 7,500 seeds per ounce. The supplier should furnish information on the amounts needed for your meadow site—be sure to ask. Forbs and grasses can also be purchased as nursery stock, but they are rather expensive to buy this way.

Most meadow perennials take at least two years to mature and bloom, spending the first season growing good root systems or lying dormant before sprouting the following spring. You may, therefore, want to mix some easy-annual seed with your basic grass so your meadow will look pretty the first year. Good choices would be bright blue bachelor's buttons (*Centaurea cyanus*), sunny yellow calliopsis (*Coreopsis tinctoria*), or golden orange California poppies (*Eschscholzia californica*). The first year might also be the time to buy a couple of those more expensive nursery plants. Clumps of butterfly weed (*Asclepias tuberosa*) or a planting of northern sea oats (*Uniola latifolia*) will soon look very attractive.

PLANTING

When winter loosens its grip on the earth, the time has come to seed the meadow. The process is similar to

ABOVE: *A meadow of western wildflowers dominated by orange California poppies* (Eschscholzia californica) *and spikes of blue California sky lupines* (Lupinus nanus).

ABOVE: *A colorful meadow in early summer.* BELOW: *The same meadow in autumn features dried grasses and flower seed heads.*

sowing lawn but does not require quite as much preparation. Meadow grasses and forbs do not need—in fact do not like—the rich, heavily fertilized soil demanded by grass lawn. Meadow plants like to be lean and hungry. Still, there must be good drainage and aeration, and in order for the seeds to penetrate the topsoil, some preparation is needed. Before beginning, decide whether the soil needs improvement or adjustment by having a soil analysis done through your Cooperative Extension agency. Then make any necessary changes. Slow-draining clayey soil may require increased organic matter; plow under a 2-to-4-inch layer of peat moss or other humus. The drainage of mildly problematic soil can be enhanced by adding gypsum, a soil conditioner, before turning the ground under. (For more on soil improvement, see

the chapter on Adjustments and Improvements, pages 238–41.) If you are replacing lawn with meadow, you will have to remove the sod or plow it under. Once this is done, prepare the ground as if there had never been lawn.

Preparation is best done in two stages. First, turn under the soil to a depth of 4 inches. For small areas, you can use a Rototiller (easily rented at most garden centers); for large fields you may want to hire someone with a tractor and plow. Once the ground has been cultivated, you will have unwittingly created the perfect environment for weeds. To give your wildflowers and meadow grasses a better chance of competing with them, hold off on sowing. Instead, water the raw earth thoroughly and wait for a good two weeks or until the inevitable weed seeds, dormant in the soil, have germinated. At this point you are ready for stage two: pulling out the weed seedlings by hand or hoe, or turning the ground under again with Rototiller or plow.

Now you are ready to sow. By hand, broadcast the meadow seeds as evenly as possible, working in two directions—north to south, and east to west. You can use a commercial seed spreader, although seeds of certain forbs have downy coverings that will not easily pass through the spreader. If your seeds are tiny, mix them with sand before spreading to get an even covering.

After the seed is sown, rake the ground smooth to cover the seeds lightly with soil, and water thoroughly with a fine spray. If possible use a heavy lawn roller to tamp down the ground, to retain moisture, and to level the area. Another optional but recommended step is

to cover the soil with an organic mulch. This will help assure constant moisture during the first three weeks while the seeds are germinating. I like to use a 1-to-2-inch layer of straw, which is both inexpensive and readily available. It will shelter the seeds and will also keep them from being dislodged in a heavy rain.

On steeply sloped banks, a little extra preparation is required to hold the seed in place. You can, if you wish, follow the lead of highway departments; they cover slopes with netting to prevent soil and seeds from running off in a hard rain and to hold tender new seedlings in place. Such a net should be made from organic material such as fine cotton string, which will eventually break down and become incorporated into the soil. If it seems too troublesome to spread and anchor a net, an alternative would be to use a meadowlike ground cover such as crown vetch (*Coronilla varia*), a vining plant, instead of seeding with meadow plants.

During the first three weeks or so, by virtue of daily hosings, sprinklers, or the certain cooperation of Mother Nature, you must keep the meadow moist to assure germination. Then, water twice a week for a month, and once a week for another month, giving the ground a good soaking each time. Because weather conditions vary not only from region to region but from year to year, use this schedule only as a general rule, letting your own climate be your ultimate guide. Once the meadow is well established, it may need no extra water at all except in drought years. Meadows survive with as little as a single foot of rainfall per year,

much less than the average in most places.

MAINTENANCE

Meadow management is a minimal affair. Largely self-sufficient, a meadow needs little more than an annual mowing to look its best. Some people do this in August, when the hay is harvested, but I like to wait until late fall, after the seeds of meadow plants have dropped naturally to the ground to await spring germination. If you do mow in the fall, rake up most of the cuttings, leaving a thin layer to act as mulch. On the other hand, a winter meadow, left uncut, has its own appeal. It can be a rich cloak of golden grasses that ripple in the chill autumn winds and stand statuesque against fresh snow. A dried meadow also provides winter cover for

ABOVE: *A simple grass meadow looks well-tended when a path is kept carefully mown.*
BELOW: *The mown path adds control and formality to nature's most informal creation. The path also allows you to pick flowers, wander, and halt the meadow spread.*

wildlife and allows you to locate and remove woody seedlings that may have gotten a start among the meadow plants. If you do let the meadow winter over, plan on mowing in the very early spring. You must carry away the clippings before bulb foliage emerges if you have naturalized daffodils or other spring bulbs in the meadow.

Whatever schedule you decide on, the grasses and forbs and especially any unwanted woody seedlings, will most likely prove too much for a conventional lawn mower. Do-it-yourselfers can practice the ancient art of scything by hand or can rent a mowing machine, but for large spaces hire a professional, easily found through your garden center or yellow pages. This service is usually inexpensive.

Burning the meadow is another way to control successional growth. This procedure absolutely requires a professional, usually located through your fire department or garden center. Check local ordinances; burning is prohibited in some areas, notably the suburbs. The benefits of burning are that it clears all plant material in one sweep, discourages unwanted woody seedlings from taking hold, and adds a beneficial layer of ash. Grasses and forbs seem to appreciate the extra close cropping a fire gives them; they are usually both larger and healthier the season following a burn. For more information and advice, contact your Cooperative Extension agent.

Another part of maintaining a meadow is controlling its spread. Mowed strips make good boundaries, but they do need weekly or biweekly passes with the mower. Permanent edging—of brick, wood, or stone—or paths enclosing and containing the meadow, require much less maintenance. An interesting alternative to these methods is to use densely rooted plants that create a barrier to the spreading meadow. Planted between meadow and grass lawn, for example, goldenrod (*Solidago* spp.), a much-maligned plant, is one of the best such barrier plants. (Goldenrod's reputation as a hay fever source is undeserved; in fact, its pollen is

very heavy and never airborne, but the yellow flower is confused with ragweed [*Ambrosia*], a notorious scourge of hay fever sufferers.)

The sun smiles on a well-planned and planted meadow, and the meadow seems to smile back. Writers, naturalists, poets, and painters have been inspired by such meadows. Vincent van Gogh was especially taken by these sunlit golden landscapes—writing to his brother Theo he once said he had "done two new studies: a farm by the highroad among cornfields, and a meadow full of very yellow buttercups, a ditch with irises, green leaves and purple flowers, the town in the background, some grey willows, and a strip of blue sky. If the meadow is not cut I should like to do this study again, for the subject was a very beautiful one . . . A little town in the midst of a countryside all flowered over with yellow and purple . . . can't you see it?"

ABOVE: *A naturalized planting of daylilies introduces the jumble of plants in a meadow left deliberately wild to shelter the house beyond. The white posts are remnants of a fence.*

Blazing star (Liatris spicata)

Goldenrod (Solidago *spp.*)

Carolina lupine (Thermopsis caroliniana)

Seedpod of purple coneflower (Echinacea purpurea)

Calliopsis (Coreopsis tinctoria)

Joe-Pye weed (Eupatorium maculatum)

Pasture thistle (Cirsium vulgare)

Annual cosmos (Cosmos bipinnatus)

Whorled loosestrife (Lysimachia quadrifolia)

Dill (Anethum graveolens)

Full seed head of Queen Anne's lace (Daucus carota *var.* carota)

Dandelions (Taraxacum officinale)

ABOVE: *Victoria Borus takes a pail of water with her on early morning cutting expeditions. In autumn, seeds can be collected by covering seed heads with a small paper bag and shaking.*

MEADOWS:
A SELECTION

Anethum graveolens, dill

Asclepias tuberosa, butterfly weed

Centaurea cyanus, blue batchelor's buttons

Cichorium intybus, chicory

Cirsium pumilum, pasture thistle

C. vulgare, bull thistle

Coreopsis tinctoria, yellow coreopsis

Coronilla varia, crown vetch

Cosmos bipinnatus, cosmos

Daucus carota, Queen Anne's lace

Echinacea purpurea (*Rudbeckia purpurea*), purple coneflower

E. purpurea 'Alba', white purple coneflower

Eschscholzia californica, California poppy

Eupatorium maculatum, Joe-Pye-weed

E. purpureum, sweet Joe-Pye-weed

Festuca ovina var. *glauca*, blue fescue

Hemerocallis hybrids, hybrid daylily

H. flava, lemon lily

H. fulva, tawny lily

Liatris spicata, gay-feather

Lupinus arboreus, California lupine

L. namus, sky lupine

L. polyphyllus, perennial lupine

L. texensis, Texas bluebonnet

Lysimachia quadrifolia, whorled loosestrife

Macleaya cordata, plume poppy

Papaver rhoeas, corn poppy, Flanders poppy

Pennisetum alopecuroides, fountain grass

Rudbeckia hirta, black-eyed Susan

R. hirta var. *pulcherrima* (*R. bicolor*), gloriosa daisy

Solidago spp., goldenrod

Thermopsis caroliniana, Carolina lupine

Vernonia noveboracensis, New York ironweed

TREES, SHRUBS, AND WOODLAND AREAS

A well-established wood-
land recalls the forest primeval that haunts
the human imagination. John Fowles, in his book
The Tree, calls the forest "the green coral," in
which "experience, adventure, aesthetic
pleasure, I think I could even say truth, all lie for
me beyond the canopy and exterior wall of
leaves." He finds in trees a "natural correspondence
with the greener, more mysterious processes of
mind . . . they seem to me the best, the most

PRECEDING PAGES: LEFT, *The forest floor in autumn;* **RIGHT,** *European white birches* (Betula pendula) *in winter.*

revealing messengers to us from all nature, the nearest its heart."

While most of America's virgin forests have disappeared over the past one hundred years, falling to the ax and giving way to the plow, the country today is blanketed by beautiful, reborn forests from which the natural gardener can derive inspiration—from the hardwood forests of the East and Midwest where oak, sugar maple, American basswood, and beech trees grow, mixed in with a few conifers, to the ponderosa pine forests and vast conifer forests of the great American West. Oddly enough, there are more of these "new wild" forests than there were a century ago.

People have always had a special love for trees for their practical and commercial value, of course, but even more for their beauty and ornamental value. No one is immune to their strength and majesty, even in winter when their leafless branches etch intricate linear shadows onto the freshly fallen snow. Your choice of trees and woodland plants will depend not only on your location but also on what you want from the woodland garden. If you want a picturesque view or a dramatic panorama to watch from the

window, plant the many trees and shrubs that have beautiful flowers in spring and brilliant foliage in fall. Will the woodland act more as a lush backdrop for the In-Between and Inner Areas than a focal point on its own? In that case, evergreens would probably be the best choice. If space allows only an edge-of-the-woods planting, choose a staged planting of shrubs and flowering perennials that mimic the woodland border. If you have enough room to create a woodland that includes a path and small clearing, you will want to plant wildflowers and other eye-catching plants. On the practical side, is energy saving a concern? Some deciduous trees have denser foliage than others, but all will provide some shade in the summer and let in light in winter. If you want complete privacy, a way to cut yourself off from the world around you, evergreens, especially a staggered planting, will provide it. Any such questions should be considered as part of the process of plant selection.

When choosing trees for your Natural Garden, whether in the Outer, In-Between, or Inner Area, you should consider the merits of deciduous or evergreen plants. Deciduous plants—trees, shrubs, and

OPPOSITE: *Tulips add seasonal color under gray birch* (Betula populifolia). *Other hardy birches* (B. albosinensis, B. costata, B. papyrifera, B. ermanii) *display a range of bark colors, from pink to orange.* **ABOVE:** *The hardwood forest floor.*

ABOVE: *Patterns of branch and bark on an Amur cork tree* (Phellodendron amurense). *Paperbark maple* (Acer griseum) *and lacebark pine* (Pinus bungeana) *also have exceptional bark.*

vines—shed their leaves seasonally, usually in the fall, following a blaze of colorful foliage. The familiar hardwoods—oaks, elms, maples, hickories, chestnuts—are all deciduous. Evergreens keep their foliage year-round. Most of the needle-leaved, cone-bearing plants—pines, firs, cedars, spruces—are evergreen. There are also broadleaf evergreens, rhododendrons for example, and some plants are semi-evergreen, losing their leaves only in the coldest parts of their range. Mimosa (*Acacia* spp.) for example are semi-evergreen. Suitable trees and shrubs of all types will be found listed under Plant Selection (pages 242–83).

In deciding between evergreen and deciduous trees for your home-site, make certain to consider each candidate's other qualities as well. Will the tree allow in the light or provide the deep shade you desire, act as a sight barrier or sound buffer if that is what you need, or will its optimum height be appropriate for

your setting? The eventual size of the trees will be of some consequence especially if you are starting from scratch creating a wooded area. There plant a mass of trees—more than you will ultimately need; they will benefit from each other in the beginning, when they are most vulnerable, providing shelter and protection. In time you will be able to thin them out, harvesting half or more for trellises, furniture, or firewood.

THE STRUCTURED WOODLAND

Although trees are the most obvious feature of wooded areas, forests are not made of trees alone. Forests have justly been called nature's cathedrals; woodland architecture is as carefully arranged as anything man has constructed. From top to bottom, the forest is in layers—canopy, understory, and floor—each with its own vegeta-

ABOVE, LEFT TO RIGHT: *Three views of sugar maples (Acer saccharum) in autumn. Depending on conditions, their foliage turns scarlet, brilliant orange, or yellow.*

tion. Trees make up the canopy, their upper branches meeting to form a green and leafy forest rooftop. In the understory are woody shrubs, and carpeting the forest floor are wildflowers, ferns, mosses, and other herbaceous plants. All three layers are present in most forests to one degree or another, and in planning your woodland, you should try to represent them as well.

This structured woodland might dominate the Outer Area of your property, providing a wilderness retreat and acting as a buffer zone between you and the surrounding properties. Even a small patch of ground on the perimeter will do. Not long ago, I visited Page Dicky, a natural gardener in Westchester County, New York, and she took me on a walk through her wild, woodland garden. We traveled a footworn path that seemed to ramble on and on through the trees. Here and there wildflowers put on their show, and we observed the intricate patterns, varied textures, and range of green colors of the many nonflowering plants. Some twenty minutes later, when we emerged from our forest ramble, I was amazed to discover that in fact we had not gone far at all. The woods were really nothing more than a narrow strip surrounding the homesite, but by careful placement of a meandering path and of richly varied woodland plants, this talented gardener had created a spirited world far removed from its tame suburban surroundings.

If you have an existing woodland, as Page Dicky had, begin by analyzing the site, identifying the trees, shrubs, and floor growth. You may need to thin out the plantings, cutting off the lower limbs of some of the trees to let in more light. You should also consider planting some young trees as eventual replacements for older ones—because you cannot predict when an aged tree will require removal, unless you plan ahead, you may have to wait twenty or thirty years for its

successor to mature. Once you know what is already there, you can decide what new plants to add and what features you wish to emphasize—a rock outcropping, a small clearing, a streamside area—and what route your path will take. Each woodland site is unique and will suggest its own solutions to design questions.

If your property has been completely cleared, and you are starting from scratch, there is no quick and easy way to establish a mature woodland. It takes anywhere from ten to twenty years for new plantings to begin to resemble forest. Although you could speed up the process by purchasing and planting a few older trees, this is a very expensive method. Instead it is usually more practical to let nature be your guide and begin with a meadow

planting that will give you almost immediate enjoyment.

In nature the meadow is one stage of forest development, part of the reclamation process for land cleared by a forest fire or other natural disaster. When not controlled by an annual mowing, woody shrubs and tree seedlings become established in the meadow and eventually shade the sun-loving meadow plants until they can no longer compete. Their remains, with the twigs and leaves falling from maturing trees, decay and form a rich humus, the perfect growing medium for the shade-loving shrubs and wild plants of the forest floor. With patience and planning you can follow nature's example. Plant a meadow as described in Meadows, positioning very young trees, as many as the space allows and you can afford, in

an arrangement that pleases you. They can be planted thickly because you will be thinning them out in time. Choose a variety of trees, some fast-growing and some slow-growing, some deciduous and some evergreen, and leave space for a future clearing or winding path. If the new woodland is along a property line, evergreen shrubs at the outermost edge will ensure privacy.

As the years pass and the meadow gradually becomes shaded you will have to move the sun-loving meadow perennials that you wish to keep to other parts of your garden. Each fall, study the trees' progress. You may want to add trees or, as the trees mature, to thin them selectively, choosing weak or badly positioned ones to cull. Eventually, when there is sufficient shade, perhaps after six or seven years, you

can begin to plant woodland wildflowers. A woodland prepared in this way is a long but ultimately satisfying project.

An evergreen border is not only useful in the Outer Area but closer to the house it will act as a buffer against noise and wind. Position the tallest plants to the rear, smaller ones in the front—this is known as a staged planting—and select plants for color and texture as well as height to create a planting that will be beautiful throughout the year. A staged planting of evergreens is lovely in smaller landscapes that are visible from many windows in the house. It also forms a perfect background for the color plantings of the In-Between Area.

Like the evergreen border, individual trees have their place in other parts of your Natural Garden.

In the Inner Area close to the house and the In-Between Area within view of the house, it is particularly important to choose trees with the most ornamental potential. A very good choice for these highly visible locations would be one of the flowering crab apple trees (*Malus* spp.). Cultivars produce white, pink, or red flowers in the spring, bear colorful fruits in late summer, explode in rich crimsons or oranges in fall, and in winter, in silhouette, reveal craggy, gnarled, and twisted trunks.

For year-round color, plant evergreens—few of them have pest problems and none has foliage to rake in the fall or shapes that need pruning (at least not in the Natural Garden). If you select shaggy evergreens, be certain to place them where an informal appearance will be an advantage. Large specimens will need sufficient space in which to spread their boughs. There are also varieties that grow into symmetrical shapes without pruning: *Juniperus virginiana* 'Sky-rocket', a juniper, forms a perfect column of silver blue, and the hinoki cypress (*Chamaecyparis obtusa* 'Crippsii') creates a tight pyramid whose leaves are tipped with gold.

You may think of evergreens exclusively as pines and related needled conifers, but there are hundreds of others. Some of them flower, such as the beautiful broad-leaved magnolia of the South, *Magnolia grandiflora,* with its glossy evergreen leaves and fragrant bowl-shaped white flowers in summer. Eucalyptus (*Eucalyptus* spp.), bottlebrush (*Callistemon* spp.), and loquat (*Eriobotrya japonica*) are other flowering evergreen choices for the warmer regions of the country (zones 8–10).

In the dry parts of the country, outside the deserts proper, there are many good dry-climate trees, some of which are cousins of trees that thrive in moist ground elsewhere. The California live oak (*Quercus agrifolia*), an evergreen, and the valley oak (*Q. lobata*), a deciduous tree, for example, are good choices for the dry near-desert regions of California. In the Great Basin states—parts of Arizona, Colorado, Utah, New Mexico, and Nevada—where water is scarce most of the year, good shade trees or windbreaks include the cottonwood (*Populus Fremontii*), in Spanish called the alamo tree. This is the largest tree in the area. Lone specimens or groups growing along streambeds are dramatic sights to behold, especially in autumn, when the triangular foliage turns a brilliant yellow. In the old Pueblo village of San Ildefonso, in New Mexico's Rio Grande valley, there is an enormous old cottonwood that is the centerpiece of the village's central plaza. Under its branches more than a century of Indian dancing has been staged.

Other trees that thrive in this region include the Pinyon pine (*Pinus monophylla*), serviceberry (*Amelan-*

chier utahensis), mountain mahogany (*Cercocarpus montanus*), and the cherrystone and Rocky Mountain junipers (*Juniperus monosperma* and *J. scopularum*), all of which grow well in high altitudes. The Russian olive (*Elaeagnus angustifolia*) and desert apricot (*Prunus Fremontii*) also do well in these dry regions. Both were introduced into the Southwest by the Spanish missionaries who settled much of the region.

Whether you are creating a woodland from scratch, adding to an existing one, or siting individual trees in the Inner and In-Between Areas, it is better to buy young trees than mature ones. Even if you want to save money to buy an older tree in several years, plant some in-expensive young ones now. You will be surprised at how quickly they will grow; very soon they will equal the size of the more expensive nursery stock you had originally considered. The prices of mature nursery trees vary according to age, size, and rarity. Not long ago, I saw two Japanese cut-leaf maples for sale in East Hampton, New York. They were beautiful, matched specimens, at least twenty-five years old, offered as a pair for $50,000. That is a lot to pay, especially because transplanting fully mature trees is risky. If you lose the tree, you lose your investment as well. And that brings me to a peripheral consideration: trees contribute more to property values than any other living thing.

TREES: A SELECTION

Acacia spp., mimosa

Acer japonicum, Japanese cut-leaf maple

A. palmatum 'Dissectum', Japanese cut-leaf maple

A. palmatum 'Aconitifolium'

A. saccharum, sugar maple

Betula pendula, European white birch

Cornus florida, dogwood

C. kousa, Japanese dogwood

Elaeagnus angustifolia, Russian olive

Eriobotrya japonica, loquat

Eucalyptus spp., eucalyptus

Magnolia grandiflora, Southern magnolia

M. x *loebneri* 'Merrill', Merrill magnolia, star magnolia

M. x *soulangiana,* saucer magnolia

M. stellata, star magnolia

Malus spp. and hybrids, crab apple

Phellodendron amurense, Amur cork tree

Prunus serrulata, weeping Japanese cherry tree

P. yedoensis and varieties, Japanese cherry tree

Pyrus calleryana 'Bradford', Bradford pear tree

Quercus virginiana, live oak

SHRUBS: THE UNDERSTORY

The shrubs that make up the forest understory are an aesthetic necessity in a woodland garden. From flowers to foliage to form, they have incredible variety. Some, such as the yews (*Taxus* spp.), have pinelike needles; others, such as the heavenly bamboo (*Nandina domestica*), not really a bamboo, have bamboolike leaves. Still others add color to the landscape: yellow-leaved *Berberis thunbergii* 'Aurea', a barberry cultivar, or wine-colored *Cotinus coggygria* 'Purpureus', the purple smokebush. Many shrubs—bayberry, holly, serviceberry, cotoneaster, viburnum, and winterberry—add seasonal interest with their vividly colored fruits.

Left unpruned—as they should be in the Natural Garden—shrubs, like evergreen trees, have wonderful shapes. Yews, for example, arch and flow, cascading and spreading at will. Some shrubs do need a bit of pruning, but I refuse to see this task in a negative way. When I prune my lilac shrubs, I am not really pruning, I am gathering a fragrant spring bouquet for my studio.

Various shrubs bloom in every season of the year, and their flowers take many forms. There are the rose forms, not only roses themselves, but evergreen gardenias and camellias as well. Snowball forms show up in viburnums and hydrangeas. Long, arching sprays distinguish other shrubs, such as spiraea, while wispy ribbon-shaped flowers appear in winter on the witch hazel. Colors range from forsythia's brilliant yellow to *Vitex divaricata's* true blue to the magenta of the butterfly bush (*Buddleia davidii*). As a bonus, many shrubs are exquisitely fragrant as well.

One of the easiest shrubs to

ABOVE: *Forsythia* (Forsythia x intermedia) *sited for easy-care. Its "untamed" look when it is not pruned provides a pleasing transition from water to woodland.*

grow, both for low maintenance and all-round appeal, is the sumac (*Rhus* spp.). Yet, despite its virtues —fernlike foliage, magnificent fall color; lovely, sometimes fragrant flowers; and handsome ornamental fruits—it is rarely seen in garden settings. Perhaps this is because several botanical scourges are also sumacs, including poison ivy and poison oak. This should not dissuade you from considering other members of the genus. The smooth sumac (*Rhus glabra*) and staghorn sumac (*R. typhina*), for example, make welcome additions to the home garden. Both are found growing wild along highways and are easily started from seed. The fernleaf sumac (*R. typhina* 'Lanciniata') is more refined in appearance than its wild cousins and is one of the few sumacs readily available from mail-order companies. North America has other native sumacs as

well: the squawbus sumac (*R. trilobata* var. *malacophylla*), for example, is a western native cultivated by the Hopi Indians for food, medicine, dye, and basketry. (For more on sumacs, see Plant Selection, page 249.)

At almost the opposite extreme from the sumac is the rose. Most roses are difficult to grow and all too many are included in home gardens. There is good reason for their presence, of course. The flowers are undeniably lovely and usually quite aromatic. They make the most elegant bouquets. Unfortunately, roses must be coddled—protected from winter weather, fed, and pruned regularly—and their caretakers must be ever vigilant for a wide range of pests and diseases. Obviously none of these characteristics recommend the rose to the natural gardener, but if a love of roses demands their presence in your garden, look for one of the named

ABOVE: *A successful planting of mixed heathers and heaths. These slow-growing subshrubs bloom by variety in every month of the year. If properly situated with excellent drainage, they can be low-maintenance plants.*

ABOVE: *Hybrid azaleas and rhododendron in a woodland garden where they are used as understory along a ramble;* RIGHT: *as edge plants, between water and forest;* BELOW: *and beside a small stream.*

hybrids listed on page 161. These hybrids have been bred for disease and pest tolerance if grown in the right conditions. In siting roses, remember that they will need a good six hours of sun a day in order to thrive. They may do best in a sunny Inner Garden where they are constantly in view and any problems will be quickly spotted and remedied. There they will also add a lovely reminder of earlier times, a touch of tradition in a modern garden, not to mention a beautiful floral display and a sweet fragrance to the summer air.

When selecting any shrub, consider not only its sun and soil requirements but also its ultimate size and how compatible it will be with the color and size of the plants around it. Shrubs of different shape, texture, and color can be grouped together in a woodland garden to create unusually beautiful arrangements. For small, enclosed areas, there are slow-growing, compact plants as well as many hybrids, dwarf forms of the more familiar shrubs.

Shrubs individually or in groups also play a role in other areas of the Natural Garden. In the Inner Area, a naturalistic shrub border near the house might camouflage its less favorable aspects. In such a border, evergreen and deciduous shrubs, chosen for foliage, texture, color, flowers, size, and form, are staged, with small plants cascading in front of naturally compact, medium-sized ones, and tall specimens rising in the back. Flowering herbaceous perennials are especially nice in this in-

formal border. For staged borders, you should do some planning on paper before planting. Elsewhere in the garden, in both the Inner and In-Between Areas, individual shrubs may act as natural sculptures, or focal points (see the many arrangements in the gardens in A Portfolio of Natural Gardens).

Dwarf maple (Acer palmatum *'Dissectum Aconitifolium'*)

Weigela (Weigela florida)

Mollis hybrid azalea (Rhododendron *x* kosteranum)

Oak-leaf hydrangea (Hydrangea quercifolia)

Star magnolia (Magnolia stellata)

Linden viburnum (Viburnum dilatatum)

Smokebush (Cotinus coggygria)

White, pink, and red hybrid rhododendrons

Russian olive (Elaeagnus angustifolia)

Vanhoute spirea (Spiraea *x* vanhouttii)

Witch hazel (Hamamelis *x* intermedia *'Jelema'*)

Staghorn sumac (Rhus typhina *'Laciniata'*)

Japanese pittosporum (Pittosporum tobira *'Variegatum'*)

SHRUBS: A SELECTION

Acer palmatum, cut-leaf maple

A. palmatum 'Dissectum', Japanese cut-leaf maple

Berberis thunbergii 'Aurea', barberry cultivar

Buddleia davidii, butterfly bush

Callistemon spp., bottlebrush

C. citrinus, bottlebrush

Camellia japonica, camellia

Chamaecyparis obtusa 'Crippsii', hinoki cypress

Cotinus coggygria, common smokebush

C. coggygria 'Purpureus', purple smokebush

Elaeagnus angustifolia, Russian olive

Eriobotrya japonica, loquat

Euonymus alata, winged euonymus

E. atropurpureus, burning bush

E. fortunei hybrids, creeping euonymus

Forsythia x *intermedia*, forsythia

Hamamelis x *intermedia* 'Jelema', witch hazel

Hydrangea macrophylla, big leaf hydrangea

H. quercifolia, oak-leaf hydrangea

Ilex aquifolium, English holly

Juniperus virginiana 'Skyrocket', juniper

Kerria japonica 'Pleniflora', Japanese kerria

Mahonia aquifolium, Oregon grape holly

Magnolia x *leobneri* 'Merrill', Merrill magnolia, star magnolia

M. stellata, star magnolia

Nandina domestica, heavenly bamboo

Pittosporum tobira 'Variegatum', Japanese pittosporum

Rhododendron calendulaceum, flame azalea

R. catarofonsis, Caratofa rhododendron

R. 'Exbury hybrids', Exbury hybrid azalea

R. kaempferi, torch azalea

R. 'Karume hybrids', evergreen azalea

R. x *kosteranum*, Mollis hybrid azalea

R. nudiflorum, pinxter-flower, pink azalea

R. roseum, honeysuckle azalea

R. yakusimanum, Yaho rhododendron

Rhus typhina, staghorn sumac

Rosa banksiae, Lady Bank's rose

R. 'Carefree Beauty', carefree beauty rose

Spiraea x *vanhouttei*, Vanhoute spirea

Syringa vulgaris, common lilac

Taxus spp., yew

Viburnum dilatatum, Linden viburnum

V. sieboldii, Siebold viburnum

Vitex divaricata, summer lilac

Weigela florida, weigela

DISEASE-RESISTANT ROSES

In the case of roses, disease resistance is difficult to pin down. A particular rose may be extremely resistant to ailments such as black spot and mildew in the Northeast, but be especially susceptible to the same fungi in the Northwest. Diseases such as these depend to a great degree on weather. Generally, moist air and a lack of air circulation leads to problems. Below is a list of rose varieties that have, over years of observation, proved to be disease and pest tolerant. You can assume that species roses, polyanthas, and some of the new breakthrough or landscape roses are more robust, and that the fancy hybrid tea roses are more delicate.

Landscape Roses

Betty Prior	Hansa	*Rosa Rugosa*
Bonica	Nearly Wild	(and varieties)
Carefree Beauty	Robin Hood	Sea Foam
Cecile Brunner		The Fairy

Grandifloras and Floribundas

Anne Harkness	First Edition	Queen Elizabeth
Apricot Nectar	Gene Boerner	Razzle Dazzle
Cathedral	Iceberg	Rose Parade
Charisma	Intrigue	Sarabande
Dorothy	Ivory Fashion	Saratoga
Wheatcroft	Montezuma	Showy Gold
Europeana	Prominent	Sunsprite
Evelyn Fison		Trumpeter

Hybrid Tea Roses

Chicago Peace	Miss All-American	Portrait
Duet	Beauty	Pristine
Evening Star	Mister Lincoln	Proud Land
First Prize	Olympiad	Seashell
Funkuhr	Pascali	Sunfire
Futura	Peace	Tiffany
Konrad Henkel	Pink Peace	Viva
Queen Elizabeth		Voodoo

LEFT: Yellow Lady Bank's rose (Rosa banksiae 'Lutea') and common lilac (Syringa vulgaris) blooming together, their colors perfectly complementary. BELOW: Landscape rose, 'Carefree Beauty'.

THE FOREST FLOOR

Deciduous trees allow sunlight to flood the understory and forest floor throughout the winter and early spring. In summer it will only dapple the ground, glinting through the canopy. This happy arrangement allows you to select from a wide range of plants from spring-blooming wildflowers and naturalized bulbs to the shade-loving plants of summer —lush ferns, mosses, and ground covers.

Most wild woodland-floor plants require loose, friable, somewhat acidic soil, with a high organic content and good drainage. They also need filtered, not full sun, and protection from strong winds. These requirements are all met by the typical woodland arrangement of canopy and understory growth. Many wildflowers have an undeserved reputation for being delicate, probably based on the fact that most will not grow in situations unlike their native habitats or will not transplant well from the wild. For the latter reason alone, it is better to purchase seeds or seedlings than to collect. Try to purchase from reputable firms that do not collect but rather propagate their stock (see Source Guide, pages 287–92). In the proper location, seeded or seedling wildflowers should thrive.

Naturalized bulbs are right at home in a deciduous woodland. Because they require some sun, choose varieties that bloom very early in the spring and will have finished their cycle by the time the trees have leafed out. Masses of grape hyacinth (*Muscari*), dainty white snowdrops (*Galanthus nivalis*), or clumps of delicate little *Iris reticulata* come to mind, but there are others, including the hybrids (see Plant Selection, pages 242–83).

And what woodland would be complete without ferns? Select ferns whose growth cycles complement the development of your bulbs and spring-blooming wildflowers. The fiddleheads—delicately curled new fern fronds—should be emerging when your bulbs and flowers are in full bloom. By the time the ferns have fully uncurled, their fronds unfolded, they will actually enhance the early bloomers whose foliage may not look its best in hot weather. And when summer's heat is at its worst, few sights are more soothing than a sea of cool green ferns rippling gently on the woodland floor.

OPPOSITE: *In a planting by Rosemary Verey, a pagoda lily (Erythronium tuolumnense) blooms beneath a weeping Japanese cherry (Prunus serrulata).* **BELOW:** *The plants of the forest floor bask in filtered light.*

Wild Sweet William (Phlox divaricata), *columbine* (Aquilegia *hybrid*), *and forget-me-nots* (Myosotis alpestris).

Virginia bluebell (Mertensia virginica)

Yellow lady's-slipper (Cypripedium calceolus)

White fringed-leaf bleeding heart (Dicentra eximia)

Great blue hosta (Hosta sieboldiana 'Elegans')

Corsican hellebore (Helleborus corsicus lividus)

Wake robin (Trillium erectum)

Bloodroot (Sanguinaria canadensis)

Japanese painted fern (Athyrium goeringianum)

Variegated hosta (Hosta montana '*Aurea marginata*') just emerging in spring

WOODLAND PLANTS: A SELECTION

Aquilegia canadensis columbine

Arisaema triphyllum, jack-in-the-pulpit

Athyrium nipponicum 'Pictum', Japanese painted fern

Cypripedium calceolus, yellow lady's-slipper

Dicentra eximia, fringed-leaved bleeding-heart

Dicksonia squarrosa, tree fern

Erythronium tuolumnense, pagoda lily

Helleborus corsicus lividus, Corsican hellebore

Hosta montana 'Aurea marginata', variegated hosta

H. sieboldiana 'Elegans', great blue hosta, Siebold plantain lily

Iris reticulata, iris reticulata

Matteuccia pensylvanica, ostrich fern

Mertensia virginica, Virginia bluebell

Myosotis alpestris, forget-me-not

Phlox divaricata, wild Sweet William

Sanguinaria canadensis, bloodroot

Trillium erectum, wake robin, red trillium

EDGES

Where forest meets meadow lives a special community of plants—semi-sun-loving creatures of the forest edge. On many homesites, there is no room for a forest proper, but there may be a small area where a few trees, shrubs, and border plants can be grown.

Edges can be staged like herbaceous borders with low-growing plants in front, and taller ones (large shrubs and small trees) in back. If the edge faces south or west, choose plants that thrive in sunny, dry locations. The taller species should be able to tolerate a bit more moisture for they will have their feet in soil shaded somewhat by the front plants. If the edge faces north and east, plant species that need less light and more moisture.

WOODLAND MAINTENANCE

In the first few years, as a newly established woodland develops, add fallen leaves and peat moss or compost to hurry along the formation of that humus so necessary to woodland plants. Areas of moss, however, should be kept leaf-free with a gentle sweeping or hand clearing, because leaves will encourage decay. You will probably want to keep the path swept clear of forest litter as well. And you must keep an eye out for the invasive undesirables of the plant world—poison ivy and Hall's honeysuckle, for example—which are best removed by gloved hand as soon as they are identified. Use mulches around shrubs and trees and as a path surface to further reduce maintenance (see Ground Covers, pages 59–75).

Once a woodland is established, it needs very little care. Most chores, such as keeping leaf litter off mossy areas or removing fallen twigs and branches from the path, can be incorporated into woodland rambles, an activity that will easily become a regular part of your life.

THE SHADE GARDEN

In almost every garden there is at least one unchangeable area of shade. It might be in a highly visible part of the Inner Garden, where the house blocks the sun for much of the day, or between the house and the garage where there is a densely shaded walkway, or in a city garden where a neighbor's fence or garden wall creates a pocket of shade. You may be able to increase the light somewhat in such a place by painting the permanent element white or a light color, thus bringing in reflective light, but you will never have direct sun.

To solve the planting of this area, therefore, look to the natural solution. What grows on the densely shaded forest floor, or in the semishade at the forest edge will also grow in the shaded areas of your garden. A staged planting, similar to that at the brink of the woods, where forest meets field, will also camouflage or soften an otherwise unattractive, unyielding element such as a fence or wall.

OPPOSITE: *A transitional planting of hostas, daylilies, and small maples leads to the forest beyond.* LEFT: *Variegated leaves simulate dappled shade in a sunless garden.*

WATER IN THE GARDEN

*S*ay, *you are in the country, in some high land of lakes. Take almost any path you please, and ten to one it carries you down in a dale, and leaves you there by a pool in the stream. There is magic in it. Let the most absent-minded of men be plunged in his deepest reveries—stand that man on his legs, set his feet a-going, and he will infallibly lead you to water, if water there be in all that region. . . . Yes, as everyone knows, meditation and water are wedded for ever.*

—From Moby Dick *by Herman Melville*

The ancient Persians would have agreed with Melville's "aquacentric" view of creation. Their poets called water the soul of the garden. Water in a garden creates drama, movement, and light. A reflecting pool mirrors a captive piece of sky, a fountain adds a background of music, floating water lilies soothe and entrance. Water is magical, yes, but its use in the landscape is a challenge. Flora and fauna, water, soil, and stones must all be arranged in a special symbiosis wherein no one component overwhelms the others. A water garden in perfect balance has a clean, fresh look.

STILL WATER, MOVING WATER

Whether you prefer a tranquil pool or a restless stream (symbolized perhaps by a bubbling fountain), a naturalistic approach to the landscape works best. If you already have a pond or stream on your property, I envy you, for you can simply pick and choose the easy-care plantings and permanent elements you want without having to create a setting from scratch.

If you are pondless, you can still have a bit of open water, but you will have to concoct it yourself. No garden is too small for some kind of contained water. A garden

pool might be as small as a galvanized tub sunk in the ground, planted with a single water plant, and camouflaged with a border of handsome rocks. Pools can be almost any shape and be as shallow or deep and costly or inexpensive as you want. All pools should, however, be watertight, and if large, they should have a drain or sump area. If they are to support water lilies, they must be at least 18 inches deep, and situated so that they bask in the sun for at least five hours a day. A shaded woodland pool or pond sounds appealing, but it is more difficult to keep fresh and buoyant than exposed pools, which will not become clogged

with falling leaves in autumn.

A large-scale "natural" pond can be created by digging a hole in the shape and depth desired and keeping it filled with water by means of an underground system of hoses and recycling pumps. If you are interested in such a project, consult with a pond specialist (see Source Guide, pages 290–91, or locate a consultant through your garden center). However, since one of the primary objectives in the Natural Garden is to make the most of what you have, it might be better to take a low-key, small-scale approach to a water garden. Therefore, unless you have a stream that can be dammed to create a pond (see page 179), con-

ABOVE: *Still water captures the sky in a central California garden designed by Zierden Waterfalls of Sacramento.*

RIGHT: *A stream was dammed over fifty years ago to form an In-Between Area pond in Alice Barnhart's garden.*
BELOW: LEFT, *A round pool, by the Rockwater Company of Amagansett, Long Island, is fed by a man-made "stream." The rock edging will soon be softened by plants.*

BELOW: CENTER, *Water and a bridge of weathered wood provide a transition from an Inner to an In-Between Area;* RIGHT, *A woodland stream rushes through a sunny clearing in an Outer Area, where yellow globeflower (Trollius europaeus) is in bloom.*

tent yourself with one of the modest pools described in Permanent Elements, pages 207–32.

The surface of a pool or pond can be enhanced by a variety of plants, the best known and perhaps best loved of which is the water lily. Gertrude Jekyll considered her water garden designs incomplete unless they included tranquil water lilies. Many people think that growing water lilies is a tricky business, destined to fail, but with careful selection and preparation, they can be grown with minimal care.

There are hardy water lilies, and tender, tropical varieties, including many night-blooming specimens in unusual colors. In the mildest parts of the southern United States (zones 8–10), tropical water lilies can be left in place year-round. Throughout most of the country, however, these tender plants must be lifted from the water and suitably wrapped and stored during the winter. If you do not mind the extra labor, these extraordinary tropical varieties can be added as a high-care planting. If, like me, you are likely to forget this necessary chore, you can still plant beautiful hardy water lilies which, once established, will thrive and bloom over the years in zones 3 to 9. Among the best of the easy-care hardy lilies are *Nymphaea odorata*, which is beautifully fragrant, *N.* x *marliacea*, and *N. gladstoniana*. The species flowers are white, with yellow or pink hybrids also available.

Culture for water lilies is usually carefully spelled out in plant catalogues and often included with mail orders. In general, if you have a natural pond in the appropriate climate zone, you can plant specimens directly into the pond bottom. I find it both neater and easier, however, and essential in man-made ponds and pools, to plant lilies and other plants with submerged roots in containers. Many mail-order suppliers offer perfect water lily containers (see Source Guide, pages 287–92); they are plastic tubs about 12 inches deep that hold 12–14 quarts of soil. The potting medium should be a highly organic mix of two parts garden loam to one part "pond muck" (scooped from the leafy humusy shallows along the pond's edge). If muck is unavailable, thoroughly rotted cow manure will do. Also, most water garden nurseries sell potting mix, and some will even pot your plants for you. Under no circumstances

LEFT: *In the corner of a city garden, a pink miniature Momo Botan lotus (*Nelumbo nucifera *'Momo Botan Minima') emerges from a small, almost hidden tub of water.*

A seedpod of native lotus (Nelumbo lutea)

Victoria water lily (Victoria cruziana)

Lotus (Nelumbo nucifera 'Alba Grandiflora')

Marliac water lily (Nymphaea x marliacea)

A night-blooming water lily (Nymphaea 'Wood's White Knight')

Miniature lotus (Nelumbo nucifera 'Momo Botan Minima')

OPPOSITE: *The round leaves of tropical water lilies (Nymphaea 'Leopardess'), foreground, and an ornamental, pink-flowered lotus (Lotus nucifera 'Momo Botan'), background, are contrasted by the spikey foliage of sweet flag narrow-leaf cattail (Typha angustifolia), left, and (Acorus calamus variegatus), right.*

use peat moss—it is too acidic and will also float out of the container.

To pot a lily tuber, fill the container halfway with your mix. Then place the tuber at one edge, growing tip pointed toward the center, so it has room to "creep." Add more soil to about 2 inches below the container rim and gently press in place. Saturate the soil with water and cover it with a 1-inch layer of gravel. This stabilizes the soil and prevents it from floating out and clouding the water. Now lower the container very slowly to the bottom of the pool or pond and set it at the correct depth—12–14 inches for dwarf lily tubers and 24 inches or so for others. The container can be set on submerged cinder blocks or bricks if necessary to bring it to the appropriate depth. Because some

lilies have a tendency to be invasive, container growing is a good idea, as it keeps the size of the planting manageable.

Aside from lilies there are other floating water plants that will add texture and variety to a pond. One of my favorites is the native lotus (*Nelumbo lutea*). Its incredible matte leaves, which are flat and round, rise several feet from the water. Raindrops spin into beads on the leaves, roll to the centers, gather, and fall to the pool. Above the foliage are magnificent bowl-shaped flowers, whose petals eventually drop to reveal large seed pods that are decorative not only on the plant but also when cut and dried for indoor arrangements. Arrowhead (*Sagittaria latifolia*), whose three types of leaves emerge successively

ABOVE: *A boggy planting at the Berkeley Botanic Garden, with the impressive large-leaved gunnera (Gunnera manicata), and blue iris (Iris versicolor) growing in the shallows.*
LEFT: *The familiar pond frog is a natural check on mosquitoes and other insect pests.*

from the water, or the water snow-flake (*Nymphoides indica*), which has tiny white blooms throughout the summer, are also good choices. (For more water plants, see Plant Selection, pages 242–83.)

By now you may be wondering how relatively still water keeps from becoming stagnant water. Pumps that add oxygen and keep water moving are part of the answer. Even tiny pools will benefit from some water movement. In my smallest pool, only 20 gallons, an aquarium pump (priced under $10) provides bubbling air through a concealed tube. The pump itself hides under an inverted flower pot. The rest of the answer has to do with the balance of plant and animal life in the pond. As oxygen in the water is used, certain plants replen-ish it. Such oxygenators help keep the water fresh, and are added for their maintenance value. Container-grown frogbit (*Elodea canadensis*), the water starworts (*Callitriche* spp.), or the lovely water violet (*Hottonia palustris*), whose little lilac flowers dance on the surface of the water, all fit the bill. A small school of goldfish will feast on insect larvae and keep insects, especially mosqui-toes, from becoming a problem. Their presence enriches the life of the pool and their droppings are natural fertilizer for the plants. In the North, if the water is deep enough, the fish can winter over; otherwise you will have to give them winter quarters in an indoor fishtank. In a small contained pool, a few snails or fresh water clams will help keep the sides and water

ABOVE: *Bridging a bog garden in an In-Between Area.*

ABOVE: *A "nat-ural" swimming pool. The cascade of rocks, right, provides a home for rock-garden plants. The swimming area of the pool, fore-ground, is edged with flat slabs of the same rock, and un-derwater surfaces are painted black.*

BELOW: *A collection of dwarf evergreens surrounds Ann Johnson's swimming pool, completely concealing it from view.*

fairly free of algae. Depending on the size of the pool, the water may also attract other wild guests—frogs and newts. All these lowly creatures have a contribution to make. Look in mail-order catalogues for information about pond supplies, plants, fish, even pollywogs and other creatures beneficial to pond life (see Source Guide, pages 287–92). Catalogues are also invaluable sources of inspiration.

Another approach to still water is the plant-free swimming pool. If you are installing a new pool, you have a golden opportunity to choose an informal design that will make a definite contribution to the Natural Garden. Pool design and technology have undergone great changes in recent years, and pools can now be constructed to simulate a rock grotto or be custom shaped to nestle into any location. When not in use the swimming pool becomes a reflecting pool.

If you already have a pool, chances

are it is a traditional, rectangular swimming pool. It may seem to be a contradiction in the Natural Garden, but you can integrate it into its surroundings. Paint the bottom a dark color instead of that bright, jarring aqua blue. A gray, deep blue, or black pool recedes into the landscape, reflects the sky, and absorbs the sun's warmth. Edged with rocks or cut stones and with poolside plantings of evergreen or grasses that screen it from view and act as wind buffers, a standard pool takes on a softer profile but still adds a classical touch to the garden, a formal counterpoint to your wilder plantings.

Like the rectangular pool, fountains are formal by definition. Natural law dictates that water flow downhill, moving skyward only through evaporation. A fountain of water defies nature and is therefore an imposing element. Even so, a simple single jet of water can be quite charming. The sweet sound of water, even if artificially produced by a fountain, is always romantic, and in an urban garden it is also practical, because it creates "white noise" that masks unwelcome sounds—traffic for example—and enhances privacy.

You may prefer moving water in its natural form—a brook or stream —which gives the garden a feeling quite different from that of a still

LEFT: *Plants for the water's edge in Beth Chatto's garden in England include yellow skunk cabbage* (Lysichiton americanum) *and white skunk cabbage* (Lysichiton camtschatcense).

water pool. In *Wind in the Willows,* Mole "thought his happiness was complete when . . . suddenly he stood by the edge of a full-fed river. Never in his life had he seen a river before—this sleek, sinuous, full-bodied animal, chasing and chuckling, gripping things with a gurgle and leaving them with a laugh. . . . All was a-shake and a-shiver—glints and gleams and sparkles, rustle and swirl, chatter and bubble . . . a babbling procession of the best stories in the world, sent from the heart of the earth to be told at last to the insatiable sea." Mole's excitement is real; I feel it myself when I stand mesmerized beside a country stream. If you have a babbling brook on your property you possess a valuable, irreplaceable design element. It can be enhanced with plants that demand moving water—watercress (*Nasturtium officinale*), or wild rice (*Zizania aquatica*), for example—and streamside plantings, stepping stones, a bridge, or a seating area on its banks.

If the property is large enough, you can even create a stream-fed pond or quiet backwater—the old swimming hole of fact and fiction—which is often more inviting and easier to maintain than its man-made concrete counterparts. Essentially, creating a pond means damming the stream to widen and deepen it at one point before it continues its

downstream journey. This is not a very complicated process but the siting, damming, and pond bottom preparation (12 inches of hard-packed, watertight clay) must be properly done. It is usually best to leave it to an expert, found through your local garden center or Cooperative Extension agent (also see Source Guide, pages 290–91).

If you plan to take an occasional plunge into your new swimming hole, you can improvise a beach by dumping sand at the pond's edge and raking it smooth. The sand should extend into the pond for a few feet—a sandy bottom underfoot is far pleasanter than squishy clay—and you may need to add sand each year to replace washout. Where the beach ends, delineate the edge with natural rocks. Leave open pockets here and there in which to plant such waterside lovelies as yellow flag iris (*Iris pseudacorus*), pickerel weed (*Pontederia cordata*), and horsetail (*Equisetum* spp.).

ABOVE: *Geese promenade past a spring-fed "swimming hole." Stone edging and a stone slab used as weir for overflow create a modern variation on this familiar theme.*

LEFT: *In April, before trees shroud the view, it is clear how Beth Chatto's In-Between Area pond flows into the lake in the Outer Area.*

OPPOSITE:
Brown spikes of cinnamon fern (Osmunda cinnamomea) *and golden ragwort* (Senecio aureus) *form a small wet meadow in an area just beyond a pond. The flowering shrub, left, is a mountain rosebay* (Rhododendron catawbiense)

THE WATER'S EDGE AND BEYOND

Many plants enjoy getting their feet wet and are right at home at the water's edge. The choice of plants will depend largely on the size of the pool or pond. A very small one will be enhanced by plantings of pretty little marsh marigolds (*Caltha palustris*) and clumps of one or more of the low grasses or grasslike plants such as sweet flag (*Acorus gramineus*). Many of these plants—like the iris, pickerel weed, and horsetail at the pond's edge—grow happily in shallow water (see Plant Selection, pages 242–83). The same little plants might look lost beside a large body of water or a wide stream and for these places choose more sizable plants: a "flock" of ostrich ferns, for example, along the banks of a stream or lake looks striking. Some of the taller grasses, reeds, and cattails are also good choices. In seaside gardens, where marsh water or the water of inlets can be brackish (on the salty side), there are some lovely plants that will tolerate such conditions. Rose mallow (*Hibiscus moscheutos*), for example, which has a showy red-centered white flower, is such a plant.

Away from the water's edge in bogs and wet meadows, many of these same plants can be grown. A true bog is the result of millions of years of geological evolution. It may once have been a lake, now filled with decaying plant material, or a wooded glen destroyed by fire; it will still have a constant course of water, an underground stream perhaps, and is cool and shady, with acid soil. If you have

ABOVE: *Two varieties of naturalized Japanese primrose (Primula sieboldii) bloom in a wet meadow.*

such a wetland, treasure it instead of fighting it, for it is the perfect environment for wonderful exotics such as pitcher plants (*Sarracenia purpurea*), blue flag iris (*Iris virginica*), showy lady's-slipper (*Cypripedium reginae*), and many others. Overhead, a bog can be shaded by water-loving trees and shrubs— swamp birch, dogwood, blueberry, Canada yew, and others.

The sunny wet meadow is not as wet and has less acid soil than the bog. It occurs where the water table is high and the soil stays damp, though not sopping wet, during the hottest summer months. Some of the showiest sun-loving meadow plants can be grown here: turk's cap lilies, milkweed, and Joe-Pye weed in full sun; wild geranium, wood

anemone, and trout lilies in shady pockets. Several tall grasses and forbs also enjoy the wet meadow.

The secret to success with wetlands is to select beautiful plants that need constant moisture and also to learn to see the beauty in many previously unsung plants. The humble skunk cabbage (*Symplocarpus foetidus, Lysichiton* spp.), for example, has a beauty all its own. It is among the earliest spring bloomers, its huge yellow, white, or mahogany-colored spathes hugging the cold earth and surrounding hundreds of tiny flowers. Later it has lush apple-green leaves. Many people are dismayed to find wetland on their property, but, as you see, they can grow splendid water-loving plants there denied to others.

WATER IN THE GARDEN: A SELECTION

Sweet Joe-Pye weed (Eupatorium purpureum)

Water Plants

Callitriche spp., starworts

Eichhornia azurea,
water hyacinth

Elodea canadensis, frogbit

Nasturtium officinale,
watercress

Nelumbo lutea, native lotus

N. nucifera 'Momo Botan',
Momo Botan lotus

N. nucifera 'Momo Botan
Minima', miniature Momo
Botan lotus

N. nucifera 'Shirokunshi',
tulip lotus

Nymphaea cv. 'Wood's
White Knight',
night-blooming water lily

N. gladstoniana

N. 'Leopardess', leopardess
water lily

N. marliacea

N. x *marliacea* (*n. alla* x *n.
odorata*), Marliac water lily

N. odorata, water lily

Nymphoides indica,
water snowflake

Victoria cruziana,
Victoria water lily

Common skunk cabbage (Symplocarpus foetidus)

Bog Plants

Acorus calamus variegatus,
sweet flag

A. gramineus, sweet flag

Arisaema triphyllum, swamp
jack-in-the-pulpit

Caltha palustris, marsh
marigold

Campanula carpatica,
bellflower

Cypripedium reginae,
lady's-slipper

Equisetum hyemale, horsetail

Erythromium spp.,
dog-tooth violet

Gunnera manicata, gunnera

Hosta fortunei hybrids, hosta,
plantain lily

Iris pseudacorus,
yellow flag iris

I. versicolor, blue iris

I. virginica, blue flag iris

Lilium speciosum 'Rubrum',
rubrum lily

L. superbum, Turk's-cap lily

*Lysichiton (Lysichiton)
americanum,* American skunk
cabbage

L. (Lysichiton) camtschatcense,
Japanese skunk cabbage

Matteuccia pensylvanica,
ostrich fern

Osmunda cinnamomea,
cinnamon fern

Pontederia cordata, pickerel
rush

Primula denticulata,
drumstick primrose

P. japonica, Japanese
primrose

P. sieboldii, Japanese
primrose

Sagittaria latifolia, arrowhead

Sarracenia purpurea, pitcher
plant

Senecio aureus, golden
ragwort

Symplocarpus foetidus, skunk
cabbage

Trollius europaeus,
globeflower

Typha angustifolia,
narrow-leaf cattail

T. latifolia, cattail

Zizania aquatica, wild rice

Pitcher plant flowers (Sarracenia purpurea)

Shrubs

*Arundinaria variegata (Sasa
variegata, S. fortunei),* dwarf
white stripe bamboo

Hibiscus moscheutos,
rose mallow

Rhododendron catawbiense,
catawba rhododendron,
mountain rosebay

Vaccinium deliciosum,
blueberry

**A north Canadian peat bog that was cut when frozen
and reassembled in a Montreal exhibition**

ROCK GARDENS

Windswept slopes high in the Rocky Mountains, exposed rock faces along the Pacific coast, acres of sunbaked scree—they may seem barren and hostile, but a closer look reveals plant communities that, challenged by nature, have adapted well to the harsh conditions. With a little planning and preparation, a rock garden with lovely plants can be created on almost any property.

Rock gardens became popular early in the

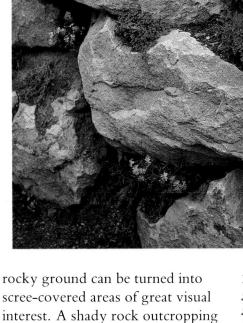

twentieth century, and right from the beginning they were intended to simulate nature. Writing in 1913, E. H. Jenkins, an English horticulturist, defined the rock gardener as a person "of the widest sympathies, a close observer of Nature and Nature's ways. . . . [who] will see to it that a certain informality whether of rock or general outline, exists everywhere [in the rock garden]." The same can be said today.

PLACES

Rock gardens are versatile—they can be established as theme gardens covering large areas, or as accents and focal points. Like meadows, they provide a good solution to spaces that might otherwise be unusable. Flat exposed patches of

rocky ground can be turned into scree-covered areas of great visual interest. A shady rock outcropping in a woodland, a rock grotto built beside a pool, a dry stone wall embankment, can all host a wide variety of plants.

A steep, sunny slope can be terraced with rocks, interplanted with cascades of flowering plants, such as yellow basket-of-gold (*Aurinia saxatilis*), candytuft (*Iberis sempervirens*), and moss pink (*Phlox subulata*), three dependable, easy-care choices for a rock garden. The helter-skelter rock-strewn look of such a hillside is actually achieved by careful positioning of the rocks so that the striations, fissures, and crevices all run in the same direction, as in nature. The rocks should be of the same type, preferably of local origin.

Most of the largest ones are set near the base of the slope, with an occasional oversized one jutting out from the upslope surface. Arrange the stones in groups, leaving open "meadow" areas, establishing pathways for easy access, and positioning an occasional stone step, log, or treated lumber riser to make the climb more comfortable. The rocks should be set into the earth at a backward slant so that rainwater is directed to the roots of your plants. Soil (its composition depending upon the plants' needs) is packed between the rocks as you go, creating pockets that simulate crevices and fissures, and in which you will spread seed or set out plants, including, for example, groups of small bulbs, such as snowdrops (*Galanthus nivalis*) or the dainty little dwarf daffodil (*Narcissus triandrus albus*). Clumps of low-growing ornamental grasses such as sheep fescue (*Festuca ovina*) look enchanting.

If you are patient and arrange the rocks thoughtfully, your slope will provide a variety of conditions: some areas will be in full sun, others will be partly or fully shaded by the surrounding rocks; some areas will be exposed, others protected. There are plants to suit each location. Most true rock garden plants need somewhat sandy soil that assures excellent drainage, which is of greater importance to them than a high nutrient content.

When preparing a rock garden on flat ground, you can create interest by suggesting hills. Dig depressions and heap the soil behind and beneath your rock arrangement. A suitable shrub, such as a juniper, planted behind a hillock will complete the illusion of a tiny slope.

Another way to build a rock gar-

den on the flat is by simulating scree. *Scree* is a Scandinavian word that means "landslide." According to Webster's, it is a "heap of stones," and describes an area of loose rock and soil found at the base of a hill. To create scree in a truly flat area, put down a 6-inch base of small rocks or builder's rubble to assure adequate drainage. Cover the base with sod, face down, and on top of it spread your scree—two parts gravel and pebbles to one part garden loam and one part peat moss or compost. Be sure to include some large rocks (tilted into the ground as on the slope), either singly or in small arrangements, to assure a natural look and add interest to the setting. They will also help keep the soil cool, for scree tends to

TOP: *Slabs of rock positioned vertically assure drainage for the long roots of alpines.*
BOTTOM: *An often photographed planting of subshrubs and herbaceous perennials in silver, gray, lavender, and blue thrive above a stone-and-mortice wall in Oxford, England.*

ferns, and other shade-loving species such as native bloodroot (*Sanguinaria canadensis*), bleeding-heart (*Dicentra eximia*), or foamflower (*Tiarella cordifolia*). A dramatic addition to a clifflike outcropping is a pool at its base. Without too much trouble you can also create a small waterfall by installing a circulating pump (available from many water garden suppliers; see Source Guide, pages 287–92). The atmosphere near such an arrangement is always fresh and buoyant, and many moisture-loving plants will thrive when perched on a ledge by the side of the waterfall. To keep maintenance to a minimum, limit the size of the pool; otherwise you will be spending too much time cleaning out leaves, twigs, and other woodland debris.

In small spaces, a rock garden adds a touch of the wild. A stone wall that may be the focal point of the Inner Area or a backdrop in the In-Between Area of an urban garden, becomes most agreeable when used as a stage for your rock garden plantings. In New England, many properties have tumbledown stone walls, relics of a bygone era when much of the Northeast was cleared farmland. If you can be sure that the plants will not dry out completely, such a wall can be planted top and sides with species needing perfect drainage. Pack sandy soil as tightly as you can into the planting pockets to secure the plants. If the wall is upright, freestanding, with straight sides and a flat top, it is usually best to plant only along the flat top. You could also use succulents such as *Sempervivum* or *Sedum,* but use them sparingly, pricking out places for seeds or seedlings. Eventually these plants will cover the top and cascade down the sides.

TOP: *Alternating steps of stone and herbs, including, from left, lamb's-ears* (Stachys lanata), *wormwood* (Artemisia spp.), *and opal basil* (Ocimum basilicum 'Dark Opal'). **BOTTOM:** *A dry wall of stone stacked without mortice, planted along the top with pinks* (Dianthus spp.).

heat up in the full sun. Plants with deep root systems, requiring excellent drainage and full sun, can be grown in scree. Species of western *Phlox* such as *P. alyssifolia* and *P. andicola,* which can be difficult to grow under normal conditions, will do well in scree, as will the easy-care moss pink (*P. subulata*) of the East.

A shady rock garden is the ideal treatment for a natural rock outcropping in woodland. Use rocks and plants to create an attractive formation ascending in terraced stages into the hillside. Trees can be integral parts of the rock garden if you prune them high—removing the lower limbs—to increase the light. Add large rocks and scree to the area in front of a particularly sheer outcropping, and plant moss,

PLANTS

While you shape and analyze your rock garden site, you should also be selecting plants that will thrive in the setting you create.

At high elevations, in the mountainous regions of the country, you can grow true alpines in the fissures of your rock garden. Among the most incredible and beautiful of plants, they demand the severe conditions of their mountain homes: short growing seasons, cool temperatures and cool soil all summer long, plenty of snow cover in the winter, rain in the spring, and very fast drainage. Alpine plants show very little growth above ground; their small size and tough little leaves are adaptations that assure survival. Below ground, however, they have extensive root systems that search out crevices and fissures where moisture and nutrients are found. A tiny 4-inch plant above ground may have a root system spread over several square yards underground, and a taproot that extends many yards down into the cool moist face of the slope or rock.

True alpines are difficult if not impossible to grow outside their native regions. Traditionally, they are pot grown in specially regulated glass houses, hardly in keeping with the Natural Garden aesthetic. They have also been successfully grown in raised beds contained by stone walls, or in banks behind similar stone walls. Both treatments can be attractive but are not easy projects for most gardeners.

However, the term *alpine* has come to mean rock garden plants in general, plants that need good drainage. Succulents are among the more interesting of these species.

Some grow naturally on the lower slopes of mountains or in rocky woodlands, others grow in mild flatlands or in the desert regions. I am occasionally asked the difference between succulents and cacti. All cacti are succulents, but not very many succulents are cacti. Any xerophytic plant, that is, one that has the capacity to store moisture, is a succulent. Even garden geraniums (*Pelargonium* spp.) are succulents. Cacti have evolved and modified to the extent that they no longer have leaves, and their stems have swollen to store water. Cacti can be recognized by their areoles, the sunken or raised areas from which the spines emerge. Some noncacti succulents have spines and others do not have leaves, but cacti are the only succulents that have areoles. All cacti are also indigenous to the Americas.

The structure of succulents enables them to grow in places where most other plants cannot survive. Some thrive in arid regions subject to drought; others live high in the mountains on rocky ledges exposed to the hot noonday sun and drying winds. There are epiphytic succulents that grow in the forest canopy, and even more curious species that are at home in bogs or areas of occasional flooding, where they use their water-storing ability to keep from drowning. Clearly many succulents can be used in the Natural Garden, especially in sunny rock gardens. The sedums and hen-and-chickens and even some hardy cacti are appropriate. The prickly pear (*Opuntia fragilis*), for example, has beautiful flowers and grows in areas of gritty soil from the Dakotas to South America. Hardy *Opuntias* are found in Canada, in British Columbia and Manitoba.

ABOVE: *A rock garden in the Berkeley Botanical Garden includes mesa prickly pear (Opuntia littoralis) and other cacti from the Americas, planted with succulents from the Mediterranean region and Africa.*

FAR LEFT: *Close-up view of* Sedum, Crassula, *and* Cotyledon *in a rock garden.*
LEFT: *Plants that love a dry region, agaves and aloes, form a planting that resembles a flowing stream.*

Edible prickly pear (Opuntia ficus-indica)

RIGHT: *Abstract pattern of lichens on a wall*

Golden barrel cactus (Echinocactus grusonii)

Deep blue harebell (Campanula alpina)

A selection of hen-and-chickens (Sempervivum *spp.*)

Moss pink (Phlox subulata), *blue forget-me-not* (Myosotis alpestris), *pale lavender wild Sweet William* (Phlox divaricata), *and yellow basket-of-gold* (Aurinia saxatilis)

A hardy cactus in a Connecticut garden

Stonecrop hybrid (Sedum spectabile 'Autumn Joy') *in spring*

Moss pink (Phlox subulata)

LEFT: *A magnificent jumble of rock-garden perennials planted by Marco Polo Stufano and John Nally.*

ABOVE: *A secret grotto enhanced by subtropical woodland plants and the sound and sight of water.*

ROCK GARDENS: A SELECTION

Perennials

Achillea spp., yarrow

Artemisia spp., wormwood

A. schmidtiana 'Silver Mound', silver mound

A. stellerona, beach wormwood

Aurinia saxatilis (*Alyssum saxatile*), basket-of-gold

Bergenia cordifolia, bergenia

Campanula alpina, harebell, bellflower

C. barbara, harebell, bellflower

Dennstaedtia punctilobula, hay-scented fern

Dianthus spp., pinks

Dicentra eximia, bleeding-heart

Festuca ovina, fescue

Geranium spp., geranium, cranesbill

Hosta lancifolia, narrow plantain lily

H. plantaginea 'Grandiflora', peace lily

Iberis sempervirens, candytuft

Myosotis alpestris, forget-me-not

Phlox divaricata, wild Sweet William

P. subulata, moss pink

Polemonium caeruleum, Jacob's-ladder

Primula spp., primrose

Salvia memorosa (*S. x superba*), sage, "East Friesland" sage

Sanguinaria canadensis, native bloodroot

Stachys lanata, lamb's-ear

Tiarella cordifolia, foamflower

Succulents

Aeonium arboreum aeonium

A. arboreum 'Atropropureum', purple aeonium

Agave spp., agave

Aloe spp., aloe

Lampranthus spectabilis, ice plant

Opuntia fragilis, prickly pear

Sedum spp., sedum

S. spectabile (*S. spectabile x telephium*) 'Autumn Joy', live-forever

Sempervivum spp., hen-and-chickens, houseleek

Shrubs

Andromeda polifolia, bog rosemary

Caragana arboriscens, Siberian pea

Cotoneaster spp., cotoneaster

Daphne cneorum, rose daphne

Euonymus fortunei 'Kewensis Variegata', creeping euonymous

Genista spp., broom

Juniperus horizontalis, creeping juniper

Pinus mugo var. *mugo*, Mugo pine

Rhododendron impeditum, dwarf rhododendron

R. imperator, dwarf rhododendron

R. indicum, azalea

Santolina chamaecyparissus, lavender cotton

EDIBLE PLANTS AND SPECIAL ATTRACTIONS

One aim of a Natural Garden is unity with nature, the creation of an environment in harmony. As such, a garden provides for the earth's creatures. It will provide for you, too, if you choose to grow edibles; some people would consider a garden incomplete without a few delectables to harvest for the table. Gardens can also provide for the cheerful, often comforting presence of birds and butterflies. A garden of ornamentals is a

carefully composed still life, await-
ing the unpredictable beating of
winged species to set it all in motion.

THE EDIBLE
LANDSCAPE

Growing food plants in the Natural
Garden means selecting those with
the greatest ornamental appeal and
the fewest care requirements. A
full-scale vegetable garden is not the
goal, although if you do enjoy the
work—and the rewards—of a vegetable garden, by all means include
one in your plans. It should, however, be situated away from the
house and the ornamental plantings.
If, on the other hand, you simply
want to grow a few hard-to-find or
superior-tasting fruits and vegetables, they can be incorporated right
into the Natural Garden. Once freed
from the vegetable garden's rigid
row-on-row design, most of these

food plants look quite beautiful
tucked into island beds or borders.

There are three annual vegetables
that I have come to plant regularly:
podded peas or snow peas, which I
grow to eat; okra, which I grow
mainly as an ornamental; and ruby
chard, which I grow for both pur-
poses. The early spring podded pea
known as "sugarsnap" is my favorite   I tell myself I grow it for the
light green foliage trailing over a
trellis behind spring bulbs, but in
fact I simply could not do without
the pea pods. They are so delicious
that most are eaten right from the
vine and rarely make it to the
kitchen. Any undiscovered pods
that mature and grow tough are
simply tossed to my dog, Peter, who
also considers them a rare treat.

Okra, on the other hand, is a true
horticultural lovely but, for me, an
unappealing edible (although my
mother is fond of it). A relative of
the enchanting tropical hibiscus,
okra (*Abelmoschus esculentus*) produces pale yellow blooms with
maroon centers.

Of the perennial vegetables, one
of the best is also one of the longest
lived—asparagus, which comes
back faithfully every spring for
twenty years or more. Not only is
this plant a true gourmet delicacy,
but the spears that are left to mature, as some must be to prepare for
the next year's harvest, will become
soft airy plumes, 3 to 5 feet tall.
They make a lovely foil for ornamental perennials and a delightful
addition to late summer flower
arrangements.

Rhubarb (*Rheum rhabarbarum*), another highly ornamental plant, is
grown for its delicious stalks which
also happen to be a luscious rosy
pink in the spring. If they are not

picked, the stalks grow into enormous elephantine platters—tropical, primeval-looking, dramatic, and also poisonous. The flower is a strange cluster atop a large stalk rising from the center of the clump of leaves. Rhubarb is a rare attention-getter. Make a trench planting—in a row 1 foot wide and as long as you like—at the rear of a sunny border or along the edge of a pool.

Many perennial herbs, especially when used as ground covers, are also appropriate to the aesthetics and easy-care requirements of the Natural Garden. In her journal, Colette called on gardeners to "let the mint plants, the tarragon, and the sage push up their spikes, just so high that a drooping hand, as it crushes their slender leaf stems, can set free their impatient scents. Tarragon, sage, mint, savory, and burnet opening your pink flowers at noon, then closing them again three hours later, I love you certainly for yourselves—but I shall not fail to demand your presence in my salads, my stewed lamb, my seasoned sauces; I shall exploit you."

Herb leaves often contain aromatic oils that actually repel insects while filling the air with a heavenly fragrance. Angelica, a giant herb, is also an easy-to-grow biennial. In its second season, huge green pom-pom flowers shoot up about 6 feet. Despite its size, its subtle coloration makes it a wonderful addition to an island bed. With herbs especially, the line between ornamental and practical becomes blurred.

Some true ornamentals can also double as food plants. My favorite edible flower is also one of my favorite perennials—the daylily. In the Orient, its buds, which taste rather like asparagus, are picked un-

ABOVE: *An orchard of semi-dwarf apple trees in full bloom.*

opened before they show color and served steamed or stir-fried. Loving the flowers as I do, I haven't the heart to harvest the buds. Instead, I wait until they open and pick the flowers that same evening, shredding them into salads or using them whole as garnishes. The flowers taste like sweet lettuce.

The best and most obvious edible ornamentals are fruit-bearing trees and shrubs. Of the shrubs, berries are my favorites, and of the berries, raspberries are by far the most rewarding. I really can't imagine my own garden without a small stand of raspberry shrubs. They are very easy-care, and their high price in the market, which reflects the difficulty of shipping, not growing, is another argument for planting your own. If you have the space, try more than one variety. If not, choose an everbearing red or gold variety such as red 'Heritage Ever-

BELOW: *Leek* (Allium prasum) *allowed to go to seed.*

American cranberry bush (Viburnum trilobum)

bearing', 'Indian Summer', or yellow 'Fallgold', a relatively small, thornless shrub that produces fruit twice in one season. 'Fallgold' fruit, extra sweet and low in acid, is also borne on the outside of the canes, making harvest especially easy.

Fruit trees produce clouds of flowers in the spring and decorative and delicious fruits later in the season. Unfortunately, fruit trees can be demanding. Some need to be sprayed against insects and disease, or to be pruned, or protected from foraging wildlife, requirements that make them unsuitable for the Natural Garden. Commercially-grown apples are sprayed about ten times a year: from flower petal drop to dormant-oil-spray in winter. However, you need only search out the easy-care, disease-resistant varieties such as the 'Liberty' apple, and you'll soon be growing and picking your own.

Fraises-des-bois (Fragaria vesca)

Two promising new fruit trees for the Natural Garden are now looming on the horizon. One is the Asian pear, which is beginning to show up in fancier markets. The trees are disease-resistant, self-pollinating, and very handsome. Fruits are round, firm, and juicy. Unlike American pears (*Pyrus communis*), oriental pears (*P. pyrifolia*) ripen on the tree. The best variety for northern gardens is the extremely hardy 'Chojuro'.

The other newcomer is the hardy kiwi. Fuzzy brown tropical kiwis have become a familiar sight in the produce market, and many *Actinidia* vines are used as ornamentals in northern gardens. Now the sub-tropical fruit meets the hardy ornamental in *A. arguta*. These plants are tenacious growers, and may become rampant in some locations. They might, therefore, need some con-

Beach rose hips (Rosa *rugosa*)
Dwarf everbearing fig (Ficus carica *'Brown Turkey'*)

Highbush cranberry (**Viburnum opulus**)

Everbearing raspberry (**Rubus idaeus 'Heritage'**)

Loquat (**Eriobotrya japonica**)
Rhubarb chard (**Beta vulgaris**)

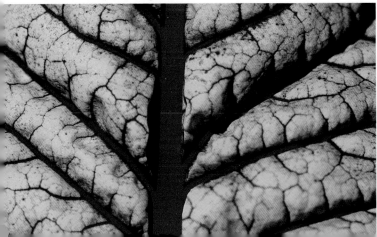

trol, but in general they will perform well on their own. Their large, heart-shaped leaves grow quickly, creating dense shade beneath. The stems are a splendid wine red, and the fruits, about the size of grapes, are smooth skinned and do not require peeling. You will need both male and female vines, so try to buy them in pairs.

Bamboo is another exotic edible. Although it can be problematic because of its spreading habits, one easy way to keep bamboo under control is to harvest the shoots in the early spring. The sweetest-tasting bamboos are *Bambusa oldhamii*, which grows in manageable clumps, *Phyllostachys pubescens, P. dulcis* 'Sweetshoot bamboo', and *P. bambusoides*. (For more on bamboos, see Ornamental Grasses, pages 113–19.)

In the South, in zones 9 and 10, you can grow citrus plants, a pleasure denied those of us who garden in the colder North. There is, however, a hardy citrus relative that will thrive as far north as Montreal—the trifoliate orange (*Poncirus trifoliata*). This slow-growing, thorny, shrubby tree is handsomely gnarled and produces fuzzy yellow fruits that persist well into the fall. The fruit, while mostly ornamental, will make a tasty marmalade or garnish a cocktail.

Like the other plantings in the Natural Garden, edible plants should be customized to your location. Observe what grows in your area and experiment with the plants that appeal to you. In Hawaii this might mean growing water chestnuts (*Eleocharis dulcis*), while in South Carolina an import such as the loquat (*Eriobotrya japonica*) might be happy in your garden.

ABOVE: *Scarlet runner bean* (Phaseolus coccineus).

ABOVE: *A rustic birdfeeder at Willow-wood Arboretum.*

WINGS OVER THE GARDEN

One of the many pleasures of the Natural Garden is its attractiveness to birds, most of whom are welcome guests. Their occasional raids on the berry patch, cherry tree, or newly seeded meadow are more than offset by the loveliness of their song, the beauty of their plumage, and their appetite for bothersome insects. Thrushes, warblers, flycatchers, and woodpeckers eat many times their weight in caterpillars and mosquitoes every year. One word of warning if you are planting to attract birds—don't do so if you have a cat. It hardly seems fair to attract these beautiful creatures to a garden where they are likely to make an evening meal for the resident feline. If you have a cat,

stick to cat-watching.

There are two "sure-thing" plants for attracting birds: the mulberry tree and the Virginia creeper, a vine. A mulberry tree practically guarantees the fluttering of many wings in your garden. Its fruit ripens in early summer, lasts several weeks, and is irresistible to a wide variety of birds, some of which are among the loveliest in the bird kingdom. I have seen evening grosbeaks, rose-breasted grosbeaks, catbirds, little chickadees, and raucous blue jays all sharing a meal of mulberries from a single tree. Another advantage of planting a mulberry is that it acts as a "lure" plant, drawing birds away from your more desirable edibles— blueberries, for example, which birds find as delicious as we do. If you are locating a mulberry by a patio, however, I advise you to se-

BELOW, FROM LEFT: *A very plain birdhouse blends in with the tree trunk; a bluebird house; an elaborate birdhouse becomes a piece of garden sculpture.*

lect white-fruiting varieties, as fallen white fruits will not stain.

The other lure is a vine such as the Virginia creeper (*Parthenocissus quinquefolia*), which has attractive five-lobed leaves that turn a brilliant red in the fall. Brightly colored fall foliage often signals to birds that there are treasures lurking beneath. Virginia creeper will quickly cover a building facade, trellis, arbor, or slope, and its black fruits are said to attract thirty-seven species of bird.

As visitors or permanent residents, birds will always be at home in a garden that has a source of water, a steady food supply, and suitable nesting sites. Nesting requirements vary from species to species so if you are planning to attract certain local species, you will need to research their needs somewhat. To give you a head start, I have listed several excellent sources in the bibliography.

Butterflies and honey bees are the other winged creatures that I welcome to my garden. Some gardeners choose plants that are larval food sources; I, however,

am content to limit my choices to plants that attract adult butterflies. This may mean fewer species in my garden but it also means less damage to foliage.

One amateur lepidopterist who does not mind having her garden eaten is Jo Brewer, author of *Wings in the Meadow*. Writing in *Horticulture* magazine, she confessed that she and her husband "bought [their] present house mainly because its surroundings seemed admirably suited to attracting butterflies." After a few seasons of planning and planting, she counted twenty-six species of butterflies visiting or homesteading in a single acre of her garden. She recommends that you learn something of the butterfly's habits, and she does provide larval food as well as abundant nectar sources.

Butterflies are perching feeders. Because they light on a flower to drink its nectar, drooping or enclosed blossoms do not suit them. Instead, they like broad-headed flowers such as *Asclepias tuberosa*, one of the milkweeds, aptly given

the common name of "butterfly weed." The flower is orange, which, along with magenta, seems to be a preferred color for many butterflies. (One August, several years ago, a friend of mine from art-school days floated a huge fluorescent orange tarpaulin on a lawn for a performance piece. Within minutes, dozens of butterflies were dancing in the air above it. I don't recommend that you shroud your garden in orange tarps, but orange flowers are a must.) Another orange flower, a popular nectar source for swallowtail butterflies and others, is also my favorite perennial and edible flower—the tawny daylily. Butterflies fold their wings and squeeze into its orange blossoms.

Most people do not think of attracting moths, which are usually rather drab creatures, grayish or beige, that appear only at night fluttering around the porch lights. One notable exception is the hummingbird sphinx moth (*Hemaris* spp.). It is large for a moth, and as its name implies it does resemble a hummingbird, particularly in its feeding habits. It actually hovers in front of its food source and refuels in midair. The sphinx is nocturnal, but appears in the late afternoon, and loves nicotiana, a night-scented, trumpet-shaped flower.

It is not necessary to include any of these special touches in a Natural Garden, but they do add depth to your plantings. A garden alive with birds and butterflies and heavy with fruits and delectables for the table has a wholeness that a purely ornamental garden may not.

ABOVE: *A small white butterfly visits Dr. Robert Zuck's mass planting of lavender* (Lavandula angustifolia). LEFT: *Trumpet vine* (Campsis radicans).

EDIBLE PLANTS AND SPECIAL ATTRACTIONS: A SELECTION

Annuals

Abelmoschus esculentus, okra
Beta vulgaris, rhubarb chard
Brassica spp., mustard
Lathyrus, garden pea
Nicotiana alata, flowering tobacco, nicotiana*

Phaseolus coccineus, scarlet runner-bean
Tropaeolum nanum, nasturtium

Perennials

Allium prasum, leeks
Asclepias incarnata, swamp milkweed*
A. tuberosa, butterfly weed*
Asparagus officinalis, asparagus
Echinops ritro, globe thistle*
Eleocharis dulcis, water chestnut

Fragaria vesca, fraises-des-bois
Mentha rotundifolia 'Variegata', pineapple mint
Nepeta cataria, catmint
Rheum rhabarbarum, rhubarb
Thymus vulgaris, common thyme

Shrubs

Bambusa oldhamii, bamboo
Buddleia alternifolia, butterfly bush*
B. davidii, butterfly bush*
Lavandula angustifolia, lavender
Phyllostachys bambusoides, bamboo
P. dulcis 'Sweetshoot bamboo', bamboo

P. pubescens, bamboo
Poncirus trifoliata, trifoliate orange
Rosa rugosa, beach rose
Rubus idaeus, everbearing raspberries 'Heritage', 'Fallgold', 'Indian Summer'
Viburnum opulus, highbush cranberry

Trees

Eriobotrya japonica, loquat
Ficus carica, edible fig ('Brown Turkey')

Pyrus communis, American pear
P. pyrifolia, oriental pear

Vines

Actinidia arguta, kiwi
Campsis radicans, trumpet vine*

C. radicans 'Flava', yellow trumpet vine*
Parthenocissus quinquefolia, Virginia creeper*

Birds and Butterflies

Asclepias incarnata, swamp milkweed
A. tuberosa, butterfly weed
Buddleia alternifolia, butterfly bush
B. davidii, butterfly bush
Campsis radicans, trumpet vine

C. radicans 'Flava', yellow trumpet vine
Echinops ritro, globe thistle
Nicotiana alata, flowering tobacco, nicotiana
Parthenocissus quinquefolia, Virginia creeper

*These plants are not edible.

ABOVE: *Butterfly weed (Buddleia alternifolia) attracts bumblebees as well.*

BELOW: *Nicotiana (Nicotiana alata cv.), a favorite of the sphinx moth, blooming above variegated mint.*

BELOW: *Carpetlike common thyme (Thymus vulgaris).*

PERMANENT ELEMENTS

Permanent elements—
paving, paths, steps, fences, pools, furniture,
and so on—are just as important to the garden
as flowers and trees. Their artful selection,
like the thoughtful mix of color and texture
in the plantings, adds cohesiveness to your
design. Visually, permanent elements can pull
the overall scheme together. Their aesthetic
contribution, however, should not override
another necessity—easy care. The hard surfaces

of high-traffic areas, furniture, and the decorative finishing touches, are all chosen not only to complement your natural plantings, but also to reduce maintenance.

PAVING

Paving materials, perhaps more than any other single feature, make outdoor space useful and easy to maintain. A well-designed patio or terrace in the Inner Area creates an extension of the house. Determine what your needs are and how you will use the space, compiling a list of elements as you go. Do you want an outdoor eating area, a play area for children, a sunny terrace, a shaded retreat for reading, a sculpture platform, a fountain niche? Evaluate what you already have, deciding what should remain, what must be removed or altered, and how much of your wish list you can realistically accomplish. Next, select the materials. Depending on your choice, you may be able to do the work yourself, or you may have to hire a contractor.

LOCATION AND DESIGN

The location of your patio or terrace will be determined by the way you plan to use the space. Most people, for example, want the patio to be a second dining area and perhaps a

second cooking space as well. Easy access to the kitchen may therefore be a priority. Other people use the patio for more formal entertaining and do not want the nearby rattle of pots and pans. They prefer the outdoor space to flow from the living room. If small children are using the outdoor area, you will want to plan for the traffic of muddy feet from terrace to house, and for easy access to the ground floor bathroom. You may also want the children's paved and planted play area to be within view of the room you spend the most time in—den, home office, or kitchen perhaps.

The patio's use will also largely determine its size. An intimate area for family meals or solitary sunbathing can be quite small, but a space that can comfortably hold a party of twenty-five guests will be a good deal larger. In either case, you will need room for tables and chairs, with a margin of circulation space (usually 3 feet all around). Be sure to plan extra space for plants tucked into pockets in the paving, container-grown plants, pieces of sculpture, or other ornaments.

Environmental factors will also influence the location and conformation of the space. Certain positive elements should not be overlooked: a spectacular view, for example, which will more than compensate for a few extra steps from house to patio. A worthy botanical element, such as a majestic tree, may be allowed to grow right through the deck or terrace floor. The negative aspects of your future patio space must also be identified, and compensation made. If the ground slopes, a raised deck or elevated garden floor may be the best, indeed the only, solution. Your aim

is to make the most of what you have by highlighting the best features and minimizing the poor ones.

Wind and water patterns also influence decisions about siting. A very strong wind can make a space practically unusable unless you install a fence. Although your Co-operative Extension agent can tell you the prevailing wind directions in summer and winter for your area, this information is only general. The house, garage, or other structures, slopes, plantings, and similar features, all affect the wind patterns on your property. Determine the direction of summer's gentle breezes, so welcome on a hot day, and orient your patio to capture them. Determine as well the drainage patterns and the locations where water collects. You can correct poor drainage by sloping the paving to draw water off in the most desirable direction. Runoff should be directed away from the house, and, if possible, toward the places where it is most needed—near deep-rooted trees, for example.

If you plan to use the patio for sunbathing, or if you want a shady corner for quiet reading, you must observe the path of the summer sun, and note the patterns of sunlight and shade. If shade predominates, you may want to thin surrounding trees to let in more light. If you have no choice but to site your patio in the sunniest area, however, create some shade by planting a suitable tree, such as a thornless honey locust. Its tiny leaves provide a gentle dappled shade that is cooling but not dense; come autumn, the leaves are easy to clean up—they simply blow away. One drawback to planting shade trees is that you may have to wait

years before they become effective. This is perhaps the time and place for a single, more mature specimen.

An arbor or trellis covered by a deciduous flowering vine will also provide shade in summer and sunlight in winter. Or you could put up a fabric canopy or create partial shade with a slatted lath roof.

SELECTION

When you install or replace a patio, you can choose among many paving materials. Your space itself may narrow the range—swampy ground, for instance, practically demands a raised deck. Climate too will guide you. In very cool climates, a dark paving material will absorb sun by day and return it to the patio by night. In warm climates, a paler material combined with shading devices would be best.

Consider existing architecture as well. The paved surface should be either a complement or counterpoint to it. The material you choose can modernize the look of an older house, soften the lines of a new house, or add interest to a plain one. The flow of traffic and space is another consideration. If the patio is in fact an extension of the living room, kitchen, or other room, choose paving that will work with the interior flooring. Some people opt for the same material, such as tile or slate, for both indoor and

ABOVE: *A newly laid patio of antique bricks. It will lose its raw look as the tiny boxwood shrubs that surround it grow larger.*

outdoor spaces. If the connecting doors are glass, the inside room visually expands when they are closed, and the entire space becomes one large room when the doors are opened to the patio beyond.

Pay special attention as well to the relationship between patio and landscape. You can formalize an Inner Area by using edging material or steps to separate it from the rest of the garden. Or you can soften the connection by using an informal asymmetrical patio shape that echoes your island planting beds. Whatever you decide, a well-designed patio and carefully chosen pavings will enhance not only the house but the In-Between and Outer Areas as well.

The paving you install will solve landscape problems and offer design options, but the selection of material must be made for durability, utility, and, of course, beauty.

BRICK. Brick is one of the best materials for paving. Made of clay, it blends naturally with its surroundings and is suitable for both formal and informal patios. Their rough texture produces a relatively nonskid surface. Brick is fairly easy to install, relatively inexpensive, and widely available. Suppliers for both new and used brick (which many people prefer) are listed in the yellow pages. Occasionally you can find a less expensive source for old brick—at some demolition sites, for example, contractors will let you have the brick just for carting it away. Old brick means irregular sizes and occasional breakage during extremely cold winters (although one or two damaged bricks can be easily lifted and replaced). Whatever the drawbacks, however, they are more than offset by the variant colors—from white to pink to terracotta to brown—that make a very beautiful paved surface. Be sure to stockpile extras to use as replacements should the need arise.

When you buy brick, try to ascertain its grade: severe-weathering brick (SW), medium-weathering (MW), or no-weathering (NW). Never use NW bricks, old or new, for outdoor areas; MW will be all right in mild parts of the country, but SW is the safest, least likely to be damaged by the elements. If you buy new brick, get the grade formulated especially for floors, known as pavers.

FIELDSTONE. New England farmers still wrestle with fieldstones, those rough and irregular stones found in fields and meadows. Because of their varied shapes and sizes, they are best for paths and stepping stones. When they are used for patios, they are usually set in cement, with small stones pushed between the larger ones to make a natural-looking, continuous surface, but they are probably better as visual accents or edging material.

FLAGSTONE. Flat, easy to walk on, and durable, flagstones have a natural and pleasing appearance, but they can be slippery when wet and because they are often irregular in shape and color, they lend a "busy" look to a large area. Depending upon the kind of stone used, the slabs range from $\frac{1}{2}$ to 2 inches in thickness; most are somewhat expensive, and all must be cut by a professional and installed with great care. Flagstones can be laid on soil and anchored in place with mortar or laid on a prepared cement bed using the "wet-mortar" method. Some suppliers will help the do-it-yourselfer by selecting and arranging the stones to your specifications, then numbering them for resetting on the site. There is usually a surcharge for this service but it is well worth it.

Bluestone is a commonly used flagstone, and if formality in the patio is your goal, slate would be an excellent choice. Large pieces of these stones can be cut into uniform rectangular shapes and are available in many shades although they may change hue over time. Large slate or bluestone flagstones are quite heavy and their installation should be left to a professional.

GRANITE SETTS. Blocks of granite, whether rectangles or 4-inch cubes, are known as setts. They are the cobblestones of yore—those rounded squares that once covered the streets of New York and many other cities, often arriving in this country as ballast on old sailing ships. Setts are installed in the same manner as brick but they cannot be cut without proper equipment, and they are expensive. However, they're extremely durable. An area paved in granite setts just never needs repaving, making their installation a one-time expense and practically guaranteeing very low maintenance.

LOOSE AGGREGATE. Pebbles or gravel spread and raked over an area is known as loose aggregate paving. It is easy to keep weed free by hand-picking invading plants, and it provides excellent drainage, with very little run-off or flooding and little splashing. It is also the easiest surface to install—you simply pour loose aggregate into an excavated area. If it is to be a permanent surface, excavate to a depth of 12 to 18 inches, or lay a sheet of black polyethylene over the bottom of a 6-inch excavation, making certain to cut several X's in the plastic for drainage. As a temporary paving, a 6-inch layer of loose aggregate is excellent; later it will double as the subbase for a more permanent paver.

As for the gravel itself, choose something that blends well with your landscape. Because of the glare, and its aesthetically disagreeable look, avoid white rock for large areas. The nicest loose aggregate, I think, is washed gravel: pebbles that are smooth and round and available

LEFT: *Chinese-style fence and decking, with an old apple tree allowed to come right through the planks.* BELOW: *Antique brick, stone, and slate.* RIGHT: *Randomly placed square-cut slate.* BOTTOM: *Granite setts and flagstone in an elaborate drive-in entryway in Charleston, South Carolina.*

matically transform it into a beautiful paving material.

LEFT: ABOVE, *A slate patio by Oehme, Van Sweden & Associates in Baltimore;* BELOW, *In this small Inner Area, brick has been laid in alternating patterns, revealing its essential formality.*

in natural colors. They should be neither so large that walking on them is difficult nor so small that they get into your shoes or are easily scattered by running feet.

MULCH. Many of the mulches listed in Ground Covers (pages 59–75) can be used in the same manner as loose aggregate. Some of them, such as small pine bark or pine needles, are very pleasant underfoot and make wonderful paths. To keep the mulch in place, excavate to a depth of 6 inches or more before spreading.

PEBBLES. The Japanese, in their justly famous gardens, meticulously arrange individual pebbles, 1 inch or more in diameter, in patterns and designs, pushing the stones into sand or soil. Just as meticulously, they continuously clean and frequently re-lay these pebbles. Such designs are exquisite but demanding. For the Natural Garden, we can borrow the idea, but reduce the maintenance by setting pebbles into concrete, thereby making a permanent, easy-care surface. Concrete is rarely used in the Natural Garden because it never looks natural and it produces a very hard, unforgiving surface, as any child with a scraped knee knows. But pebbles placed into freshly poured concrete dra-

matically transform it into a beautiful paving material. In the simplest installation, rounded pebbles are randomly mixed into a shallow surface layer of concrete while it is being laid. As the concrete begins to set, that is, to harden, it is brushed with a stiff push broom to expose the pebbles. Not surprisingly, this surface is called exposed-aggregate.

Another method, with more unusual, variable, and beautiful results, calls for setting round, washed pebbles individually as the Japanese do, however, in this case you will be pushing the stones into wet concrete instead of sand or soil. If the surface to be covered is large, have a contractor pour a slab of concrete first. Small areas are then isolated with wood frames and, one by one, covered with wet mortar, 1 inch deep, and set with stones. Before spreading the mortar, select and arrange the pebbles on a piece of paper next to the area where you will be working. Because all the stones will ultimately have to be at the same height for an even surface that is comfortable underfoot, lay a board across the small area just completed and press; this will level the pebbles and set them securely.

A pebble-and-mortar installation can be combined with other paving materials. In a brick patio, for example, you can replace a single row of bricks with a line of mortar and pebbles, or use them as a decorative edge or border or to frame a planting. Such a change in surface will also warn the unwary walker that a level change is about to occur and a stairway or ramp is ahead.

WOOD BLOCK. Pretty pavers that are too often overlooked, wood blocks are 4-to-6-inch cubes of red-

wood, cypress, or other wood that has been pressure-treated with a preservative. They are inexpensive, easy to install, and they weather well, blending nicely with the surrounding landscape. Edge blocks, about 8 inches long, are buried end up on the border to contain the paving. They should be level with the cubes, which are then laid end-grain up without mortar. Sand should be swept into the cracks. Wood blocks are nice underfoot, but they do have drawbacks. They can be slippery when wet, or slick and mossy in shady, ever-moist areas.

WOOD ROUNDS. A variation of wood-block paving, wood rounds are made from short tree sections and produce an attractive, easy-to-install paved surface. They can be cut from small trees for the patio site. Cut small log lengths, 4-to-6 inches long, well in advance, and allow them to dry thoroughly. Then soak them in a preservative such as copper naphthenate or zinc naphthenate, which are nontoxic to plants. Copper naphthenate, available under several trade names such as Cuprenol, preserves wood far better than the clear zinc preparation, but it is bright green and a full season will pass before the color has faded. The logs are laid just as wood blocks are, end-grain up. Use longer sections end on end for edging.

Very large wood rounds, 12 to 18 inches in diameter, make particularly attractive "stepping stones" when set along earthen paths or into loose aggregate.

DECKS. Wood-plank paving is called decking, and is always raised above the ground. Not only is this the best solution for moist

areas and for gaining a flat space on a sharply sloping property, but it can also be used to create an outdoor space adjoining an elevated or second-story room. Redwood or cypress, or decay-resistant, pressure-treated woods are the best choices. Any wood can be stained after installation, if desired, and should also be waterproofed with a wood sealer, waterproof coating, or preservative such as *Woodlife* or *Raincoat,* which will do all three jobs. Decks can also be painted, but once it is done, painting becomes an ongoing chore. Installation can be tricky, especially when the deck is raised quite a bit off the ground. Support posts must be laid into piers set in cement, a job best left to professionals, who will also know about obtaining permits and code variances, if necessary, for decks more than 3 feet off the ground, for example. Aside from occasional drawbacks, splinters and narrow heels caught in drainage spaces, decking is a good solution for several types of problem areas, and its relatively natural appearance makes it a good choice for the Natural Garden.

INSTALLATION

Whatever paving you select and wherever you choose to situate it, there are many instances in which you should hire a professional to in-

stall it: if the area to be paved is very large; if the site is to be elevated; if the ground slopes sharply, requiring grading or staging and more than one level; or if drainage poses a serious problem. In these cases, a contractor will do a better and faster job than the average do-it-yourselfer. A professional will also be able to facilitate the process of securing building permits and will know how to deal with code compliance and variances.

Finding a good contractor can be difficult. A recommendation from friends or neighbors is best, but if this is impossible, contractors can be found through your local nursery, lumberyard, building supply company, or Better Business Bureau. They are also listed in the yellow pages. Before you hire anyone, however, there are a few precautions you should take. Ask to see examples of the contractor's work and to talk to clients.

If you are satisfied, the next step is to insist on a written contract, including an estimate of the total costs and the builder's agreement in writing that the actual final cost will be no more than 20 percent above the estimate. A payment schedule should be spelled out so that the first payment is less than one-third of the estimate, and the final payment is made only after completion of the job. The contract should also include a completion date with a penalty clause if the date is not met, but with some leeway for unavoid-

able delays such as bad weather. Materials and their quality should be specified in writing. For example, lumber grades and any finish to be applied by the builder, whether wood preservative or polyurethane, must be stated. In fact, any promise the builder makes should be accepted only in writing, and if the contractor keeps saying, "Don't worry," then you had probably better start worrying. A verbal agreement may stand up in court, but a written agreement is best.

Hiring a professional is undeniably expensive, but you can keep the costs down somewhat by offering what is known as sweat equity. This means that you do some of the labor, such as cleaning up, removing sod and debris, and so on, and generally act as an unpaid helper. Most contractors are willing to work with you this way to help you meet your budget.

By now you may be feeling that a do-it-yourself patio is impossible in the Natural Garden. This is not so. If you have chosen loose aggregate, brick, or wood blocks or rounds for your paving material, and are fairly handy, you can tackle the job successfully. When you stand on a beautifully paved patio, with bricks laid in a herringbone or basket weave pattern, it may seem complicated to produce, but the steps are actually quite simple. Essentially, you outline the area to be paved, dig a shallow, level foundation, cover it with a layer of gravel and a

ABOVE, LEFT TO RIGHT: *Western flagstone, cut square for a formal look; Installing rugged, permanent granite setts on a bed of sand; Weathered woodrounds set in sand for temporary paving; Brick in a herringbone pattern; To expose aggregate, hardening concrete is brushed with a stiff broom.*

layer of sand for drainage, and set the bricks in place, without mortar, in straight lines or patterns. Do a little research beforehand by reading about paving procedures in one of the books listed in the bibliography.

MAINTENANCE

Paving—permanent and easy care as it is—needs some maintenance as time goes by. You must keep its surface clean, and leaf- or litter-free. Sweeping up can be transformed into sheer delight by the use of a blower. This relatively inexpensive garden tool (in gasoline- or electric-powered models) is available through most garden centers.

Even with conscientious sweep-ing, however, you will need to hose down the surface—be it wood, stone, brick, or gravel—from time to time to clear it of soot, dirt, and spills. Wooden decking will need repaint-ing or resealing as the years pass.

Weeds, (any plants in an un-wanted place) will occasionally pop up in cracks between paving mate-rials or in loose aggregate. Usually they can be pulled out, or try pour-ing boiling water onto it. As a last resort, however, you can apply a herbicide. Make sure to select a biodegradeable one for localized ap-plication. (The Safer company now offers an acceptable de-mosser.) Re-member, though, that the natural solution to any gardening problem is always the one to try first.

PLANTS FOR BETWEEN PAVING STONES

Achillea tomentosa, woolly yarrow
Aethionema warleyense, stone cress
Ajuga spp., bugleweeds
Antennaria rosea, pussy-toes
Arabis spp., rock cresses
Armeria maritima, thrift
Aurinia saxatile basket-of-gold
Campanula rotundifolia, harebell
Cerastium tomentosum, snow-in-summer
Chamaemelum nobile (Anthemis nobile), chamomile
Cymbalaria muralis, Kenilworth ivy
Dianthus spp., pinks
Gypsophila repens, baby's-breath
Hedyotis caerulea (Houstonia caerulea), bluets, quaker-ladies

Heuchera sanguinea, coralbells
Iberis sempervirens, evergreen candytuft
Lamium maculatum, spotted dead nettle
Lysimachia nummularia, creeping Jenny
Mazus reptens, mazus
Mentha requienii, Corsican mint
Muehlenbeckia axillaris, wire plant
Phlox spp. creeping varieties
Sagina subulata, pearlwort
Saxifraga stolonifera (S. sarmentosa), strawberry geranium, strawberry begonia
Sedum spp., stonecrops
Sempervivum tectorum, hen-and-chickens
Soleirolia Soleirolii, baby's tears
Thymus spp., thymes

ABOVE: *Corsi-can or creeping mint (Mentha requienii) fills the spaces be-tween large field-stones.*

PATHS, WALKWAYS, AND STEPS

You may think that paths and walkways are synonymous, but in the Natural Garden they are two distinct entities, defined by their uses. Paths meander through the landscape with no particular goal other than to take you on a ramble through your garden. They can be little more than a packed-earth trail through a sun-dappled woodland, covered with leaf litter or mulch, or perhaps a whimsical arrangement of wood rounds or fieldstones leapfrogging through a meadow.

Walkways, on the other hand, have a more practical aim. They move with purpose, connecting two or more spaces—the garage, say, and the house, or the front door and the sidewalk. While they should almost never follow a rigid straight line, they should take you on a fairly direct route from one

place to the other. Walkways should also be paved with a hard material that guarantees an even surface for guests in high heels or returning shoppers laden with packages. A path can be just wide enough for a solitary walker, but a walkway must be wide enough for at least two people to walk comfortably abreast—that is, about 3 feet.

When the landscape is on more than one level, a path or walkway may lead to a flight of steps. Blandly put, the purpose of steps and stairways is to link one level of space with another, but their effect is often more than just physical— stairs can have a powerful aesthetic and psychological impact, and often become dramatic sculptural elements. Long stairs winding through a landscape are an integral part of its design, while a short flight of very wide steps creates the feeling of gliding grandly through the garden. Staircases also influence the way space is perceived. A small garden

RIGHT: *Brick steps with plants at FILOLI in Woodside, California.* MIDDLE, FROM LEFT: *A Lutyens-style staircase of bricks, slate, and stone provides a transition from formal to informal areas. An archway frames a stairway of the same brick. Paving and steps of ex-*

posed aggregate and concrete in an unusual zigzagging entryway designed by Ron Lutsko, Jr. BOTTOM, FROM LEFT: *A shredded fir-bark path in a woodland garden. Red New Jersey stone pavement echoes the walls of the gardener's cottage.*

ABOVE: *Wood-rounds set in loose aggregate turn a straight path into a decorative element.*
BELOW: *Loose aggregate contained by an edging of concrete at the Blake garden in California.*

can seem larger and more elaborate than it really is when there is a change in level and a break for a staircase. In an urban area, steps may heighten the sense of transition from the chaotic outer world, making the garden seem a faraway retreat. Any staircase, whether long and dramatic, or short and elegant, should be softened with appropriate plantings to ensure that its look is delightful and inviting.

The design of your outside staircase will depend on what feeling you want to create, and on the difference between the levels you are connecting. There is, therefore, no hard and fast rule about the best proportions for outdoor stairs. However, I use the following formula as a guide: the width of the tread—the horizontal plane—plus twice the height of the riser—the vertical plane—should equal 26 inches. This means that if you want a 12-inch tread, the risers should be 7 inches. A longer, more gradual staircase may have 16-inch treads and 5-inch risers. Outside steps should also have a ¼-inch forward pitch to allow for good water run-off. To decide what sort of steps you want, study the staircases in your area, in parks or neighbors' gardens, and analyze them. Perhaps you will see exactly what you want and be able to reproduce it, but if not, you will at least get a good idea of the possibilities.

Outdoor stairs can be made of many natural materials. Use the same paving you used for your Inner Area patio to make stairs linking it with another space. For long stairs leading up a rock garden or meadow slope, you can use fieldstones, or lengths of 4-by-4 or 6-by-6 lumber soaked in nontoxic wood preservative, as risers, with packed earth as treads. If you plan an elaborate staircase, made from heavy materials such as slate, flagstone, or brick, you should probably hire professional help.

OPPOSITE: *An elegant white gate provides a year-round focal point in the formal Inner Area of a Long Island garden designed by Innocenti and Webel.*

FENCES AND WALLS

A fence or wall usually has a practical function—ensuring privacy, delineating space, acting as a wind buffer, holding back a slope —but in the Natural Garden it may also be a purely sculptural ornament, over which disease-resistant roses ramble or vines cling.

The most natural fences are living ones—shrubs and evergreens. Sometimes, however, a living wall is not the best choice. In that case, there are many materials to choose from. Your preference will depend not only on the function of the fence but on the style of your garden and the architecture of your house. Bamboo timber, for example, works wonderfully well with rock garden plantings or with a paving of pebbles set in concrete, echoing the Oriental note in such a garden. In a woodland garden, on the other hand, a rustic fence of saplings would be more complementary, while naturally aged redwood looks good in almost any setting.

Fences are often used as wind barriers. Recent experiments have shown that more wind protection is offered by an open slat fence than a solid one. Solid fences create a reverse flow eddy that makes it almost as windy on the inside of the fenced area as it is on the outside. Another potential problem with a solid wind barrier is that in an area of constant wind the continual pressure may loosen the fence posts, allowing the fence to come down eventually in a strong gust. A vertical, louvered fence will, therefore, give the best wind control over a very large area.

A classic split-rail fence, whitewashed and adorned with wisteria

Diagonal lines give this split-rail fence support and an unusual look

A formal iron gate ornaments a walkway and entry planting
A little fence keeps dogs from napping in the flower bed

A heavy stone wall is interrupted by an airy garden gate

A simple, low-maintenance fence makes an inviting entryway

An old dry wall enlivened by a landscape rose, 'The Fairy'
A rustic fence at Mohonk Mountain House in New York State

A popular design for a windbreak is the basketweave fence, so called because the slats are woven in front of and behind a series of spacers, taming the wind but not completely blocking the flow of air.

Under ordinary circumstances, however, fence slats can run either horizontally or vertically. Horizontal lines will make the fence itself seem lower and sometimes make the space seem longer and wider, a useful illusion, especially if you must have a screen 5 feet or more high. Vertical lines, on the other hand, emphasize height and can make a space appear somewhat narrower.

Horizontal and vertical fence lines can also be used to unify the plantings or other elements in the garden. For example, in the Sheffield garden on pages 21–25, vertical and horizontal fences are used in combination. The vertical fence echoes the slender grasses planted against it, while on the other side of the patio, the horizontal fence complements the horizontal planes of the table, seating, and raised planter.

As a simple space delineator, the inexpensive split rail fence is a natural. Unless you have wandering livestock, such a fence is used almost purely for visual effect. It gives no protection from wind or sun, and offers no privacy. But it can clearly show where one area leaves off and another begins. It may, for example, define the limit of an island bed in the In-Between Area or the start of a sweep of meadow in the Outer Area. The split rail fence can also support vines or act as a backdrop to naturalized bulbs or easy annuals, adding a rustic, informal note while still reflecting the comforting presence of

many areas of the country, retaining walls higher than 3 feet are subject to building codes and must be professionally engineered.

MAN-MADE POOLS AND FOUNTAINS

The tranquil charm and beauty of a garden pool is universally appealing, which must explain why pools and fountains have been part of the domestic landscape since ancient times. They are found in gardens around the world, from the carefully designed natural pools in Japanese gardens to the grand, formal reflecting pools of the great English and European estates. Water has not been ignored in American gardens, either. Thoreau called his beloved lake "the earth's eye," an apt metaphor, for still water does seem to capture the sky in its gaze.

Many types of pools blend well into a landscape. Some are very easy to install. One uses a fiberglass liner, available in many predetermined shapes and sizes at pool supply stores and through mail-order catalogues. The pool is simply sunk into a pit in the ground. These pools are truly permanent easy-care elements, but they are expensive; a small circular pool, 58 inches in diameter, 11 inches deep with a 125-gallon capacity, will cost upwards of $250.

For a less costly "instant" pool, which also has the most flexible design potential, consider a plastic liner. Such a pool is little more than a hole in the ground lined with a sheet of soft plastic such as vinyl (PVC, not polyethylene which becomes brittle with age and may crack in cold weather). The mate-

humanity in the landscape.

One of the structures most compatible with natural aesthetics is the stone wall, especially if it is made from stones wrested from the surrounding earth and stacked without mortar. If you have no stones on your homesite, find a local supplier of native stone dug from quarries. The supplier will also be able to find you an artisan adept at stacking stone walls. Whatever the source of the stone, a wall stacked without mortar is called a dry wall. You can build one as a retaining wall, to break the slant of a slope and incidentally to provide an ideal setting for succulents and other rock garden plants. A freestanding dry wall is very impressive when left untouched but it is also lovely when used as the foundation for a rock garden. Dry walls can be built by amateurs, but bear in mind that it is heavy, lengthy work. Also, in

RIGHT: *A man-
made rock grotto
and pool fit comfort-
ably in a woodland
garden. The tree
trunk has been
integrated into the
design.*

rials you need to construct a plastic-
lined pool are sold through the mail
(see Source Guide, pages 287–92).

More difficult for a beginner to
install is the small concrete pool,
used to showcase water lilies and
other aquatic plants. Indisputably a
permanent element, this type of
pool can be cunningly disguised.
The simplest is shaped like a giant
soup bowl—or a miniature pond—
with rounded sides that slope
downward toward the center and
facilitate cleaning. The pool's diameter can be anywhere from 5 to 10
feet. Installation begins with excavation. The chosen site is dug to a
depth of 18 to 24 inches, or 8 inches
deeper than the deepest part of the
pool. Its exact depth will depend on
which water plants you plan to
grow. A 2-inch base of gravel is
then spread on the bottom, over
which a 3-inch layer of concrete is
poured. A sheet of wire mesh or
hardware cloth is then smoothed
over the surface, bent, and shaped
to conform to the bowl. This will
act as reinforcement. Then pour another 3 inches of concrete. You
must let the concrete cure slowly by
keeping it moist with wet rags or a
wet tarp for the few days it takes to
harden. In the preplastic age, the
rags were misted with water from
time to time, and were themselves
covered with burlap or straw.
Today, however, a sheet of plastic,
laid over the rags or tarp and
weighted down at the edges, is
standard, and no further wetting is
required.

If you want to grow plants or
stock the pool with fish or other animals, its pH must be adjusted.
Concrete is so alkaline that it can
burn your skin. Therefore, once it
has completely dried, spray the surface with a 50/50 solution of vinegar
and water to make it habitable for
fish and plants. Cured concrete can
also be painted any color. Better
still, to avoid future repainting simply add a *nontoxic* dye to the wet
concrete while it is being mixed.
Your dealer can advise you about
dyes and paints, and the instructions
on the package of concrete will give
you valuable advice about mixing,
pouring, and curing.

Working with cement can be
frustrating for the inexperienced,
even though the process is simple in
theory. The proportions of cement
to sand to gravel to water must be
carefully determined, you must
have the facilities to mix the desired
amount, and once cement is mixed
up into concrete it must be poured
quickly, for it hardens quickly. Unless you are really keen to try it,
you might be better off leaving this
part of the job to a professional.

FINISHING TOUCHES

The basic theme of the Natural Garden is "reduce maintenance by working with nature." This is no less important in the selection of finishing touches that it is when you choose trees or grasses. Furniture, garden structures, lighting, sculpture and ornament, even paint must be long-lasting and easy-care. They must also beautifully enhance your house and landscape.

FURNITURE

Like other permanent elements, furniture should be made from natural materials that blend well with the surroundings. Wood and cloth are the most comfortable materials for outdoor seating.

CLOTH has certain maintenance drawbacks—it should be protected in foul weather; its colors are liable to fade in the sun; and eventually the fibers will wear out. However, heavy-duty canvas in natural colors can be considered a medium-care element in the Natural Garden.

WOOD is more permanent than cloth. The best woods are cedar, cypress, and teak, all of which will last a long time if properly treated for outdoor use. Teak, if well protected, is rumored to last a century. After it weathers to a natural gray, the wood you select should be painted with automobile primer and finish-coat paint or, preferably, treated with a clear wood preservative. Painted or unpainted wood fits well into most garden settings. Rustic wood benches and chairs that reflect their forest origins can be as romantic as a field of wildflowers. Today, more and more of this rustic, handmade furniture is available. Delicate pieces will last longest if used in sheltered spaces, such as a breezeway or porch. Otherwise, plan to store it away from the elements in winter. If the furniture has not already been treated with a sealer or wood preservative, you should do so yourself.

STONE, another good natural material, can also be used for furniture. A simple stone-slab table, for example, is a dramatic sculptural element. As seating, however, stone should be used only for a temporary perch. It is simply not a comfortable seating material. In a shady corner, a stone bench can be cold and clammy and, in full sun, that same bench can be blisteringly hot.

ARCHITECTURE

Garden architecture, which does not carry the same burden of seriousness as other architectural forms, has gone through many delightful phases. The planned picturesque ruin, appropriately known as a folly, sprang from the eccentric leanings of the upper-crust gentry in eighteenth-century England. They dotted their landscapes with bits of antiquity, real or fabricated, some of which still survive. Occasionally these pseudohistorical garden buildings cunningly camouflaged practical structures such as stables, gate houses, game-keeper's lodges, and later, garages. More often, they were erected to add visual interest to the landscape —some say to turn reason to folly, others say the opposite—and were merely whimsical, if expensive,

LEFT, CLOCKWISE FROM TOP: Teak benches at the Worcester County Horticultural Society Botanic Garden in Massachusetts. A small chair is tucked into a dry wall. Laura Cadwallader covered tree stumps with a plank to create a contemplative seat. A rustic chair nestles beneath a Pee Gee hydrangea(Hydrangea paniculata 'Grandiflora').

BELOW: A simple wooden bench that will weather to the same color as the natural rock outcropping in a garden by Leonore Boronio of Rye, New York.

ABOVE: The simplest garden bench imaginable is made of "found" slabs of stone.

ABOVE: *A gazebo inspired by Andrew Jackson Downing's works and made of New Jersey cypress is still standing after more than a century (only the roof has been replaced). Built over an old icehouse and with an open "chimney," it has always been a cool spot on hot summer days.*

open-air summerhouses, places to spend an afternoon reading, having tea, or watching the sun set. By the Victorian era, belvederes and gazebos, which usually commanded views, were almost standard on large estates. They provided welcome relief from the very formal life within the Victorian household.

The concept of a folly is still appealing today, although the real thing may be quite costly. A scaled-down version, however, could be made of a rough-hewn iron-wood such as cypress, cedar, or redwood, fashioned to complement both house and landscape. Many companies now sell natural wood gazebos and garden rooms. They are expensive, but if this is a dream of yours that must be realized, or if the outdoor season in your area is very long, you will be able to justify the investment. Like its ancestors, today's garden room may camouflage a necessary service structure—a toolshed or solar collector, for example. Or it may be nothing more than a romantic retreat.

LIGHTING

The nighttime garden is often sadly overlooked. Yet in summer it is perfectly enchanting when carefully and delicately lit. Lighting not only extends the daily time you can spend in the garden, but extends the season and the perceived size of the garden as well. But, while aesthetics may be your first consideration, do not overlook safety and security.

When selecting lighting, the most important thing is to keep it as natural as possible. Try to simulate moonlight or filtered sunlight. Think in terms of background light, focal-point light (in which one or two features are brightly lit), and "brilliant" light that adds highlights and sparkle. The most successful lighting designs are also the most discreet—the light is seen but not the fixtures themselves. This may mean placing fixtures in trees to wash light down to the ground, or pointing them up into trees for a dramatic effect. Both these installations will make the garden seem larger. Light washing across the surface of a fence, wall, or facade will reveal textures that give these elements a completely new look at night. Along walkways, hide fixtures among the plants so that their light will guide your way.

Light in the garden also opens up the view from the house. Instead of throwing back a mirror image of the room, a window frames a night garden. In winter when there is snow, the view can be especially beautiful. Shadows or silhouette lighting can also be very effective in winter. If you light a wall behind a naked tree, the tree will appear as a line drawing in the garden. A light placed in front and perhaps to the side of the same tree will cause its shadow to fall across the wall.

In a water garden, there are many opportunities for dramatic or subtle lighting. Illuminated plants above the pool will be reflected on the water's surface. Specially sealed immersible lights placed directly in the water can be lovely, if the water is immaculately clean.

All outdoor lights should be independently controllable by area. Thus you could light the In-Between Area or the front walkway without having to light them both. Decorative lanterns for the Inner Area should be attached to dimmers. Utility lights—along walk-ways, at the front door, and by the garage—should be on their own line, separate from ambient artistic lighting.

One of my complaints as a gardener is the paucity of decent outdoor lighting fixtures. I find the popular mushroom lights nothing but an intrusive distraction, both night and day. A few discreet fixtures are available, but to find them you may have to consult a lighting designer.

Whatever fixtures you eventually do choose must be accompanied by reflectors of some sort. The longer the reflector, the more concealed the bare bulb will be, but the beam of light will also be more directed, pinpointing a more specific target.

Your chosen fixtures should give off only as much light as you absolutely need. Brilliant spotlights are garish and disagreeable, overpowering the mysterious beauty of a darkened landscape. As it may be too expensive to put all your lights on dimmers, seek out low-wattage bulbs and the new low-voltage units. The latter are not only less expensive than higher voltages but also less risky for the do-it-yourselfer, as lines can be laid directly on the ground without compromising safety. They use transformers that reduce voltage from 120 to about 12 or 14 volts,

LEFT: *A utilitarian lantern among rhododendrons. Sometimes a handsome, straightforward design is the least intrusive in the landscape.*

A figure by Karel Appel tucked into the soft landscape

A large oil jar is a focal point in this Mediterranean-style garden

Traditional garden sculpture at Magnolia Plantations

A magnificent gateway in the Brooklyn Botanic Garden

A "found" object becomes a permanent sculpture in a meadow

A simple planting, transformed by an old Japanese stone lantern

and they can deliver subtler light.

When it comes right down to it, the lighting I prefer is the most subtle—candlelight. A few small lanterns placed along the walk for a party are truly captivating. It is amazing how brilliant a single candle can be when separated from the glare of house lights. Perhaps the best fixtures I have yet seen were simple glass cylinders from hurricane lamps, placed over candles set on iron holders, and attached to 4-foot stakes pushed directly into the soil. (If you know a source for such lights, please write to me.)

SCULPTURE

Sculpture does not have to be a formal element, isolated on a pedestal, demanding attention. Instead, it should be integrated into the landscape, carefully obscured by plants and plantings so that its discovery is a surprise. Perhaps this will mean redefining "sculpture," looking beyond its narrowest definitions to include objects such as an antique piece of farm equipment, which looks interesting and evocative in a large meadow. Wrecking yards sell the cast-offs of another age—chunks of stone architectural details from the facades of once grand buildings—and these can be used as

the "follies" of today. Birdhouses, decorative gates, and other ornaments can also be designed, selected, and positioned to capture the serendipity of nature.

TRELLISES AND ARBORS

Trellises can change the look of a house's exterior, but they can also support vines (see Vines, page 121) and act as sun screens or wind buffers. If neighbors' windows overlook your Inner Area, you can increase your privacy by constructing an arbor—an overhead trellis—over part of the space. It will be light and airy while still providing a privacy screen. If you want to increase the shade in the Inner Area, a vine-covered arbor is an attractive way to do so. The grape arbor has traditionally served this purpose. Grapevines such as the Concord grape are heavy and the arbor should be sturdy enough to carry the weight.

One of the most charming uses of trelliswork is around the front door, with a vine growing up and over it. Choose a fragrant species such as moonflower (*Ipomoea alba*), which is night-blooming and provides a gracious greeting to evening guests.

LEFT: *A trellis arbor for pole beans in the vegetable garden at Monticello, built according to Thomas Jefferson's original plans as part of the garden restoration.*

ABOVE, FROM LEFT: *Sky color captured in paint lightens a shaded entrance. Echoing plant colors, Page Dicky's pale yellow house is warmer and more inviting than stark white. A rich barn-red suits this country cottage and is colorful year-round.*

PAINT

Paint is most definitely a permanent decorative feature, playing its part year-round. Not too long ago, most houses in rural and suburban America were painted white. Now there is nothing wrong with a white house, but neither is there any rule that states that your house *must* be white. The next time the exterior needs repainting consider using a color that may contribute more to the entire landscape, keeping in mind that all its elements should be in harmony, and no one should overpower the others.

Be adventurous in your color selection but remember the color's effect on its surroundings. A dark green, gray, or brown exterior will recede into the woods while a pale blue one will echo the sky. Try out your color on a small area first—the side of the garage or the doorway trim—before you take the plunge. Clear colors, such as rose or pale yellow, seem to be most compatible with most environments. In fact, recent scientific analysis has proved that the so-called Williamsburg palette was actually composed of clear bright colors, not the heavy, dull colors long thought to be true Colonial pigments. Two or three hundred years ago, the world was not a dull-hued place, and there is no reason why it should be so today.

LEFT: *A door is brightened by an arrangement of squashes that complements the coral color and will last for several months.*

PLANNING AND PLANTING A NATURAL GARDEN

EVALUATION
AND DESIGN

Now that you have seen and studied several Natural Gardens, and know something about the possible themes and variations, it is time to cast a critical eye on your own backyard. If you are about to build a house and have no backyard yet, so much the better; you are in an enviable position, able to incorporate the natural style into your landscape from the beginning. This style extends even to the house itself—the idea being to build the right house for the right place.

In this energy-conscious age much has been written about siting and building homes so as to use the environment itself for heating and cooling. "Energy-efficient" houses are naturally warmer in winter and cooler in summer. This is not the place for a detailed discussion of how to design such a house; for that, turn to one or more of the books listed in the Bibliography. Briefly, however, some of the things you will want to consider are the topography of the land; the path of the sun and the patterns of shade and light, both summer and winter; the direction and velocity of prevailing winds; the position and amount of fenestration on all sides of the house; and the positions of evergreen and deciduous trees. Our American forefathers understood all these issues and, if you live in the Northeast, you can look at old farmhouses and see how well the siting and landscaping follow the rules for energy efficiency.

There are also other factors to contemplate. For example, if there is a fantastic view to capture, you may not want to site the house on the center of the lot (a maxim that has been slavishly and foolishly followed for decades in home building). If you are on a very busy street, you might want to position the garage to act as a sound buffer between house and road. The garage could screen you from a too-close neighbor. Every building site suggests its own questions and answers; be sensitive to its personality and to your own needs.

This advice holds true whether you have bought an old house, a new one, or are simply reconsidering your long-lived-in landscape—the approach you take will be about the same. It begins with a thorough evaluation of your property, through observation and research. Once you know the land, you will add your dreams, sketching on paper, trying out alternative schemes, looking at catalogues and in garden centers, until you have a plan that pleases you. At the end of this process, you will probably have a fairly good idea of what you want to grow to turn your dreams into reality. The Plant Selection lists beginning on page 242 will help you find just the right easy-care plants, and the Source Guide (pages 287–92) will direct you to suppliers and experts across the country.

EVALUATION

In the beginning, there is a great temptation just to plunge in and buy everything you see at the garden center, or indiscriminately to clear away a previous garden on your property. Resist it. Restraint is the key—"plan before you plant," as the adage warns. Planning carefully will spare disappointment and hard work later on, when your impulse garden gets out of hand, or fails to live up to your expectations.

The best strategy, especially for those with newly built or purchased homes, is to observe the landscape for a full growing season before making any changes. New owners are often pleasantly surprised by such things as an area of spring-blooming bulbs or a slope covered with summer daylilies, and long-time homeowners may discover hidden plant treasures growing unnoticed. This is the time to start a garden notebook and to make a line drawing, a map, of your land as it is now. Use the builder's or architect's plan, or a survey map of your homesite if you have one. If not, borrow or buy a 100-foot tape measure and approximate a plan, showing boundaries, house, driveway, and so on. Be as accurate as possible; later you will use this map to help design your new garden. You can make the map fairly large, but I like to have it reduced to about 11 by 14 inches, and to duplicate several copies for recording my observations.

With your notebook, a camera if you like, and a couple of maps in hand, walk the land. Examine every foot of garden space, noting the terrain, from rock outcroppings, to elevation changes, to moist and dry areas; the man-made permanent elements, from swing sets to sheds, paved surfaces, patios, and footpaths, to stone walls and fences; the location and condition of existing plants; the microclimates and general soil conditions; and the patterns of sun, shade, and wind. You can use separate maps for different categories of things and take photographs to be pinned to the maps and studied later. Do not expect to accomplish everything in a single ramble. Instead, make several trips, looking at the environment from different vantage points, at different times of year. Some features that you may at first have considered problems, especially the immutable permanent elements, may be turned into assets, as you have seen in earlier chapters.

EXISTING PLANTS

To identify plants, you will probably need a field guide to wildflowers for your area, and one or another of the plant identification guides (see Bibliography). On the map note plant names and locations, indicating those that are doing especially well. If a particular plant thrives on your property, you may want to plant more specimens or related varieties. Also make special note of any surprises—native wildflowers or ferns, for example.

Pay particular attention to the shrubs, noting those that need work, pruning, thinning out, or even possible removal (a final option for diseased plants). If you have a pruned, formal hedge you will probably want it to revert to a more natural state. This should be accomplished in stages. Shrubs simply left free after years of pruning will thin out at the bottom so much that they lose their effectiveness as privacy screens. To achieve a successful renaturalization, you will have to cut back about 50 percent of the old wood. Thin and weak growth should be cut to the ground, the sturdy vertical pruned back by one to two thirds. After this drastic trimming, new growth will be thick, luxuriant, and natural.

Catalogue your trees as well, and note those that are crowded, insect-infested, old and weak, or obscured by lesser plants. Much later, after careful thought, some of them may have to be thinned, pruned, or removed. My advice again is not to move too quickly. At this point you are simply observing and evaluating.

CLIMATE

The zone map (page 241) will tell you what to expect as an annual average minimum temperature for your homesite. It is a useful tool for choosing plants and should never be ignored, but actually it gives only a general idea of your climate. Other factors will greatly affect how plants grow in different places. For example, many plants that, by zone, should be easier to grow in New Jersey (zone 6) than in Maine (zone 5) in fact do better in Maine. This is because Maine's consistently low temperatures and its natural winter-long "mulch" of snow are far less destructive to plants than New Jersey's fluctuating temperatures. Freezing and thawing and frost heaves can push perennials right out of the ground. Another variable is large bodies of water. Oceans, large lakes, rivers, canals, and inlets heat and cool more slowly than the surrounding air and therefore modify the climates of nearby gardens. Even smaller lakes or large ponds affect directly adjacent areas. Most will stay warmer later in the fall and be cooler in

the spring and summer.

All gardens also have microclimates. Low areas may hold pockets of cold air, shortening the growing season. High ground may stay warmer, but might catch the wind, which can shorten the growing season in spite of higher temperatures. A location protected from both extremes would most likely have the longest growing season. The south side of a house will be the warmest and brightest, the north, the coldest and darkest. Certain plants prefer the north side, where they are unlikely to break winter dormancy too early in the spring before the weather settles. Nothing is more disheartening than early buds destroyed by a freak spring snowstorm or cold snap. As you observe your landscape through the year, you will begin to understand its microclimates and how the temperatures relate to your zone number.

While charting the climate, keep track of the wind patterns as well, for they too affect how plants will grow. Your Cooperative Extension agent can tell you the seasonal direction and average velocity of the prevailing winds in your area, but local terrain and buildings can influence those patterns dramatically. Steady winds dry out the vegetation. If this is the case on your homesite, select tough, drought-tolerant plants or temper the wind with a screen of evergreens or fence (see Permanent Elements, pages 207–32).

AVAILABLE LIGHT

When planning outdoor spaces and selecting plants, it is vital to know the amount of sunlight you can count on, especially in summer. With the exception of mosses, some ferns, and the like, few plants can grow in complete shade. On one of your maps, note areas that get full sun (eight or more hours of unobstructed daily sunlight, usually from the south), partial sun (about six hours of morning or afternoon sun, usually at an east or west exposure), partial shade (about three hours of direct sun, with indirect or filtered sun the rest of the day), and deep shade (no direct sun, but strong, even light all day, usually on the north side of the house or the garden floor under a canopy of tall trees). Again, as with the Zone number, this will give you only a

general idea of the growing conditions in your garden. You must also determine the quality of the available sunlight. The full sun of the Arizona desert, for example, is not at all the same as the full sun of a Connecticut meadow. Plants have to be selected with this in mind.

SOIL ANALYSIS

Any gardener who lives in Connecticut has had hands-on experience with "Connecticut potatoes," those round rocks deposited by ancient glaciers. Georgia is famous for its red clay soil, and certain other parts of the country have equally obvious soil problems. There are also those problems that go unseen until plants do poorly—soils that drain too fast or too slowly, that contain insufficient organic material, or have little nutritional content, or are too acidic or alkaline for most plants.

All soils are composed of the same ingredients in varying amounts—particles of stone from disintegrating rocks and minerals, humus (decaying organic material), water, air, microorganisms (bacteria and fungi), and dissolved mineral salts. Soils are usually classified by the size of the mineral particles in their makeup: fast-draining sandy soil has large particles, slow-draining clayey soil has minute particles. Particle size not only affects drainage, but also determines how easily the soil can be worked, how well plants' roots can penetrate, how much nutrition is retained, and how quickly soil warms in the spring. The best soils are at neither extreme—neither too sandy nor too clayey. They have a good mix of particle sizes, good drainage, and good moisture-holding capacity. The perfect soil is called loam. It is a balanced mixture of sand, clay, and humus, possessing the good drainage of sandy soil and the moisture retention of clayey soil. The humus makes it spongy and friable and provides a home for the microorganisms that benefit plants.

For a complete profile of your soil, send samples to your area's soil testing laboratory, easily found through your Cooperative Extension Service (which may even provide this testing itself). There will be a nominal fee but it is well worth it. Your Cooperative Extension agent will tell you how to prepare and send samples. Samples are usually collected from several different places, and marked "A," "B," "C," and so on. If you have any questions, send them along with your sample.

DESIGN

By season's end, your "garden file" should be bulging with ideas—your notebook full and your maps well-covered with observations. Now you are ready for the next stage, preparing the design of your new garden. Many people believe that it is best to design a garden spontaneously, and for some, depending upon their experience, this may be true. In most cases, however, landscapes that evolve in piecemeal fashion—a flower here, some shrubs over there—rarely possess satisfying aesthetic cohesiveness. Rather than risk disappointment, use all that you have learned during a year of observation, and draw upon the inspiration in this book, to work up a master plan for your future garden.

THE BASE PLAN

Review the maps you have been using and make a single map, to scale, on a large sheet of graph paper. This will be your base plan. Indicate the location of windows, doors, outdoor faucets, and electrical outlets. Also note the areas of full sun, partial sun, and shade; the prevailing wind conditions; the soil pH of tested areas; and spots that are either very wet or very dry. You should have several overlay sheets on hand, and you may want to have different colored pens or pencils as well, for color-coding of plants, permanent elements, or any other category of change you plan to make. If you have them, gather together photographs of your property, showing the terrain and elevations as they currently exist.

Armed with your notes, maps, base plan, and photographs, and a stack of mail-order catalogues (see Source Guide, pages 287–92), hold a family meeting that includes everyone, perhaps even friends who will be enjoying the garden. Their interest and ideas

may surprise you, and the landscape will be that much more satisfying if it is designed with the full participation of the group. At the meeting, compile a dream list of everything everyone wants in the new garden—from plants to permanent elements and so on. Let imaginations run free; later the list will be trimmed and fine-tuned to coincide with the actual landscape and budget.

THE THREE AREAS

When you are designing, it helps to think in terms of the three areas of the Natural Garden: Inner Area, In-Between Area, and Outer Area. Be certain that you understand and can explain to the group the differences between them.

The Inner Area is psychologically and aesthetically the most important, for family and friends will probably spend the most time here, relaxing, entertaining, and just enjoying themselves. Consider how each member of the group will conduct those activities. Will there be large parties or is there

---

SAMPLE PLAN FOR A RAISED ISLAND BED IN GRASS LAWN

Plan for color and seasonal bloom, but consider foliage, texture, and form as well. Spikey iris; heart-shaped hosta; and ruby-colored, semi-evergreen, scalloped heuchera leaves, for example, would be good choices. Repeat types of plants to enhance the planting's structure (three colors of day-lilies, for example).

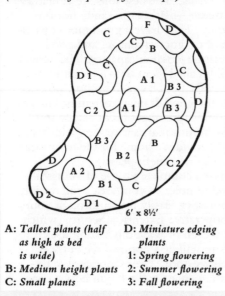

6' x 8½'

A: *Tallest plants (half as high as bed is wide)*
B: *Medium height plants*
C: *Small plants*
D: *Miniature edging plants*
1: *Spring flowering*
2: *Summer flowering*
3: *Fall flowering*

A SMALL GARDEN IN A BIG CITY
(See garden on page 20)

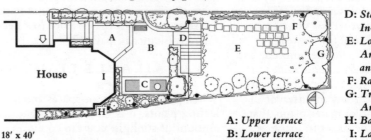

18' x 40'

A: *Upper terrace*
B: *Lower terrace*
C: *Pool with urn*
D: *Stairs to In-Between Area*
E: *Lower In-Between Area with grasses and rudbeckia*
F: *Raspberries*
G: *Trees of Outer Area screen*
H: *Bamboo screen*
I: *Large picture window*

A GARDEN FOR COLOR
(See garden on page 14)

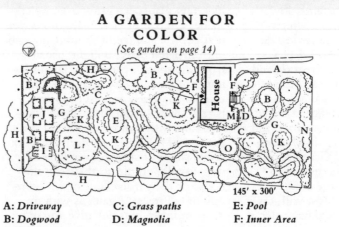

145' x 300'

A: *Driveway*
B: *Dogwood*
C: *Grass paths*
D: *Magnolia*
E: *Pool*
F: *Inner Area*
G: *In-Between Area*
H: *Outer Area*
I: *Raspberry patch*
J: *Flower beds*
K: *Island beds*
L: *Beech tree*
M: *Greenhouse*
N: *Forsythia screen along street*
O: *Rhododendron and azalea above retaining wall*

more need for private space? Would plantings of woodland wildflowers and ferns or great splashes of color set the right tone? What permanent elements will satisfy the various needs? How will the views be best used or camouflaged? How can privacy be assured? Should there be paths or stairs?

The In-Between Area, as you know, is for your most ambitious plantings. Encourage horticultural imaginations; look at the gardens in this book. You should think in terms of broad sweeping plantings and seasonal color. Remember to plan recreation areas—open spaces that may be planted over when the children are older.

Now consider the Outer Area. This is where you will frame your garden, preferably with the most naturalistic and informal plantings. Be sure to think about the access to this area, what view there is of it from the house, and the inclusion of permanent elements. You might want a bench in a clearing or even a rustic summer house.

By the end of the family meeting, you will know pretty well what you

and the rest of your group think of as the ideal garden. Pick the ideas that are most appealing, most feasible, most wanted, and sketch them in on a fresh overlay. Use separate overlays for different categories of data—for example, evergreen plants, deciduous plants, seasonal plants, island beds, permanent elements—or fit everything onto a single plan. Clip little squares from the catalogue pictures of flowering plants to details of In-Between Area plantings and arrange them on the plan to get an idea of how the colors will work together.

When you are fairly satisfied with the shape of the plans, begin to work on the budget. Estimate the cost of the major changes first—installing new paving or a pool, building a deck, or erecting a prefabricated gazebo, for example. Some of these costs can be found in catalogues, but at this point you may need to talk to experts at your garden center or lumberyard to get a closer estimate. Then, working with the catalogues, begin to estimate the cost of new plants. If the costs are way

over your budget, don't despair, remember that you can do much of the work yourself. And you need not complete everything the first season.

Decide to make at least one major change in the first season, a change that will make a significant difference in the garden—paving the Inner Area with bricks or installing a pool, for instance. Also add a few of the plants that will require several seasons before they begin to look their best. This may be all you can afford in the first season, but it does not mean that your garden need be unattractive. You can choose and sow some of the easy annuals for summer color, and can spend the time continuing to study your land, making changes and improvements to the plan.

When you see a lush garden of perfectly matched plants and complementary permanent elements, remember, every garden evolves gradually with a guiding spirit to keep it focused. The evaluation-and-design process outlined in this chapter makes you that guiding spirit in your own garden, armed with a blueprint for success.

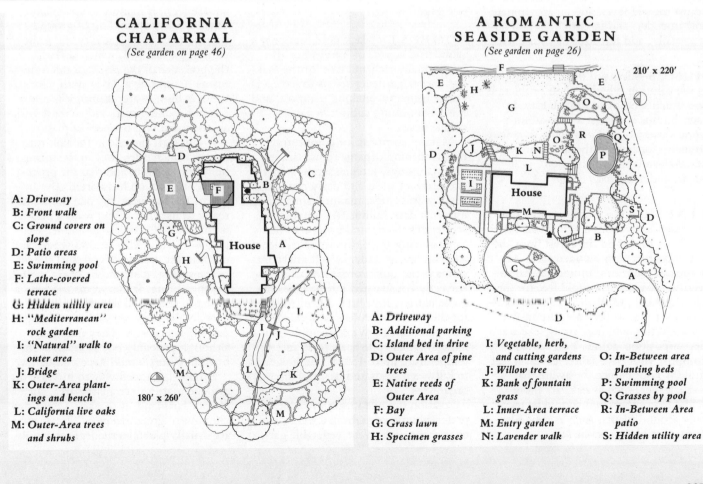

CALIFORNIA CHAPARRAL
(See garden on page 46)

A: *Driveway*
B: *Front walk*
C: *Ground covers on slope*
D: *Patio areas*
E: *Swimming pool*
F: *Lathe-covered terrace*
G: *Hidden utility area*
H: *"Mediterranean" rock garden*
I: *"Natural" walk to outer area*
J: *Bridge*
K: *Outer-Area plantings and bench*
L: *California live oaks*
M: *Outer-Area trees and shrubs*

180' x 260'

A ROMANTIC SEASIDE GARDEN
(See garden on page 26)

210' x 220'

A: *Driveway*
B: *Additional parking*
C: *Island bed in drive*
D: *Outer Area of pine trees*
E: *Native reeds of Outer Area*
F: *Bay*
G: *Grass lawn*
H: *Specimen grasses*
I: *Vegetable, herb, and cutting gardens*
J: *Willow tree*
K: *Bank of fountain grass*
L: *Inner-Area terrace*
M: *Entry garden*
N: *Lavender walk*
O: *In-Between area planting beds*
P: *Swimming pool*
Q: *Grasses by pool*
R: *In-Between Area patio*
S: *Hidden utility area*

ADJUSTMENTS AND IMPROVEMENTS

During the evaluation process, you undoubtedly uncovered some problems or potential problems on your property, and you may also have noticed conditions that need improving if your design is to succeed. Although one of the basic tenets of the Natural Garden is to choose plants that suit the existing conditions, relatively minor adjustments will widen the range of plants you can use.

SOIL

In most gardens, problems center around the soil—its content and quality and soil is one element that can be adjusted and improved somewhat. To improve the soil overall, add humus; to adjust the pH level, add an appropriate soil amender; and to enrich the soil nutritionally, add fertilizer of your choice.

HUMUS—decayed organic matter—is the solution whether your problem is too much sand or too much clay. In fact, humus is almost a cure-all for a wide variety of soil problems. It comes in many forms, but the three most readily available are leaf mold, peat moss, and compost.

LEAF MOLD is nothing more than partially decayed leaves. It forms the top layer of soil on the forest floor and is always found in wooded areas. In some communities, municipal leaf collection provides leaf mold free for the carting. Find out from your local sanitation service, as they are responsible for collecting and depositing leaves at a decomposition dump. You can also compost your own fallen leaves. If leaf mold is your choice, be aware that some leaves, such as oak, are more acidic than others and should be used only around plants, such as rhododendron, that like an acidic soil.

PEAT MOSS—decayed sphagnum moss and other swamp plants—is rich in organic material, very absorbent and moisture retentive, relatively free of unwanted weed seeds and harmful fungi, and, perhaps most significant, widely available. Choose the coarsest grade, sometimes known as poultry grade because it is strewn in chicken coops. The large lumps will break down more slowly, providing better long-term aeration than fine-grade peat. Peat moss is not a perfect additive; it is acidic, and has almost no nutritional content. To neutralize peat, add limestone; to increase nutritional content, add compost or fertilizer. Another disadvantage is that although it is sold dry, it must be applied wet and is difficult to moisten (see page 74).

COMPOST is black gold, not only a wonderful source of humus but also nutritionally rich and free for the making. Every gardener seems to have a favorite recipe for making compost, and it is a continuing subject in garden magazines.

Making compost, or composting, means turning organic refuse (leaves, grass clippings, kitchen scraps with the exception of meat and dairy products, small wood chips, manure, and so on) into rich dark humus. A compost pile accelerates the natural process of decay by providing the optimum ingredients and conditions under which microorganisms break down organic matter. A correctly constructed pile includes organic matter, moisture, air, nitrogen for the microorganisms, and the organisms themselves. While the process is underway, the pile heats to an internal temperature up to 150° F., high enough to kill weed seeds and harmful disease organisms.

Position the pile in sun or shade, preferably out of sight in a utility area, or perhaps next to the vegetable gar-den, if you have one. A compost pile can be almost any size, but I find 3 feet square or 3 feet in diameter and 3 feet high to be reasonable for the average home. I also prefer contained piles to free-flowing ones; an enclosure of chicken wire, open-slatted fencing, or both, has a neat appearance and still provides the necessary aeration.

Of the many recipes for compost, I like the following one best. Start with a bottom layer of about 6 inches of coarse twigs and branches, to assure aeration. Next, add a 6-inch layer of plant refuse (from garden or kitchen, grass clippings or leaves), and over this spread a 1 inch layer of manure, or a sprinkling of high-nitrogen fertilizer such as 10-6-4 (apply 1 ounce to a surface of 12 square feet), if manure is unavailable. Finally, add a sprinkling of ground limestone to reduce acidity and a shovelful of garden soil, which will assure the presence of the essential microorganisms. Continue to layer until your pile is 3 feet high; water it until it is moist but not soaking wet, and cover it with an anchored tarp or sheet of plastic.

If you start the pile in the fall, turn it over with a garden fork in the spring to be sure it is damp and that the process of decomposition has started. By the end of the summer, the pile should be ready to use, but if you want a fine-textured compost you should let the pile work through a second winter and use it in the spring. If you start the pile in the spring, it should be ready the following spring. If this seems too long a process, you could try one of the compost accelerators, which are sold at garden supply centers. They may help, although probably not as much as the manufacturers would have you believe.

An old-fashioned way to increase the organic matter over a large area, such as former farmland, is to plant a *cover crop,* known as "green manure." These crops are usually plants in the legume family that, working with certain soil bacteria (*Rhizobia*), have the ability to increase the nitrogen in the soil. *Rhizobia* absorb nitrogen from the air; when they touch a root hair of the legume they cause a slight irritation that becomes a nitrogen-rich nodule. When the cover crop is turned under into the soil, nitrogen, and a humusy texture, are added. In fact, a good cover crop of legumes can provide up to 150 pounds of nitrogen per acre, the equivalent of adding 12½ tons of cow manure.

Some legumes combine with bacteria found readily in the soil; others must combine with a specific bacteria, or not only will they not produce nitrogen, they will not survive. In such cases, the appropriate bacteria can be purchased at a good garden center or through the mail (see Source Guide, pages 287–92). Before sowing the seed, mix the bacteria (it comes in powder form) with water and coat the seeds. Instructions for use will accompany both seed and bacteria.

Before sowing, prepare the ground as for a meadow (see Meadows, pages 131–43). Allow the cover crop to grow just short of maturity and then turn it under, using a Rototiller. There are two good reasons not to allow the crop simply to go to seed and die back: the nitrogen nodules are at their peak just before the plant forms seed and some of these plants, if allowed to develop seed, will self-sow, later appearing unexpectedly in undesirable places. Different cover crops have different schedules for sowing and turning under. Choose the one that will work best for you.

You will also have to consider the *pH reading* of your soil. The pH of anything is a measurement of the concentration of hydrogen ions it contains. You need not understand the chemical basis for this scale, only that it indicates how acidic or alkaline the soil is. The scale runs from 3.5 to 8.5, with a reading of 7 being neutral, higher numbers are alkaline, lower numbers are acidic.

The acidity or alkalinity of soil can be adjusted somewhat. You will not be able to alter drastically the existing conditions on your property in order to grow acid-loving plants in areas with alkaline soil. You can't grow rhododendrons in desert soil, for example. You can make minor adjustments, however,

that will allow you to grow a greater range of plants.

Soil testing kits are available at any garden center. They are simple to use and give an idea of the general soil pH as well as some nutritional information. A soil profile obtained through your Cooperative Extension Service will be more detailed and specific, a good reason to have your soil tested professionally.

If your soil is alkaline, add organic substances that will lower the pH—oak leaves, leaf mold, peat moss, composted coffee grounds, or tea. Adding 1 pound of sulfur or 3 pounds of iron sulfate per 100 square feet of surface will lower the pH level by .5. The exact amount of sulfur you should add will vary according to soil type. (Aluminum sulfate has been widely used, and is readily available for this purpose, but it may have a residual toxicity and for this reason its use has been questioned.)

For soil that is too acidic for certain plants, add bonemeal and ground egg shells, two organic substances that will raise the pH. Dolomite limestone applied at a rate of 5 pounds per 100 square feet will raise the pH by .5. Again, the exact amount of dolomite you should add will vary according to soil type. Hydrated lime and other kinds of limestone will also work, but dolomite is best for this purpose.

No matter how loamy your soil or how well the pH suits your plants, if you do not add *food* from time to time, the plants will not thrive. People often tell me how poorly their plants are doing, but when I question their fertilizing practices, they are taken by surprise. Watering is about the only care they give their plants. Most plants, however, do need nutritional supplements. Tiny amounts are supplied by water and by decaying organic material on the soil surface or generated by lightning, but usually this is not enough for garden plants to perform at their best.

Of the several nutrients plants need, the three that concern us are nitrogen (N), phosphorus (P), and potassium (K). Simply stated, nitrogen aids vegetative growth, meaning leaves and stems; phosphorus encourages flower, fruit, and seed production; and potassium (sometimes called potash) builds

strong roots and helps plants resist disease. "Complete" fertilizers have all three ingredients in varying amounts, and commercial mixes give the percentages of each, N-P-K, in that order. A preparation that lists a ratio of 15:30:15 contains 15 percent nitrogen, 30 percent phosphorus, and 15 percent potassium. The higher the percentages, the stronger it is—the higher the ratio to inert ingredients.

I rarely use high-nitrogen fertilizers. Because they encourage green growth, plants may need pruning or staking or may outgrow their space too rapidly. Instead, I like to use an even mix (20:20:20) or a mild one with slightly more phosphorus (5:10:5). Some plants also respond to "foliar feeding" — spraying a water-soluble fertilizer such as Rapid-gro directly onto the foliage (on a cloudy day or early in the morning). Commercial products come in many forms, from grains to time-release capsules or pellets to water soluble powders. Choose whichever you prefer. Follow the manufacturer's recommendations for the correct amount to use, keeping in mind that it is far safer to underfeed than to overfeed. Too much fertilizer can have a disastrous effect. The best time to apply fertilizer is in the spring when the plants are actively growing. For this reason, I also top-dress the soil around plantings with well-rotted cow manure in the fall so they will have a head start the following spring.

You may want to use an organic fertilizer. There are many of them available, but to obtain a complete fertilizer (with nitrogen, phosphorus, and potassium), you will have to use a few organic substances in combination. If you use manure or food waste, it should be well-rotted through composting. Fresh manure will burn plant roots and kitchen scraps may attract scavengers.

WATERING is just as important as fertilizing. Although your plants are selected for their durability under adverse conditions, at certain times, such as during a dry spell or drought, you simply cannot expect them to survive without a helping hand on the watering can or, better yet, the soaker hose. It is tempting when the weather is dry to give the garden an occasional quick drink, but don't do it. Shallow watering encourages roots to grow close to the soil surface, making them more susceptible to drought damage and putting them solely in contact with the nutrient-poor top layer of soil. It is far better to give the plants a thorough, deep watering, at a slower rate over a longer period of time and at less frequent intervals. In the long run this even saves water. It is practically impossible, however, to water a garden this way by hand. An automatic device is not only easier but also better. Such devices range from a simple plastic jug perforated with small holes, sunk in the ground, and filled with water to automatic irrigation systems hooked up to a timer or moisture sensor (see Source Guide, pages 287–92).

As a general guide, plants need about an inch of water per week on average. Set a straight-sided pan in the path of a sprinkler and see how long it takes for the water to reach a depth of 1 inch. From then on, water for that length of time and you will have delivered adequate moisture for a week.

LIGHT

To some extent, the amount of light your property gets can be adjusted to suit your plants. Usually, you will have to add or subtract from the landscape—cutting down or thinning the lower branches of trees to let in more light, planting trees or shrubs in appropriate places to reduce sunlight.

If an Inner Area adjacent to the house gets too much sun, for example, attach an awning or other shading device to the building. If it is away from the house, you might construct an arbor or lathe house to filter the sun. A lathe house is a wooden roofed structure made of slats with equal open spaces between them. Rain comes through, and the sun's striped rays are always moving across the plants' leaves. Plants grown beneath a lathe house receive only half as much sun as plants grown in the open. If too little sun falls on an Inner Area, however, there is little you can do. White painted surfaces will help reflect what light there is and will brighten the space, but the best strategy is to choose plants that do well in shade.

PROBLEMS, PREVENTIONS, AND CURES

Innumerable diseases can afflict plants, and many pests can infest them. The situation is not hopeless, however. If you choose disease- and insect-resistant varieties of plants, and use natural means to control harmful insects and undesirable critters, you should not have too much trouble.

Preventing problems is, of course, the ideal. The first step in prevention is having healthy plants—plants that are happy in their environment, getting enough water and sun, and living in healthy nutrient-rich soil. If your plants are healthy, they will be able to fend off many diseases and insects by themselves. The next step is to enlist your natural allies—beneficial insects—in the battle against pests.

The friendliest and most familiar predator allies are the *ladybug* and the *praying mantis*. Ladybugs eat thousands of aphids as they journey through the garden, and a praying mantis will eat just about anything.

The shiny black *ground beetle* that scurries around the garden, darting out when rocks are moved, devours cutworms and other nocturnal nuisances. The beautiful *lacewing* has an enormous appetite for tiny pests. *Mosquito hawks,* which look terrifyingly like gigantic mosquitoes, are also allies—harmless to humans while their larvae eat hundreds of mosquito larvae. *Dragonfly nymphs* feast on mosquitoes and mosquito larvae. Give such creatures free run of your garden, and do not destroy them, either intentionally or inadvertently. I make it a rule never to kill a spider, for instance; it more than earns its keep by dining on garden foes.

Many such beneficial insects can be purchased from mail-order sources, usually at a minimal one-time expense (see Source Guide, pages 287–92). The ladybugs and praying mantises I introduced in my garden five years ago have returned every year since. While on the subject, I should also note that every garden pool should be stocked with *goldfish* and every bog have a resident *frog* or two. Both are insectivorous predators with a particular taste for mosquitoes—larvae and adults. *Tadpoles* also gobble up mosquito larvae.

Goldfish will actually reduce the general population of these pesky insects, which are attracted to water where the fish then devour every larva and mosquito in their midst.

It occasionally happens, unfortunately, that an insect problem will demand human attention. In that case, I always begin with the mildest, least dangerous remedy and escalate from there if necessary. A strong spray of plain water, for instance, will dislodge many pests from their feeding perches on plants. If that fails, I move on to soapy water, using one teaspoonful of dish detergent to one quart of water, applied with a sprayer. This treatment will often take care of simpler problems, but if not, or if favorite plants are seriously threatened, then, and only then, do I resort to stronger measures.

In recent times, entomologists and horticultural scientists have been turning more and more to biological pest controls, many of which do no harm to the environment or to beneficial insects. Some are specific to a single target foe. The Japanese beetle, for example, may be captured in beetle traps that use a sex lure and floral scent to attract only Japanese beetles. Another way to get rid of Japanese beetles is purposely to introduce milky spore, a host-specific insect disease, into the area where they are active, spraying the liquid on the ground. This will not be fully effective for about three years, but a treated area will then be free of Japanese beetle grubs for the next twenty years. Another host-specific disease, BT (*Bacillus thuringiensis*), kills insects that have a caterpillar stage. It does not harm beneficial insects or humans and is available from several manufacturers under various brand names including *Attack. Attack* also makes BT *isrealiensis,* a safe spray for mosquitoes.

A new insecticidal soap (*Safers*), a "fatty acid," will help with many insect problems, specifically white fly, scale, and mealy bug, and is safe for beneficial insects, pets, and humans. It has even been approved for food crops, but as with all insecticides, read the label carefully and follow instructions to the letter.

Many stronger insecticides are derived from natural sources—poisonous plants. They should be used with care. Rotenone, for example, is made from

Lonchocarpus, a South American leguminous plant. Used as a dust, it controls aphids, thrips, and Japanese beetles. Pyrethrum, made from the *Pyrethrum* daisy, and *Ryania,* from a South American shrub, are two other poisons. If you must use them, do so safely and responsibly. Wear gloves and even a mask, measure carefully, and thoroughly clean everything that has come in contact with the poison. Because cleaning tools and disposing of containers can be a real problem, the Sudbury company now makes "uni-bottle" insecticides: premeasured individual doses of various insecticides in tiny bottles, sold eight to a package. Organic pesticides such as pyrethrum degrade quickly in the environment.

Old-fashioned home remedies will often work against some of the more ubiquitous garden pests. Slugs, for example, are attracted to beer. If empty tuna fish cans are filled with it and sunk into the ground, slugs will crawl in and drown. Dry wood ashes discourages slugs when spread across their paths or around susceptible plants such as hosta. Diatomaceous earth, another natural product, kills slugs with its sharp-edged particles. It's available through mail-order suppliers.

Large, warm-blooded garden scavengers—deer, woodchucks, racoons, rabbits, and so on—are the bane of a vegetable garden, but are not quite the same problem in a Natural Garden unless it is largely an edible one. Squirrels will dine on bulbs, birds make raids on berry shrubs, and deer nibble the tender ends of yew and buds of trees.

In some rural areas, or in years of overbreeding, deer can become a major nuisance. I generally try to follow a live-and-let-live philosophy, but if such visitors really are damaging your plants, do not reach immediately for a shotgun. Your Cooperative Extension agent can give advice on humane methods of control. Home remedies are often the best, however, and there are many of them to try—from sprinkling dried blood meal on the ground to hanging net bags of human hair at nose level in trees or on stakes. Hanging strong-smelling deodorant soaps such as *Dial* or *Safeguard* also seems to work well. Try commercially available scented repellents for cats, dogs, and squirrels. Or, mix garlic and cayenne

pepper with water in a blender. Strain it, and add a drop of dish detergent (to make it spread on the leaves). Then spray the scavengers' favorite plants with the mixture. *Miller Hot Sauce* diluted with water is a good repellent spray. An inexpensive commercial product, *Hinder,* which contains fatty acids and ammonium soaps, is very effective. Moth balls sprinkled around the garden may also help. Such treatments discourage the animals and do no harm to the environment.

HELP

Some of the work you must do to improve and later to maintain a garden may require outside help. Felling a large tree, removing a dead one, or installing a concrete pool, for example, is more than many gardeners want to tackle. And, although your plants have been selected for low maintenance, there will still be times when their care may have to be left to someone else—when a busy schedule prevents you from doing the normal chores or when you are on vacation.

Very few people who do landscape work today are as familiar with plants as were the trained gardeners of yesteryear. The new styles and concepts of the Natural Garden may also be foreign to them. To an inexperienced or uneducated eye, your treasured wildflowers may look like weeds, and your shrubs, so lovingly encouraged to grow free, may appear simply unruly. A mower

or pruning shears in the wrong hands could ruin your beautiful landscape. I have heard many sad stories of ground covers mowed down, ancient vines hacked to stumps, and delicate shrubs turned into poodle shapes.

The best defense is to go over every job in detail. Walk the property with your hired help, making a list of what is to be done and what is to be left alone. Explain the concept behind your Natural Garden. If possible, make frequent checks on the progress of the work. If you are going on vacation, be sure the hired helper, or kind friend, makes a trial visit beforehand, so you can observe and correct the work as necessary. That way, there will be no unpleasant surprises upon your return.

By following this advice, I have always been fortunate in entrusting my garden to others, and in the years that I had my rooftop garden it came to mean almost as much to its occasional caretakers as to its creators. That garden is gone now, the plants dispersed, some to a community center, others—along with the greenhouse—to a senior center. My cherished plants, those closest to my heart, have moved with me to a new home, and like me, are settling in.

The new garden is still raw, but I treasure its potential as I study the patterns of life behind a brownstone in Brooklyn. As the garden evolves, I apply many of the lessons I learned in my old garden and in writing this book —it will be a Natural Garden, without question.

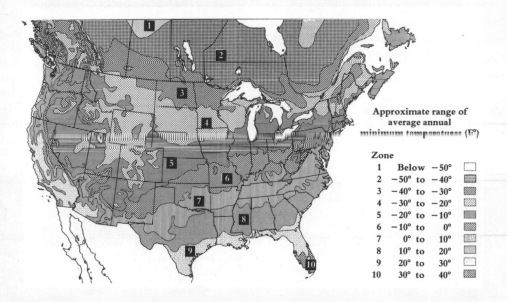

Approximate range of average annual minimum temperatures (F°)

Zone		
1	Below −50°	
2	−50° to −40°	
3	−40° to −30°	
4	−30° to −20°	
5	−20° to −10°	
6	−10° to 0°	
7	0° to 10°	
8	10° to 20°	
9	20° to 30°	
10	30° to 40°	

PLANT
SELECTION

On this master list of plants for a Natural Garden, the species, hybrids, and cultivars, whether natural or man-made, have been chosen with several criteria in mind. Essentially, these plants are easy to care for. This does not mean "no-care"—a phenomenon that simply does not exist—but low care. For the most part, I have not included fussy, finicky plants that demand staking, dividing, deadheading, heavy feeding and watering, extra protection in winter, or any other special, constant attention in order to look their best. Plants that are susceptible to extensive damage by pests or disease are also not included. And, except for the annuals, these are all long-living plants; they will come back faithfully year after year.

To follow these criteria, of course, I had to leave out several of the most familiar garden plants: petunias, most of the roses, and tulips, for example. However, like most rules, the rules of plant selection are occasionally broken. Some plants are simply so beautiful that they are worth the extra trouble. If you are drawn to such plants, you just have to accept the necessity for extra care. If a plant species, genus, or group of hybrids not on the list does well for you, then by all means include it in *your* Natural Garden. Your specific climate and location may suit a plant that we found difficult.

The list is arranged according to broad categories of plant types or applications:

Trees	Ornamental
Shrubs	Grasses
Herbaceous	Ground Covers
Perennials	Ferns
Biennials	Vines
Easy Annuals	Water Plants
Bulbs	Edible Plants

Individual plants are arranged alphabetically by their Latin names, using *Hortus Third*, the bible of plant growers, professional and amateur. Help was also provided by Lothian Lynus of the New York Botanical Garden and her resources. Needless to say, few of us know every plant by its formal name, and so plants, listed by their common names, will be found in the index.

There is no separate category for wildflowers, which instead are scattered throughout the lists. I do not see wildflowers as an isolated phenomenon, but imagine them, both natives and aliens, rubbing shoulders happily with all manner of varieties and hybrids. (However, if you would like to establish a woodland wildflower garden, see the boxed list on page 165.)

In the master list, a heading to each entry includes certain basics about the plant: its hardiness zone (indicated by USDA zones), height, flower color, season of bloom, and occasionally some facts about cultivation. Not all information is given for every category of plant; it will vary from section to section according to what is relevant to specific kinds of plants. Nor is every listing annotated; I have only annotated those plants of special interest or with qualities of note. Plants not annotated are either easily grown in limited areas—the subtropical plants, for example—or are valuable additions not annotated simply because space does not permit more detailed description here. However, wherever you live, whatever your gardening tastes, you will find a wide range of plants—both familiar and unusual—from which to choose. And read new catalogues to find recommended hybrids of the plants listed that are new, particularly distinguished, or especially suited to your site's conditions.

Key: Z = hardiness zone; Ht = maximum height; L = length; C = culture; Fl = flower; Fr = fruit; S = season; W = water; cv. = cultivar; var. = variety; E = evergreen; D = deciduous; spp. = species.

TREES

DECIDUOUS TREES

Acer campestre, hedge maple. Z: 5–9. Ht: to 35'.

A. griseum, paperbark maple. Z: 4–8. Ht: 20'.
The main interest of this small, slow-growing species native to China, is its bark, which exfoliates in flakes to reveal the young bark underneath. Trunk colors range from cinnamon red to cork brown to gleaming honey orange on the same tree, and the fall foliage is a striking red and orange.

A. negundo, box elder. Z: 3–9. Ht: 50'–70'.

A. palmatum, Japanese cut-leaf maple. Z: 4–9 (by cv.). Ht: 20'–50'.
There are many cultivars of this aristocratic plant. Most are small and slow growing, many have red foliage throughout the growing season; some are pendulous, with multiple trunks and branches that arch to the ground, others have straight single trunks. They are expensive to buy, but even a single showcased specimen is beautiful and impressive, making a spectacular display. 'Dissectum' maples are the tiny "thread leaf" varieties.

A. saccharum, sugar maple. Z: 3–8. Ht: 130'.
This is one of my favorites of the more than 200 *Acer* species. Its leaves are handsome when green, and brilliantly colored in autumn, turning red, orange,

or yellow depending upon the individual, its location, and the weather conditions. A shapely tree, with or without foliage.

Aesculus x carnea 'Briotii', red horse chestnut. Z: 5–8. Ht: 60'–80'. Fl: bright scarlet panicles.

Aesculus flava, yellow buckeye. Z: 4–8. Ht: 60'–75'. Fl: yellow panicles 5"–7" long in late spring.

Albizia julibrissin, mimosa. Z: 6–10. Ht: 40'.
A fast-growing, relatively short lived tree (40 to 60 years), the mimosa may not be a perfect plant—its flowers are a bit messy, sticking to other plants and to walkways beneath them—but its drawbacks are more than offset by its long blooming period, its cream and pink powder puff flowers, their intoxicating peachlike fragrance, and the delightful quality of the light shade its foliage creates. Its tiny leaves simply blow away in autumn, leaving little to clean up.

Amelanchier canadensis, Juneberry or serviceberry. Z: 4–7. Ht: to 25'. Fl: white flowers followed by blueberry-like edible fruits.

Betula platyphylla japonica 'Whitespire', Whitespire Japanese, white birch. Z: 4–7. Ht: 40'.
Many birch species have problems, but the beauty of their bark and their overall form make them desirable as specimens. This white birch, which is insect resistant, is a good candidate for the Natural Garden. Like other birches, it grows well in cold areas, in moist, well-drained soils. Plant several against a backdrop of evergreens. Because they are relatively short-lived (50 to 70 years), consider planting a second set some fifteen to twenty years after the first. European white birch, *B. pendula*, is a common species.

Carpinus betulus, European hornbeam. Z: 5–7. Ht: 40'–60'.

C. caroliniana, American hornbeam. Z: 3–4. Ht: 35'.

Cercidiphyllum japonicum, Katsura tree. Z: 5. Ht: to 100'.

LATIN NAMES:
BREAKING THE CODE

Latin plant names may look bewildering at first, but there are several reasons to learn and use them. First, common names may change from region to region (some familiar names are quite localized), but the Latin name is consistent the whole world over. Also, some plants share the same common name—for instance, hundreds of different plants are called *daisy*—and the Latin name makes clear the horticultural distinctions. The best reason, however, is that knowing a plant's true name allows you to treat it as an individual, and such familiarity is one of the secrets of successful gardening.

Latin names are always set up the same way: The first word refers to the genus of which the plant is a member, and the second word is usually descriptive of its color, form, or habit of growth. *Echinacea purpurea*, for example, is purple coneflower (*purpurea* means purple). *Echinacea purpurea* 'Alba' is white purple coneflower (*alba* means white).

Listed below are several of the most-used Latin words and their meanings. As you begin to recognize these words, you will find that you instantly know something about a given plant. The Latin names are used throughout this book so that you will be able to find plants in catalogs or at nurseries, regardless of the common name. (Incidentally, I find that the use of a Latin name on a tag at a nursery or in a mail-order catalog is a sign of quality. If the proprietors care about accuracy, they often care about the condition of their plants as well.)

alba, albus: white
aurea, aureus: gold-colored
caerulea, caeruleus: sky blue
campanulata: bell-shaped
chinensis: originating in China
citrinus: lemon-colored or lemon-like
citriodora: lemon-scented
coccineus: bright scarlet red
cordata: heart-shaped
cornuta: horned
crassifolius: thick-leaved
cretaceus: chalky white
cristata: crested
curvifolius: with curved leaves
cyaneus: bright blue, azure
densus: thick
divaricata: diverging, branched
dulcis: sweet
edulis: edible
elatus: tall in comparison to allied plants
elegans: very pretty

erectus: upright
falcata, falcatus: with flat leaves curving to a point
fastigatus: columnar
flava, flavus: yellow
fulva, fulvus: tawny, dull yellow
giganteum: gigantic
glauca, glaucus: bluish gray
gracilis: graceful
grandiflorus: with large flowers
grandifolius: with large leaves
grandis: large
hirta: hairy
humilis: low-growing
japonica: originally from Japan
labiata: lipped
latifolia, latifolius: with broad leaves
longifolius: with long leaves
lutea, luteus: pale yellow
macranthus: with broad, large flowers
macrophylla: with large leaves
majalis: May-flowering

major, majus: larger than others in the genus
maritima: from the seaside
microphylla: tiny-leaved
minor: smaller than others in the genus
mollis: soft and hairy
multiflora, multiflorus: with many flowers
nani: dwarf
niger, nigra: black
nobilis: famous
nocturnus: night-blooming
ordorata, odoratus: fragrant
ovata: egg-shaped
pendula, pendulus: drooping
perennis: perennial
praecox: early-blooming
procumbens: trailing
pubescens: hairy
purpurea, purpureus: purple
pyramidalis: shaped like a pyramid
quinquefolia: with five leaflets
radicans: rooting along the stem

repens: trailing or creeping
reptens: trailing or creeping
roseus: rose-colored
rotundifolia: with round leaves
ruber, rubra, rubrum: red
salicifolia: with willowlike leaves
sanguinea, sanguineus: blood red
scandens: climbing
sempervirens: evergreen
sinensis: from China
spicata, spicatus: with flowers on spikes
stellata, stellatus: star-shaped
tomentosa: covered with densely matted hairs
umbellatus: with flowers forming a flat flowerhead
variegata, variegatum: with variegated leaves
vera: true
virens: bright green
viridus: bluish green
zebrinus: striped

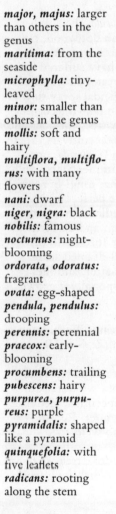

Cercis canadensis, eastern redbud. Z: 4–9. Ht: 40'.
A North American native, the redbud has spring flowers of deep pink; its leaves are heart shaped, turning yellow in fall. Because it likes cool, moist, well-drained soil and tolerates light shade, it is a good candidate for the transitional edge of an Outer Area woodland.

Chionanthus virginicus, white fringe tree. Z: 5–9. Ht: 12'–20'. Native.

Cladrastis lutea, yellowwood. Z: 4–8. Ht: 50'. Fl: native tree with white wisterialike flowers in late spring.

Cornus kousa, kousa dogwood. Z: 4–9. Ht: 20'.
Unfortunately, *C. florida,* the familiar and beloved American dogwood, cannot be recommended. In recent years, these treasured trees have suffered from blight, a disease that can be controlled with a systemic fungicidal spray such as benomyl. Rather than take the chance of a potentially sickly tree, consider one of the resistant *C. kousa* cultivars. These will bloom later than *C. florida;* one cultivar, *C. kousa* 'Summer Stars', will even flower all summer long. In zones 6, 7, and 8 they make perfect understory plants in a woodland, but farther north, they prefer sun, and do better on the sunny edge of the forest. All the dogwoods like a well-drained acidic soil rich in organic matter, and they need ample water, especially if grown in full sun.

Crataegus phaenopyrum, Washington thorn tree, hawthorn. Z: 4–8. Ht: to 25'.
This is a native that can be used as an untrimmed hedge for a windbreak or can be featured as a specimen. Red fruit in the fall lasts into winter. Red and orange fall foliage is also welcome.

Davidia involucrata, dove tree. Z: 6–8. Ht: 40'. Fl: produces 7-inch-long white flowers in spring.

Fagus sylvatica, European beech. Z: 5–7. Ht: to 100'.
Some insect and disease problems, but beautiful.

Franklinia alatamaha, Franklin tree. Z: 5–9. Ht: 30'.
A beautiful, easily grown, but often overlooked native American tree. It was first found in 1777 growing in a small stand on the banks of the Alatamaha River in Georgia. A specimen was sent to John Bartram in Philadelphia, who named the plant after his old friend Benjamin Franklin. In the wild the plant has never been found anywhere but in the original site, and the last one seen there was in 1803, by John Lyon. All of today's plants are descendants of Bartram's original specimen. *Franklinia* has a spread of 15 feet. Its 3-inch white flowers are fragrant, and resemble giant versions of the common mock orange. They appear from late summer until frost nips the buds in the fall, after the foliage has turned crimson. *Franklinia* can stand an Ohio winter and can be grown in protected sites as far north as Michigan. It likes full sun or partial shade and soil with very good drainage.

Fraxinus americana, white ash. Z: 3–9. Ht: 50'–80'.

Ginkgo biloba, ginkgo, maidenhair tree. Z: 3–9. Ht: to 120'.
The ginkgo, a conifer, is a living fossil, known to have existed millions of years ago. Its unique fan-shaped leaves resemble those of the maidenhair fern from which it derives its common name. Tolerant of city conditions, it makes an ideal street tree; it has virtually no pest problems, is disease resistant, and transplants easily—a true survivor. Its only drawback is that the female plant has foul smelling, though edible, fruit (considered a delicacy in the Orient) that creates a litter problem in the fall. Nurseries, however, are well aware of this characteristic and usually offer only male plants. Cultivars have various spreading habits, from wide to narrow (fastigiate), the former suitable for open landscape, the latter best for the small spaces available along city streets.

Gleditsia triacanthos var. *inermis* (and cvs.), honey locust. Z: 3–9. Ht: 75'.
The honey locust is an extremely useful all-purpose tree, and this variety has the best attributes. Its tiny leaves create a light, cool shade and simply blow away in the fall; its shape is pleasing at maturity; it is fast growing with nondestructive roots; and, like several other varieties, it is both thornless and nonfruiting. (The long brown pods of varieties that have not been vegetatively grown from nonfruiting stock are attractive on the tree but a nuisance when they fall to the ground.) 'Halka' is an excellent cultivar.

Halesia carolina, wild olive, Carolina silverbell. Z: 5. Ht: 45'.

Koelreuteria paniculata, golden-rain tree. Z: 5. Ht: to 45'. Fl: attractive yellow flowers and pale green pods.

Laburnum x watereri, golden-chain tree. Z: 5–7. Ht: 20'. Fl: long yellow racemes in spring.

Lagerstroemia indica 'Indian Tribes', crape myrtle. Z: 7–10. Ht: 25'.
New disease-resistant variety of famed southern bloomer.

Liquidambar styraciflua, sweet gum. Z: 6–9. Ht: 75'–100'. Smooth, maplelike leaves.

Liriodendron tulipifera, tulip tree. Z: 4–9. Ht: to 150' or more.
A straight, stately tree and a native hardwood, it has orange and green flowers that are tulip shaped, resembling magnolia. Situated in the Outer Area, to be viewed close up on woodland rambles, and also enjoyed from afar. Source of telephone poles.

Magnolia x soulangiana, saucer or Chinese magnolia. Z: 5–9. Ht: to 25'.
Of the many magnolia species, this one is the most familiar, growing in gardens all over America. Its large white, pink, and purple tulip-shaped blossoms arrive in early spring with the daffodils. Use it as a single specimen in the Inner or In-Between Area, or position several along the house-facing edge of the Outer Area. It is easy to grow, tolerant of city conditions and partial shade, but does best in full sun. Other magnolias to look for are: *M. grandiflora,* Southern magnolia, which is an evergreen in warm regions only; *M. stellata* and *M. x loebneri* 'Merrill' (Z: 3–8), which are deciduous and have white star-shaped flowers that bloom before the other varieties; and finally *M. virginiana,* sweet

bay magnolia (Z: 5–9), a much prized native plant that is evergreen in the South and semievergreen in the North, and that has fragrant green and white flowers followed by fruits that turn red in autumn.

Malus spp., crab apple. Z: 4–8. Ht: 6'–30'.
Any small-fruited *Malus* species is known as a crab apple; they are grown for flowers rather than fruit. Some are little more than shrubs, others are substantial trees; some are disease and insect resistant. Flower colors range from white to pink to salmon to red, and forms can be single or double. There are dozens of available species, varieties, and cultivars appropriate for a Natural Garden. A good choice would be *M. floribunda,* the showy crab apple, and its varieties. Introduced from Japan, it grows to 25 feet and has rose-colored flowers. Others include: *M.* 'Adams'; *M.* 'Donald Wyman'; *M. hupehensis; M.* 'Mary Potter'; and *M.* 'Professor Sprenger'.

Metasequoia glyptostroboides, dawn redwood. Z: 4–8. Ht: to 100'.
Until 1944 this tree, known only by its fossilized remains, was thought to be extinct. That year, however, living specimens were found in Szechuan, China, and the tree has since gained in popularity. It has an elegant pyramidal form, resembling an evergreen conifer with bright green needles, but it is deciduous, turning a coppery apricot gold before shedding its needles to reveal a soft silhouette. It prefers ample room and moisture but will tolerate city pollution, a fact I know from personal experience, having identified one of these redwoods in the Chelsea section of New York City.

Oxydendrum arboreum, sourwood, sorrel tree. Z: 4–9. Ht: to 80', usually much smaller.
This is an excellent ornamental throughout its growing season. Its fragrant hanging white flowers, borne in summer, are long lasting, remaining on the tree while the foliage begins to change from green to crimson to rust. Twigs are scarlet in winter. It is very slow-growing, likes full sun, and tolerates a wide variety of soil conditions.

Parkinsonia aculeata, Mexican palo verde. Z: 9–10. Ht: 40'. Fl: ferny foliage, yellow pea flowers.

Phellodendron amurense, Amur cork tree. Z: 3–7. Ht: 30'–45'. Widespread; interesting bark.

Prunus spp., stone fruits. Z: 4–8. Ht: varies, usually no more than to 25'. (See EP)
There are some 400 species and cultivars of these flowering ornamental trees. Among them are peaches, plums, apricots, nectarines, cherries, and almonds. They have different flower colors and plant forms—from weeping to upright, from shrubs (such as *P. tomentosa,* Nanking cherry) to trees. In some cases, flowers precede leaves; in others, leaves rival flowers for color. *P. cerasifera* 'Newportii', a cherry plum, (Z: 4–8; Ht: to 25'), for example, has white flowers, red leaves, and edible fruit, and grows from Maine to Florida. *P. subhirtella,* Higan cherry (Z: 6–8; Ht: to 25'), is from Japan, is disease and insect resistant, has many cultivars, including upright and pendulous ones, and is very floriferous. Perhaps the most famous cherry trees in America are those that surround the Tidal Basin in Washington, D.C. They are *P. yedoensis,* Japanese flowering cherry (Z: 6–8; Ht: to 25'), a gift from Japan to the United States many years ago. Other cultivars include: *P.* 'Okame'; *P. sargentii.*

Pseudolarix kaempferi, golden larch. Z: 5–7. Ht: 30'–50'.
Deciduous conifer.

Pyrus calleryana 'Bradford', Bradford callery pear. Z: 6. Ht: to 30'.

Quercus alba, white oak. Z: 4. Ht: to 100'.
There are many mighty oaks, suitable to virtually every part of the country. Of these, the white oak is perhaps our best species. It has easily identified gray bark, grows very slowly, and lives well over a century, becoming a monument among trees. The nation's champion oak is a white oak in Wye, Maryland, that is some 107 feet high with a girth of 414 inches. Another northern oak is *Q. rubra,* the red oak (Z: 4–8; Ht: to 80').

Q. palustris, pin oak. Z: 4–8. Ht: to 80'.
This is an excellent, fast-growing street tree, with attractive bright green leaves. Fall leaves (brown) persist through winter. Another good choice for an urban location is *Q. phellos,* the willow oak (Z: 6–9; Ht: to 60'), which has light green shiny leaves that are not lobed.

Robinia pseudoacacia, black locust. Z: 3–7. Ht: to 50'. Fl: native tree has fragrant white flowers. Mimosalike leaves turn yellow in fall.

Salix babylonica, weeping willow. Z: 2–9. Ht: to 50'.

Sorbus aucuparia, European mountain ash. Z: 3–6. Ht: to 30'.

Stewartia koreana, Korean stewartia. Z: 6–7. Ht: 20'–25'.

S. monadelpha, tall stewartia. Z: 6–8. Ht: 70'.

Styphnolobium japonicum, Japanese pagoda tree, Chinese scholar tree. Z: 5–8. Ht: to 80'.

Styrax japonicus, Japanese snowbell. Z: 5. Ht: to 30'. Fl: beautiful white bell-shaped flowers, egg-shaped fruits.

Syringa reticulata, Japanese tree lilac. Z: 4–7. Ht: 30'. Most trouble-free lilac.

Zelkova serrata, Japanese zelkova. Z: 5. Ht: to 100'.
This Japanese timber tree is easy to cultivate and has many of the qualities of the elm tree that has nearly disappeared from the American landscape, victim of the devastating Dutch elm disease. Zelkova, while not as tall and majestic as the elm, has similar leaves and provides excellent shade under its widespreading branches.

EVERGREEN TREES

Abies concolor, white fir. Z: 3–7. Ht: 30'–50' average; 100' maximum.
A Rocky Mountain native, with blue-green needles and a handsome columnar shape, the white fir is a tough tenacious tree that does well in difficult places. It thrives in its native habitat—

the dry soil of wind-swept mountain slopes. Seek other species.

Acacia spp., acacia, mimosa. Z: 9 (hardy to 20°). Ht: Varies.
There are some 800 acacia species, for the most part small, flowering semievergreen trees (subject to temperature); some are deciduous. Their small leaves resemble the northern "mimosa," *Albizia julibrissin*.

Araucaria araucana, monkey-puzzle. Z: 7–10. Ht: 70'.
Good lawn specimen.

A. bidwilli, Bunya-Bunya. Z: 9–10. Ht: 50'.
Good windbreak for dry, desert regions.

A. heterophylla, Norfolk Island pine. Z: 9–10. Ht: reaches 80'.
This is a familiar container-grown houseplant; unrestricted, it becomes a pinelike tree that grows well in moist places in the warmer regions of the country.

Arbutus unedo, strawberry tree. Z: 8–9. Ht: 30'. Rough, red ornamental fruits.

Bauhinia forficata, white orchid tree. Z: 9–10. Ht: 20'–30'. Fl: White.

Cedrus atlantica, Atlas cedar. Z: 6–9. Ht: 100'.
This native of Spain has bluish needles and branches that grow from the base of its trunk to the tip, forming a near-perfect pyramid. The best cultivar is *C. atlantica* 'Glauca'.

C. deodara, Deodar cedar. Z: 7–9. Ht: 70'.
Beautiful tree. Magnificent in winter. Pest free.

C. libani, cedar-of-Lebanon. Z: 7–9. Ht: 100'.
A tall, wide-spreading evergreen that, along with *Cedrus deodara*, is a good choice for the warmer zones, especially California.

Chamaecyparis lawsoniana, Port Orford cedar, Lawson cypress. Z: 6–9. Ht: 100'.
This is a "false cypress." It is pest free,

seldom needs pruning, and forms a shaggy pyramid with branches beginning at the base of the trunk. It requires moist, slightly acidic soil, and resents strong winds, so is not a good choice for a windbreak.

C. obtusa, hinoki false cypress. Z: 4–9. Ht: 120'.
Similar attributes and requirements as *C. lawsoniana,* but grows into a perfect cone, usually around 50 feet tall. A good cultivar to choose is *C. obtusa* 'Crippsii'.

Chamaerops humilis, European fan palm. Z: 9. Ht: 5'–20'.
A small tree, it is drought-tolerant but likes moisture.

Cibotium chamissoi, Hawaiian tree fern. Z: 10. Ht: 25'.
A subtropical plant, one of the tree ferns suitable to warm humid regions, such as Florida and the Gulf states.

Citrus spp. Z: 9–10. Ht: approx. 20'.
There are about sixteen species of citrus plants that will grow in the country's warm regions: *C. aurantiifolia,* lime; *C. limon,* lemon; and *C. reticulata,* tangerine, are three good choices for an edible landscape. They have beautiful glossy leaves and are lovely small trees. Oranges, kumquats, and grapefruits are also available; if you are in the right zone, ask your nursery for resistant cultivars.

Cupressus arizonica, Arizona cypress. Z: 7-10. Ht: 40'.
A tree for warm regions; forms silver pyramids.

C. macrocarpa, Monterey cypress. Z: 7–10. Ht: 50'. California native.

C. sempervivens, Italian cypress. Z: 8–10. Ht: variable to 50'. Perfect columns.

Cycas revoluta, Sago palm. Z: 9–10. Ht: variable. Palmlike prehistoric cycad.

Dicksonia squarrosa, tree fern. Z: 10. Ht: 20'. Similar to *Cibotium chamissoi.*

Eriobotrya japonica, loquat, Japanese plum. Z: 7–9. Ht: 25'.

Lovely loquats line the streets of Charleston, South Carolina. They have large quilted leaves and produce cream colored or yellow fruits that are both ornamental and edible. A good choice for an edible garden in the South.

Eucalyptus spp., gum trees. Z: 8–10. Ht: 20'–100', by variety.
This wonderful Australian genus deserves an entire book to itself. All species have fragrant foliage, *E. citriodora*'s leaves are lemon scented when crushed. Some species grow tall, others are quite small and will not outgrow a site. *E. cinerea,* for example, the silver-dollar tree and the florists' eucalyptus, is a small, silver-leaved plant of great beauty. The young plants need plenty of moisture. *E. globulus* is the common giant, now "wild" in California.

Feijoa sellowiana, pineapple guava. Z: 9–10. Ht: 18'.
This plant has attractive small evergreen leaves, and colorful flowers, and edible fruit. It needs moisture when young but is drought-tolerant when established.

Ficus spp., ornamental figs. Z: 9. Ht: varies.
There are some 800 species of *Ficus,* some with edible fruit. In the North, they are grown indoors as potted plants, but they can tolerate temperatures to around 30°. All need moisture. Two elegant choices are *F. benjamina,* the Benjamin tree, and *F. macrophylla,* the Australian banyan, which grows to 50 feet.

Grevillea robusta, silk oak. Z: 9–10. Ht: 150'. Fl: orange masses in spring.
This is one of my favorite trees; because it needs moisture and warmth, it will grow only in a greenhouse in the North, but it makes a lovely city tree in California, Florida, and Hawaii.

Ilex opaca, American holly. Z: 5–9. Ht: 50'.
Overharvested for its Christmas greenery, the holly has actually become hard to find in its native North American habitats. Nonetheless, it is widely available from nurseries and very attractive; make certain to plant both male and female plants to assure production of berries. *I. opaca,* 'Wayside's Christmas

Tree', forms a perfect cone without pruning, and there are many other varieties and imports from England, Korea, Japan, China, and elsewhere. The Korean varieties are interesting; they resemble boxwood and might substitute for it in cold climates. *I.* x *aquipernyi* and *I. pedunculosa* are especially pest and disease resistant.

Jacaranda mimosifolia, jacaranda. Z: 9–10. Ht: 50'.
Not as pretty as *Acacia* or *Albizia,* which it resembles, the jacaranda does have exquisite blue flower clusters. It needs moisture and is briefly deciduous in the spring.

Juniperus chinensis, 'Columnaris' and other cv., juniper. Z: 4–9. Ht: to 60'.
In general, the junipers are a hardy lot, practically indestructible and very versatile. Some species are good ground covers, others are tree sized; there are junipers for sun and for shade, and for just about every zone in the country. This cultivar is American bred, of a Chinese species. It becomes a perfect dense column of blue, usually reaching about 20 feet.

J. virginiana, eastern red cedar. Z: 2–9. Ht: to 50'.
This is a hardy, tall American native that has many available cultivars. Despite its common name, this is a juniper and like other tree-type junipers, it does well in dry soil, tolerates salt spray and smog, never needs pruning, and makes a good windbreak. Also, like most junipers, it is sometimes stricken by diseases carried by other plants; position it well away from apple trees, cotoneasters, and hawthorns. Junipers have foliage ranging from blue to purple, often changing in cold weather; females produce attractive berries. Seek varieties.

Ligustrum lucidum, glossy privet. Z: 8–10. Ht: 30'.
Most species of this genus are shrubs, but this one is a small tree with dense foliage and fabulous fragrant flowers. It needs moisture and will tolerate partial shade.

Magnolia grandiflora, southern magnolia. Z: 7–10 (Z: 6, sheltered). Ht: 90'.
Deep glossy green large leaves. Huge cream-colored fragrant flowers. *M.*

grandiflora 'Edith Bogue' is the best hybrid for zone 6.

Olea europaea, common olive. Z: 8–10. Ht: to 25'.
A slow-growing, long-living tree with silvery foliage and interesting gnarled trunks, the olive is grown in California, Arizona, and wherever there is a Mediterranean-like climate. Its flowers are fragrant, but its fruits do cause litter, and suckers must be removed annually.

Phoenix canariensis, Canary island date palm. Z: 9. Ht: to 50'.
This tree grows in central California, northern Florida, and the Gulf states. It likes fertile, moist soil, has massive trunks when mature, and will need some grooming. A slightly hardier date palm is *P. dactylifera,* which is taller and thinner and produces commercial edible dates. It needs ample moisture but is hardy to 20°.

Pinus spp., pine trees.
There are pines for all parts of North America. The following are those that will do well with the least amount of attention. *P. nigra,* Austrian pine (Z: 4–8; Ht: to 100'), is used in problem areas such as along highways or by the seashore where windbreaks are needed. It thrives on neglect, has long needles and decorative brown cones and can tolerate many soil conditions as well as salt spray and pollution. *P. resinosa,* red or Norway pine (Z: 3–7; Ht: to 90'), grows well in the eastern states and west to Michigan. *P. strobus,* white or eastern pine (Z: 2–7; Ht: to 120'), towers above houses in northern suburban and rural areas. Valued for its timber, it grows tall, has blue-green needles, and is a good background plant. Cultivars range from dwarf to dense, trailing, conical, or umbrella shaped. *P. sylvestris,* Scotch pine (Z: 3–7; Ht: to 100'), is bluish green and prized as a Christmas tree when young. *P. thunbergiana,* Japanese black pine (Z: 4–8; Ht: to 130'), is another tenacious plant. It grows in places where no other evergreen tree will survive, such as on windswept dunes. Pruning will give it a distinctly oriental look, befitting its name. *P. cembra,* Swiss stone pine (Z: 3–7; Ht: to 75'), is another slow-growing, low-maintenance evergreen.

P. cembra, P. koraiensis and *P. parviflora* are the most disease and pest resistant species.

Pistacia vera, pistachio. Z: 9. Ht: to 30'.
There are many pistachio trees but this is the one that produces the commercially available nuts. It is grown in the western United States and is a good choice for an edible landscape.

Podocarpus macrophyllus, podocarpus. Z: 8–10. Ht: 30'–50'. Excellent long-needled evergreen for warm climates.

Quercus agrifolia, California live oak. Z: 9–10. Ht: 30'–50'.

Q. virginiana, live oak. Z: 7. Ht: to 60'.
This is an evergreen or semievergreen oak and a truly beautiful tree. It needs moisture when young but no maintenance once established. Lives for 1,000 years.

Rhus lancea, African sumac. Z: 9. Ht: to 25'.
A relative of the deciduous American sumac, this small tree has greenish white flowers in dense panicles.

Roystonea regia, Royal palm. Z: 10. Ht: 50'–70'. Needs moisture.

Sciadopitys verticillata, umbrella pine. Z: 5–8. Ht: to 30' in cultivation.
Often overlooked for the home landscape, the umbrella pine would be elegant in an Inner Area where its flat whorls of shiny long needles could be viewed close up. It is slow growing, never needs pruning, and produces only minor litter from dropping needles. It likes a moist, neutral to slightly acidic soil, and can tolerate full sun except in its southernmost range, where it needs shading from the afternoon sun and will prefer a position perhaps on the east facing side of the house.

Sophora secundiflora, Texas mountain laurel. Z: 8–10. Ht: 25'. Fl: Violet-blue fragrant flowers in early spring. Pest free.

Strelitzia spp., bird-of-paradise. Z: 9–10. Ht: to 18'.
These are not really trees, but the spe-

cies, notably *S. alba* and *S. nicolai*, are large enough to include here. They will grow where there is rich soil, ample moisture, and partial shade, with night temperatures averaging about 50° Temperatures below 20° will kill them. The bird-of-paradise many florists carry comes from *S. reginae*, which is trunkless and grows to 36 inches.

Trachycarpus fortunei, windmill palm. Z: 8. Ht: to 40′.
This is the hardiest of the palm trees, able to withstand temperatures as low as 10°; I've seen them growing on the coast of Virginia. They need ample water and occasional grooming.

Tsuga canadensis, Canada hemlock. Z: 4–7. Ht: to 80′.
This is the hardiest of the hemlocks, and among the best of the carefree and versatile evergreens. Planted in the open, it is a graceful tree, with shaggy branches sweeping the ground. Grown in clumps in the Outer Area, it forms a thick background for other plantings and makes an effective privacy screen. It is disease and insect resistant, likes full sun or partial shade, moist, well drained, slightly acidic soil, and loves the cold (down to -30°). Do not use it as a foundation planting near the house, because it will rapidly outgrow the space. Countless cultivars available.

Washingtonia filifera, Desert or California fan palm. Z: 9–10. Ht: to 40′.
This is a familiar palm, native to Arizona and California; its old leaves form a shag "petticoat" around the trunk. *W. robusta*, the Mexican Washington palm or thread palm, is similar in habit, but faster growing, a bit less hardy, and will do better on the coast; it lines the streets of Los Angeles.

Yucca brevifolia, Joshua tree. Z: 8–10. Ht: to 40′.
This desert-loving plant grows from California to Utah and is right at home in a dry, arid garden. *Y. gloriosa*, the palm lily, is another handsome, well-mannered member of the genus suitable for warm dry climates. It has multiple trunks from the bottom (a habit known as a basal clump), and grows to about 8 feet, with 3-foot flower spikes covered with white bell-shaped flowers. In the North, it is grown as a houseplant.

SHRUBS

DECIDUOUS SHRUBS

Abelia x grandiflora, glossy abelia. Z: 6–10. Ht: to 6′. Fl: white to pink. S: spring to fall.
Excellent hedge—good for erosion on slopes.

Acanthopanax sieboldianus, five-leaved aralia. Z: 4–9. Ht: 6′.
Impervious to disease, insects, and adverse environmental conditions, the aralia has small clusters of bright green leaves. It rarely needs pruning.

Acer spp., maples.
Some of the small maples can be grown as shrubs. See Deciduous Trees.

Aesculus parviflora, buckeye. Z: 4–8. Ht: to 15′. Fl: white. S: summer

Aralia spinosa, devil's-walking stick. Z: 4–9. Ht: 20′. "Tropical" looking foliage.

Berberis thunbergii, Japanese barberry. Z: 5–9. Ht: 3′–6′. Fl: yellow. S: early spring.
Small maroon leaves are distinctive on some cultivars.

Buddleia davidii, butterfly bush. Z: 5–9. Ht: 3′–6′. Fl: assorted. S: summer to fall.

Callicarpa japonica, beautyberry. Z: 5–8. Ht: 4′–6′. Incredible purple berries in fall. Must be seen.

Calycanthus floridus, Carolina allspice. Z: 4–9. Ht: 8′. Fl: brown. S: spring.

Caryopteris incana, blue mist shrub. Z: 5–10. Ht: 3′–5′. Fl: blue. S: summer.

Chaenomeles speciosa, flowering quince. Z: 4–8. Ht: 4′–6′. Fl: assorted. S: spring.

Chimonanthus praecox, wintersweet. Z: 7–10. Ht: 8′. Fl: yellow and purple. S: late winter.

Clethra alnifolia, sweet pepperbush. Z: 3–8. Ht: 4′–8′. Fl: white to pink. S: summer.

Cornus alba 'Sibirica', red-twig dogwood. Z: 3–10. Ht: to 10′.
This red-twig dogwood is grown primarily for its bright magenta twigs that stand out against winter snow. Its flowers are borne in flat umbels and are followed by black berries, making it a very ornamental shrub. *C. sericea*, the red-osier dogwood (Z: 2–8; Ht: 8′), is another nice red-twig dogwood. *C. sericea* 'Flaviramea' has yellow twigs.

Corylopsis spicata, winterhazel. Z: 5–8. Ht: 10′. Fl: yellow pendant. S: late winter.

Corylus avellana 'Contorta', corkscrew hazel. Z: 4–7. Ht: 6′.
Contorted branches and twigs give it unusual winter interest.

Cotinus coggygria, smokebush. Z: 4–8. Ht: 15′. Fl: in plumes. S: summer. 'Notcutt's Variety', 'Royal Purple' are purple-leaved varieties.

Cotoneaster apiculatus, cranberry cotoneaster. Z: 5–9, evergreen in South. Ht: 3′. Fr: red berries. S: summer to winter.

Cytisus x praecox, Warminster broom. Z: 6–10. Ht: 10′.
Broom, which gets its name from the wispy stems that bear its tiny deep green leaves, thrives in dry sandy soil where pests and other plants cannot live, and it never needs pruning. A legume, it increases the soil nitrogen and has yellow, pealike flowers. (Other varieties have wine- or cream-colored flowers.)

Daphne spp., daphne. Z: 4–7. Ht: 6″–4′ by variety. Flower: rose to pink. S: early spring.
Seek varieties for your area. *D. cneorum*, *D. odora*, *D. x burkwoodii* are good choices for northern states.

Elaeagnus angustifolia, Russian olive. Z: 2–7. Ht: 15′–20′. Fl: small, yellow. S: spring.
Prized for silver-gray foliage, and tolerance of variety of difficult situations.

Enkianthus campanulatus. Z: 4–8. Ht: 4′–6′. Fl: pink. S: spring.

Euonymus alata, winged spindle tree,

burning bush. Z: 3–9. Ht: to 8'.
Of the many wonderful deciduous and evergreen shrubs in this genus, *E. alata* is one of the best. It is easy to grow, virtually pest free, likes almost any soil or location, and has brilliant cherry red foliage in autumn. Grown in full sun or partial shade, it is a favorite of municipalities. *E. alata* 'Compacta' is a dwarf form suitable to small domestic plantings; it grows into a shaggy little mound.

Forsythia x *intermedia* 'Lynwood', forsythia. Z: 5–9. Ht: to 10'.
This is one of the best cultivars of the familiar forsythias. Forsythias are very easy to grow, growing so large so fast that it can almost become a problem. Some of them must be hacked back unmercifully from time to time; if so, do it after the spring flowering. Forsythias need plenty of room as some can reach 10 feet; however, they take on a pleasant fountain shape and look best with very little pruning—as with lilacs, simply cut a large bouquet of stems for the house. Forsythia is also easy to force in the winter for an early touch of spring. Just bring some stems indoors one to six weeks before their natural spring blooming; smash the bottom of each stem with a hammer or slice it vertically with a knife, and place in a vase of water. Before long, their buds will plump and open. *F.* x *intermedia* 'Densiflora' has lemon yellow flowers on a weeping plant.

Fothergilla major. Z: 5–8. Ht: 4'. Fl: white. S: spring.

Hamamelis mollis, Chinese witchhazel. Z: 5–8. Ht: 10'. Fl: orange-red. S: winter.

H. vernalis, spring witchhazel. Z: 4–8. Ht: 6'–10'. Fl: yellow. S: late winter.

H. virginana, witchhazel. Z: 4–8. Ht: 10'–20'. Fl: yellow. S: fall.

Hibiscus syriacus, rose-of-Sharon. Z: 6–9. Ht: 6'–10'.
This is the hardiest member of the hibiscus family. Once established, it is a free blooming, upright shrub; there are many cultivars offering white, pink, red, and even almost blue flowers (*H. syriacus* 'Bluebird'). For the first few

years after planting in the colder parts of zone 6, give the young plant a winter mulch.

Hydrangea paniculata 'Grandiflora', hydrangea "peegee". Z: 6–9. Ht: to 30'.
There are so many splendid members of this family that to choose just one is difficult. This cultivar, however, nicknamed "peegee," is one of the toughest, able to withstand almost any environmental adversity. It has huge cone-shaped flower clusters that turn from green to white and finally to pink. They can be as large as 18 inches long and 12 inches wide. They dry beautifully, lasting for several years—to do so, simply cut and place in a vase without water. *H. quercifolia,* the oak-leaf hydrangea tolerates shade and has large conical white flowers in late spring and bronzy wine-colored fall foliage. *H. macrophylla* is the familiar large blue-flowered kind, a bit too showy for Natural Gardens, but a fine specimen plant.

Hypericum prolificum, broombush. Z: 6–8. Ht: 5'. Fl: yellow. S: summer.

Ilex verticillata, winterberry. Z: 4–8. Ht: 8'. Fr: red berries. S: fall to winter.

Kerria japonica, Japanese rose. Z: 5–7. Ht: 4'–6'. Fl: yellow. S: late spring.

K. japonica 'Pleniflora'. Z: 4–9. Ht: 5'. Fl: double form, deep yellow. S: spring, and sporadic repeat blooms.

Kolkwitzia amabilis, beautybush. Z: 5–8. Ht: to 10'.
An easy care, fast-growing shrub that takes full sun or partial shade in any well-drained soil. It bursts into bloom in spring with large sprays of pink flowers, followed by brown seedpods that last until fall. This is nice at the edge of an Outer Area woodland.

Lagerstroemia indica, crape myrtle. Z: 7–10. Ht: 15'–20'. Fl: assorted. S: late summer to fall.
'Indian Tribes' is a new super hardy and disease-resistant variety.

Lavandula angustifolia, English lavender. Z: 6–10. Ht: 8"–24". C: sun; well-drained soil. Fl: lavender. S: summer. (Subshrub, often grown as an herbaceous perennial.)

Lonicera, honeysuckle.
The no-maintenance honeysuckle shrubs are good choices for the Outer Area, beneath or beside the trees. They are practically indestructible; they tolerate wet or dry soil, full sun or shade. Blooms are small and in a range of pinks or white, some fragrant; they are followed by red, white, or black berries, favored by many species of bird. Good honeysuckle choices include: *L. maackii* (Z: 3–9; Ht: to 15'; Fl: white to yellow; Fr: dark red), *L. tatarica,* tatarian honeysuckle (Z: 5; Ht: to 10'; Fl: pink or white; Fr: red), and *L. fragrantissima* (Z: 4–9; semievergreen in South; Ht: to 8'; Fl: white and very fragrant; Fr: red).

Magnolia stellata, star magnolia. Z: 3–8. Ht: 15'.
Shrublike tree can be kept small.

Myrica cerifera, southern bayberry. Z: 7–9. Ht: 15'.

M. pensylvanica, bayberry. Z: 5–8. Ht: to 9'.
This is a common seaside plant, which thrives in very sandy soil and tolerates salt air. It needs little attention and no pruning and in some areas is semievergreen. Its white flowers are followed by aromatic waxy gray berries from which candles are made and which attract migrating birds.

Philadelphus coronarius, mock orange. Z: 5–9. Ht: 10'. Fl: white. S: late spring.

Photinia villosa. Z: 4–8. Ht: 15'. Fl: white. S: spring.

Poncirus trifoliata, hardy trifoliate orange. Z: 5–10. Ht: 10'.
Spring shrub with deep green 3-part leaves and yellow golf ball-sized fruits in fall that persist after leaves fall. Excellent free-form security hedge.

Potentilla fruticosa, shrubby cinquefoil. Z: 2–7. Ht: 3'–4'. Fl: yellow and white. S: summer.

Prunus glandulosa, flowering almond. Z: 4–8. Ht: 4'–6'. Fl: pink or white. S: spring.

P. maritima, beach plum. Z: 3–8. Ht: 6'. Fl: white. Fr: purple. S: spring.

P. tomentosa, Nanking cherry. Z: 2–6. Ht: 8'. Fl: white. Fr: red. S: early spring.

Rhamnus frangula, 'Columnaris', tall-hedge buckthorne. Z: 3–8. Fr: red. Glossy leaves. Used as hedge planted two feet apart, or as specimen. *R. alaternus,* evergreen, black-fruited species.

Rhododendron spp., deciduous azaleas. Most people envision the showy, broad-leaved evergreen plants when they think of rhododendrons. There are, however, many deciduous members of this large genus, including the azaleas. Among the nicest are: *R. calendulaceum,* flame azalea (Z: 5–9; Ht: to 10'), an American native that still grows wild in the Appalachian Mountains. In gardens, it is at home from Pennsylvania to northern Georgia. Flowers range by individual from yellow to red. *R. periclymenoides,* pinxterbloom (Z: 3–8; Ht: 6'–9'), is another native of eastern woodlands, and a good plant for the forest understory. Its small fragrant pink flowers appear in early spring. *R. vaseyi,* pinkshell azalea (Z: 3–8; Ht: to 15'), is my favorite. It likes the swampy areas of mountain valleys, and should be grown in a moist spot in the garden. Clusters of delicate pink flowers appear in early spring; its foliage turns crimson in fall. There are many imported species and hybrids to look for, including the *Lionel de Rothschild* 'Exbury' hybrids (Z: 5–8) which are the most striking of this group of plants. They have enormous floral heads, in pink, red, orange, gold, yellow, or white. I think the palest ones, yellow and pink, look best in the Natural Garden. Other good choices are: Knap Hill Hybrids, Windsor Hybrids, Mollis Hybrids, *R. kaempferi,* and *R. schlippenbachii,* the royal azalea. (For cultural requirements, see *Rhododendron* listing under *Evergreen Shrubs.*)

Rhus spp., sumac. Z: 2–10. Ht: varies. Members of this genus are among the best easy care North American shrubs, yet they are rarely seen in our gardens despite fernlike foliage, magnificent fall color, lovely sometimes fragrant flowers, and ornamental fruits. This may be because of two all too familiar members of the group: poison ivy (*R. toxicodendron*) and poison sumac (*R. vernix*).

These two monsters aside, several sumacs make welcome additions to the home landscape. *R. glabra,* smooth sumac (Ht: to 20'), and *R. typhina,* staghorn sumac (Ht: to 30'), are familiar species that often line the highways. *R. glabra* has smooth branches and insignificant flowers but abundant red fruits in the fall. *R. typhina* has fuzzy velvety branches that resemble deer antlers and huge chartreuse trusses that become berried spears persisting well into fall. A relative, *R. typhina* 'Laciniata', the fernleaf sumac, is refined and ornamental. Its foliage is deeply serrated and, in fall, blazes with color; shades of yellow, orange, and red are all present on a single plant. A western sumac, *R. trilobata* var *malacophylla,* the squawbush or lemonade sumac (Z: 8–9; Ht: to 4') was grown by the Hopi, Navaho, and Apache; they ground flour from its berries, made medicine from its roots, turned its leaves into dye, and used its branches to weave baskets. Its flowers are yellow and the branches are strongly scented when broken. With the exception of fernleaf sumac, these plants are rarely offered by mail-order companies; one such source is Mellingers (see Source Guide). Although sizable plants are difficult to transplant from the wild, sumacs are easy to propagate by seed. Simply collect the berries, wash off the fuzzy coating in warm water, and sow outdoors in the fall in a protected spot. The very young seedlings *can* be successfully transplanted.

Rosa cvs.
Of the many thousands of hybrid roses, some do well when used right in the landscape instead of as isolated specimen plants. 'The Fairy' (Z: 5–10) blooms almost continuously with a double flower in shades of pink; 'Seafoam' (Z: 5–10) has white flowers and blooms almost but not quite as long as 'The Fairy'. 'Carefree Beauty' (Z: 5–10) is virtually pest free with bright pink flowers that appear in June and then intermittently; it puts on another big show in late summer. 'Bonica' is a new addition. 'Iceberg' (Z: 5–10), a *R. floribunda* cultivar, has cheery white flowers and is a centerpiece in the white garden at Sissinghurst in England as well as in Lady Caroline Somerset's famed vegetable

garden. My own 'Iceberg' plants are pest free and bloom from June until well into the fall. (See list on page 161).

R. rugosa, beach rose, Japanese rose. Z: 2–10. Ht: to 6'.
A high tolerance for salt spray and wind make this attractive plant a standby of seaside gardens, although it also grows well elsewhere. It has crinkled, pleated foliage, magenta flowers, and edible bright orange hips that are high in vitamin C.

Salix discolor, pussy willow. Z: 3–9. Ht: to 20'.
Produces catkins in early spring. There are several other species in cultivation, including ones with pink catkins and black ones.

Spiraea prunifolia, bridal-wreath. Z: 4–10. Ht: to 6'.
Most members of the *Spiraea* genus are appropriate for a Natural Garden. *S. prunifolia* has long arching boughs of white flowers in spring. It looks wild yet controlled and is insect and pest free. It thrives in well-drained soil and partial shade, although the more sun, the greater the flower display.

Syringa x persica, Persian lilac. Z: 4–7. Ht: 5'–6'. Flower: lilac. Season: spring.

S. vulgaris, common lilac. Z: 4–9. Ht: 10'–20'. Fl: fragrant, lilac-purple. S: spring. Many hybrids available.

Tamarix parviflora, tamarisk. Z: 2–9. Ht: 15'. Fl: pink. S: spring. Salt spray tolerant.

T. ramosissima 'Rosea', summer glow tamarisk. Z: 2–8. Ht: 8'. Fl: rose. S: summer.

Vaccinium angustifolium, lowbush blueberry. Z: 3–8. Ht: under 2'. Fl: white. Fr: edible. S: early spring.

V. corymbosum, highbush blueberry. Z: 3–8. Ht: 12'. Flower: white. Fr: edible. S: early spring.

Viburnum spp.
Of the many worthy members of this genus, some grow as far north as zone 2, although most thrive in zones 4–9. Some viburnum have fragrant flowers,

mostly in white, flat or snowball-shaped umbels. Fruits can be red, white, or black; fall foliage is attractive. For an edible landscape choose *V. trilobum,* the American cranberry (Z: 2–9; Ht: to 10'). Others include *V.* x *carlcephalum,* fragrant snowball (Z: 5–9; Ht: 7'; Fl: white; S: early spring), and *V. carlesii,* the Korean spice viburnum (Z: 4–8; Ht: 4'–6'; Fl: white to pink; S: early spring). *V. plicatum* var. *tomentosum* is the doublefile viburnum that resembles a dogwood and is a useful replacement for *Cornus florida. V. rhytidophyllum* (Z: 5–8; Ht: 15') is the leather-leaf viburnum. *V. dilatatum* (Z: 4–8; Ht: 10') is the linden viburnum and has the best berry display. *V. opulus* 'Sterile' (Z: 3–8; Ht: 10') is the widely planted "snowball."

Vitex agnus-castus, vitex or chaste tree. Z: 7–9. Ht: 10'. Fl: blue. S: summer. Vitex provides the best blue color for late summer. 'Alba' is a white-flowered form; 'Rosea' is a pink one.

Weigela spp. Z: 5–8. Ht: 6'–8'. These are fast-growing, arching, and wide-spreading. They like well-drained soil, and full or partial sun. The showy blossoms resemble large azalea flowers, and colors range from pink to purplish to carmine to white. The interior growth, which browns with age, needs an occasional thinning. Wait until after flowering to do so because the flowers appear on twigs of preceding year's growth. This is an easy, durable plant.

EVERGREEN SHRUBS

Arbutus unedo, strawberry tree. Z: 8–10. Ht: 8'–30'. Fl: white. Fr: red. S: late summer.

Buxus microphylla, littleleaf boxwood. Z: 6–9. Ht: 3'–6'. The boxwoods all impart a formal air to a garden; they look pruned without pruning, forming near perfect balls, and are very slow growing. *B. microphylla* is a good choice; it has many cultivars and varieties such as *B. microphylla* var. *japonica* and *B. microphylla* var. *koreana.* It likes well-drained soil and partial shade and is hardy to zone 6, but may be damaged in severe winters. *Buxus* spp. do best in zones 7–9. (See *Ilex crenata* following).

Callistemon citrinus, bottlebrush. Z: 9–10. Ht: 20'. A drought-tolerant ornamental with spectacular red flowers.

Calluna vulgaris, Scotch heather. Z: 4–6. Ht: 2'. Fl: white, pink. S: late summer to fall.

Camellia japonica, common camellia. Z: 7–9. Ht: to 10'. Given a location that suits them, the camellias, a genus that includes the Asian plant whose leaves we brew as tea, can be easy to grow. This species seems most resistant to problems. It likes an acidic soil and the bright light of open shade. It will bloom in late winter to spring, bearing either single or double rose-form flowers, in shades from white to pink to red, sometimes variegated. The leaves are deep green and glossy and very attractive. *C. sasanqua* has smaller leaves, blooms late fall, and is a bit more hardy.

Ceanothus coeruleus, California lilac. Z: 8–10. Ht: 20'. Fl: blue. S: spring.

C. dentatus, California lilac. Z: 8–10. Ht: 6'. Fl: blue. S: spring, summer.

C. thyrsiflorus, California lilac. Z: 8–10. Ht: 1'. Fl: blue. S: spring. Good ground cover. There are over 40 species of *ceanothus.*

Euonymus fortunei, winter creeper. Z: 5–8. Ht: 30". Spreading creeper. Many varieties have variegated foliage that turns pink to purple in winter.

Gardenia jasminoides, gardenia. Z: 8–10. Ht: 6'. Fl: white, familiar waxy florist flower. S: spring to midsummer.

Ilex cornuta 'Burfordii', Chinese holly. Z: 7–9. Ht: to 15'. This is one of the smaller hollies, a dwarf that needs no pruning. It is self-fruiting, which means that you do not need male plants in order to assure the orange or red fruits so desirable in the genus. It is fast growing, reaching 10 feet in as many years, and grows well from New Jersey southward.

I. crenata 'Helleri', Japanese holly. Z: 6–9. Ht: to 3'.

This is a slow growing, dwarf cultivar that becomes a 3-foot-wide low mound. Another cultivar, *I. crenata* 'Convexa', also forms a low mound but slightly larger—6 feet wide and 4 feet high. *I. crenata* 'Hoogendron' is another good choice. These plants can be used as "box" *(buxus)* substitutes for cold climates. Watch for red spiders though, in dry climates.

I. glabra, inkberry. Z: 4–9. Ht: to 10'. This is the hardiest of the evergreen hollies, tolerating temperatures down to −30°. It also tolerates partial shade, sandy soil, and a seaside location.

Juniperus chinensis and cvs. See Evergreen Trees.

J. communis, common juniper. Z: 2–9. Ht: to 30'. Fr: dark blue berries. S: fall.

J. horizontalis, creeping juniper. Z: 4–10. Ht: 1'–2'. Many cultivars for ground covers including 'Wiltonii' or 'Blue rug'.

J. procumbens 'Nana' is an exceptionally lovely, tight-needled low grower that lends a decidedly Japanese effect.

Kalmia latifolia, mountain laurel, calico bush. Z: 4–9. Ht: to 10'. This familiar American plant is found growing wild in woodland. It blossoms in late spring, producing abundant deep rose buds that become light pink flowers. It likes acidic soil and some shade, but can take full sun if the ground is kept moist. Not drought-tolerant, it is susceptible to red spider mite infestation if kept dry. Many cultivars available.

Laurus nobilis, sweet bay. Z: 8–10. Ht: 6'. This is the plant that produces the familiar bay leaf used in cooking.

Leucothoe fontanesiana, doghobble, drooping leucothoe. Z: 4–6. Ht: 3'–5'. Fl: white. S: spring. Varieties have colorful foliage.

Ligustrum amurense, Amur privet, hedge privet. Z: 3–7. Ht: 15'. Fl: white. S: early summer. Pollution tolerant—good for city streets.

L. japonicum, Japanese privet. Z: 7–10. Ht: 10′–15′. Fl: white. S: summer.

L. lucidum, glossy privet. Z: 7–10. Ht: 25′. Fl: white. S: early summer.

Lonicera nitida, box leaf honeysuckle. Z: 7–10. Ht: 6′. Fl: white. S: late spring.

Mahonia aquifolium, Oregon grape. Z: 5–10. Ht: 6′. Fl: yellow. S: spring. Ornamental blue fruits through winter.

M. bealei, leatherleaf mahonia. Z: 5–8. Ht: 5′. Fl: pale yellow. S: spring. Leaves, hollylike. Berries are sky blue.

Nandina domestica, sacred or heavenly bamboo. Z: 7. Ht: to 8′.
This bamboo look-alike grows well in California and gardens in the South; it is hardy to zone 7 but can be killed to the ground in very severe winters. It usually makes a valiant comeback however, growing new canes that eventually equal the original growth. Sometimes it is deciduous, exhibiting bright red fall foliage; its new growth is also tinged red. Its pink flowers are borne on large panicles, and are followed by red berries that last for a year. It likes shade or sun and should be well watered.

Nerium oleander, common oleander, rosebay. Z: 8–10. Ht: 20′.
In warm regions where there is no danger of a freak winter cold snap, oleander is a terrific flowering evergreen. Its flowers may be white, yellow, peach, red, or a combination, and are almost continuous, with a brief winter hiatus. The plant grows quickly in any soil and defies heat, wind, and pollution. Because all parts of the oleander are poisonous, it is not recommended for a garden in which small children will play.

Osmanthus fragrans, sweet olive. Z: 8–10. Ht: to 30′.
This often overlooked shrub can reach tree size but more often it remains small, about 4 to 6 feet. It has nice serrated foliage and flowers all winter long; its tiny flowers have a rich exotic fragrance like fresh apricots and jasmine. It is hardy to South Carolina where it is called tea olive.

O. heterophyllus, holly olive. Z: 7–10. Ht: to 15′. Fl: white. S: early summer.

Photinia serrulata, Chinese photinia. Z: 7–9. Ht: to 30′. Fl: white. S: spring.

Pieris japonica, Japanese pieris, andromeda, lily-of-the-valley bush. Z: 4–8. Ht: 10′. Fl: white. S: early spring. Many varieties available.

Pittosporum tobira, mock orange, Japanese pittosporum. Z: 8–10; Ht: to 18′.
This southern evergreen likes moist, well-drained soil but will tolerate drier conditions once established. It can take heat and pollution and thrives in either sun or shade. Its white-to-lemon-colored flowers are very fragrant, smelling like orange blossoms. Varieties are available with variegated foliage, gray-green and cream.

Podocarpus macrophyllus, podocarpus. Z: 8–10. Ht: to 50′, but as it grows slowly, can be easily kept as shrub. Long evergreen needles. Superb hedge for screening.

Raphiolepis indica, Indian hawthorn. Z: 7–10. Ht: 6′. Fl: pink or white. S: spring.
Large waxy leaves, can be sheared, but no pruning necessary. Easy shrub in appropriate zones.

Rhododendron spp. and cvs.
Too often the members of this large genus, both deciduous and evergreen but especially the latter, are installed in a garden without sufficient thought to their placement and cultural requirements. This is unfortunate because proper siting is the key to their success. Their native habitats are the cool misty slopes of the Himalayas and the humid forests of the Carolinas. In the United States, they do well in the Pacific Northwest and the central mountainous region. Wherever they are grown, they need acid soil (pH 4.5–5.5)—add acid peat or oak leaves to the soil when planting. Choose a location where the soil will be moist and well drained, to benefit their shallow root systems; to keep the nearly exposed roots cool and moist, use a mulch around the plants and do not position them near shallow rooted trees such as maples that will compete for moisture and nutrients.

Some rhododendrons like full sun, some like partial shade or even dense shade. Outside favored locations, though, they should be sheltered from noonday sun in summer, which can scald their leaves, and early morning sun in winter, which can warm them enough to permit later cold damage. They can be grown in the forest understory, beneath delicate-leaved trees that will filter the sunlight, or very tall trees, such as oak or pine. They can also be sited on the north side of a building where, if they are near a window, they act as a casual thermometer —on cold days the leaves curl inward to conserve moisture; very tightly rolled leaves indicate temperatures below 20°.

These growing restrictions may seem to rule out rhododendrons as easy-care plants but the trouble you take in siting and planting them will be worthwhile because they provide color, texture, and sculptural form. There are thousands of cultivars of rhododendron (and more of azalea, the subgroup; see *Rhododendron* under Deciduous Shrubs), but it seems fitting here to concentrate on some of the American natives. By all means however, investigate the imports and hybrids, such as the Ghent Hybrids (also known as *R. x gandavense*), Glen Dale Hybrids, or Kurume azaleas. These and many others are listed exhaustively in catalogues such as the one from Greer Gardens (see Source Guide).

R. carolinianum, Carolina rhododendron. Z: 5–8. Ht: 6′.
This is a lovely small native shrub that looks good in front of natural plantings in the Outer Area. In midspring, it bears enormous numbers of pale petticoat pink flowers.

R. catawbiense, catawba rhododendron or mountain rosebay. Z: 4–8. Ht: to 6′.
Native to the eastern mountain regions, from Virginia to Georgia, this plant has been used widely in hybridization, the cultivars having white, lavender, purple, crimson, or red flowers. A very easy, widely tolerant group to grow.

R. impeditum, dwarf rhododendron. Z: 6–9. Ht: 1′.
This remarkable dwarf with tiny fragrant foliage has violet-blue flowers in

spring. Slow growing, excellent for rock gardens.

R. maximum, great laurel or rosebay. Z: 4–8. Ht: 15′.
This is the hardiest and most familiar native species. It bears huge flower clusters from late spring into summer in shades of white, pink, or rose. Because of its size, it is best in an Outer Area woodland.

Skimmia japonica. Z: 7–9. Ht: 4′. Fl: white. Fr: red berries. S: spring.

Taxus spp., yew. Z: 4–8. Ht: varies. The yews owe their popularity to their ease of culture, durability, tolerance for full sun or partial shade, and ability to thrive in a variety of soil conditions (though they do best in slightly acidic soil) as long as there is good drainage. Unfortunately, they are most often used as brutally pruned foundation plants, especially *T. baccata*, the English yew (and they are a favorite browsing shrub of deer). Grown away from the house, however, *T. baccata* can be left unpruned. One low-growing variety, *T. baccata* 'Repandens', the familiar spreading English yew (Z: 6–8; Ht: to 4′), has long arching deep green branches. *T. canadensis*, the ground hemlock (Z: 3–10; Ht: to 6′) is also relatively low growing and hardier than the English variety. Other species and cultivars have even tidier, if taller, growing habits than this variety. Without pruning they still retain a nice shape. *T. cuspidata* 'Capitata', the Japanese yew (Z: 4–6; Ht: to 15′), grows into a perfect pyramid. *T.* x *media* 'Hicksii', Hicks yew (Z: 4–6; Ht: to 20′), becomes a perfect column; planted in a group these shrubs make an excellent wind or privacy screen. Female yews of all species bear red berries if both sexes are planted; the berries are poisonous and children should be warned.

Thuja occidentalis, American arborvitae. Z: 3–10. Ht: 6′.

Tsuga canadensis, Canadian hemlock, dwarf hybrids. Z: 3–7. Ht: 1′–2′.
The species is a tree growing 75 feet tall with tiny needles; but there are many dwarf forms such as *T. canadensis* 'Pendula', Sargent's weeping hemlock, and

T. canadensis 'Bennets', which forms short whorls of needled branches. Dwarf varieties are excellent for rock gardens and containers.

SHRUBS FOR HOT REGIONS

The shrubs listed here are tough specimens that will grow in the warm and dry areas of zones 8–10. Many are suited to desert climates; others prefer the kind of climate found in northern California. Some become drought-tolerant and will need extra water only when young; others need extra water intermittently throughout their lives. Such watering needs are noted. The season indicates the time of most ornamental interest; plants without flower, fruit, or season noted are grown primarily for their foliage.

Baccharis sarothroides, desert broom. E. Ht: 8′. Fl: white. S: fall. W: when young.

Bauhinia variegata, orchid tree. D. Ht: 20′. Fl: white, pink. S: winter/spring. W: regularly.

Caesalpinia pulcherrima, Barbados-pride. E. Ht: 5′–10′. Fl: red and yellow. S: all. W: moderate.

Callistemon citrinus, crimson bottle-brush. E. Ht: 10′–25′. Fl: red. S: spring. W: when young.

Carissa grandiflora, natal plum. E. Ht: 5′–18′. Fl: fragrant, white. S: spring/summer. W: regularly.

Cassia artemisioides, feathery cassia. E. Ht: 4′–6′. Fl: yellow. S: early spring. W: moderate.

C. wislizenii, shrub senna. D. Ht: 5′. Fl: yellow. S: all. W: little.

Cercidium floridum, palo verde. D. Ht: 25′–30′. Fl: yellow. S: spring. W: moderate.

Chamaerops humilis, European fan palm. E. Ht: 5′–15′. W: little to moderate.

Cocculus laurifolius. E. Ht: 15′–20′. W: moderate.

Cotoneaster spp. E. Ht: 1′–20′, by variety. Fr: red berries. W: moderate.

Cycas revoluta, sago palm. E. Ht: 6′–10′. W: moderate.

Dodonaea cuneata, hopbush. E. Ht: 10′. Fr: decorative seed. W: moderate.

Elaeagnus angustifolia, Russian olive. D. Ht: 20′. Fl: yellow. Fr: silver. W: little to moderate. Silver foliage.

Euonymus fortunei, winter creeper. E. Ht: 2′–20′, can climb. W: moderate.

Fouquieria splendens, coach-whip. D. Ht: 12′–20′. Fl: red. S: spring. W: when young.

Gardenia jasminoides, common gardenia, Cape jasmine. E. Ht: 6′. Fl: fragrant, white. S: spring. W: regularly.

Hibiscus rosa-sinensis, Chinese hibiscus. E. Ht: 5′–15′. Fl: assorted. S: all. W: regularly.

Myrtus communis, true myrtle. E. Ht: 5′. Fl: white. S: spring. W: moderate.

Philodendron selloum, selloum philodendron. E. Ht: 4′. W: moderate.

Platycladus orientalis, oriental arborvitae. E. Ht: 3′–40′, by variety. W: moderate.

Punica granatum, pomegranate. D. Ht: 8′. Fl: orange. Fr: red, edible. S: early spring. W: widely tolerant.

P. granatum cultivars: 'Alba Plena' (double white flowers, fruitless); 'Double Red' (double red flowers, fruitless); 'Nana' (dwarf, single orange flowers, fruit); 'Wonderful' (best for fruit).

Raphiolepis indica, Indian hawthorn. E. Ht: 2′–6′, by variety. Fl: pink. S: spring/summer. W: moderate.

Rhus ovata, sugarbush. E. Ht: 10′. Fl: white. S: spring and fall. W: moderate. Red buds.

Rosa banksiae, Lady Banks' or Banksia rose. Semievergreen. Ht: Climbs to 30′. Fl: yellow, thousands. S: spring. W: moderate.

Rosmarinus officinalis, rosemary. E. Ht: 2'–4'. Fl: lavender blue. S: winter/spring; reblooms in fall. W: little. *R. officinalis* 'Fastígiatus', also known as 'Miss Jessopp's Upright', is a good cultivar.

Santolina chamaecyparissus, lavender cotton. E. Ht: 2'. Fl: yellow. S: summer. W: moderate.

Strelitzia reginae, bird-of-paradise. E. Ht: 2'. Fl: showy orange and purple. S: fall, occasionally winter. W: moderate.

Vauquelinia californica, Arizona rosewood. E. Ht: 10'. Fl: white. S: summer. W: when young.

Yucca aloifolia, Spanish-bayonet. E. Ht: 10'. Fl: white. S: summer. W: little.

HERBACEOUS PERENNIALS

Acanthus mollis, artist's acanthus. Z: 8–10. Ht: 3'. C: full sun to partial shade; moist, well-drained soil. Fl: lilac. S: midsummer.
Grown for foliage—famed as motif of Corinthian column capitals.

Achillea spp., yarrow. Z: 2–9. Ht: 4'. The yarrows are very dependable. They have ferny foliage and bright yellow flower heads, though some species are white or deep pink. They need full sun and well-drained soil, and they bloom from late spring to late summer. The only potential drawback is that some species grow so tall that they require staking, so choose carefully. A good cultivar is *A. filipendulina* 'Coronation Gold', fernleaf yarrow, which has large yellow flower heads, grows to about 36 inches and rarely needs staking. 'Goldplate' is a similar but larger fernleaf cultivar. Cultivars of *A. millefolium,* milfoil (Z: 3–10; Ht: 3'), with pink to red flowers, are also popular. *A. filipendulina* 'Moonshine' has pale yellow flowers and silver foliage—very choice. *A. tomentosa,* woolly yarrow, is suitable for rock gardens (Ht: 4"–8").

Aconitum spp., monkshood. Z: 3–8. Ht: 4'–5'.
Most members of this genus have blue flowers that resemble monks' hoods, as their common name suggests. They

like rich soil and full sun but will tolerate partial shade. Blooms appear in summer or fall, according to species; plants benefit from a winter/spring mulch. Their roots are poisonous but this rarely poses a problem. I recommend *A. carmichaelii* (pure blue flowers) and cultivars of *A. napellus* (flowers ranging from pale to deep blue, some bicolor), with handsome feathery foliage.

Agapanthus africanus, African lily. Z: 8–10. Ht: 1'–2'. C: needs sun to partial shade; average soil. Fl: blue or white. S: summer.

Alchemilla vulgaris, lady's-mantle. Z: 3–9. Ht: 18". C: sun to partial shade; humusy soil. Fl: chartreuse. S: early summer.
Foliage gray-green, broad leaves catch water droplets.

Amsonia tabernaemontana, bluestar. Z: 3–8. Ht: 24"–30". C: sun or shade; average soil. Fl: steel blue. S: spring.

Anemone x hybrida cvs., Japanese anemone. Z: 5–10. Ht: 3'. C: partial shade; average soil. Fl: white, pink, or rose. S: late summer to early fall.

A. vitifolia, grape-leaved anemone. Z: 4–10. Ht: 30"–36". C: partial shade; average soil. Fl: light pink. S: fall.

Aquilegia caerulea, columbine. Z: 3–8. Ht: 2'. C: needs partial shade to full sun; moist, well-drained soil. Fl: blue and white. S: late spring.

A. canadensis, columbine. Z: 2–8. Ht: 2'. C: needs partial shade to full sun; average soil. Fl: red and yellow. Self-sows. Suitable for rock gardens.

Arctotheca calendula, Cape gold, cape dandelion. Z: 10. Ht: 10". C: needs sun; moist soil. Fl: yellow. S: all.

Arabis spp., rock cress. Z: 6–10. Ht: 1'. C: sun; well-drained soil. Fl: white to pink. S: spring. Suitable for rock gardens.

Arenaria montana, sandwort. Z: 4–9. Ht: 2"–4". C: partial shade; moist, well-drained soil. Fl: white. S: late spring. Suitable for rock gardens.

Armeria maritima cvs., thrift. Z: 2–10. Ht: 3"–5". C: sun; well-drained soil. Fl: pink to white. S: early summer. Suitable for rock gardens.

Artemisia lactiflora, white mugwort. Z: 4–8. Ht: 4'–5'. C: sun; average to poor, well-drained soil. Fl: white; foliage, gray. S: mid- to late summer.

A. schmidtiana 'Nana', and 'Silver Mound'. Z: 4–8. Ht: 1'. C: sun; average to poor, well-drained soil. Fl: foliage, silver. S: summer.

Aruncus dioicus, goatsbeard. Z: 5–9. Ht: 4'–5'.
Despite its beauty—tall feathery foliage and white floral plumes—and its ease of care, *Aruncus* is often overlooked. The plants, which resemble giant *Astilbes,* are long-lived and never need dividing; they like rich soil and a moist, partially shaded site.

Asclepias tuberosa, butterfly weed. Z: 3–9. Ht: 15"–20".
This drought-tolerant American native likes full sun and fast-draining soil of the typical meadow, but it will also do well in a sunny flower bed. Once planted, it never needs dividing and, in fact, resents being disturbed so position it thoughtfully. Its clear, bright orange flowers bloom all summer and attract butterflies.

Aster novae-angliae and **A. novi-belgii,** New England aster, New York aster. Ht: 3'–5'. C: needs sun and average to poor soil. Fl: pink to purple/violet. Tall, floppy plants, good for the meadow.

Astilbe x arendsii cvs., astilbe. Z: 4–8. Ht: 24"–30". C: partial sun or shade; moist humusy soil. Fl: white, pink, rose, peach, or red. S: early to mid-summer.

A. taquetii 'Superba', astilbe superba. Z: 4–8. Ht: 3'–4'. C: partial to full sun; moist humusy soil. Fl: mauve. S: summer to late summer.

Aurinia saxatilis cvs., basket-of-gold. Z: 3–10. Ht: 10"–18". C: sun; well-drained soil. Fl: yellow. S: spring. Subshrub suitable for rock gardens.

Baptisia australis, blue false indigo. Z: 3–10. Ht: 2′–3′. C: tolerates almost any light or soil but appreciates sun and moisture. Fl: blue, pealike flowers. S: spring. Very easy.

Belamcanda chinensis, blackberry lily. Z: 5–9. Ht: 36″–42″. C: sun; well-drained soil. Fl: orange, with ornamental "blackberry" fruits. S: midsummer.

Bergenia cordifolia. Z: 3–8. Ht: 1′. C: sun; any soil. Fl: pink-rose. S: spring. Large evergreen leaves, pink-tinged in winter. Good edging plant.

Brunnera macrophylla, (*Anchusa macrophylla*), Siberian bugloss. Z: 3–8. Ht: 18″. C: sun or partial shade; average soil. Fl: blue. S: spring.

Campanula latifolia 'Superba', bellflower. Z: 5. Ht: 3′. C: full sun to partial shade; average, well-drained soil. Fl: violet-blue. S: early summer.

C. poscharskyana. Z: 3–8. Ht: 1′. C: partial shade to full sun; sandy soil. Fl: blue. S: late spring to frost. Suitable for rock gardens.

Cassia marilandica, wild senna. Z: 4–10. Ht: 3′–5′. C: sun; average soil. Fl: yellow. S: midsummer.

Centaurea macrocephala, globe centaurea. Z: 3–9. Ht: 3′–4′. C: sun; dry soil. Fl: 3½″ thistlelike, yellow. S: early summer. Specimen plant.

C. montana, perennial cornflower, mountain bluet. Z: 4–8. Ht: 2′. C: full sun; average to poor, well-drained soil. Fl: blue. S: spring to summer. Cut back for rebloom.

Centranthus ruber, red valerian. Z: 5–9. Ht: 3′. C: sun to partial shade; any soil. Fl: scarlet. S: summer.

Chelone glabra, turtlehead. Z: 4–9. Ht: 30″–36″. C: partial shade; rich, moist soil. Fl: pink-white. S: summer.

C. lyonii, pink turtlehead. Z: 4–9. Ht: 36″–40″. C: partial shade to full shade; moist soil. Fl: pink. S: late summer.

Chrysanthemum x morifolium, florist's chrysanthemum. Z: 5–9. Ht: 1′–4′. C: sun; well-drained soil. Fl: assorted. S: late summer to fall. Needs early pruning, mulching, and regular dividing.

Chrysogonum virginianum, golden star. Z: 6–9. Ht: 4″–6″. C: partial shade to full sun; rich, moist soil. Fl: yellow. S: spring to fall.

Cimicifuga racemosa, black cohosh. Z: 3–9. Ht: 4′–6′. C: sun to partial shade; average soil. Fl: white. S: midsummer. Excellent background plant.

C. simplex, black snakeroot, kamchatka bugbane. Z: 3–9. Ht: 2′–4′. C: sun to partial shade; average soil. Fl: white fuzzy racemes. S: fall.

Coreopsis spp. Z: 4–9. Ht: 6″–48″ by var.
Members of this genus are real sun worshipers. Their abundant, bright yellow, daisylike flowers bloom all summer long. Of the many varieties, all are yellow but some have mahogany-colored centers. Some coreopsis have needle foliage and are as short as 6 inches; those that reach 48 inches should be avoided because they may need staking. New cultivars, such as the award-winning *C. grandiflora* 'Sunray', have double flowers. 'Sunray' also tolerates heat and drought. One of my favorites is *C. grandiflora* 'Sunburst', which grows to about 24 inches, blooms all season, and has somewhat evergreen foliage, which makes it useful as a winter reference point in the garden. A similar cultivar, *C. grandiflora* 'Goldfink', is only 9 inches tall. All coreopsis appreciate well-drained soil, but they are not finicky and will do well in almost any sunny location. *C. verticulata* 'Moonbeam' has pale yellow flowers and thread leaves. *C. auriculata* 'Nana' grows only 6 inches tall. Suitable for rock gardens.

Corydalis lutea, yellow corydalis. Z: 3–8. Ht: 12″–25″. C: sun to partial shade; rich, moist, well-drained soil. Fl: yellow tubular flowers on lacy foliage. S: spring to late summer. Suitable for rock gardens.

Cynoglossum nervosum, hound's tongue. Z: 4–7. Ht: 30″. C: sun; dry soil. Fl: blue. S: midsummer.

Dianthus spp. 'Brilliant', maiden pinks. Z: 4–8. Ht: 4″–6″. C: full sun; well-drained alkaline soil. Fl: pink. S: late spring.

Dicentra spectabilis, bleeding-heart. Z: 3–9. Ht: to 2′.
This familiar and romantic early spring bloomer produces pendulant heart-shaped flowers on arching stems that last for about six weeks. Less familiar is *D. eximia,* wild bleeding-heart, an especially beautiful American native whose lovely ferny foliage is handsome from April to frost. It blooms intermittently throughout the growing season, unlike *D. spectabilis,* and it self-sows readily. New plants can be easily moved to other parts of the garden. While it does best in moist, well-drained soil, it is widely tolerant of conditions and will take full sun or partial shade, moist soil or dry. A good cultivar is *D.* x 'Luxuriant', which produces rose-colored blooms on 18-inch stems that are held above 10 inch mounds of foliage and appear from April to October.

Dictamnus albus (formerly **D. fraxinella),** gas plant, dittany. Z: 3–8. Ht: 30″–36″.
In early spring it emerges with asparagus-like shoots that quickly reach their maximum height. Throughout the growing season it produces white or pink (*D. albus* 'Rubra') flowers on spikes held above the foliage. The common name, gas plant, comes from the belief that on hot days the flowers produce vapors that can be ignited with a match. I've personally never witnessed this phenomenon.

Digitalis grandiflora, perennial foxglove. Z: 4–8. Ht: 30″. C: sun to partial shade; moist acid soil. Fl: yellow. S: early summer. Short-lived, self-sows.

Doronicum cordatum and cvs., leopard's-bane. Z: 4–7. Ht: 18″–24″. C: sun to partial shade; rich, moist soil. Fl: yellow. S: spring. Suitable for rock gardens.

Echinacea purpurea, purple coneflower. Z: 3–9. Ht: 3′.
I often think that this is one of my favorite flowers. Coneflowers increase yearly, are wonderful for cutting, and attract butterflies and bumblebees who

sleep cosily on the stiff petals, nestled against the cones. They are very easy to grow and are equally at home in a meadow, flower bed, or island planting. They do like full sun but will bloom in partial shade. Although they accept various soils, because they are drought-tolerant they prefer a very well drained medium. The flowers themselves resemble black-eyed Susans *(Rudbeckia hirta)* but are longer lasting —an individual flower will last up to a month. The purple variety I've listed is the easiest to grow, but there are white varieties (*E. purpurea* 'Alba' or 'White Luster'), contrarily called white purple coneflowers, that are very beautiful. *E. purpurea* 'Bright Star' is a redder version of the species. New cultivars are on the horizon.

Echinops ritro, small globe thistle. Z: 4–9. Ht: to 2'.
Jagged gray foliage and spiny ball flowers give this plant its common name. Flowers emerge from spiky steel blue balls to form perfect, large spheres; after flowering, the showy bract-balls last for months and are wonderful in flower arrangements. *Echinops* likes full or partial sun and will tolerate almost any soil, but prefers a moist one.

Epimedium spp., barrenwort, bishop's hat. Z: 4–8. Ht: 10"–12". C: partial shade; acidic soil. Fl: assorted. S: spring. A perfect ground cover for partial shade.

Erigeron speciosus, fleabane. Z: 4–8. Ht. 18". C: needs full sun; light, sandy, well-drained soil. Fl: blue, daisylike. Other cvs. are white and pink.

Eryngium spp., sea holly. Z: 4–10. Ht: 1'–4', by var.
These are thistlelike plants with spiky bluish flower bracts, blue stems, and thorny foliage. They are easy to grow and accept ordinary soil as long as there is good drainage (not surprising in a drought-tolerant seaside plant). The common name, sea holly, actually refers to one of the species, *E. maritimum,* which is a good choice for a coastal location.

Eupatorium coelestinum, mist flower, hardy ageratum. Z: 3–10. Ht: 24"–30". C: sun or partial shade; moist soil. Fl:

blue, white. S: late summer to early fall. Naturalizes readily.

E. purpureum, Joe-Pye weed. See Water Plants.

Euphorbia epithymoides, cushion spurge. Z: 3–9. Ht: 18". C: sun; well-drained soil. Fl: yellow. S: spring.

Filipendula rubra, queen-of-the-prairie. Z: 3–9. Ht: 4'–6'. C: sun; average soil. Fl: pink. S: early summer. Native of the prairies. Naturalizes in moist soil.

F. ulmaria, queen-of-the-meadow. Z: 3–9. Ht: 4'. C: sun; average soil. Fl: white. S: early summer.

Gaillardia x *grandiflora* cvs., blanket flower. Z: 3–10. Ht: 6"–36". C: sun; average to poor, well-drained soil. Fl: red, yellow, or various. S: late spring to late summer.

Gentiana asclepiadea, willow gentian. Z: 4–8. Ht: to 2'. C: partial shade; moist soil. Fl: blue. S: mid- to late summer. Seek other species.

Geranium spp., cranesbill. Z: 4–10, by var. Ht: to 20".
These are not the popular houseplant geraniums (which are *Pelargonium),* but rather the true geraniums, which are hardy perennials. *Geranium* species grow in mounds that spread into low herbaceous "shrubs." Some like full sun, others partial shade; many will bloom from spring to fall in a range of colors. *G. himalayense,* lilac cranesbill (Ht: 1'), has nearly blue flowers; *G. endressii* 'Wargrave Pink' (Ht: 18") produces clear pink blooms. Cranesbills are easy to grow in ordinary garden soil; once established they do not like to be disturbed.

Gypsophila paniculata 'Bristol Fairy', baby's breath. Z: 4–8. Ht: 3'. C: sun; alkaline soil. Fl: double white. S: midsummer.

Helenium autumnale 'Butterpat'. Z: 3–9. Ht: 3'. C: sun; rich, moist soil. Fl: yellow daisies. S: late summer to early fall.

Helianthemum nummalarium, rock rose. Z: 5–9. Ht: 10". C: sun; well-

drained alkaline soil. Fl: variable by var. S: early summer. Suitable for rock gardens.

Helianthus x *multiflorus,* perennial sunflower. Z: 3–9. Ht: 6'. C: sun; average soil. Fl: yellow sunflowers. S: late summer. Can be invasive.

Heliopsis helianthoides subspecies *scabra* cvs., false sunflower, oxeye. Z: 4–9. Ht: 36"–40". C: sun; dry soil. Fl: yellow. S: midsummer to fall.

Helleborus niger, Christmas rose. Z: 4–6. Ht: 1'–2'. C: partial shade; rich, moist, well-drained soil. Fl: greenish white. S: late winter. Do not transplant; self-sows for new plants.

H. orientalis, Lenten rose. Z: 4–8. Ht: 18". C: partial shade; rich, moist, well-drained soil. Fl: pink. S: early spring, evergreen.

Hemerocallis spp. and hybrids, daylilies. Z: 3–10. Ht: varies.
Daylilies form the backbone of perennial plantings in the Natural Garden. They tolerate intense summer heat and bitter winter cold, live through drought, survive flooding, and accept a wide range of growing conditions. They will take full sun but many will bloom best in partial shade. An eastern location with unobstructed sun is best, but the open sun of a southern exposure or afternoon sun of a western one are also good, although flowers may fade a bit. Daylilies prefer a sandy loam but will tolerate almost any soil makeup as long as there is good drainage, a necessity for a plant whose root system resembles a bunch of carrots. These root clumps are so dense that daylilies can be used to fight erosion on a slope; occasionally a saw is needed to divide the clumps for propagating. Such division can be done at any time of the growing season, but early spring is best, to assure blossoms that same year. In most cases it is a simple matter of lifting the roots with a garden fork and pulling sections apart for replanting. Although individual flowers, as the common name suggests, last but a day, each plant produces so many flowers that it actually blooms for three to six weeks. By selecting different cultivars you can have season-long blooms. In my zone 6

garden, various daylilies are in flower from May to November. The species include smallish plants such as *H. flava,* the lemon daylily (Ht: to 2'), a spring bloomer with pale yellow flowers, and large ones such as *H. fulva,* the familiar tawny daylily of the roadside (Ht: to 5'). Aside from species plants, there are also some 10,000 named varieties and cultivars, from dwarf, midget, and miniature to large-sized plants, with a wide range of color choice. There are also new tetraploid cultivars that have very large, thick, fleshy flowers, borne on extra-sturdy, well-branched stalks. Whatever your taste, there will be a daylily to satisfy it.

Heuchera sanguinea, coralbells. Z: 4–10. Ht: to 2'.
Delicate bell-shaped flowers held above a low mound of wavy foliage appear on this plant from spring to fall. These shallow-rooted plants need moist soil with good drainage. They can be left undisturbed for five years or more, but if they become crowded they are easy to lift and pull apart for repositioning. They make a good edging for island beds in the In-Between Area. Seek out named varieties such as *H. sanguinea* 'Fire Sprite' (rose red flowers), 'Freedom' (rose pink), 'June Bride' (white), 'Pluie de Feu' (bright red), or 'Rosamundi' (coral), and Bressingham hybrids. Suitable for rock gardens.

Heucherella alba. This is a cross between *Heuchera* and *Tiorella.* Z.: 3–8. Ht: 12". C: same as *Heuchera.* Fl: pink, in sprays.

Hibiscus moscheutos cvs., hardy hibiscus, mallow rose. Z: 4–9. Ht: 4'–8'. C: sun; moist soil. Fl: red, pink, white, as big as a dinner plate. S: late summer.

Hosta spp., plantain lily. Z: 3–10. Ht: by var.
Dependable perennials for shade, the plants have broad dense foliage and tall flower spikes whose blossoms range from white to purple to blue. Some bloom in early summer, others well into fall. They are attractive foliage plants, with lance- or heart-shaped leaves, in an incredible variety of sizes and colors, including variegated. They do well in any garden soil but fare best in moist loam, rich in organic matter.

They also need space, from 3 to 4 feet between plants. Beyond these few requirements they rarely need dividing or other attention. If they do have a problem, it is that they are sometimes attacked by slugs who love the succulent foliage. There are many species and cultivars: *H. sieboldiana* 'Elegans' (Ht: to 30") has huge blue-green leaves and fragrant pale lilac flowers, and loves full shade. *H. sieboldiana* 'Frances Williams' is the most popular variegated hosta; *H. plantaginea* 'Grandiflora' (Ht: to 30") has enormous white lilylike flowers that are also very fragrant.

Iberis sempervirens and cvs., evergreen or edging candytuft. Z: 3–10. Ht: 9"–12". C: sun; well-drained soil. Fl: white. S: spring. Suitable for rock gardens.

Incarvillea delavayi, hardy gloxinia. Z: 5–10. Ht: 18"–24". C: sun or partial shade; well-drained soil. Fl: pink. S: spring.

Inula ensifolia, swordleaf inule. Z: 3–9. Ht: 16". C: sun; average, well-drained soil. Fl: yellow, daisylike. S: summer.

Iris sibirica, Siberian iris. Z: 3–10. Ht: to 45".
All irises are easy to grow, are resistant to insects and disease, and have attractive foliage. They do, however, have a drawback that keeps them off most limits of best low-maintenance plants: many need frequent division. *I. sibirica* is an exception; it can be left in place almost indefinitely. It will grow in shade but will be truly floriferous in full sun. While it prefers moist, rich, well-drained soil, it will survive in any soil. When I do want to divide it, I use a saw, plunging it into the ground on one side of the clump and cutting through to the other side. Then I lift half with a garden fork and saw it into as many other divisions as I want for repositioning. Making divisions in March means some bloom in May, but most irises are planted in late summer when they are semidormant, and this is the traditional time to divide them as well. Other easy-care irises are: *I. kaempferi,* the Japanese iris (Ht: 2'); *I. pseudacorus,* yellow flag (Ht: to 5'), and *I. cristata,* the dwarf crested iris (Ht: 1"–3"), which is useful

as a ground cover and suitable for rock gardens. *I. tectorum,* roof iris, is used to hold thatch in Japan. It has large flat flowers that can be white or violet, tolerates partial shade, and is suitable for rock gardens. *I. spuria,* butterfly iris, and *I. dichotoma,* vesper iris, are also recommended. Californians can select from among their natives and cultivars.

Kniphofia cvs. (*Tritoma*), torch lily, red-hot-poker. Z: 7–10. Ht: 18"–48". C: sun; well-drained soil. Fl: orange, red, yellow, white. S: summer.

Liatris spicata, gay-feather. Z: 3–10. Ht: 18".
This is the most familiar species of this genus of easy-care meadow plants. Its spikes of rosy lavender flowers bloom in July, and all the *Liatris* species bloom from the top of the flower spike downward, unlike most spike-bearing plants. They like full sun but will tolerate partial shade; they need good drainage but will accept a wide range of soil types. *L. pycnostachya,* the Kansas gay-feather, grows to a towering 72 inches and blooms in the fall, but I'm not fond of its fussy "button" flowers. I do like *L. spicata* 'Kobold', which reaches 18 inches and has the usual lavender flowers.

Ligularia x przewalski 'The Rocket', rocket ligularia. Z: 4–8. Ht: 5'–6'. C: partial shade; rich, moist soil. Fl: yellow, on spires. S: late summer to fall.

Limonium latifolium and cvs., sea lavender. Z: 3–10. Ht: 20". C: sun; well-drained soil. Fl: lavender-blue, pink, white. S: late summer.

Liriope spp., lilyturf. Z: 5–10. Ht: 6"–24". C: sun to partial shade; average soil. Fl: violet, white, with evergreen leaves. S: mid- to late summer. See Ground Covers.

Lupinus perennis, wild lupine. Z: 4–8. Ht: 1'–2'. C: sun to partial shade; deep sandy soil. Fl: blue. S: late spring. Resents transplanting, best from seed; self-sows.

Lupinus subcarnosus, Texas bluebonnet. Z: 7–9. Ht: to 1'. C: sun; sandy prairie soil. Naturalizes. Fl: blue. S: late summer to fall.

Lychnis chalcedonica, Maltese-cross. Z: 3–10. Ht: 24″–30″. C: sun; well-drained soil. Fl: scarlet. S: summer.

L. coronaria, see Biennals.

Lysimachia clethroides, gooseneck loosestrife. Z: 4–8. Ht: 2′. C: partial shade to sun; average soil. Fl: white. S: midsummer.

L. punctata, yellow loosestrife. Z: 4–8. Ht: 30″. C: partial shade; average soil. Fl: yellow. S: early summer. Very easy, but can grow out of bounds.

L. quadrifolia, whorled loosestrife. Z: 4–8. Ht: 1′–3′. Fl: yellow. C: sun to partial shade; any soil. Yellow stars surround central stems. This is an easy plant for meadow or garden.

Lythrum salicaria, purple loosestrife. Z: 3–9. Ht: 18″.
This is a very useful plant, which blooms in zone 6 from June to September, is practically indestructible, and has no enemies in the garden. A single plant produces twelve or more spikes completely covered with tiny purple flowers. The only problem with loosestrife is that it can overwhelm other plants; in fact, this European native has naturalized so successfully that in the Northeast, it has crowded out some of our native plants. Not only does this threaten the future of these plants, but it also endangers the wildlife that may depend on them for food. In the garden, loosestrife can easily be controlled by sawing it up (see *Iris sibirica,* above). It is a sun lover but will do well in partial shade, and it prefers moist nutrient-rich soil. Hybridizing has produced cultivars in a range of colors from soft pink to rich violet; there are also dwarf cultivars such as *L. salicaria* 'Robert' (Ht: 2′; rose red) and 'Happy' (Ht: 18″; deep pink). 'Morden's Pink' (Ht: 3′; pink), 'Morden's Gleam' (Ht: 3′; carmine), and 'Dropmore Purple' (Ht: 3′; purple) are larger, desirable hybrids that are *very controllable.*

Macleaya cordata, plume poppy. Z: 3–10. Ht: 5′–8′.
An easy to care for, but often overlooked perennial, the plume poppy is an unusual plant. In midsummer, bronze buds on foot-tall stalks appear atop the plants and become pink or white airy plumes. These flowers have no petals but only pollen-bearing stamens. Seedpods form, which look like the flowers; and last until frost. Deeply lobed cordate leaves are gray-green on top, beige underneath, and can be as wide as a foot near the bottom of the stalk tapering to a mere 3 inches near the top. The only potential problem with the plume poppy is its *invasiveness.* This can be resolved, however, by using it as planting in a wild place. Because of its large scale, it will also look best treated this way. Extra plants can be pulled out in early spring. It grows in sun or partial shade and likes a rich, moist soil.

Malva alcea 'Fastigiata', hollyhock mallow. Z: 3–9. Ht: 24″–30″. C: sun to partial shade; average soil. Fl: pink. S: summer to fall.

Mertensia virginica, Virginia bluebell. Z: 3–8. Ht: 18″–24″. C: partial shade; moist soil. Fl: blue. S: spring.

Monarda didyma cvs., bee balm. Z: 4–9. Ht: 2′–3′. Fl: lavender, pink, white, red. S: summer. Spreads fast, may need dividing.

Nepeta x faassenii, catmint. Z: 3–8. Ht: 18″. C: sun; well-drained, sandy soil. Fl: violet-blue with tiny gray foliage. S: summer. Forms handsome, controlled clump.

Oenothera missourensis, evening primrose. Z: 4–9. Ht: 15″. C: partial shade to sun; average soil, widely tolerant. Fl: yellow. S: early summer. Seek related species, wild throughout the United States.

Paeonia lactiflora cvs. and related spp., peonies. Z: 3–9. Ht: 18″–36″.
Most of the common herbaceous peonies are cultivars of *P. officinalis.* They are very long-lived perennials that never need dividing or replanting. Once established they have been known to thrive and bloom in the same place for a century. They flower in the spring, with flowers lasting two to three weeks; by selecting early, mid-, and late-season cultivars, you can be assured of a six-to-nine-week season. Stay away from the enormous double blossom cultivars which may need staking, and from those whose garish hues, such as bright red, look almost artificial. Instead choose pale pink, white, and the light apricot shades. 'Mrs. Franklin D. Roosevelt' has apricot petals that curve in on themselves making soft ball-shaped blooms. I like single-flowered cultivars of *P. lactiflora* such as 'Krinkled White', which is white and looks like a fried egg, sunny-side up. When flowering is over, all peonies have attractive shrubby foliage that forms a herbaceous hedge and dies to the ground each fall. They like full sun, but will tolerate a touch of shade, and they thrive in any soil that has good drainage, but prefer a rather heavy well-drained clayey loam. They do need to be fed: add bone meal to the planting hole and apply a general purpose fertilizer (5-10-5, for example) twice each season—when the new shoots are about 10 inches tall and after the plants have bloomed. Peonies must be planted in the fall, when they are dormant. Be certain to set the "eyes" (the little pink buds that are the next season's growth) one to two inches below the soil surface. If they are set deeper or shallower, the peonies will not bloom. Peonies have few problems; the ants that are attracted to the buds are harmless. Peonies can contract botrytis fungus during rains, but a dusting with benomyl will control it. Other species to look for are *P. tennifolia,* fernleaf peony (Z: 3–8; Ht: 18″–24″; Fl: assorted) and *P. arietina* (Z: 3–8; Ht: 2′; Fl: pinks, gray-green leaves).

Penstemon gloxinioides 'Ruby King'. Z: 7–10. Ht: 2′. C: sun; gravelly soil. Fl: red. S: summer.

P. heterophyllus 'True Blue.' Z: 5–9. Ht: 15″. C: sun; gravelly soil. Fl: blue. S: summer.

Perovskia atriplicifolia, Russian sage. Z: 3–9. Ht: 2′. C: sun; well-drained to dry soil. Fl: blue. S: late summer. Subshrub with silver foliage.

Phlox carolina 'Miss Lingard', thick-leaf phlox. Z: 3–9. Ht: 30″. C: sun to partial shade; well-drained soil. Fl: white. S: late spring to late summer.

Physostegia virginiana 'Alba', obedience. Z: 2–8. Ht: 18"–24". C: sun; average soil. Fl: white. S: midsummer to fall.

P. virginiana 'Bouquet Rose'. Z: 3–10. Ht: 36"–42". C: sun; average soil. Fl: pink. S: midsummer to fall. Earlier bloomer than 'Alba'.

Platycodon grandiflorus, balloon flower. Z: 3–9. Ht: 2'. C: sun; well-drained soil. Fl: blue, white. S: mid-spring to late summer.

Polemonium caeruleum, Jacob's-ladder. Z: 3–10. Ht: 18". C: partial shade; moist soil. Fl: blue. S: spring.

Polygonatum biflorum, Solomon's-seal. Z: 3–8. Ht: 2'–3'. C: partial to full shade. Fl: white. S: spring. Seek variegated leaf form as well.

Polygonum cuspidatum var. compactum, Japanese knotweed. Z: 4–9. Ht: 12"–18". C: sun; any soil. Fl: pink. S: summer to fall.

Potentilla nepalensis, cinquefoil. Z: 5–8. Ht: 1'. C: full sun to partial shade. Fl: rose. S: spring to frost.
Varieties have yellow or white flowers, strawberrylike leaves. Look for other cinquefoils: *P. x tonquei* (Ht: 3"; Fl: apricot), *P. verna* 'Verna' (Ht: 3"; Fl: yellow), and *P. fruticosa,* a common hedge plant. All are suitable for rock gardens.

Primula denticulata, primrose. Z: 4–8. Ht: 1'. C: partial shade; rich moist acid soil. Fl: lavender, purple. S: spring.

P. japonica, Japanese primrose. Z: 5–8. Ht: 2'. C: partial shade; rich moist acid soil. Fl: white, pink, rose, crimson, terra-cotta. S: spring.

P. x polyantha, polyanthus primrose. Z: 3–8. Ht: 8"–12". C: partial shade; rich moist acid soil. Fl: assorted with contrasting center. S: spring. Look for *P. florindae* and *P. acule,* also.

Pulmonaria saccharata, Bethlehem sage. Z: 3–9. Ht: 6"–12". C: partial shade; moist soil. Fl: reddish violet. S: spring.

Romneya coulteri, California tree poppy. Z: 8–10. Ht: 4'–8'. C: sun; dry soil. Fl: white with yellow center. S: spring to early fall.

Rudbeckia spp., coneflowers. Z: 3–10. Ht: to 3'.
The best known and loved of this genus is *R. hirta,* black-eyed Susan. It and other species and cultivars are easy to grow, long blooming, and at home in meadows, in broad sweeping plantings, in perennial beds, and a wide variety of other settings. Coneflowers multiply by self-sowing, and their underground clumps will spread. All like well-drained soils and full sun or a touch of shade. The flowers are lovely and so are the dried cones in winter against the snow. In addition to *R. hirta,* the American wildflower, there are many good cultivars, the best of which originated in Europe. *R. fulgida* 'Goldsturm', for example, has the familiar yellow petals and brown cone; it grows a little over 24 inches once established and will spread and increase over the years. *R. laciniata* 'Goldquelle', goldenglow (Ht: 30"), has double yellow blossoms. Other cultivars are known as gloriosa daisies, and have very large brick red and mahogany flowers. They work well in meadows or in flower beds of the In-Between Area.

Salvia farinacea cvs., mealy-cup sage. Z: 7–10. Ht: 2'–3'. C: sun; well-drained soil. Fl: light to dark blue. S: early summer to fall. Used as an annual in the North.

S. pratensis, perennial sage, meadow clary. Z: 3–9. Ht: 3'. C: sun; well-drained soil. Fl: bluish violet. S: early summer to fall.

S. x superba 'East Friesland'. Z: 4–9. Ht: 18". C: sun; *very* well drained soil. Fl: deep violet-blue.

Sanguinaria canadensis, bloodroot. Z: 3–8. Ht: 6". C: partial shade to full sun; rich humusy acid soil. Fl: white. S: midspring.

Santolina chamaecyparissus, lavender cotton. Z: 6–8. Ht: 1'. C: sun; average to poor, sandy, well-drained soil. Fl: yellow buttons above silver furry foliage (scented). S: late summer. (Woody subshrub often used as herbaceous perennial.)

S. virens, green lavender cotton. Z: 6–8. Ht: 1'. C: sun; average to poor, sandy, well-drained soil. Fl: pale yellow buttons over deep green foliage. S: late summer. (Woody subshrub.)

Scabiosa caucasica cvs., pincushion flower. Z: 3–8. Ht: 2'. C: sun; average soil. Fl: blue, white, lilac. S: summer.

Sedum spectabile and cvs., stonecrop. Z: 3–10. Ht: 18". C: sun; well-drained soil. Fl: red, rust, pink, white. S: late summer to fall.

Sidalcea malviflora cvs., checkerbloom, false mallow. Z: 5–10. Ht: 3'. C: sun; well-drained soil. Fl: pink, white, purple. S: early summer.

Solidago spp. and cvs., goldenrod. Z: 3–10. Ht: 18"–40". C: sun; any soil, prefers average to poor, well drained. Fl: yellow, white. S: late summer. There are more than 100 American forms.

x Solidaster luteus, solidaster. Z: 5–10. Ht: 2'. C: sun; average soil. Fl: yellow. S: mid- to late summer. Cross between aster and goldenrod.

Stachys byzantina, (S. lanata) lamb's ears. Z: 3–10. Ht: 1'. C: sun; well-drained soil. Fl: purple, silver leaves. S: midsummer. Look for flowerless cultivar.

Stokesia laevis and cvs., Stokes' aster. Z: 5–8. Ht: 15". C: sun to partial shade; well-drained soil. Fl: blue, lilac, white. S: midsummer to frost.

Teucrium chamaedrys, germander. Z: 5–9. Ht: 15". C: sun; average, well-drained soil. Fl: rose. S: summer.

Thalictrum aquilegifolium, meadow rue. Z: 5–8. Ht: 3'. C: partial shade to sun; rich humusy soil. Fl: lavender. S: spring.
Use at meadow's edge; also seek other species.

Thermopsis caroliniana, Carolina lupine. Z: 3–9. Ht: 3'–4'. C: sun; any soil. Fl: yellow. S: late spring to early summer.

Tiarella cordifolia, foamflower. Z: 3–8.

Ht: 1'. C: partial to full shade; rich humusy soil. Fl: white. Best in naturalized colonies.

Tradescantia x andersoniana, spiderwort. Z: 4–9. Ht: 24"–30". C: sun to partial shade; average to rich soil. Fl: white, purple, blue, pink. S: summer. Seek *T. virginiana* cvs.

T. virginiana cvs. Z: 4–9. Ht: 12'–20'. C: sun to partial shade; well-drained soil. Fl: white, purple, blue, pink. S: summer.

Trillium erectum, wake robin. Z: 4–8. Ht: 1'. C: full shade; rich, moist, humusy, well-drained soil. Fl: maroon. S: early spring.

T. grandiflorum, large, white trillium. Z: 4–8. Ht: 15". C: full shade; rich, humusy, moist soil, well drained. Fl: white. S: early spring.

Trollius europaeus cvs., globeflower. Z: 4–9. Ht: 2'. C: partial shade; moist to wet soil. Fl: yellow. S: spring; may bloom more than once in a single season.

Valeriana officinalis, garden heliotrope. Z: 4–8. Ht: 4'. C: sun to partial shade; average, moist, well-drained soil. Fl: white, pink, lavender, fragrant. S: summer.

Verbascum hybrids, mullein. Z: 4–10. Ht: 3'–4'. C: sun; well-drained soil. Fl: pink, white, yellow, amber, purple. S: midsummer to early fall.

Veronica spicata and cvs., speedwell. Z: 3–10. Ht: 14"–18". C: sun; well-drained soil. Fl: blue, white. S: summer. Seek other species and hybrids.

Yucca filamentosa, yucca, Adam's-needle. Z: 4–10. Ht: 5'–6'. C: sun; well-drained soil. Fl: white. S: early summer.

BIENNIALS

Biennials are hardy plants (Z: 3–7) that have a two-year cycle, producing vegetative growth in the first year and blooming usually in the second.

Alcea rosea, hollyhock. Z: 4. Ht: to 10'. Fl: white to pink or purple, sometimes yellowish. S: mid- to late summer.
Seeds of *A. rosea* sown in seedbeds in June of the first year will bloom after they are transplanted to a permanent location the following spring. There is also a so-called annual hollyhock that will bloom the first year if started indoors in February.

Bellis perennis, English daisy. Z: 5. Ht: to 6". Fl: white to rose. S: spring to early summer.
Seeds planted in the spring will bloom the following year.

Campanula medium, Canterbury bell. Z: 7. Ht: to 3'. Fl: blue. S: summer.
Some of the old-fashioned "singles" will bloom in one season. Unfortunately, Canterbury bells are susceptible to diseases and insects.

Daucus carota var. carota, Queen Anne's lace. Z: 3. Ht: to 3'. Fl: white. S: mid- to late summer. Often flowers first year.

Dianthus barbatus and cvs., sweet william. Z: 6. Ht: to 2'. Fl: wide range from white to pink, rose, red, violet. S: summer.

Digitalis spp. and cvs., foxglove. Z: 4. Ht: to 6'. Fl: white, yellow, dusty rose, or pink. S: late spring to early summer. Self-sows.
There are perennial foxgloves but the most beloved are the biennials. Many of them, such as the Shirley Hybrids that can grow to 6 feet are hybrids of the European wildflower, *D. purpurea.* Although at least one hybrid, 'Foxy', may bloom a bit in the first year, for the most part foxglove spend the first season as rosettes of textured foliage. The following spring, flower spikes make their appearance, usually preceding other tall-growing flowers. Old varieties of foxglove have bell-shaped or elf-hat flowers on one side of the stalk; on newer varieties, such as Excelsior Hybrids, flowers encircle the spikes. They do well in full sun, partial shade, or even full shade, and most bloom in late spring or early summer, with occasional rebloom.

Lunaria annua, honesty or silver-dollar. Z: 5–7. Ht: to 3'. Fl: white to purple. S: late spring. Self-sows. Plants are easy to start from seed. They produce attractive flowers the second spring, and also mature into the silver-colored papery seedpods that inspired the plant's common name and look wonderful in dried bouquets.

Lychnis coronaria, rose campion. Z: 3–8. Ht: to 3'. C: partial shade to full sun. Fl: deep pink. S: late summer. Self-sows. This plant is actually a short-lived herbaceous perennial. *L. coronaria* 'Alba' is a white form.

Myosotis sylvatica, forget-me-not. Z: 3–7. Ht: to 2'. Fl: pale blue. S: spring. Self-sows.
Forget-me-nots naturalize so easily that they can become invasive. They grow in almost any location but prefer damp, woodsy soil and a bit of shade. Seeds sown in July and August will bloom the following spring.

Papaver nudicaule, Iceland poppy. Z: 2–7. Ht: 1'. Fl: white with yellow at base; can be orangy or reddish. S: early summer.

Verbascum spp., mullein. Z: 4–10. Ht: to 5'. Fl: yellow. S: midsummer. Self-sows.
Sophisticated species and hybrids, come in colors including bronze, pink, terra-cotta, and salmon, but I still prefer the lowly wild species, *V. phlomoides* (Ht: 4'), which grows happily along the highways. Each year, the spikes appear in the garden, covered with little pale yellow, buttercuplike flowers. The first-season they are rosettes of fuzzy, gray-green leaves. A more refined mullein is *V. phoeniceum* (Ht: 5'), which has lavender to mauve flowers.

EASY ANNUALS

Annuals all complete their life cycles —from germination to maturity— within a single season. Those listed here are suitable to all parts of the United States; and will grow under almost any conditions, although most do best in full sun. Included are: so-called hardy annuals that can be planted before the last frost; half-hardy annuals that can be planted outdoors before full warm weather begins; and tender annuals that must be started indoors or planted outdoors only when it is truly warm. It is best to plant annuals in masses, rather than in small groupings. Some varieties will self-sow.

Calendula officinalis. Ht: 1′–2′. Fl: orange to yellow. Hardy, self-sows.
The common name and Latin name are the same. Calendulas were once called pot marigolds. They resembled marigolds, and people added their petals and leaves to the soup pot. They are fast growing, and can be sown directly in the garden. They prefer cool temperatures and may stop blooming in very hot weather, but they will start up again in late summer and fall when many put on their best show. In Northern California they behave as perennials, blooming almost year-round.

Catharanthus roseus, vinca or periwinkle. Ht: about 10″. Fl: rose-pink to white. Tender.
Periwinkle is actually a perennial but is treated as an annual. It resembles impatiens, with a contrasting "eye" in the center of the blossom, and will bloom continuously throughout the summer. These relatively low-growing plants spread 12 to 24 inches, making them useful as temporary ground covers.

Centaurea cyanus, cornflower or bachelor's button. Ht: 2′–3′. Fl: blue, pink, white. Hardy, self-sows.
These flowers bloom very quickly, meaning almost instant color in the garden. Seeds can be sown in the fall for overwintering and they start up early in the spring. Because the blooming period is brief, it is a good idea to scatter seed in the garden or meadow every two weeks or so until midsummer to extend the season. Of the traditional blue cornflowers, 'Blue Boy' (Ht: about 3′), is especially nice. There are also dwarfs that reach only about 12 inches; one attractive floriferous dwarf is 'Polka Dot' (Ht: 16″), which produces flowers in the full color range.

Chrysanthemum parthenium (Tanacetum parthenium) feverfew. Ht: 1′–3′. Fl: white and daisylike. Half-hardy, self-sows. *C. paludosum* is a long-blooming "mini-marguerite" useful for many situations.

Cleome hasslerana, spider flower. Ht: 3′–5′. Fl: white to deep pink, by variety; some bicolor. Half-hardy, self-sows.
The delicate lacy flowers, borne on columnar flower heads, have long stamens and pistils that radiate from the stems. Varieties are available in white ('Helen Campbell'), deep pink ('Rose Queen'), and mixed. Remember that these long-blooming plants grow very tall,

Coreopsis tinctoria, calliopsis Ht: 8″–36″. Flower: yellow to red. Hardy, self-sows readily.
Coreopsis are good meadow plants, tolerating poor soil, normal rainfall, and partial shade. The daisy-formed flowers are most often deep yellow, but some varieties and mixes have zoned flowers (two colors on a single blossom) of red against yellow.

Cosmos spp. Ht: to 6′. Fl: red to white. Tender, self-sows.
Cosmos bloom continuously and self-sow, are heat-resistant, tolerant of almost any soil, need no special care, and are excellent as cut flowers. They can be grown a mere 12 inches apart and should be sited with their height in mind; the tallest varieties are cultivars of *C. bipinnatus.* The new shorter, intensely colored varieties should be used with discretion because their colors dominate any scheme.

Cynoglossum amabile, Chinese forget-me-not. Ht: 18″–24″. Fl: blue. Hardy, self-sows.

Dianthus chinensis, rainbow pink. Ht: 1′. Fl: white, pink, peach, scarlet maroon, purple, cerise, bicolors, and more. Hardy, self-sows.

Eschscholzia californica, California poppy. Ht: 1′. Fl: orange. Hardy, self-sows.
California's state flower carpets the coastal hillsides in the spring with its single, 3 inch wide, cup-shaped blossoms. Flowers last for several weeks in cool springs, but if you do not mind the extra work of deadheading you can extend the season well into summer. These poppies require an alkaline soil and naturalize well; include some in a meadow mix. There are also mixes available in yellow, pink, deep rose, and white.

Gaillardia pulchella cvs., blanket flower. Ht: to 3′. Fl: yellow to brick red. Hardy, self-sows in mild climates.
The annual blanket flower and its cultivars, like the perennials, are natives. The flowers have a daisylike form with a central "button," usually in a contrasting color. Most cultivars have an 18-inch spread, and tolerate heat and drought, making them good candidates for meadow or prairie plantings. Deadheading will extend the blooming season.

Gazania rigens and cvs., treasure flower. Ht: 3″–10″. Fl: varied. Tender.
These plants are perennials in zones 9 and 10 but in most gardens they are treated as annuals. Easily grown from seed started indoors, they do take quite a long time to mature. You may prefer to purchase them in flats in the spring. Because they are extremely heat-tolerant, they make an especially good edging along an exposed walkway or driveway where radiant heat can be intense. Flowers are daisylike, 3–4 inches wide, and come in an incredible range of colors—khaki and gray against yellow, pink, or red, for example. Among the named varieties are 'Chansonette', 'Sunshine', 'Golden Marguerita', 'Mini Star Yellow', and 'Sundance'.

Gomphrena globosa and cvs., globe amaranth. Ht. and color vary. Tender.
This is one of my favorite plants. From seeds sown in mid-May, plants begin to flower in early June and continue until frost, needing virtually no care at all. The tall varieties, such as 'Globosa Mixed' (Ht: 3′), are usually available in color mixes and are perfect for massing in sunny areas. There are dwarfs, such as 'Buddy' (Ht: 6″–8″), available in magenta. The flowers retain their color when dried; pick them just before frost and hang them upside-down in an airy place.

Helianthus and cvs., sunflower. Ht: 4′–10′. Fl: varies. Hardy, self-sows.
What could be sunnier than a sunflower? Sunflowers are very easy to grow: just plant a seed one inch below soil level to keep the birds from reaching it, and you will get a flower. It's as simple as that. *H. giganteus,* is the enormous, edible-seeded variety that towers

to 10 feet or more, is invariably yellow, and is almost always relegated to the vegetable garden. There are also smaller varieties in a range of colors. *H. annuus,* 'Italian White', (Ht: 4'), for example, has smallish 3–4-inch-wide flowers in a wonderful cream color, with a fine yellow halo and a nut-brown center. Other varieties come in a range of solid colors, and zoned flowers are available in mahogany, gold, yellow, and red. Sunflowers are sure to attract birds; some alight on the faded flower head and peck at the seeds, others, ground-feeders such as mourning doves, feed on dropped seeds. Flowers from self-sown seeds rarely duplicate the look of the first year's flower; instead, they begin to revert to the original form from which they were hybridized, and often this means even more beautiful second-year flowers.

Impatiens spp. and cvs. Ht. and color vary. Tender.
Neither self-sowing nor easily grown from seed, impatiens are still a must for a shade garden. They bloom profusely and are available in an incredible range of colors, mostly in the white to purple-red family, including candy-striped ones that I consider too fussy. *I. wallerana* cvs. are lovely. Pay close attention to height in selecting—'Elfin' hybrids are a mere 8 inches tall, while 'Tangeglow', which is a lovely soft orange, reaches 24 inches. Avoid New Guinea impatiens, which require full sun; they are plagued by red spider mites.

Lobularia maritima and cvs., sweet alyssum. Ht: 4"–6". Fl: white, pink, rose, purple. Hardy, self-sows.
Flowers appear in only four weeks after germination and continue as long as the garden is cool. In hot areas, plants stop blooming in full summer but start up again in the fall. All varieties are very fragrant and make nice edgings, or cascades among rocks. When sited near a patio, their honey scent fills the evening air.

Mirabilis jalapa, four-o'clock.
Ht: 2'–3'. Fl: white to yellow to orange to magenta—on the same plant! Tender.
The Latin *mirabilis* means miraculous and in this case refers to the astonishing habit of differently colored flowers ap-

pearing on a single plant. The common name reflects the fact that flowers open in the late afternoon. When planted on an eastern exposure, however, they can be tricked by the early shade into opening earlier, and when it is cloudy they will remain open all day. Children love these unusual, bushy plants, which may pique their interest in the wonders of horticulture. These plants may act like perennials in protected spots, and often self-sow.

Nicotiana alata and cvs., nicotiana or jasmine tobacco. Ht: 30"–54". Fl: varies. Tender, self-sows.
This is another favorite plant. It comes in a range of soft colors including mauve, cream, dusty pink, and maroon. All are evening scented, with a spicy aroma. *N. alata* 'Sensation' (Ht: 30") looks like the old-fashioned plants but its flowers remain open during the day; 'Really Green' and 'Lime Green' as their names suggest, produce green flowers that look wonderful in large drifts. To plant nicotiana, scatter seeds in midspring for June blossoms that continue into late summer and beyond. Stay away from bright, short, unscented varieties, such as 'Nicki Hybrids'.

Portulaca grandiflora, portulaca or moss rose. Ht: 6". Fl: varies. Self-sows.
The spreading habit of portulaca makes it useful as a ground cover or low edging plant. It is a sun loving, heat- and drought-tolerant plant that is also at home in a rock garden. Flowers may be double or single, depending upon variety. Plants are everblooming and available only in color mixes that can include white, cream, pink, magenta, red, yellow, or orange.

Rudbeckia hirta, 'Gloriosa Daisy' and other cvs. Ht: to 3'. Fl: varies. Half-hardy, self-sows.
These cultivars of that North American native, the black-eyed Susan, are treated as annuals. They bloom quickly from seed and naturalize easily in meadows where poor soil and dry conditions may prevail. While yellow with a brown center is the usual color combination, there are also mahogany reds and zoned flowers. One variety, 'Irish Eyes', has yellow petals and a beautiful light green center.

Salvia splendens, annual salvia.
Ht: 24"–30". Fl: red. Tender, self-sows.
This easy annual can be grown in partial shade. It flowers for months without deadheading, and hybrids allow a great choice of color—from deep purple to cream-white. Bright red varieties, however, rarely look natural. The perennial salvia *S. farinacea* can be treated as an annual in the North (zone 4–6). It comes in clear blue and white and is ever-blooming. All salvias are heat-tolerant but can take humidity as well.

Tagetes spp. and cvs., marigolds.
Ht: 6"–36". Fl: varies. Half-hardy, may self-sow.
Marigolds are difficult to blend into a Natural Garden, as their strong colors seem to dominate any planting. They are so easy to grow, however, that it is worth seeking out the more subtly colored cultivars: 'Cinnabar' has red flowers delicately outlined in yellow with yellow centers; and 'Snowbird' is all-white, long thought an impossible color for marigolds. Its breeder, Alice Vonk, an amateur, claimed a ten-thousand-dollar prize that the Burpee Seed Company had offered for fifty years. Watch for new creamy-white varieties as they develop.

Tithonia rotundifolia cvs., Mexican sunflowers. Ht: to 6'. Fl: orange. Collect seeds and resow the following year. These rarely grown annuals are incredibly easy and bloom continuously, producing shimmering orange flowers that are good for cutting. They do not produce edible seeds nor do they self-sow. Their height should be considered when siting them, although one variety, 'Sundance', is just 36 inches. The variety 'Torch' bears the deepest orange flower.

Tropaeolum majus cvs., nasturtium.
Ht: 1'–6'. Fl: varies. Hardy.
All nasturtiums like well-drained, nutrient-poor, sandy or rocky soil. In rich loam they languish. Other than this, they grow everywhere but the hottest places, and they are exquisite. In cool climates they bloom continuously in a range of colors: orange, yellow, red, white, pink, or mahogany. Some are dwarfs of 12 inches, some are vines of 6 feet, and all are edible. The flavor

of both flowers and leaves is peppery; they liven up a salad. I like to use the flowers as garnish for summer soups, floating a single leaf and a yellow flower in, say, a bowl of gazpacho. In California they are perennial.

Viola pendunculata (V. tricolor), Johnny-jump-up or wild pansy. Ht: 1'. Fl: yellow. Hardy, self-sows.
This may be last in the list but should be a first choice. The plants produce hundreds of tiny pansylike flowers that bloom from spring to fall, stopping only if the weather gets too hot. One of the best varieties is *Viola tricolor,* 'Helen Mount', a tricolored flower of purple, lavender, and yellow, with tiny black "whiskers" brushed across the petals. Other varieties are hard to find, and you may have to collect them from seed exchanges or from friends' gardens. Seeds are easy to harvest and germinate in the ground almost anywhere in the garden; some will overwinter and sprout the following spring. These are perennials, but for me, plants are always self-sown seedlings in full flower by mid-spring.

BULBS

Each heading includes how deep to plant the bulb and how far it should be spaced from other bulbs (Dp x Sp).

Agapanthus spp., such as *A. africanus* (African lily or lily-of-the-Nile), and cvs. Z: 8–9. Ht: 20"–30". Fl: blue. S: midsummer. Dp x Sp: 4" x 6".

Allium spp., wild onion. Z: 4–9. Ht: 1'–2'. Fl: color varies. S: spring to fall. Dp x Sp: 4" x 8".
These close relatives of the garden onion are perfect for naturalizing. They not only produce bulbils (small bulbs that develop from the main bulb) but they also self-sow. Most like full sun and well-drained soil, and produce foliage that grows close to the ground, with flowers borne on tall spikes. Their oniony smell is released only if plants are crushed or cut and it quickly fades. Among the nicest is *A. canadense,* or garlic chive (also wild garlic). It bears pretty white flowers in late summer and its long-lasting faded flower heads are equally decorative. *A. schoenoprasum,*

the familiar edible chive, blooms in spring with dainty purple flowers on 24-inch stalks. *A. triquetrum* is one of the few members of the species that does well in shade. It is small, with 18-inch flower spikes, white star-shaped flowers striped in green, and often with a rosy keel.

Anemone spp., windflower or anemone. Z: 4–8. Ht: 6". Fl: varies. S: midspring. Dp x Sp: 3" x 3".
The most widely available species, *A. blanda* (Ht: 4"–6"), needs full sun and has daisylike flowers of pink, white, or violet-blue. *A. apennina* is similar with more intense colors, but a little rarer and taller. Anemones demand fast-draining soil. Soak the bulbs before planting them.

Bulbocodium vernum, spring meadow saffron. Z: 8–10. Ht: 4"–6". Fl: violet-purple and crocuslike. S: spring. Dp x Sp: 3" x 12".

Camassia spp., camass. Z: 3–8. Ht: 2'. Fl: white, blue, blue-violet. S: late spring. Dp x Sp: 8" x 12".

Chionodoxa luciliae, glory-of-the-snow. Z: 4–8. Ht: 3"–6". Fl: blue with white stripes. S: early spring. Dp x Sp: 4" x 3".
All the members of this genus are very hardy. *C. luciliae,* the most common, produces its flowers on 6-inch stems just after the crocuses bloom. It likes moist soil, full sun or partial shade, and must be planted about 4 inches deep, 1–3 inches apart. The variety 'Alba' has all-white flowers; 'Rosa' is pink-lilac.

Clivia miniata, kaffir lily. Z: 9–10. Ht: to 18". Fl: orange. S: early spring. Dp x Sp: 4" x 12".
This is a close relative of the amaryllis but it does not go completely dormant —its attractive strappy foliage is evergreen. *C. miniata* produces huge umbels of orange, trumpet-shaped flowers. These plants are wonderful as ground covers in shady spots in warm climates. They spread from offsets that can be divided and planted elsewhere. In colder climates they make excellent pot or greenhouse plants.

Colchicum autumnale, meadow saffron or autumn crocus. Z: 4–9. Ht: to 1'. Fl:

pink, lilac, or white. S: late summer. Dp x Sp: 3" x 12".
These unusual plants produce large flowers, 2–8 inches in diameter, late in the season. They like loamy soil and sunny or partly shady locations, and work best along out-of-the-way meadow edges, beneath shrubs, or beside lawn borders where they can grow undisturbed. They would also add a note of color popping up through an evergreen ground cover.

Convallaria majalis, lily-of-the-valley. Z: 3–7. Ht: 8". Fl: white. S: late spring. Dp x Sp: 1" x 4".
Grown in full sun or partial shade, in moist acid soil, lily-of-the-valley will multiply and spread rapidly, making a dense ground cover in just a few seasons. The extremely fragrant flowers are excellent for cutting—wait until about a quarter of the flowers on the spike have opened. Plant the pips—little rhizomes—1 inch deep, 4 inches apart. There is now a pink variety—*C. majalis* 'Rosea'.

Crocus spp. Z: 3–8. Ht: about 5". Fl: varies. S: early spring. Dp x Sp: 3" x 3".
There are fall-blooming crocuses, but the spring-blooming varieties are the most appealing. Crocuses are one of the first signs of spring and are available in many varieties and colors—white, lilac, purple, pink, yellow, gold, and stripes. Plant corms in sun or partial shade. Crocus hybrids bloom later in the spring with various flower colors: blue, yellow, white, or purple.

C. speciosus. Z: 6–9. Ht: 6". Fl: lavender. S: fall. Dp x Sp: 4" x 4".

Endymion spp. **(Hyacinthoides** spp. **Scilla** spp.**),** bluebells, squill. Z: 4–8. Ht: 3"–20", according to type. Fl: mostly blue. S: early spring. Dp x Sp: 5" x 4".
Scilla are beautiful for their strappy deep green foliage as well as their nodding bluebell flowers. Look for *S. peruviana,* the Peruvian bluebell (actually a native of the Mediterranean area), which is 12 inches tall and has very small bluish purple flowers that surround the stalk and wide foliage; it somewhat resembles *Agapanthus* and is handsome when planted either in small clusters or in large groups. For the

coldest regions *S. siberica,* the Siberian squill (Ht: 3″–6″) is best; it produces brilliant bluebells that look wonderful under magnolia trees. Plant scillas in sun or partial shade in moist locations at a depth of 4 inches, 6–8 inches apart, except for *S. peruviana* which should be set at 5–6 inches deep, 10 inches apart.

Eranthis cilicica and E. hyemalis, winter aconite. Z: 3–9. Ht: 2½″–3″. Fl: yellow. S: early spring. Dp x Sp: 2″ x 3″. Honey scented, single flowers, with interesting "collars" formed by their bracts, resemble their relatives, the buttercups. They arrive early, sometimes pushing up through the snow, and prefer sun or partial shade and soil that stays somewhat moist all summer. Tubers should be soaked for 24 hours before planting. *E. cilicica* is the better choice for naturalizing, but *E. hyemalis* blooms a bit later.

Erythronium americanum, dog-tooth This is perhaps the most familiar of these exquisite wildflowers. It has lovely mottled foliage and is also known by a prettier common name— trout lily. ("Dog-tooth" actually refers not to the flower but to the shape of the little bulbs.) There are several other *Erythronium* species, both native and alien. All of them like moist conditions and are perfect for naturalizing at the edge of a pond or pool. Bulbs dry out quickly, so plant them immediately. Because they are so pretty, they make fine individual specimens. They are also at home in moist, shady nooks in a rock garden. It can take up to five years for the new plants to flower; to speed up the process, place a flat stone beneath each bulb you plant.

Fritillaria meleagris, checkered lily. Z: 3–8. Ht: to 9″. Fl: veined red-purple. S: midspring. Dp x Sp: 3″ x 4″.

Galanthus nivalis and G. elwesii, snowdrop. Z: 3–8. Ht: 4″. Fl: white. S: very early spring. Dp x Sp: 3″ x 3″. Snowdrops are among the very first flowers of spring. They return year after year with no care at all and look especially pretty bordering a path or walkway where they can be seen close up. They can be grown in sun or partial shade. *G. nivalis* grows to about 6 inches, while *G. elwesii,* the giant

snowdrop, is about 12 inches tall.

Iris reticulata and cvs. Z: 4–9. Ht: 6″–8″. Fl: deep violet-purple and others according to cultivar. S: early spring. Dp x Sp: 6″ x 4″. This is a good rock garden bulb.

Leucojum spp., snowflakes. Z: 3–8. Ht: 12″–15″. Fl: mostly white. S: according to species. Dp x Sp: 5″ x 6″. These bulbs, although very easy to grow, are rarely seen. They like full sun or partial shade and prefer not to be disturbed. *L. vernum,* its white bell-shaped flowers tipped with green, blooms in the spring; *L. aestivum* flowers in the summer; and *L. autumnale*'s pinkish blooms appear in the fall, but it does not do well in warmer zones.

Lilium spp. and cvs., lilies. Z: 3–8. violet. Z: 4–9. Ht: 8″–12″, by var. Fl: yellow, tinged pink. S: late spring. Dp x Sp: 5″ x 4″.
Ht., Fl., and S. according to variety. (June–August.)
There are so many lilies to choose from that it is impossible to list them all. In general, the simplest forms look best. One exception is the very dramatic cultivar 'Black Dragon Strain' which grows 5–6 feet tall and produces huge, flaring, trumpet-shaped, fragrant flowers that are white inside and maroon-brown outside. Two or three plants positioned together actually look quite natural; each mature plant will produce as many as twenty blooms. Lilies can be successfully naturalized, but the mixes available for this purpose are too brightly colored. Instead, make your own mix of muted shades, choosing from the several native and alien species. For example *L. canadense,* the Canada lily (Ht: 5′), produces exquisite yellow or red nodding flowers and pretty whorled leaves. *L. superbum,* the Turk's-cap lily (Ht: 8′) is one of the best for naturalizing; and the familiar and stately *L. tigrinum* (now known as *L. lancifolium;* Ht: 6′), the tiger lily with its black-spotted orange flowers, also naturalizes easily, even in partial shade, by producing little bulbils along its stem, which eventually fall to the ground and grow into new plants. Most lilies like sunny locations and moist, rich, well-drained soil. Plant bulbs 4–6 inches deep, 9–18 inches

apart, depending on the ultimate size of the plants.

Lycoris squamigera, magic lily. Z: 5–8. Ht: to 2′. Fl: pink. S: late summer. Dp x Sp: 5″ x 5″.
Leaves appear in early spring, become dormant during the summer, and are followed by flower spikes.

Muscari botryoides and M. armeniacum, grape hyacinth. Z: 3–8. Ht: 4″–12″. Fl: blue. S: spring. Dp x Sp: 3″ x 3″.
These easy-care bulbs, some of the most beloved of spring flowers, like sun or partial shade and do well as a spring ground cover on an embankment or along a walk or in a rock garden. They are also lovely in spring bouquets. *M. botryoides* (Ht: 4″–8″) is bright blue; the 'Alba' variety is white; *M. armeniacum* (Ht: 6″–12″) is deep blue; and there are purple and wedgwood blue varieties. Plant as many bulbs as you can afford.

Narcissus spp. and cvs., daffodil. Z: generally 4–8, but not in the hottest part of Florida. Ht: 12″–18″. Fl: white to yellow. S: spring. Dp x Sp: 8″ x 6″. The list of Narcissus species and cultivars is exceedingly long, with flower shapes ranging from trumpet and cupped to double flowered and more, and colors from white and palest yellow to deep golden hues. I myself prefer the most natural-looking species and the small-flowered hybrids. *N. bulbocodium,* the yellow cup-shaped "petticoat" daffodil (Ht: 15″), has grasslike foliage, while *N. juncifolius,* the rush-leaved daffodil, produces 6-inch cylindrical rushlike leaves; both blend well in lawns or meadows. *N. triandrus,* angel's-tears (Ht: 1′), has small clusters of white to pale yellow flowers, with some all-white varieties; and *N. jonquilla,* is the familiar, fragrant yellow jonquil. These species are hardy from zone 6 southward. For zones 8–10, try hybrids of *N. tazetta* such as 'Paper White', a bulb commonly forced for indoor blooming in northern climes.

Daffodils are the best bulbs for naturalizing in great sweeps. Plant them in full sun or beneath deciduous trees that leaf out as the daffodil foliage matures. Set small types 4 inches deep, 4–6 inches apart and large types 6–8 inches deep, 6–10 inches apart.

Ornithogalumnutans, star-of-Bethlehem. Z: 4–9. Ht: 15″. Fl: white. S: late spring. Dp x Sp: 2″ x 3″.

O. umbellatum, star-of-Bethlehem. Z: 3–9. Ht: 9″. Fl: white. S: late spring. Dp x Sp: 2″ x 3″.

Puschkinia scilloides. Z: 4–8. Ht: 6″. Fl: white, blue. S: spring. Dp x Sp: 3″ x 3″. Good for rock gardens.

Sternbergia spp. Z: 4–10. Ht: 1′. Fl: yellow. S: spring (*S. fisherana*); fall (*S. lutea*). Dp x Sp: 5″ x 4″. C: likes dry sunny locations and heavy soil.

Zantedeschia, calla lily. Z: 8–10. Ht: to 3′. Fl: white, pink, yellow. S: early spring and sporadically through fall. Dp x Sp: 3″–4″ x 12″–24″.
Calla lilies are especially beautiful in southern gardens where many of them naturalize well. *Z. aethiopica,* the florist's white calla lily, is often grown in southern and coastal California as a single specimen, a living sculpture in the Inner Area. Smaller varieties—such as *Z. aethiopica* 'Minor' (white), *Z. elliottiana* (yellow), and *Z. rehmanii* (pink)— would be happy by a garden pond or pool. All like moist soil and partial shade. Watch out for snails in California's central coastal regions.

ORNAMENTAL GRASSES

PERENNIAL GRASSES (AND GRASSLIKE PLANTS)

Andropogon gerardii, big bluestem grass. Z: 4. Ht: 4′–7′.
This is one of the great prairie grasses of America. It takes two years to grow from seed. After frost it turns a light reddish brown.

Arrhenatherum elatius var. *bulbosum* 'Variegatum', bulbous oat grass. Z: 5. Ht: 5″–18″.
A slender, erect grass, this cultivar has variegated white and green leaves. There are "bulbs" on the lower stem from which new plants are produced and in which water is stored. This grass is a good choice for spring and fall interest.

Arundo donax, giant reed grass. Z: 7–9. Ht: 14′. S: blooms in early fall.

Briza media, quaking grass. Z: 5–9. Ht: 1′–2′.
This is the perennial form of quaking grass.

Calamagrostis epigejos, reed grass. Z: 5–9. Ht: 3′–4′.
The variety 'Karl Foerster' grows to 6 feet and like all reed grasses, it makes a lovely sound.

Carex conica 'Variegata', variegated sedge. Z: 5–9. Ht: 6″. S: year-round interest.

C. morrowii var. *expallida,* Japanese sedge grass. Z: 5–9. Ht: 1′–2′.
Although actually a sedge and not a grass, this plant has a grasslike appearance. Its leaves are striped white and it is grown along borders or in clumps or as a ground cover. This cultivar is sometimes sold as 'Variegata' or *C. conica* 'Variegata'. Another cultivar, *C. morrowii* 'Aurea-variegata' or 'Old Gold', has yellowish leaves striped in green along the edges. It is somewhat less hardy than *expallida.*

Cortaderia selloana, pampas grass. Z: 7–9. Ht: to 14′.
This dramatic grass forms a towering fountain and looks wonderful as an isolated specimen planting, such as is often found in California and the South. Its feathery plumes range from silvery white to pink; the female plant has showier flowers.

Cymbopogon citratus, lemongrass. Z: 9–10. Ht: to 6′.
This aromatic grass grows in the tropics, especially in the Far East where it is used in cooking. Anyone who has sampled the cuisine of Thailand has come across its distinctive flavor in soups and curries. Lemongrass oil is used in perfumery and medicine.

Dactylis glomerata 'Variegata', striped orchard grass. Z: 5–9. Ht: 1′–2′.

Elymus glaucus, wild rye grass. Z: 5–9. Ht: 1′–3′.
A dune grass, wild rye is used in coastal areas to stabilize sand dunes. It is blue in color.

Erianthus ravennae, plume or Ravenna grass. Z: 5–9. Ht: to 14′.

If you love pampas grass (*Cortaderia selloana*) but your zone is not warm enough to grow it successfully, Ravenna grass would make a good substitute. It is fountainlike, its silvery plumes turning a beautiful golden brown in the fall, and standing erect into the winter.

Festuca ovina var. *glauca,* blue fescue. Z: 4–9. Ht: 6″–12″.
This, and the several other fescues (*F. cinerea* or *F. caesia,* for example) are grown for their attractive blue or silvery foliage. They can be grown in dainty clumps in a rock garden, or as edging along a path or island bed. *F. rubra,* red fescue, is red or purple tinged. To give you an idea of this genus's variations, Kurt Bluemel Nurseries in Maryland (see Source Guide) offers 35 species!

Hakonechloa macra 'Aureola'. Z: 5–9. Ht: 1′–2′.
This Japanese species resembles bamboo but does not have the invasive growth habit. It likes partial shade.

Helictotrichon sempervirens, blue oat grass. Z: 5–9. Ht: 2′.

Hystrix patula, bottlebrush grass. Z: 5–9. Ht: 3′–4′.
This grass is native to wooded areas of the Northeast. It likes shade and damp soil and is a good choice for a woodland wildflower garden.

Imperata cyclindrica rubra, Japanese blood grass. Z: 5–9. Ht: 1′–2′.
Like the fescues, this grass is fairly short and grows in a clump. In the middle of summer, it turns a stunning red, beginning at the tip ends of its blades, until it is fully ablaze by midfall, adding a dramatic note to the garden.

Koeleria glauca, blue hairgrass. Z: 4–9. Ht: 1′.
This grass resembles *Festuca* but blooms very early, in June, and keeps its golden dried flowers for months.

Miscanthus sinensis, eulalia grass. Z: 5–9. Ht: 8′–12′.
Of the many cultivars of this species, my favorite is 'Zebrinus', zebra grass, which has dark green blades dashed with pale yellow at 6-inch intervals. It

reaches about 7 feet tall and does very well by the water's edge. 'Variegatus', another cultivar, has white or yellow stripes rather than bands, and 'Gracillimus', maiden grass, a popular choice, has deeply channeled light green blades. 'Giganteus' grows to 15 feet. All are robust growers that form thick clumps and spread slowly via rhizomes; they make very good privacy screens and are handsome against the snow in northern winter gardens. The miscanthus plants are of Asian origin as the name suggests (*sinensis* means Chinese); in Japan, the stems are used to make brush handles and parts of kitchen utensils.

Molinia caerulea **var. altissima,** purple moor grass. Z: 5–9. Ht: 4'–6'. S: blooms in midsummer and lasts through winter.

Panicum virgatum, switch grass. Z: 5–9. Ht: 3'–5'. S: blooms from midsummer to early winter.

Pennisetum alopercuroides, fountain grass. Z: 6–9. Ht: 3'–4'.
This perennial pennisetum is undeniably attractive. And the purple color of the flowers makes it all the more worthwhile. This is one of the best grasses for beginners.

Phalaris arundinacea **var. picta,** ribbon grass. Z: 4–9. Ht: 3'–4'.
Ribbon grass has beautiful flat blades of variegated pale green and white. It is easy to grow under a variety of conditions but will spread in all directions unless it is contained or the soil is of poor quality. A good water plant, it will even grow with its roots submerged.

Phragmites australis, reed grass Z: 4–9. Ht: to 15'.
This is the reed that is found round the world, from Asia to America, growing in ditches and in poor soil everywhere. Fossil evidence also gives it a long history. It is easy to transplant by simply digging up a bucketful.

Schizachyrium scoparium, little bluestem grass. Z: 4. Ht: 3'–4'.
This grass grows in clumps, turns a golden red-brown in the fall, and produces attractive small flowers for dried bouquets.

Sorghastrum avenaceum, Indian grass. Z: 5–9. Ht: 5'. S: blooms late summer to early winter. This grass naturalizes well.

Spodiopogon sibiricus, spodiopogon. Z: 5–9. Ht: 4'–5'. S: blooms from summer to late fall. This is a vigorous grower with red leaves.

Uniola latifolia (Chasmanthium latifolium), northern sea oats. Z: 5–9. Ht: 3'. C: tolerates partial shade. S: blooms from late summer to late winter.
This is a wonderful grass for dried flowers. The plant forms incredible seedpods in August—green chevrons that turn golden in early fall and then become a rich, chestnut brown. They dangle from arching spires and dance in the wind, or if dried, in the gentlest of breezes.

ANNUAL GRASSES

The plants on this list can be grown throughout the country. In short-season climates, starting the seeds indoors in early spring will extend the season, and in the warmest zones, some of these plants are perennial. Seed packages provide most of this information.

Agrostis nebulosa, cloud grass. Ht: 1'.
This delicate-looking grass, a native of Spain, is handsome in dried bouquets and will grow well in partial shade.

Avena sterilis, animated oats. Ht: to 3'.
This species earns its common name from the curious way in which the bristles on the fruits twist and untwist when in contact with a moist surface.

Briza maxima, big quaking grass. Ht: to 2'.
A half-hardy grass that, although rather tall and sometimes ungainly, is attractive in bouquets. Grow it in the Outer Area.

B. minor, little quaking grass. Ht: to 16".
An erect-growing grass; its lower flower parts are striped with purple.

Coix lacryma-jobi, Job's-tears. Ht: 3'–4'.
Related to corn, Job's-tears is grown in

Asia as a food plant. In Europe, it is an ornamental, but the beadlike grayish white fruits are also strung into rosaries and necklaces. It has a long history as an ornamental, dating back to the fourteenth-century in Europe, and earlier in Asia. Job's-tears tolerates partial shade and some moisture, self-sows in the South, and can be started indoors elsewhere. Germination takes three to four weeks.

Eragrostis spp., love grass.
Of the annual members of this species, *E. amabilis* (Japanese love grass) is fairly low growing (Ht: 20"), and *E. suaveolens,* which it resembles, reaches about 36 inches. Both are grown as ornamentals and for bouquets.

Lagurus ovatus, Hare's-tail grass. Ht: 18"–24".
This Mediterranean native has light green foliage with a downy covering on both stems and leaves. The sturdy flower heads are long lasting in bouquets or in a winter garden.

Lamarckia aurea, goldentop. Ht: to 16".
Another Mediterranean grass, goldentop produces a golden yellow to purplish flower that turns silvery as it matures.

Pennisetum setaceum, fountain grass. Ht: to 4'.
This is a perennial in zone 9, where it can be invasive. Elsewhere, it is a very pretty annual, prettier some say than the perennial *P. alopecuroides* which it resembles (see above). It is most useful in areas that are newly planted with a perennial grass needing a year to take hold. *P. setaceum rubrum* is deep red.

P. villosum, feathertop grass. Ht: 2'–3'.
This too is a perennial in zone 9, an annual elsewhere. When picked fresh its feathery form combines well in a bouquet with astilbe and other summer perennials.

Setaria italica, foxtail millet. Ht: 2'–4'.
This ancient grain crop is known to have been grown in China, in 2700 B.C. It was brought to Europe in the Middle Ages, when trade with China began, and came to the United States in the

mid-nineteenth-century. It is still grown as a fodder crop for livestock, but it also makes an admirable ornamental.

Sorghum bicolor var. technicum, broomcorn or black sorghum. Ht: 10′–15′.
This tall grass is grown commercially as a source of bristles for brooms or brushes. Another old crop, it was plentiful in ancient times. Its shiny black panicles make it an attractive ornamental.

BAMBOO

These long-lived, woody evergreen grasses grow in clumps or spread along rhizomes. The heights given below are the maximum heights under optimum conditions; most plants will be considerably shorter; their vertical growth can be further controlled by trimming in the summer. The horizontal spread, particularly of hardy aggressive, running-types, can be stopped simply by stepping on the new shoots as they appear in the spring. Or, if you have a taste for bamboo shoots, you can harvest them for stir-fried dishes.

Arundinaria disticha (sometimes sold as *Sasa disticha*), dwarf fernleaf bamboo. Z: 8–10. Ht: 2′–3′. Runs.
A delicate, ferny plant; a rampant grower that can be cut to the ground if it becomes leggy.

A. humilis (sometimes sold as *Sasa humilis*), low bamboo. Z: 7–9. Ht: 1′–3′. Runs.
A small graceful plant that spreads quickly and makes a good ground cover on a hillside.

A. pygmaea (sometimes sold as *Sasa pygmaea*), pygmy bamboo. Z: 7–9. Ht: 12″–18″. Runs.
In colder parts of its range, this small plant is semideciduous; otherwise it is an aggresive spreader that can be used to hold a slope.

A. variegata, dwarf whitestripe bamboo. Z: 6–8. Ht: 2′–3′. Runs.
This bamboo has white stripes on its leaves and stems that are a mere quarter-inch in diameter. It is a fast spreader and can be used as a ground cover.

Bambusa glaucescens (sometimes sold as *B. multiplex*), hedge bamboo. Z: 8–10. Ht: 15′–25′. Clumps.
Interesting cultivars of this species include 'Alphonse Karr' (Ht: 15′–30′) which has yellow stems streaked with green; 'Fernleaf', a small plant (Ht: 10′–20′) which has fernlike foliage; 'Golden Goddess' another small plant (Ht: 6′–10′) with a graceful dense growth habit; 'Stripestem Fernleaf' (Ht: 25′–30′) which resembles 'Fernleaf' but has bolder green stripes on stems. *B. glaucescens* var. *riviereorum*, Chinese-goddess bamboo (Ht: 5′–8′) has tiny fernlike leaves and is both dainty and graceful. Seek also *B. beecheyana*.

B. oldhamii (also sold as *Dendrocalamus latiflorus*), Oldham, or clump giant timber, bamboo. Z: 9–10. Ht: 20′–40′. Clumps.
A single clump can be used to form a dramatic accent; otherwise, this species grows densely and is useful as a screening hedge. For such a hedge, position clumps 4–5 feet apart.

B. ventricosa, Buddha, or Buddha's-belly, bamboo. Z: 9–10. Ht: 15′–30′. Clumps.
The common name was suggested by the swollen internodes that appear on the stalks when this bamboo is grown in tubs or poor, dry soil. It is a very vigorous grower.

Phyllostachys aurea, golden, or fishpole, bamboo. Z: 5–8. Ht: 15′–25′. Runs.
This has long been the most widely grown bamboo in the United States. It has been known to survive temperatures to −26°F; to look its best, it needs moist conditions but can tolerate occasional dryness. It is an invasive plant; however, since its shoots are mild flavored, it can be controlled by harvesting new shoots for the kitchen in midspring. Mature stalks are quite strong and in the Orient are used as walking sticks and umbrella handles, as well as the fishing poles suggested by its common name.

P. aureosulcata, yellow-groove, or stake or forage, bamboo. Z: 5–8. Ht: 15′–25′. Runs.
Slimmer and more open than *P. aurea*, this too is a hardy bamboo. When

young, its stems are green with yellow grooves.

P. bambusoides, giant timber, or Japanese timber, bamboo. Z: 7–9. Ht: 25′–70′. Runs.
This is a large hardy timber bamboo, its dark green stems growing to an eventual 6 inches in diameter and forming an attractive grove effect if kept thinned. Its edible shoots appear in late spring and are grown and sold commercially. The cultivar 'Castillon' has bright yellow stems marked with bright green vertical bands, and has been known to flower in western states. Once bamboo flowers, it often dies back dramatically; however, this cultivar has also been known to recover its vigor after a few years of conscientious watering and fertilizing.

P. dulcis, sweetshoot bamboo. Z: 7–9. Ht: 20′–40′. Runs. Favorite edible species.

P. nigra, black bamboo. Z: 7–9. Ht: 10′–25′. Runs.
As the name suggests, stems can be a dense black; they are sometimes green, dotted with black. Needs afternoon shade in the warmer parts of its range.

P. pubescens, moso bamboo. Z: 7–9. Ht: 40′–60′. Runs.
This is one of the largest of the timber bamboos, attaining not only a 60-foot height but also stem diameters up to 8 inches. Its leaves are feathery and cloudlike, and its shoots are a delicacy.

P. viridis, green bamboo. Z: 6–8. Ht: 20′–30′. Runs.
This is a rather slow-growing runner. It has a slender, curving stem and produces fernlike foliage. The cultivar 'Robert Young' is a more vigorous grower and can be invasive but also has attractive yellow stems with green stripes and a green ring at each node.

Pseudosasa japonica, metake, arrow bamboo. Z: 7–9. Ht: 10′–20′. Runs.
A good screen plant when grown in a thick hedge; leaves are large with long points. It can also be used to hold a hillside.

Sasa palmata, palmate bamboo. Z: 7–9. Ht: 8′–12′. Runs.

Grows tallest in the cool moist areas of its range; under other conditions it rarely exceeds 3 feet in height. It has broad, attractive leaves, shaped like the palm and fingers of a hand.

GROUND COVERS

Most people think of ground covers as ground-hugging plants, and for the most part those listed below are low-growing. This definition, however, has always seemed somewhat narrow to me—there are places where a plant with more height or bulk is desirable. For example, on a slope, certain shrubbier prostrate junipers can make admirable ground covers. In fact, anything that spreads by one means or another to cover a given area can accurately be described as a ground cover. I prefer this broader definition and have thus included several plants that are knee-high and higher. These taller plants are the only ones for which I've given heights in the headings below. All others are under one foot tall.

Acaena microphylla, New Zealand bur. Z: 7–9.

Achillea tomentosa, Woolly-yarrow. Z: 3–8. C: full sun; well-drained soil. Fl: yellow, all summer.

Acanthus perringii, bear's breech. Z: 8–10. Ht: 18″. C: partial shade. Fl: red snapdragonlike, all summer.

Aegopodium podograria variegatum, goutweed. Z: 3–9. C: full sun or shade; poor, dry soil.

Agapanthus africanus, lily-of-the-Nile, agapanthus. Z: 8–10. Ht: 2′, leaves 4′. Fl: blue. See Bulbs.

Ajuga reptans and spp., bugleweed. Z: 4–9. Flowers: blue.
Bugleweed is a good ground-hugging cover for shady areas. The leaves are rich green, bronze, or a variegated cream and gray-green; plants spread by runners (and can be a bit invasive if planted near lawn grass). If the location is moist, bugleweed will produce impressive blue flower spikes, about 10 inches tall, in the spring. These tough little plants can withstand some foot traffic, making them true lawn alterna-

tives. There are, however, many varieties from which to choose, so if, for example, you want a plant to tuck into the rock garden, or as edging along an island bed, look for *A. genevensis* and *A. pyramidalis* or another of the ajugas that does not spread.

Alchemilla vulgaris, lady's-mantle. Z: 3–8. Ht: to 18″. Fl: yellow-green. Popular in England, but rarely used here, lady's-mantle has large, lobed, gray-green foliage that is beautiful in early morning or after a rain when beads of water form perfect jewels in the center of each leaf. The tiny flowers are an unusual shade of yellow-green, blooming in great profusion to form lime-colored clouds. Cut off faded blossoms. They cannot be walked upon, but are useful as edgers for an island bed or along walkways. Able to thrive in sun or partial shade, each plant spreads to about 2 feet in diameter.

Antennaria dioica 'Rosea', pussy toes. Z: 2–8. C: full sun; dry soil. Fl: pink in spring

Anthemis nobilis, camomile. Z: 3–9.

Andromeda polifolia, bog rosemary. Z: 2–6. Ht: 12″. C: full sun to partial shade; wet, acid soil; evergreen. Fl: pink in early spring.

Arabis alpina, Rock cress. Z: 3–7. C: full sun; moist, well-drained soil. Fl: white in spring. Suitable for rock gardens.

Arctostophylos franciscana, Laurel hill manzanita. Z: 7–9.

A. hookeri, Hooker manzanita. Z: 7–10. Ht: 18″.

A. uva-ursi, bearberry. Z: 2–8. Ht: 12″. C: full sun; well-drained soil. The foliage turns a bright red in fall.

Arctotheca calendula, cape weed. Z: 8–10. Evergreen. Fl: yellow.
This plant, which is often grouped with the African daisies, is a tenacious cover that can survive extremes of heat and dryness, making it good for southern and western gardens. Its coarse gray-green foliage is, to many, not very attractive, but it produces sunny yellow

2-inch flowers in late spring. To improve its overall appearance, try planting cape weed with ivy or another cover, to soften its appearance.

Arenaria verna caespitosa, Moss sandwort. Z: 2–8. C: partial shade to sun; well-drained, moist soil.

Armeria maritima, thrift. See Herbaceous Perennials.

Artemisia schmidtiana, Silver Mound. See Herbaceous Perennials.

A. stelleriana, beach wormwood. Z: 2–8. Ht: 18″–24″. C: hot sandy soil; a seashore plant.

Asarum europaeum, wild ginger. Z: 4–8. C: partial to deep shade; rich, moist humusy soil.
This species is grown for shiny foliage.

Asparagus densiflorus 'Sperengeri', Asparagus fern. Z: 9–10. C: sun to partial shade; well-drained soil; drought-tolerant.

Astilbe chinensis 'Pumila'. Z: 4–8. Ht: 15″. C: partial shade and moist soil; forms a solid mat. Fl: pink in late summer.

Aurinia saxatilis, basket-of-gold. Z: 3–8. Ht: 10″–18″. C: full sun and well-drained soil. Fl: yellow, gold, or white.
This perennial subshrub is easy to grow; it thrives in dry rocky soil and looks especially lovely when allowed to drape over a wall or a tumble of rocks. The plants have silvery foliage and brilliant flowers that bloom in early spring.

Berberis thunbergii 'Crimson Pygmy'. Z: 5–8. Ht: 1′. C: full sun for best foliage color, drought-tolerant.

Bergenia cordifolia. Z: 4–9. C: from full sun to partial shade; dry soil to moist. Evergreen. Fl: magenta, white, pink.
Bergenia cordifolia grows well in a variety of situations and has large deep green leathery leaves often touched with magenta. In spring, 15- to 20-inch flower spikes shoot up, covered with flaring bell-shaped flowers. As a bonus, plants tend to rebloom sporadically throughout the season.

Bruchenthalia spiculifolia, spike heather. Z: 5–9.

Brunnera macrophylla, dwarf anchusa, forget-me-not. Z: 1–8. Useful, large leaves

Calluna spp., heather. Z: 5–8. Ht: 6″–24″. C: full sun; sandy soil. This heather has deep roots that help prevent soil erosion. It can withstand salt air. Must have good drainage.

Campanula rotundifolia, harebell. Z: 3–8. Fl: blue. Suitable for rock gardens.

Cerastium tomentosum, snow-in-summer. Z: 2–8.

Ceratostigma plumbaginoides, plumbago. Z: 5–9. C: full sun. Fl: blue. As one seed catalogue proclaims, "If you can't grow *Ceratostigma,* give up gardening!" Although it does like sun, this versatile plant will grow in nearly any situation. Each plant is about 4 inches tall and creeps along to form a dense mat from 12 to 18 inches in diameter. It flowers profusely in late summer and fall, and its leaves turn a deep mahogany, in late summer.

Convallaria majalis, lily-of-the-valley. See Bulbs.

Cornus canadensis, bunchberry. Z: 2–8. Fl: white. This native wildflower is a member of the dogwood family and one of the berried ground covers. The plants, which grow to 9 inches, spread by woody rhizomes. Their white flowers appear in late spring or early summer, and red berries brighten up the fall.

Cotoneaster dammeri 'Skogsholmen'. Z: 5. Fl: white. This prostrate evergreen is drought and wind tolerant, and spreads several feet each year, sending out roots where its branches touch ground. Its leaves are leathery, a lovely dark shiny green with a lighter shade on the underside; it blooms in the spring and produces red berries in the fall. (Beware of red spider in dry climates, also susceptible to scale.) Suitable for rock gardens.

Cymbalaria muralis, Kenilworth ivy. Z: 5–10.

Daboecia cantabrica, Irish heath. Z: 5–8. Ht: 18″.

Daphne Cneorum, rose daphne. Z: 4–8. Ht: 12″.

Dianthus spp., pinks. Z: 2–8.

Dicentra eximia, fringed bleeding-heart. Z: 3–7. Ht: 15″.

Dichondra carolinensis, dichondra. Z: 8–10. Lawn substitute; will take foot traffic.

Duchesnea indica, mock strawberry.

Epigaea repens, trailing arbutus. Z: 4–8.

Epimedium spp. Z: 4–8, by species. Ht: to 15″. Fl: star-shaped, white, red, rose, lilac, pink, or pale yellow; some two-toned.
These hardy plants are tolerant of shade and of moist, acid conditions, making them a good choice for planting near evergreens or rhododendrons. In sheltered situations, the plants are semievergreen. They spread by underground runners or rhizomes, which can be divided for new plants, and they form mounds about 12 inches in diameter. The trilobed, clear green leathery leaves are tinged red in the fall. Waxy flowers appear in the spring. *E. grandiflorum,* bishop's hat or barrenwort, the most widely available species, can be planted in spring or fall. It requires only an occasional spring trimming before the new growth appears.

Ericaceae family, heathers.
When properly sited, members of the heather family require almost no care. Like their relatives, the rhododendrons, all heathers require acid, well-drained soil that is rather moist—add peat and sand if necessary and mix in some pure forest floor soil. Most heathers also need full sun and ample water. Hardiness varies greatly from species to species and is probably the single most important factor to consider when choosing a heather; for those listed below, I have given the minimum temperature they will tolerate.
This is a rewarding family of plants to include in your garden; some have colorful foliage—grays and greens, yel-

lows, reds, and gold—and all have enchanting flowers from white to deep pink to purple. By selecting carefully you can have heathers in bloom in every season.

Bruckenthalia spiculifolia, spike heather. Hardy to 10°F. Compact, 10″ tall. Fl: pink in midsummer.

Calluna vulgaris and cultivars, Scotch heather. Hardy to −35°F. Needle-type foliage, height ranges from a few inches to 3 feet by cultivar. Flowers range from purple, pink, or white, to crimson, with some double varieties. Bloom in summer to early autumn.

Daboecia cantabrica, Irish heather. Hardy to −10°F. At a height of 2 feet, this is a tall heather. Its shiny foliage and half-inch purple flowers appear in late summer to fall. Good in rock gardens.

Erica carnea, spring heath. Hardy to −10°F. Ht: 12″. As the name suggests, blooms in the spring; flowers are red.

E. cinerea, twisted heath. Hardy to −10°F. Ht: 24″. Blooms in summer to early fall; flowers are purple to blue. Many cultivars.

E. x darlyensis, darley heath. Hardy to −5°F. Ht: to 24″. Fl: pink in spring.

E. tetralix, cross-leaved heath. Hardy to −35°F. Ht: to 24″. Rose-colored flowers in summer to autumn.

E. vagans, Cornish heath. Hardy to −15°F. Ht: 12″. Fl: purplish pink. This native of Europe has been naturalized on Nantucket Island.

Euonymus spp., winter creeper. Z: 4–9.
There are countless varieties of euonymous, with small-leaved semievergreen foliage—both solid green and variegated. Used as creeping ground covers, these varieties range in height from 2 to 12 inches. Scale insects bother some cultivars. Dormant oil spray is safe and effective. Seek dwarf *E. fortuni* cultivars.

Festuca ovina **var.** *glauca,* blue fescue grass. See Ornamental Grass.

Fragaria spp., strawberries. Z: 3–8. Ht: 6″–10″ by spp. See Edible Plants.

F. californica, wood strawberry.

F. chilohesis, sand strawberry.

F. vesca americana, American strawberry.

F. virginiana, Virginia strawberry.

Galium odoratum (Asperula odorata), sweet woodruff. Z: 4–8. C: partial shade; moist humusy soil. Fl: white in spring.
This is a good ground cover to plant under trees. As an herb, it is used in flavoring May wine.

Galox aphylla, galax, florist's galax. Z: 3–8.
This plant is grown primarily for its dark green leathery leaves—like lily-pads.

Gaultheria hispidula, creeping snowberry. Z: 3–8.

Gaultheria spp., wintergreen. Z: minimum by species 2–5. Ht: 4″–15″ by species.

Glecoma hederacea, gill-over-the-hill. Z: 2–8. Can be invasive.

Gypsophila repens, creeping baby's breath. Z: 3–8.

Hedera helix, English ivy. Z: 3–10.
This is one of the royal triumvirate of evergreen ground covers, sharing the throne with *Pachysandra* and *Vinca minor.* English ivy will grow just about everywhere. As a ground cover it is most attractive beneath trees and shrubs where it thrives in the bright light of partial shade. In addition to the broad-leaved English ivy species there are others from which to choose: '238th Street', developed by T. H. Everett of the New York Botanical Garden, will grow in any situation and holds its leaves well in winter (as does 'Baltica'); *H. marmorata,* marbled ivy, and *H. aureo-variegata,* golden-leaved ivy, have pretty variegated leaves. In warmer climes, try Canary Island ivy.

Helxine soleiri, baby's-tears. Z: 8–10.
Baby's-tears forms a dense mat.

Hemerocallis spp. and hybrids, day-lilies. See Herbaceous Perennials.

Heuchera sanguinea, coralbells. See Herbaceous Perennials.

Houstonia caerulea, bluets. Z: 2–7. Good for shaded rock crevices.

Hypericum calycinum, creeping St. John's-wort or Aaron's-beard. Z: 5–9. Ht: 12″. Evergreen. Fl: yellow.
This useful plant can be grown in poor soil and tolerates occasional drought although it prefers humid, coastal climates. It also likes moist soil; in fact, in dry conditions spider mites can be a problem. Its tight-knitting roots, which can compete with tree roots, will anchor an embankment. The plant spreads 12 inches a season and produces delightful 3-inch wide yellow blossoms, buttercuplike with many fuzzy stamens. They look very showy against the shiny, richly colored 4-inch long leaves. Mowing this plant every three years will rejuvenate it.

Iberis sempervirens, evergreen candytuft. See Herbaceous Perennials.

Ice plants. Even though there are many genera of these succulents, I have grouped them together under their common name because they all require roughly the same growing conditions. These are striking plants for warm climates, full sun, and dry soil. With one exception, the plants listed below are hardy only to 20°F., but in the right environment, they will really take off. All have startling daisy or asterlike flowers. They thrive on neglect.

Carpobrotus spp. Ht: 12″–18″. Fl: pink to yellow or light purple, by sp. Sometimes called sea fig, or even hottentot fig, their leaves are the largest of the genera. Plants will grow in pure sand but do not do well on slopes under such conditions. Beware of giving this plant too much water.

Cephalophyllum spp. This plant will tolerate slightly colder climates: it is hardy to 10°F. It has familiar clawlike foliage—reddish leaves that point straight up on 3–5-inch tall plants. Brilliant cerise flowers appear in late winter or early spring.

Drosanthemum floribunda. An excellent ice plant for erosion control, this one produces 6-inch tall plants that are virtually hidden by pretty pink flowers from late spring through early summer.

Lampranthus. Species of this popular plant are available in many flourescent colors. Shop the nurseries and garden centers in spring when the plants are in bloom to find the colors that suit your taste.

Delosperma, Malephora, Oscularia, and *Ruschia* are also hardy to 20°F. and are good candidates for a natural garden. Also investigate the *Mesembryanthemum* spp.

Juniperus spp., juniper. See Evergreen Shrubs.
Low-growing spreading junipers do well in every corner of the country. In general, they are among the most useful, dependable, low-maintenance plants you can grow. Their needle foliage comes in an incredible range of colors, from blue to plum to bright green. They can be grown on embankments or cascade over rocks and walls; they can be planted alone, freestanding, or in combination with another ground cover (perhaps a flowering one).
Junipers do well in full sun and dry soil, but will tolerate partial shade. Plants must be properly spaced—usually around 3 or 4 feet apart—even though in the beginning this may make your planting look thin. Remember—some junipers will spread as much as 6 feet, and no juniper will thrive in a crowded grouping. When making your selection, be sure to verify that the cultivar has a low-growing habit and thus will be suitable as a ground cover; otherwise you may be unpleasantly surprised. *Juniperus chinensis* for example has many low-growing varieties, but the species itself grows to 60 feet. The following list will give you a head start:

J. chinensis 'Armstrong', 'Fruitlansii', Pfitzerana', sargentii. Hardy to −20°F.

J. communis, English juniper. Hardy to −50°F.

J. communis montana, mountain juniper. Hardy to −50°F.

J. conferta, shore juniper. Many cultivars. Hardy to −10°F.

J. davurica 'Expansa'. Hardy to −30°F.

J. horizontalis, creeping juniper. Many cultivars, including 'Bar Harbor', Blue Chip', 'Plumosa Compacta', 'Wiltonii', and 'Youngstown'. Most are hardy to −30°F.

J. procumbens, creeping juniper, Japanese juniper. Many good cultivars. Most are hardy to −10°F. *J. procumbens* 'Nana' is unexcelled.

J. sabina, savin juniper. Popular low-growing cultivars include 'Arcadia', 'Blue Danube', and 'Scandia'. Hardy to −40°F.

J. virginiana 'Silver Spreader'. A dwarf form of the native Eastern red cedar. Hardy to −20°F.

Lamiastrum galeobdolon 'Variegatum', yellow dead nettle, yellow archangel. Z: 4–9.
This is a ground-hugging vine with silver foliage. It is excellent for covering spring bulb foliage. It tolerates average soil and grows in partial to full shade. Yellow flowers are borne in late spring.

Lamium moculatum, dead nettle. Z: 4–9.
Similar to *lamiastrum,* but more ruly, *lamium* is an excellent ground cover for full shade. Its foliage is silver and its flowers are usually rosy pink. One cultivar, 'Alba', has white flowers, and another, 'Beacon Silver', tolerates full shade, although it will grow well in sunny, moist locations.

Leiophyllum buxifolium, sand myrtle. Z: 4–8. Ht: 15″.

Linnaea borealis americana, twinflower. Z: 2–7.

Lippia canescens, mat grass. Z: 8–9.

Liriope muscari and cvs., big blue lilyturf. Z: 6–9. Ht: to 24″. C: likes shade. Evergreen. Fl: deep violet in late summer.
This species of lilyturf has flowers that resemble those of the grape hyacinth; it

is also the largest of the lilyturfs, with grasslike leaves that form a mound 18 inches in diameter. Black berries follow.

L. spicata and cvs., creeping lilyturf. Z: 5–9. C: shade. Fl: pale violet to white.
This small lilyturf forms a more uniform cover than *L. muscari.* It too flowers in late summer.

Lysimachia nummularia, moneywort, creeping Jennie. Z: 3–9. Can be invasive.

Mazus reptens, mazus. Z: 5–9. Pretty orchidlike tiny flowers.

Mentha requienii, creeping mint, Corsican mint. Z: 8–9.
Resembling baby's-tears, creeping mint likes good drainage. If perfectly sited, it is a perennial. It can be walked upon and is the mint used in making the liqueur crème de menthe. Some sources claim this to be hardy to zone 5, but it hasn't been my experience. I did see this wonderful ground cover growing year-round in a New Jersey garden in gravelly, fast-draining soil. However, I've found that it grows so fast that small plants, plugged-in in spring, will rapidly fill the spaces between pavers. You can cut sections with a knife and pot them up in the fall to winter over in a cool window indoors for planting outside in spring.

Moss. This is one of nature's most beautiful ground covers for places that are shady and very humid. Moss gardens, however, such as those for which the Japanese have long been renowned, are very high on maintenance. A moss gardener must spend many contemplative hours clearing leaf and tree litter from the moss surface. If the location suits it, however, moss will thrive with very little care. I recommend that you try a small patch, purchased or transplanted from a wild corner of your property; if it takes hold, you will have little difficulty encouraging it to spread. In addition to shade and high humidity, mosses need very acid soil—with a pH of about 5—and are therefore well situated beneath evergreen trees. One gardener I know, Laura Cadwallader, has had good success with new transplants

by pouring beer over them; they must like the yeast.

Two available mosslike plants are good candidates for ground covers and rock gardens: the *Areneria* and *Sagina* species—Irish and Scotch mosses—especially *A. verna* and *S. subulata* both of which are often sold as Irish moss. Both plants produce white flowers; *Arenaria* has clusters; *Sagina* bears single flowers. Both also have gold-flowered cultivars, listed as 'Aurea', which are more tolerant of more sun. Plant them in well-drained sandy soil, in cool spots in the garden.

Ophiopogen japonicus, mondo grass. Z: 7–10. Ht: 8″–18″. Similar to liriope, but recurving.

Opuntia humifusa, prickly pear cactus. Z: 6–10. C: sand, well-drained soil and full sun; will naturalize. Fl: yellow in early summer followed by red fruits on flat, spiny pods.

Pachistima canbyi, pachistima. Z: 5–8.

Pachysandra terminalis, pachysandra or Japanese spurge. Z: 3–9.
Another of the royal triumvirate of evergreen ground covers, pachysandra forms a dense carpet beneath trees and shrubs. Place rooted cuttings 8–10 inches apart and keep them well watered. They take hold rapidly, forming an almost instant cover, and will then need only minimal maintenance. Unlike ivy, pachysandra will not climb vertically.

Phlox divaricata, wild sweet william. Z: 3–8. C: partial shade; rich, humusy, well-drained soil. Fl: lavender, white.
Most people think of phlox as a tall-flowering perennial, but this wildflower is one of the exceptions. In the spring, it produces large fragrant flowers on 10-inch stems.

P. stolonifera, creeping phlox. Z: 4–8. Fl: fragrant and blue in midspring; evergreen foliage.

P. subulata, moss pink. Z: 2–9. Fl: pink.
Only 6 inches tall, this plant makes a great ground cover. In the spring it is covered with fragrant flowers, which

are usually pink but are also available in white, blue, or scarlet cultivars. This low-growing, creeping phlox is tolerant of a wide range of growing conditions throughout the United States. It is also a good choice for the rock garden or cascading over a wall. *P. nivalis* (Z: 4–8. Ht: 8″), *P. ovata* (Z: 4–8. Ht: 6″) and *P. procumbens* (Z: 4–8. Ht: 6″) are other ground-covering members of this native genus.

Polemonium reptans, Jacob's-ladder. Z: 3–8. Ht: 12″. C: partial shade to full sun; naturalizes well in shade. Fl: blue. S: mid to late spring.

Polygonum cuspidatum* var. *commpactum (P. Reynontria), fleeceflower. Z: 5–8. Ht: 12″. See Herbaceous Perennials.

Potentilla spp., cinquefoil. Z: 4–8. Ht: 3″–12″ by var.
Small shrubby plants with strawberry-like foliage and flowers of red, pink, white, or yellow by variety.

Primula spp., primrose. Z: 3–8 by spp. Ht: 8″–12″ by var.
All the primroses want partial shade and rich, moist soil. *P.* x *polyantha* (Z: 3–8. Ht: 10″) comes in every color and is well-suited to lining a path. Other species to try are *P. auricula* (alpine primrose), *P. denticulata* (Himalayan primrose), *P. japonica* (candelabra group, Japanese primrose).

Pulmonaria angustifolia 'Aurea', *P. rubra, P. saccharata,* pulmonaria, lungwort. Z: 3–8.
Pulmonarias have interesting mottled foliage often splashed with silver. Flower colors range from blue (most common) to yellow, red, and white. They bloom in early spring and require rich, moist, humusy soil, and will bloom in partial to full shade.

Rosmarinus officinalis prostratus, dwarf rosemary. Z: 8–10.

Sagina spp., Irish moss. See Moss, page 271.

Sanguiana canadensis, bloodroot. Z: 2–7.

Saturcia spp., savory. Z: 5–7–9 by spp. Ht: 6″–15″.

Saxifraga stolonifera, strawberry geranium. Z: 7–10.
Shade-tolerant ground cover, spreads by plantlets on stolons in the same manner as strawberries.

Sedum spp., stone crop.
Many sedums make excellent ground covers. Like ice plants, sedums are succulents, but they can be incredibly hardy. I have a large area of *S. acre* that thrives on poor soil, drought, and (honestly) complete neglect. I started the plant simply by breaking ¼–½-inch stem sections from a single nursery purchase and scattering them randomly over the ground in late winter. By next summer's end, the entire area was a thick carpet of fresh green. In winter the plants remain evergreen but take on a bronze cast; in June, they simply burst into bloom with thousands of half-inch yellow star-shaped flowers. In the list that follows, I have indicated height, flower color, and flowering season, and the lowest minimum temperature at which the plant can survive.

S. acre, golden-carpet. Ht: to 12″. Fl: white, early summer. Hardy to −35° F.

S. brevifolium. Ht: 2″–3″. Fl: white, early summer. Hardy to −35° F.

S. confusum. Ht: 6″–8″. Fl: yellow, spring. Hardy to 10° F.

S. dasyphyllum. Ht: 2″. Fl: white with pink undersides, early summer. Hardy to 5° F. Magnificent mosslike plant with blue-gray leaves.

S. lineare. Ht: 6″–10″. Fl: yellow in early summer. Hardy to −35° F. I consider this variety to have the most beautiful flower of all the sedums.

S. oaxacanum. Ht: 6″–8″, fast spreading. Fl: yellow in profusion. Hardy to 5° F.

S.* x *rubrotinctum (often misnamed S. Christmas-cheer). Ht: 6″–8″. Fl: yellow, winter. Hardy to 10° F. A very easy sedum to grow; jelly bean leaves that are bronze brown in sun but green if grown in shade.

S. spathulifolium. Ht: 2″–3″. Fl: yellow in late spring. Hardy to −10° F.

The leaves are silvery and borne in rosettes.

S. spurium. Ht: 3″–4″. Fl: pink to purple in summer. Hardy to −35° F. Plants have 1-inch bronzy leaves; the cultivar 'Dragon's Blood' has rose-red flowers.

Sempervivum tectorum, hen and chickens. Z: 4–10. C: full sun; well-drained, sandy soil.
These charming plants form compact rosettes, from which flower stalks (pink) shoot up to a height of about 12 inches.

Shortia galaifolia, oconee-bells. Z: 4–8. Fl: white. Use under shrubs such as rhododendron.

Teucrium chamaedrys, germander. Z: 4–8.

Thymus, thyme. Z: 3–9.
Certain species of this aromatic herb form dense ground-covering mats, and two excellent ones make true lawn alternatives: *T. praecox* subspecies *arcticus* (serpyllum), commonly called creeping thyme or mother-of-thyme, and *T. pseudolanuginosus,* woolly thyme. They spread well, can be trod upon, and can be mowed. Both are low-growing (2–6 inches) and produce small flowers— purple for the creeping thyme species and pale pink for woolly thyme—from mid- to late summer. Creeping thyme has many cultivars, which offer a range of flower color. Woolly thyme forms a furry mat. Both species need full sun and until they are established should be watered regularly.

To use thyme as a grass substitute, space plants 6 to 10 inches apart and expect to pull weeds until the plants grow together. *T. vulgaris* can also be used.

Tiarella cordifolia, foam flower. Z: 3–8. C: partial shade to full shade in rich, humusy, acid soil.
Fluffs of cream-colored stars appear in late spring above mats of maplelike leaves.

Trillium erectum, wake robin. Z: 4–8. C: full shade; rich, humusy, well-drained, moist soil. Fl: maroon in early spring.

T. grandiflorum, wake robin. Z: 4–8. Ht: 15″. Fl: white in early spring. C: same as above.

Vaccinium angustifolium laerifolium, lowbush blueberry. Z: 4–8. Ht: 12″. C: rocky, acid soil; naturalizes well. Fl: pink flowers, followed by berries; attractive red foliage in the fall.

V. vitis-idaea minus, mountain cranberry. Z: 5–8. Ht: 12″.

Verbena bipinnatifida, verbena. Z: 2–7. Ht: 8″–12″.

V. prostrata 'Heavenly Blue', Harebell speedwell. Z: 5–8.

Veronica repens, creeping veronica. Z: 4–8.

Vinca minor, vinca, myrtle, or periwinkle. Z: 3–9.
This useful and almost indestructible ground cover thrives in partial or deep shade, and has long been popular in the United States. Thomas Jefferson used vinca in his gardens at Monticello, and it has had a place in American gardens ever since. The most familiar variety has deep, glossy evergreen foliage and produces lovely violet-blue flowers in early spring. It is easily divided at any time of year: simply dig up a clump, transplant it, and water well.

Viola, violets. Z: 6–10 by var.
To use violets as a ground cover, choose fragrant varieties that are only moderately invasive: *V. odorata* 'Royal Robe' (Z: 4–8), which resembles the florist's violet, or *V. odorata* 'White Czar' (Z: 4–8), which is very easy to grow and produces white flowers veined yellow and purple.

Waldsteinia fragarioides, barren strawberry.

Xanthorhiza simplicissima, yellowroot. Z: 4–8.

FERNS

Most ferns are shade-loving plants, but they will usually thrive under many different conditions. There are hundreds of fern species that will grow throughout this country. Seek individual types that grow in the woodlands where you live. With few exceptions, the plants listed below will tolerate the cold of northern zones, although plants that are evergreen in warm zones may behave as deciduous species in colder regions. Most ferns, if provided with enough moisture and appropriate shade, will also do well south of their minimum zone.

In early spring, the newly emerging ferns are known as "fiddleheads," so named because each curled frond resembles the neck end of a violin. The fiddleheads of many species are edible, but for every fiddlehead eaten, you will have one less frond in the garden that summer.

Adiantum pedatum, maidenhair fern. Z: 3. Ht: 18″–24″.
The fronds of this native species are borne in delicate diadems, with individual leaflets that resemble the fan-shaped leaves of the ginkgo tree. It is an exquisite plant for the moist woodland garden but does equally well in dry shade.

Asplenium bulbiferum, mother fern. Z: 8–10. Ht: to 48″.
Graceful, arching fern whose fronds produce plantlets at the ends which can be separated from the main plant and rooted or planted elsewhere. Grow mother ferns in heavy to medium shade; watch out for slugs in coastal California.

A. platyneuron, ebony spleenwort. Z: 4. Ht: to 15″.
This is another native species. Its stalks are purple and its leaves are about 3 inches across with attractively rounded leaflets.

Athyrium felix-femina, lady fern. Z: 3–9. Ht: to 36″.
This plant is popular and rightly so. Its large showy leaves, in a lovely shade of green, are deeply cut, giving a lacy appearance.

A. nipponicum 'Pictum', Japanese painted fern. Z: 6. Ht: 6″–18″ by var.
This elegant species has many forms, each with its own variegation, in combinations of silver, cream, purple, green, bluish, and gray. Silvery pink is especially lovely. These ferns like partial to full shade and make admirable ground covers. (May be sold under its old name, *A. goeringianum* 'Pictum' or *A. iseanum*.)

Cyrtomium falcatum, Japanese holly fern. Z: 10. Ht: to 30″.
This fern is easily cultivated outdoors in the milder temperate regions; its glossy leathery leaves are deep green. Cyrtomium resembles the shrub, *Mahonia*.

Cystopteris fragilis, bladder fern. Z: 3–7. Ht: to 12″.
Bright green, feathery fronds. This is a good choice for open shade in the woods or moist crevices in rock gardens.

Dennstaedtia punctilobula, hay-scented fern. Z: 3–8. Ht: to 24″.
This familiar native fern has fine feathery grass green fronds that are light as air. It likes poor soil (as long as there's moisture), forms large clumps, and spreads by rhizome as well as by spores. Although it has a tendency to be too vigorous, it is easily controlled by pulling and it makes a good ground cover. One of the most beautiful ferns, and easy to grow, hay-scented fern does equally well in sun, partial shade, or full shade. Named for smell of crushed fronds.

Dryopteris austriaca var. spinulosa (sometimes listed as *D. spinulosa*), spinulose or toothed wood fern. Z: 3. Ht: to 36″.
Choose this for a shady spot.

D. cristata, narrow swamp fern. Z: 3–7. Ht: 18″–30″.
This evergreen fern adds tall accents in areas of deep shade.

D. filix-mas, male fern. Z: 3–7. Ht: to 48″.
An almost evergreen fern except in the coldest regions, this will do well in dry shade, but is happier with some moisture. Its fronds are long and feathery and the plant forms a clump about 3 feet across.

D. ludoviciana, Florida shield fern. Z: 7–10. Ht: to 24″.
This fern is an evergreen in the warm zones.

D. marginalis, marginal shield fern or leather wood fern. Z: 3–8. Ht: to 30".

Matteuccia struthiopteris, ostrich plume fern. Z: 3–7. Ht: to 5'.
This is a bold semievergreen plant, easily transplanted from the wild and easily grown in the garden. Its long graceful fronds, usually 3-feet long, sometimes reach 5 feet. This species is not as erect as *M. pensylvanica,* another American native, that can grow from 6 to 9 feet under optimum conditions (semishade, cool, moist environment, and rich loamy soil).

Nephrolepsis exalta bostoniensis, Boston fern. Z: 9. Ht: to 24".
The familiar houseplant is grown outdoors in Florida, south Texas, and the far West.

Onoclea sensibilis, sensitive fern. Z: 3–9. Ht: 12"–24".
Thickly lobed sterile fronds grow in a variety of moist, sunny places.

Osmunda cinnamomea, cinnamon fern. Z: 4–9. Ht: to 5'.
This American native has a slightly different growth habit from other ferns: it produces both sterile and fertile leaves on the same plant, the fertile leaves becoming cinnamon brown as they mature. The fiddleheads that appear in the spring are edible. All Osmundas are tough plants; they transplant well from the wild and like open shade and moisture. This is one of the few ferns that can tolerate *full* sun as long as there is ample moisture.

O. claytoniana, interrupted fern. Z: 4. Ht: to 4'.
Spores concentrated on the central pinnae of this fern's fertile fronds give its leaves an "interrupted" look. The fiddleheads of this species are also edible.

O. regalis, royal fern. Z: 3–9. Ht: to 6'.
This stately fern is found around the world. It grows well in sun and is particularly attractive in the spring when the reddish brown fronds unfurl. Its love of moisture makes it a good candidate for the bog garden. Its tough fibrous roots are chopped up and used as a growing medium for orchids.

Phegopteris hexagonoptera, broad or southern beech fern. Z: 3–9. Ht: 12"–24".
An excellent fern on moist woodland slopes, the broad beech fern has triangular fronds that are almost as broad as they are long.

Phyllitis scolopendrium (sometimes listed as *Asplenium scolopendrium*), hart's-tongue fern. Z: 4 or 5. Ht: 18".
This is a European native that has been naturalized in the United States. Its leaves are straight or curved blades, about 3 inches wide; the leaf margins are sometimes wavy. The var. *americana* grows in zone 5 of the northeastern United States on limestone and there are several other cultivars, including dwarfs.

Polypodium virginianum, rock polypody or American wall fern. Z: 4–8. Ht: to 10".
This American native is excellent for rock gardens or "cliff" faces—garden walls or boulders with pockets of earth tucked in the cracks and crevices.

Polystichum acrostichoides, Christmas fern. Z: 4. Ht: to 24".
An evergreen fern with many cultivars from which to choose.

P. munitum, giant holly fern or Western sword fern. Z: 4–8. Ht: 24"–36".
This hardy evergreen fern of easy culture has leathery leaves.

P. setiferum, Alaska fern or hedge fern. Z: 4–8. Ht: 24".
A large and vigorous grower; there are many cultivars from which to choose.

Thelypteris noveboracensis, New York fern. Z: 3–8. Ht: 12"–24".
A familiar native with feathery fronds, the New York fern naturalizes easily in moist soil in partial shade.

Woodsia ilvensis, rusty cliff fern. Z: 2–8. Ht: 3"–6".
Perfect little fern for rock garden in open shade. The name comes from small rust-colored hairs on the underside of the blade.

W. obtusa, blunt-lobe cliff fern. Z: 3–9. Ht: 12".
Narrow light green leaves and small size make this cliff-dweller good for the rock garden. Grow it in open shade and neutral soil.

VINES

Twining vines need vertical supports to wrap around; climbing vines have rootlets or holdfasts with which they affix themselves to walls or fences; vines with tendrils need an occasional horizontal support around which the tendrils can wind. By understanding the way a particular vine grows, you can provide the proper support and site the plant in an optimum location. Don't try to change the direction of twining—you can't. If you are retying a stem, note the direction and duplicate.

Actinidia polygama, silver vine. Z: 4–9. Twining, left to right. Fl: white in early summer.
This is the most commonly grown member of this species. Its fragrant flowers are followed by berries that ripen to a yellow color in the fall, but the vine is grown primarily for its decorative silvery leaves. Other varieties and members of this genus are noted for their variegated leaves.

A. chinensis, kiwi. Z: 9–10. Twining, left to right. Edible fruit.
The tropical kiwi fruit is now widely found in northern greengrocers. The plant is quite easily grown in warm climates as long as it gets a very long frost-free season.

A. kolomikta. Z: 4–9. Twining, left to right. Fl: white in late spring.
A recent import from the Orient, this plant has incredible foliage; its leaves are purple when young, and then turn to variegated shades of pink, green, and white. The vine grows from 15 to 20 feet tall; flowers are small and borne in clusters, similar to *A. polygama.* Tolerates some shade.

Ampelopsis brevipedunculata, porcelain berry. Z: 4–9. Tendrils. Ornamental fruit.
This vine has handsome grapelike leaves; its flowers are inconspicuous, but in the fall countless berries appear that begin as pale lilac, turn yellow, become an incredible porcelain blue, then aubergine and black. This plant likes sun to partial shade and almost any soil.

It is a useful vine for fall color or for camouflaging a chain link fence.

Antigonon leptopus, coral vine, queen's-wreath, or rosa de montana. Z: 8–10. Tendrils.

Aristolochia durior, Dutchman's-pipe. Z: 5–8. Tendrils.
The flowers of this northeastern native are insignificant, but tropical species such as *A. grandiflora* have enormous spotted flowers. *A. durior* has huge overlapping shinglelike leaves that provide dense shade and, when in bloom, is a favorite food plant of many species of butterfly. It climbs to 30 feet.

Bignonia capreolata, cross vine. Z: 6–9. Tendrils. Fl: orange-red in late spring.
Because it needs room to sprawl, this vine is good over a stone wall in an Outer Area, perhaps along the edge of a meadow. It is completely covered with flowers in the late spring.

Bougainvillea spp. Z: 9–10.
Most of these South American plants can be grown outdoors only in areas that are truly free of frost. *B. glabra* 'Sanderana', is found around the Gulf of Mexico. In other areas, greenhouse growing is required for most of the year. The bougainvilleas produce paper-thin lanternlike bracts in all the colors of the rainbow but blue, even on a single plant. (*B. spectabilis* 'Texas Dawn').

Campsis radicans, trumpet creeper or trumpet vine. Z: 4–9. Rootlets. Fl: orange to scarlet in summer to fall.
One of my favorite vines, the trumpet vine blooms for a long period and is easy to grow. Large tubular orange to scarlet flowers, each 3 to 4 inches long, are borne in immense clusters. The compound leaves are bronzy green and dense. Trumpet vine has been grown since colonial times, and will hold tenaciously onto brick or stone or just about anything else. Keep this vine away from shrubs and trees, and spend the first season training it to grow in the direction you want it to. Don't be dismayed by lack of foliage at the beginning of the second season—it takes this plant a long time to leaf out each year. It also prefers poor soil; in rich

earth it produces luxuriant foliage at the expense of flowers.
Hybrids include *C. radicans* 'Flava', which has breathtaking yellow trumpets, is a bit refined in appearance, and is definitely a lure for butterflies, bees, and hummingbirds. *C. x tagliabuana* 'Mme Galen' (Z: 5–9) has apricot-tinged orange flowers that are profuse and long blooming, followed by attractive fall foliage. It is perfect for covering a dead tree or stump and is another favorite of the hummingbirds.
Another species to consider is *C. grandiflora* (Z: 7–9), the Chinese trumpet creeper. It blooms in late summer and has larger flowers than the native. Because it is somewhat less vigorous than *C. radicans* it may be a better choice for an Inner Area. It does not, however, have rootlets or holdfasts and so must be given support and helped along. Plant it beside *C. radicans* or *Bignonia capreolata*; they will give it all the support it needs, and it will extend the blooming season in a given area while widening the variety of leaves and flowers. These vines may send up new vines from roots and can be invasive.

Clematis spp. and cvs. Z: 5–7. Leaf stems act as tendrils in clinging to supports.
Clematis need neutral to slightly alkaline soil, and many must have good support until they are well established. Because not all of them are easy to grow, I recommend choosing from the least finicky of this genus. You will have to provide fertilizer: work bonemeal or manure into the soil around them once or twice a year and feed them regularly throughout the growing season with a high phosphorus fertilizer (5–10–5). A winter mulch of well-rotted manure is also useful. Because they are tendril-growers, they need a support that will allow the tendrils to hang on—just about anything will do, from a cyclone fence for the stronger varieties to a small shrub or tree for the hybrids that seldom make dangerously heavy growth.

C. armandii, an evergreen clematis (Z: 7–10), is often grown in California. It produces large white star-shaped flowers above deep glossy green foliage. The flowers appear on the previous year's growth, so prune (if at all)

only just after blooming. Because it is so attractive year-round, this is a good vine to train around a doorway.

C. paniculata (C. maximowicziana), autumn-flowering clematis (Z: 5–9), can climb to 30 feet but will stay neat and orderly when it covers the top of a low fence or a trellis. In late summer to early fall, 1-inch star-shaped, fragrant flowers completely cover the vine. It likes slightly alkaline soil and can be cut for bouquets, both fresh and dried.

C. tangutica, golden clematis (Z: 5–9), is from western China and provides a long season of interest. Its soft gray-green leaves are a perfect foil for its unusual, nodding, lanternlike yellow flowers. Later these turn into silver seed clusters, larger and almost as showy as the flowers, and described by Vita Sackville-West as "Yorkshire terriers curled into a ball." The plant tolerates a wide variety of soils.

C. virginiana, virgin's bower or woodbine (Z: 4–9), is our own American wildflower. Autumn blooming, this vigorous plant will run along the ground on the edge of the forest or cover an old stone wall. It tolerates shade and damp soils that would kill other members of the species.
Also look for *C. chrysocoma* (formerly *C. spooneri*), which flowers abundantly; *C. macropetala,* which has large petaled flowers somewhat like columbines, 2½ to 4 inches wide; *C. montana,* which produces late spring anemonelike flowers; and *C. lanuginosa,* the woolly leaved clematis, which has mauve flowers blushed blue all summer long. Cultivars of all these species offer a range of flower colors and sizes.

Euonymus fortunei, euonymus. Z: 4–9. Rootlets.
This is a very easy and attractive evergreen vine or ground cover. It needs only a bit of help getting established—give it some support for vertical growth until the rootlets can take hold. Its only drawback is a susceptibility to oyster shell scale, an insect that can be controlled with dormant oil spray (a safe spray, applied in the winter, that suffocates the insects). See Ground Covers.

Ficus pumila, creeping fig. Z: 9–10. Holdfasts.
This is a vigorous grower in the South. It may get off to a slow start, but don't be fooled. A single plant can cover an entire wall or even a five-story building! Although it is easy to control, it is perhaps best located where its rambling ways will not be a problem.

Gelsemium sempervirens, Carolina jessamine or evening trumpet flower. Z: 7–10. Twining.
This jasminelike plant produces fragrant 1-inch yellow flowers from late winter to early spring.

Hedera helix and cvs. English ivy. Z: 4–9. Rootlets.
This is the most familiar evergreen ivy in northern climes. It is a vigorous grower that will cling to just about anything, from old trees to brick walls to stucco. One of ivy's best features is a preference for shade, that makes it ideal for an east or north location where it will be lush and leafy year-round. If planted in the south or west, it may be subject to winter sun scald, which makes the leaves a bit less than perfectly evergreen. Cultivars offer a range of leaf forms—from large to tiny, and from dark glossy green to variegated, including some with golden mottling. A good cultivar for cold climates is '238th Street', which seems to be the most evergreen. In warm climates, try *H. canariensis* (Z: 7–10) and its cultivar 'Canary Cream', which has waxy 5-to-8-inch leaves, half green, half cream-colored. *H. colchica* 'Dentato-variegata' has huge leaves and is often seen in California.
If the ivies have a nemesis, it is red spider, which makes the leaves look pale and dusty. Treat by spraying with a strong jet of water or with a water-dish-detergent mixture (1 teaspoon to a quart of water). To prevent infestation, provide good air circulation and keep the soil moist. Ivies can also be attacked by scale; if so, treat as for euonymus. Also see Ground Covers.

Hydrangea anomala petiolaris, climbing hydrangea. Z: 4–8. Rootlets.
This is an excellent climbing woody vine. It may need some help in the beginning but once it catches on—usually the second season—it can climb from

60 to 80 feet. Its large glossy deep green leaves, somewhat heart shaped, give the vine an almost shrubby appearance. The stem bark exfoliates each fall, leaving it reddish brown and very attractive in winter. In early summer, fragrant flat umbels of white flowers bloom all over the plant. It is very versatile, looks sensational against a brick or stone wall and equally well on an old tree, reaching into leafless branches. It will be nearly trouble free, in either sun or partial shade.

Ipomoea alba, moon-flower. Z: 10 or grow as annual in the north. Twining.
This nocturnal bloomer is in the same genus as the morning-glory. Its enormous fragrant white tubular flowers open at dusk (in about ten minutes) and close the next morning just as the morning-glories begin to open. They make perfect companion plants. Because of the moon-flower's night-blooming habit, position it near the outdoor entertaining space in the Inner Area. This species is sometimes recognized as a member of a separate genera, *Calonyction,* and may be listed in catalogues under that name.

I. tricolor 'Heavenly Blue', morning-glory. Annual. Twining.
This annual morning-glory is an excellent vine to plant if you want to try one out for a single season in a given locale. Although there are other good cultivars (for example, 'Pearly gates' with 4½-inch white flowers; or 'Scarlet O'Hara' with red flowers), I consider 'Heavenly Blue' the star. Its beautiful flowers are abundant, and close by noon or even later if the location is very sunny. All morning-glories have very hard seeds. Some people recommend filing or nicking the corner of each seed before planting, but it is gentler and easier to cover the seeds with warm water and let them soak overnight. Also look for *I.* x *multifida,* the cardinal climber.

Jasminum, jasmine. Z: 6–10 by var.
Although usually tropical, these plants are easy to grow in the right zones, with many species, such as *J. polyanthum,* from which to choose. Most are leggy shrubs that sometimes twine and almost always need support. A few species will survive even as far north as Cleveland, such as *J. nudiflorum,* winter

jasmine. A graceful vine, it blooms early with a profusion of yellow flowers before the foliage appears. If sited in a sheltered entry garden in zone 6, it might even bloom in January or February. You will occasionally need to prune off wispy shoots or redirect them to trellis or wire supports, but otherwise the plant is quite trouble free.

J. mesnyi, the primrose jasmine (Z: 8–10), and *J. officinale,* poet's jasmine (Z: 7–10), are two other species whose range extends northward. *J. mesnyi* is a slow-growing evergreen; its long arching branches are covered with pale yellow flowers from late winter to early spring. They make an attractive cascade over rocks or dangle from arches and above doorways. *J. officinale* is semievergreen, bearing fragrant white flowers in the summer.

Lathyrus latifolius, perennial sweet pea. Z: 5–9. Tendrils.
Perennial sweet pea clambers over rocks or through a meadow or up a trellis. Pealike flowers bloom over a long season in pale to deep shades of pink. This plant will beautifully cover an unsightly fence.

Lonicera, honeysuckle. Twining right to left.
Although it would be foolhardy to plant Hall's honeysuckle, (*L. japonica* 'Halliana'), which is an uncontrollably invasive plant, it would be equally foolish to exclude all members of this genus from your garden. *L. hildebrandiana,* the giant Burmese honeysuckle, for example, is an excellent choice for zones 9 and 10 or, in other zones, for wintering in a greenhouse, if you have one, and summering outdoors (as I do). All summer, this plant produces 6–10-inch long, fragrant cream-colored flowers that slowly deepen to yellow-orange.
In the colder zones, there are many worthy honeysuckles: *L.* x *brownii* 'Dropmore Scarlett' (Z: 3–9) produces masses of brilliant red, tubular flowers from summer to fall. *L. sempervirens* 'Sulphurea' or 'Flava', (Z: 3–10), a cultivar of the trumpet or coral honeysuckle, has tubular yellow flowers and blooms intermittently throughout the season. *L.* x *heckrottii* (Z: 4–10) blooms with bright carmine buds that open into creamy yellow flowers from late spring

through late fall. *L. periclymenum* 'Serotina Florida' (Z: 5–9) is similar, with crimson buds and cream-colored flowers and red fruits, tolerates some shade. Both cultivars are compact. *L. henryi* (Z: 5–9) is an evergreen ground cover that can be trained up a chain link fence for an attractive windbreak.

Parthenocissus tricuspidata, Boston ivy. Z: 4–9. Tendrils with disks that act as holdfasts.
This fast-growing deciduous vine will quickly cover a building, obliterating all traces of architecture. It is tenacious but easy to control and virtually care-free, impervious to pests and pollution. It has wonderful fall color—oranges, reds, and coppery browns. If you want a more delicate vine for an entry garden wall, try *P. tricuspidata* 'Lowii', which is an exquisite miniature that must be seen close up. Its tiny shaggy lobed leaves grow tightly on a perfect miniature vine. Another, *P. tricuspidata* 'Veitchii', has a similar pattern of growth, but the young leaves are purple. This plant is said to cling to even the slickest surface, including glass.

P. quinquefolia, Virginia creeper (Z: 3–9), is a native vine that grows happily in woods or against a building, in sun or shade. Its compound leaves turn brilliant crimson in the fall, to alert birds to its blue-black berries.

Passiflora spp., passionflower. Z: 6–10 by species. Tendrils.
Although for the most part these are tropical plants, some, such as *P. incarnata,* wild passionflower or maypop, grow throughout the South. In fact, they are so widespread as to be practically ignored, despite being truly remarkable flowers. The less common blue form, *P. caerulea,* blue crown passionflower, is a Brazilian native whose flower is 4 inches across. Like *P. incarnata,* it is hardy as far north as Virginia. In California, *P. manicata,* red passionflower, is often used to cloak a building in bright red flowers. In zones 9 and 10 you can select from some magnificent kinds such as *P. x alatocaerulea, P. quadrangularis* and *P. incense.*

Polygonum aubertii, silver lace vine. Z: 4–9. Twining.
A very fast-growing, easy-to-grow vine that climbs an incredible 10–20 feet the first year it is planted. In summer it is covered with white flowers on long panicles. Because it self-sows, you may want to plant it where seedlings will not be a problem. Although it prefers sandy, well-drained soil and plenty of sun, it also grows under the worst city conditions—in poor soil and some shade—making it a good choice for a problem location.

Rosa banksiae, Lady Banks' rose. Z: 8 (7 if sheltered) – 10.
Climbing roses such as this one are extremely attractive and if you can provide the exact right location, you will find them relatively easy to care for. Before you invest in a number of plants, however, it is best to experiment with one and see how it does. In cold climates, there may be a great deal of die-back each winter, meaning that without extensive protection these plants will never grow more than about 4 feet tall. Lady Banks' rose is a good choice for a beginner in zones 8 and 9. Like all roses, it needs an open sunny location and fertile well-drained soil with a near neutral pH. Being a climber it also needs a support—trellis, fence, post, or arbor—and will look especially attractive growing around an arbor in an entry area. (Climbing roses are just shrubs with long, arching canes.) In early spring the Lady Banks' rose is abundantly covered with double, white flowers. One catalogue claimed that almost fifty thousand blossoms had been counted on a single plant. The plant is evergreen in the warmer zones, and like all climbers and other roses, it will need to be pruned from time to time, but less severely than other roses, just enough to keep it growing close to its supports. A yellow cultivar, *R. banksiae* 'Lutea', is also available, and there are other climbing rose varieties to look for: 'Blaze', with clusters of brilliant red flowers; 'New Dawn', a hardy plant with light pink, fragrant flowers, and 'Golden Showers', an old favorite with fragrant yellow flowers, to name just a few. *R. laevigata,* the Cherokee rose, actually from China, but naturalized in the South, is also a vigorous grower.

Trachelospermum jasminoides, Confederate or star jasmine. Z: 7 (if protected) or 8–10. Holdfast roots.

Waxy green lancelot foliage, a profusion of heavily scented flowers, and a long blooming season make this a good choice for an Inner Area in a southern or western garden.

Vitis labrusca 'Concord', Concord grape. See Edible Plants (vines).

Wisteria spp., wisteria. Z: 5–9.
Wisteria is very popular and extremely beautiful, with violet-blue (or white) flowers, but it is also an aggressive and potentially invasive vine. Grow it where it can be controlled, over a fence away from trees and house. Severe pruning after bloom will help contain the plant and promote flowering. Cutting back leggy shoots to 4 inches in August will also boost bloom. An old plant can be rejuvenated by root-pruning. Insert a spade into the soil in a circle about 18 inches from the trunk. *W. floribunda* is the Japanese wisteria. *W. sinensis* is the Chinese species. These species twine in opposite directions. *W. floribunda* has longer racemes (18″), which bloom when the plant is in full leaf. *W. sinensis* is not quite as hardy, but is a bit more vigorous, and its blooms precede emerging foliage.

WATER PLANTS

Water plants are divided into those that prefer to be grown in or underwater or at the water's edge and those that do well from the water's edge to the bogs and wet meadows; there is some overlapping of groups. Each entry will include a note on the optimum location and on culture where appropriate. The oxygenators, listed in the Underwater to the Water's Edge section, are plants that release oxygen into the water, thus performing an essential function in ponds and still pools, maintaining the balance and keeping the water clear. For the most part, they are grown for this service and are not ornamental. It is best to include four or five different types in still water to assure success.

UNDERWATER TO THE WATER'S EDGE

Alisma subcordatum, water plantain. Z: 6. Ht: to 36″.
Grown for its arrowhead-shaped veined

foliage, this plant likes the shallow edges of pond or pool.

Calla palustris, water arum. Z: 3–8. Ht: to 8″.
This creeping plant has 4-inch white flowers, followed by red berries, and likes shallow water at pondside.

Callitriche spp., water starworts. Oxygenator.
This plant flowers underwater but produces rosettes of leaves that float on the surface.

Colocasia esculenta, green taro. Z: 9–10. Ht: leaves to 42″. C: shallows of 3″–6″.
The foliage is a beautiful dark green; the tubers are edible—poi is made from them—and can be stored when the plant is dormant.

Cyperus alternifolius, umbrella palm. Z: 9–10. Ht: 3′–5′.
Grassy leaves grow in whorls. If grown in colder zones, this plant is easily wintered indoors in a tray of water.

C. haspans, dwarf papyrus. Z: 9–10. Ht: 24″–30″. C: water's edge.
This is a small version of the ancient Egyptian paper plant.

C. papyrus, papyrus. Z: 9–10. Ht: 8′–10′. C: edges to underwater up to 3′ deep.
The actual plant of ancient Egypt; produces beautiful tops on lofty stems.

Eichhornia crassipes, water hyacinth. Z: 10. C: underwater 1′ deep.
Lovely blue flowers on floating plants that are very easy to grow. Be warned, however, that this is a very invasive plant that has clogged waterways in parts of the Deep South. In fact, some companies will not ship them for this reason. But they are also very beautiful and, if contained and controlled, are welcome. Since they are killed by frost, they pose no problem in northern winter gardens. A small piece can be wintered indoors. If successfully carried over, the little cutting will become a flowering colony by midsummer in full sun. It has been discovered that water hyacinth can filter water—even filter out hazardous chemical wastes, and there have been some experiments with

them as miniature waste-treatment plants.

Eleocharis acicularis, spike rush. Z: 6–9. Ht: 8″–18″. C: shallows.
This plant will also grow in boggy places; it has grasslike or quill-like foliage that is distinctly spiky, at the end of which brown roundish flowers appear.

E. dulcis, Chinese water chestnut. Z: 7–10. Ht: to 36″. C: shallows.
Stems are cylindrical, tubers are edible.

Elodea canadensis (Anacharis), water weed or frog bit. Oxygenator. Z: 5.
This is a North American native that is often included in aquarium or tank plantings. The foliage is fernlike, growing in a bunch. Plants produce both male flowers, which at the time of pollination are released to float on the surface, and female flowers, which rise to the surface and submerge again once pollinated.

Equisetum hyemale, horsetail. Z: 3–9. Ht: to 48″. C: water's edge.
A unique prehistoric plant related to ferns, with segmented hollow stems at the top of which is a conelike spore-bearing structure. It grows wild throughout the country and is easily propagated by division. It is sometimes called scouring rush because its siliceous stems were sometimes used as scouring or polishing agents.

Gunnera manicata, gunnera. Z: 7–9. Ht: 14′. Enormous rhubarblike leaves grow by the water's edge. This colossus is popular as a water feature in England.

Hottonia palustris, water violet. Oxygenator.
A floating mat of leaves, above which rise pretty little 1-inch lilac flowers with yellow throats.

Hydrocleys nymphoides, water poppy. Z: 9–10. C: shallows.
Produces 2½-inch yellow poppylike flowers held above the foliage.

Iris spp.
There are many iris, native and imported, that can tolerate moist locations. Some even love having "wet

feet." Listed below are the species, but some among these have been hybridized into hundreds of colors, shapes, and forms. Hybrids' heights also vary considerably, making them good candidates for use in a staged arrangement. Select early, midseason, and late-blooming hybrids, and position tall ones in the back, shorter ones in front for season-long blooms. Some of the iris of wet meadows and bogs listed in group 2 will also tolerate the water's edge and even shallows.

I. cristata, crested dwarf iris. Z: 4–8. Ht: to 4″–6″. C: water's edge; partial shade.
This is a native iris with fragrant violet-blue or white flowers in spring. The blue flowers have a golden crest on the down-curved falls.

I. fulva, red iris. Z: 5–9. Ht: 1′–3′. C: water's edge to shallows; full sun to partial shade.
Small, delicate flowers bloom early to late spring. Narrow, grasslike foliage.

I. pseudacorus. See From Water's Edge to Bogs and Wet Meadows.

I. sibirica. See Perennials.

Isoetes spp., quillworts. Oxygenator.
These are related to ferns, having grasslike submerged foliage.

Myriophyllum spp., water milfoils. Oxygenator.
These produce tiny flowers and have feathery underwater foliage.

Nasturtium officinale, watercress. See Edible Plants.

Nelumbo lutea, American lotus. Z: 4. C: under 2′–3′ of water.
This is the native American lotus; its pale yellow flowers stand above the surface and appear in July in the North, earlier elsewhere, with the season of bloom lasting almost two months. Flowers are followed by the cuplike seedpods that stand erect above the matte leaves. The flat, round leaves are so resistant to water that rain rolls around the leaves and settles into a ball before the leaf nods and drops the rain to the pool. This is altogether an exotic-looking plant with many foreign

species and hybrids from which to choose; all lotuses need full sun for at least six hours a day. The lotus is familiar from Egyptian art and lore and the edible tuber is used in Chinese cooking, but the plants grown for flowers are too dear to sacrifice for eating. *Nelumbo nucifera* 'Miniature Momo Botan' is a smaller plant for little pools and the garden.

Nuphar spp., spatterdock, cow lily, or pond lily. Z: 5. C: underwater, 2'–3', or at the edge of slow-moving stream.

Nymphaea spp., water lily.
Water lilies are easy to grow if their cultural requirements are met. They need full sun and warm, even temperature water. For this reason, in the home environment, they do best in an unshaded pool of shallow water, that is, about 2 feet deep. They can be planted directly into the bottom of a natural or man-made pond, but more often they are potted and the pots sunk underwater. Young seedlings are introduced into the water only when the day and night temperatures are around 70°; lower temperatures will cause the new plants to go dormant and only slowly to become established. The soil should be rich in nutrients—for example, a mixture of three parts loam, one part well-rotted cow manure, and several ounces of a high phosphorus content fertilizer to encourage blooming; or a mix of two parts loam to one part "pond muck" from the pond bottom near the edge. (For more on potting and caring for water lilies, see Water In the Garden, pages 169–83.) In the warm zones of the country (zones 9–10), you can grow a wide assortment of tropical water lilies and leave them in the water year-round; in the North these same plants must be removed to a cool basement over the winter, more trouble than most Natural Gardeners care to give them. If you are in the colder zones, choose one of the following species of hardy water lilies, all of which can be left in place over the winter in zones 3 to 10.

N. gladstoniana, Gladstone.
This is a slightly fragrant, vigorous, and fertile grower. Its blossoms are 6 to 8 inches across and its floating leaves will cover an area about 12 feet in diameter.

N. x marliacea.
This name describes a group of hybrids that are hardy and vigorous growers, with large flowers that stand above the surface. 'Marliacea Albida' has fragrant pink-tinged white flowers, is a terrific bloomer, and makes a good choice for a small pond; 'Marliacea Carnea' produces fragrant, pink to rose colored blossoms; 'Marliacea Rosea' is similar to Carnea but the leaves when young are purplish before turning dark green.

N. odorata, fragrant water lily.
This is a large (3–5 inches across) white, fragrant lily. Its blooms open early in the day and close at night with each one lasting for about three days.
N. odorata var. *gigantea* has an even larger flower and is a more vigorous grower.

Nymphoides spp. In addition to those listed below, look for other commercially grown species.

N. cristata, water snowflake. Z: 6–10. C: floats in shallow water.
Produces tiny white flowers in abundance all summer.

N. geminata, yellow snowflake. Z: 6–10. C: floats in shallow water.
Produces tiny, brilliant yellow flowers in spring and summer and has attractive chocolate brown leaves with green veins.

N. indica, water snowflake. Z: 9. C: floats in shallow water.
Produces tiny white flowers above 8-inch leaves.

N. peltata, yellow floating-heart. Z: 6–9. C: shallows.
Has attractive green and maroon variegated leaves above which yellow flowers appear throughout the summer.

Pistia stratiotes, water lettuce or shell-flower. Z: 10. C: floats.
Produces lovely matte green little cabbagelike leaves in rosettes in still ponds throughout the tropics. It spreads by stolons and can overcrowd a pool unless controlled. Flowers are inconspicuous. Outside zone 10, use this plant as an annual. Unfortunately, water lettuce is very susceptible to aphids, but they can usually be dislodged with a

spray of water and in a pool stocked with fish will be quickly eaten.

Pontederia cordata, pickerel weed, pickerel rush. Z: 3–9. Ht: spikes to 30". C: shallows to water 12" deep.
Leaves are arrowhead-shaped, flowers are blue, appearing from spring to fall. A white variety is available.

Ranunculus flabellaris, water buttercup. Z: 4–9. Oxygenator.
Grows submersed or floating and has stalks of from one to seven yellow buttercup-type flowers.

Sagittaria latifolia, arrowhead. Z: 5–10. Ht: leaves to 20", flower stalks to 48". C: water's edge to 6" shallows.
Plant has beautiful foliage, with leaves shaped like arrowheads, and tall stalks of little white flowers in the summer. A Native American plant food, its tubers are edible.

S. sagittifolia (sometimes sold as *S. natans*), Old World arrowhead. Ht: 3"–6". C: water's edge.
This is a little grasslike plant with smaller flowers than *S. latifolia*. Planted along the margins of a pond, it will keep them weed free. There is a double-flowering variety 'Flore Pleno' that is sometimes sold as *S. japonica* 'Flore Pleno' (Z: 7–10) and has double blossoms spotted with purple and leaves to 20 inches.

Thalia dealbata, water canna. Z: 6–10. Ht: leaves 36"–48"; flowers to 72". C: water's edge or shallows.
Very tall purple flowers in summer. *T. geniculata* (Z: 9–10) grows 10 feet tall.

Typha angustifolia, narrow-leaved cattail. Z: 2–10. Ht: 7'–10'. C: water's edge to shallows. Very graceful.

T. latifolia, cattail. Z: 2–10. Ht: 7'–10'. C: water's edge to shallows.
This is the familiar wetland plant. It is a vigorous grower and may need to be restrained.

T. laxmannii, graceful cattail. Z: 3–10. Ht: 4'.

T. minima, dwarf cattail. Z: 5–9. Ht: 24".

Vallisneria americana, eel grass or water celery. Oxygenator. Stoloniferous growth habit, ribbonlike foliage; requires some movement in the water in order to grow—will not survive in stagnant pools.

FROM WATER'S EDGE TO BOGS AND WET MEADOWS

Many of the edge or shallows plants listed above will also be good plants for bogs or wet meadows, along with those listed below.

Acorus calamus, sweet flag. Z: 4–10. Ht: 30″. C: bog, shallows to 6″.
Has grasslike foliage that resembles iris and emits strong lemony aroma when crushed. The curious flower resembles a cattail and emerges from the side of a leaf stalk.

Arisaema spp., jack-in-the-pulpit. Z: 4–7. Ht: 1′–3′ by spp.
Familiar trifoliate leaves and hooded spathe endear this native to all gardeners and garden visitors. It is easy to grow by the waterside in partial shade.

Asclepias incarnata, swamp milkweed. See Perennials.

Astilbe. See Perennials.

Caltha palustris, marsh marigold or cowslip. Z: 3. Ht: 12″. C: moist, boggy places.
Attractive heart-shaped leaves, bright yellow flowers, and easy cultivation recommend this plant. There is a white variety as well as a double-flower cultivar 'Monstruosa' (sometimes sold as 'Plena').

Canna cvs., water canna. Z: 7–9. Ht: 48″. C: moist soil, wet meadows or water's edge.
Of easy cultivation, cannas produce very showy red flowers, or red with yellow spots. Treat as an annual in the North, or store plants indoors over winter.

Carex spp., sedge. See Grasses.

Clintonia borealis, bluebead or corn lily. Z: 5. Ht: to 18″. C: moist, shady woods.
Glossy green leaves and greenish yel-

low flowers that nod on the stalks; fruits are blue and beadlike, as one of the common names suggests.

Crinum americanum, bog lily or southern swamp crinum. Z: 8–10. Ht: to 24″. C: moist soil, water's edge.
The very beautiful flowers are fragrant, white, and lilylike, with long petals; they appear in summer. Annual in North or store indoors over winter.

Cyperus alternifolius, umbrella palm. Z: 9–10. Ht: 3′–5′. C: moist ground or water's edge.
Produces very attractive foliage in umbrellalike whorls atop the stems. For two centuries it has found a place in water gardens and indoors as pot plants.

Darlingtonia californica, California pitcher plant or cobra plant. Z: 8–9. Ht: to 30″. C: bogs, swamps, wet meadows.
A carnivorous plant native to the West; has interesting tubular leaves in a basal rosette and a nodding dark purple flower with yellow-green sepals that have purplish veins.

Eupatorium purpuream, Joe-Pye weed. Z: 3. Ht: 36″–48″. C: sunny wet meadows.
A perennial with purplish flowers in midsummer and leaves in whorls around the stem.

Filipendula vulgaris (sometimes listed as *F. hexapetala*) 'Flore Pleno'. Z: 4. Ht: to 36″. C: Wet meadow and prairie.
Fernlike foliage; white flowers frequently tinged red appear in late spring to summer. This cultivar has double flowers.

Gentiana asclepiadea, willow gentian. See Perennials.
Nearly all gentians enjoy wet meadow conditions. *G. andrewsii,* closed gentian, is especially showy with an unequalled blue color.

Heracleum sphondylium var. *montanum,* American cow parsnip. Z: 3. Ht: to 9′. C: wet meadows.
The large dark-green foliage adds a dramatic note to the garden. Flowers are white.

Hibiscus moscheutos, rose mallow. Z: 5. Ht: to 8′. C: wet meadow. See Perennials.
This is a shrublike herbaceous perennial that attains its full height from roots each year. Its showy flowers are 4 inches across, white with crimson centers, and appear in midsummer.

Hosta spp. C: moist shady places by water's edge. See Perennials.

Hymenocallis liriosme, spider lily. Z: 8–10. C: moist soil.
Produces large white, fragrant flowers from spring to summer. *H. narcissiflora,* Peruvian daffodil, is often available in specialty bulb catalogues.

Iris spp.
Irises are among the first perennials many gardeners think of when planning a water garden. Those listed here and in Underwater to the Water's Edge are showy plants of easy culture.

I. ensata, I. kaempferi, Japanese iris. Z: 5–9. Ht: 2′–3′. C: full sun, water's edge.
There are numerous cultivars that are called simply Japanese iris. The species and most cultivars have enormous, flat flowers in various iris colors from white, purple, violet, blue, red, and yellow, in combinations. Most bloom from early to midsummer.

I. laevigata. Z: 4. Ht: to 30″. C: water's edge, shallows.
This looks very much like the Japanese iris but it actually does better if it is grown in shallow water as it needs constant moisture.

I. prismatica, slender blue flag. Z: 5–8. Ht: 1′–3′. C: bogs, marshes, partial shade.
Grasslike foliage is topped by violet and yellow flowers in late spring to midsummer. This is a native found from Georgia to Nova Scotia.

I. pseudacorus, yellow flag, yellow water iris. Z: 4–9. Ht: 48″. C: wet meadows, bogs, water's edge, shallows, full sun.
This is one of the easiest of all plants to grow. Naturalized from garden escapees, it is likely to be the only yellow iris seen wild. It needs full sun but

tolerates a range of other conditions and is a perfect plant for the bog garden. There is a very floriferous double form *I. p.* 'Flora Plena' and a variegated hybrid.

I. versicolor, large blue flag. Z: 4–9. Ht: 2'–3'. C: waterside, bog or wet meadow; full to partial shade.
This plant is very much like a garden iris. Soft blue flowers on graceful foliage appear from early to midspring.

I. virginica, southern blue flag. Z: 6–9. Ht: 24"–36". C: bog, wet meadow. Color lilac to lavender to violet. Some varieties are white.

Lobelia cardinalis, cardinal flower. Z: 5–8. Ht: 36". C: wet meadow, sunny moist borders.
Brilliant red snapdragonlike flowers in late summer.

L. siphilitica, great blue lobelia. Z: 5–8. Ht: 36". C: wet meadow, sunny moist borders.
A blue-flowered lobelia.

Lysichiton americanum, bog arum, yellow skunk cabbage. Z: 5–8. Ht: to 3'.
Has incredible, exquisite yellow flower spathes up to 2 feet. As you might imagine, it is a native. *L. camtschatcense* is a Japanese species with white flowers.

Lythrum salicaria, purple loosestrife. See Perennials.

Malva alcea 'Fastigiata', marsh mallow. See Perennials.

Matteuccia struthiopteris, ostrich plume fern. See Ferns.

Primula japonica, Japanese primrose. See Perennials.

Sarracenia purpurea, common pitcher plant. Z: 3–9. Ht: 12". C: bogs.
This is the familiar version of the native pitcher plant, found in many parts of the country. Like its western counterpart, *Darlingtonia californica,* its distinctive maroon flowers, which appear in the spring, are nodding and its leaves are tubular in a basal rosette.

Symplocarpus foetidus, skunk cabbage.

Z: 3–8. Ht: leaves to 18" long and 12" wide. C: moist, shady location.
A purple-brown ground-hugging leaf form known as a spathe encloses a thick fleshy flower spike very early in the spring while ice still clings to the stream banks. Later the foliage is large and dramatic. Its common name comes from the skunklike smell of the leaves when crushed.

Trollius europaeus, globe flower. Z: 4–8. Ht: 2'. C: waterside.
Flowers are golden orbs reminiscent of full, bulbous buttercups.

Zantedeschia aethiopica, Calla lily, arum lily, lily-of-the-Nile. Z: 9–10. Ht: 18"–42" by var. C: waterside, wet meadows, and bogs.
Callas are very popular wetlands plants in coastal California. Huge white spathes surround yellow spadix.

EDIBLE PLANTS

In the Natural Garden, edible plants are included for their ornamental appeal and ease of culture, as well as for the contribution they make to the dining table. They are arranged below by plant type—trees, shrubs, perennials, annuals, bulbs, vines, and miscellaneous—rather than by food type.

TREES

Castanea mollissima, Chinese chestnut. Z: 5–9. Ht: 60'. D.
This chestnut tree is resistant to the chestnut blight fungus, hardy to −20° F., and will grow well in average soil, on the sandy and slightly acid side. A newly planted or grafted tree should begin to bear nuts two to three years after planting.

Diospyros virginiana, American persimmon. Z: 5–9. Ht: 30'–40'. D.
This is a drought-resistant persimmon that grows well in well-drained garden loam; the only species that is truly hardy to New England. It produces greenish yellow flowers in the spring. Similar in almost all respects is *D. kaka,* the oriental persimmon, which has yellowish white flowers and is slightly less hardy (Z: 6).

Eriobotrya japonica, loquat. See Evergreen Trees.

Feijoa sellowiana, pineapple guava. See Evergreen Trees.

Ficus carica 'Brown Turkey', fig. Z: 7–10. Ht: 7'–10'.
This dwarf variety of fig bears the most wonderful sweet fruit. It will grow well in medium rich to downright poor but well-drained soil. Hardy to Washington, D.C., it can be grown as far north as New York City and Long Island if planted against a south-facing wall. Other varieties will do well in protected areas in zone 7 and very well in zones 8 and 9, and cool parts of zone 10. Better known varieties tolerant of average garden conditions are: 'Blue Celeste', bronzy purple fruits with rosy center; 'Kadota', tough yellow-green skin, fruit used mostly for canning; 'Latterula', two-crop bearing "honey fig"; 'Mission' ('Black Mission'), purple-black fruit for warmer regions; 'Texas Everbearing', purple to brown fruit, strawberry-colored pulp, second best to 'Brown Turkey'.

Malus spp., apple. Z: 4–9. Ht: varies. D.
There are many varieties of apple from which to choose; try to narrow your choices to those that are disease and insect resistant, will require the least pampering and pruning, and will thrive in your climate. Commercially grown apples are sprayed eight to eleven times annually, from before spring flowering to late autumn dormancy. For this reason alone you might want to stay away from "supermarket" apple varieties— 'Red' and 'Golden' Delicious', for example—which are sold not because they're easy to grow, but because they are easy to ship and store over long periods. Besides, it is more fun to grow an unusual variety of apple that is not readily available. One of my favorite all-purpose apples is 'Red-Stayman-Winesap' (often just called winesap). Eaten when ripe, it is very crisp, sweet, and winelike, with a hint of tartness to my liking. The apple variety reported to be most disease and insect resistant is 'Liberty', an old favorite.

Any apple tree you choose, however, will need some protection from insects, the safest and most useful being the dormant oil spray. This is simply an oil that coats the tree, after the leaves fall, and smothers many predatory insects. Once the flower buds open in the spring, avoid any spray products because they will kill the pollinator insects along with the pests. Instead, try Safer's Insecticidal Soap formulated specifically for edible crops. Because many insects are attracted to the color red, I've found that any red ball, coated with a sticky substance, such as Tangle-foot or motor oil, will act as an insect lure and trap. (Throwing a net over the tree, and hanging shiny objects and/or tying bright ribbons among the branches will help to keep birds away but is quite extreme, to say the least.)

Apples are available in a range of sizes—standard, semidwarf, dwarf, and, sometimes, miniature. These are often all variations of the same cultivar, grafted to dwarfing root stock. Your selection depends on the space you have. Dwarf varieties usually bear at a younger age than standards. Catalogues will make recommendations for your landscape and will indicate the varieties that need another variety for pollination (see Source Guide, page 287–92).

Morus nigra, black mulberry. Z: 5–8. Ht: 15'–30'. D.
Plentiful berries as appealing to birds as humans make this a good choice for gardeners wanting to attract birds to the garden. While the mulberry is fairly tolerant of soil type, it will do best in good garden loam. This species produces the largest and juiciest berries, good for jams or jellies. The berries can stain walkways and paving, however; there are white-fruited varieties that might be better in the Inner Area.

Persea americana, avocado. Z: 9–10. Ht: to 60'. E.
Even those of us who have pot-grown avocado pits know of the ornamental appeal of these plants. Where they can be grown outdoors, they turn into beautiful specimens and bear those large edible fruits treasured by cooks everywhere.

Poncirus trifoliata, trifoliate orange. Z: 5, with protection, to 8. Ht: to 20'. D.
This citrus relative is easily hardy in zone 8 but will survive in protected locations as far north as Boston. It is heavily thorned and has a shrubby growth habit, making it useful as a security hedge. It can also be pruned up into a tree. It has beautiful 2-inch,

white flowers resembling large orange blossoms, shiny deep green leaves, and curious orangelike fruit. The fruits are sour but lend a tang to a summer drink and can also be used for marmalade.

Prunus spp. See Deciduous Trees. While many of the stone fruit trees are now grown strictly as ornamentals, you can still harvest crops from those listed here; there are shrubby species in the next section and many other varieties (including dwarfs) offered by the nurseries. In making your selection, look for disease and insect resistant plants.

P. cerasifera 'Newport', cherry plum. Z: 4–8. Ht: to 25'. D.
This tree has many good things to offer: white flowers, red leaves, and edible fruit.

P. dulcis, almond. Z: 6–9. Ht: 20'–30'. D.
The flowers, appearing in the spring are white or pink; nuts mature by fall. There are dwarf varieties available.

P. persica, peach (nectarine). Z: 4–9 by variety. Ht: about 14' by variety. D. Peach trees are easy to grow, but not too fruitful if left to their own devices. To have successful yields, trees must be pruned, otherwise they tend to flower and form fruits that fail to mature or that grow too heavy at branch ends and cause the branch to break. For information on growing and maintaining peach trees, consult *America's Garden Book* (see Bibliography) or another good garden reference book.

Although thought of as southern fruits, there are many cold-tolerant peach varieties such as 'Hale Haven'. 'Belle of Georgia', a white-fleshed variety, is easily hardy to New Jersey (Z: 6). White peaches are rarely available at markets because they bruise easily in shipping, but they are wonderfully aromatic, and have a very sweet taste, which you may only be able to experience by growing your own. Consider trying a freestone variety with white flesh. Almost all peaches are self-fruiting—one variety is all you need. However, different varieties ripen at different times, so planting several kinds will extend the season.

Punica granatum, pomegranate. Ht: 8',

by var. Fl: orange. Fr: red. Full sun to partial shade. Drought tolerant. Cultivars include sterile plants with beautiful double flowers and 'Nana', a dwarf with fruit. The best edible variety is 'Wonderful'.

Pyrus calleryana 'Bradford', Bradford callery pear. Z: 6–9. Ht: to 30'. D. An atractive, easy-care pear tree that is resistant to fire blight and makes a good street tree.

Ziziphus jujuba, Chinese date, jujube. Z: 6–10. Ht: 15'–30'. D.
Hardy north to western New York, with some protection, this tree is tolerant of heavy clay soil, alkaline and with poor drainage. The fruits are preserved, sometimes sweet pickled, and used in making confections.

SHRUBS

Carissa grandiflora, Natal plum. Z: 10 (hardy to 24° F.). Ht: 2'–18'. E.
This tree bears white flowers, sometimes continuously, twelve months of the year. Some growers consider this a shrub and treated as such it makes an attractive hedge. It is not particular about soil as long as it is well drained. The fruit is used in jelly making.

Laurus nobilis, sweet bay. Z: 8–10. Ht: 6' sometimes more. E.
This is a stately ornamental shrub, the leaves of which are used in flavoring stews, soups, roasts, and so on. It is a slow grower and makes an attractive pot plant in the colder zones.

Prunus japonica, Japanese bush cherry. Z: 3–6. Ht: 4'–8'. Fl: pink. D.
More shrub than tree, this cherry makes a good hedge and will thrive on a wide variety of soils.

P. maritima, beach plum. See Deciduous Shrubs. The fruits make a wonderful jelly.

P. tomentusa, Nanking cherry. Z: 3–6. Ht: 4'–8'. D.
Also a shrubby tree that is not particular about soil.

Ribes hirtellum, gooseberry. Z: 4. Ht: 3'–4'. D.
This is an attractive fountainlike shrub

when grown out in the open. The fruits are good for jams and preserves and when very ripe can be eaten fresh. They are flavorful for about three weeks once ripe. (*R. grossularia* includes varieties of European origin).

***Ribes* cvs.,** currants. Z: all, by variety. Ht: 2'–8'. D.
There are red, white, and black varieties of currant, many having very ornamental flowers. Some sales of currants (especially the black) are restricted because they are the alternate host plant of white pine blister rust.

Rubus idaeus, red raspberry. Z: all, by variety. Ht: 3'–6', by variety. D.
This is a difficult plant to categorize; it grows and spreads by means of long thorny canes that root when they arch and touch ground. It makes a good security hedge and is one of the easiest fruiting plants to grow. The wonderful flavor of the berries simply defies description. There are many cultivars that are virus free and produce gold or everbearing red fruits. 'Fall-Gold' is an excellent everbearer (one crop in early summer, another in late summer). It is small and practically thornless, with fruit borne on the ends of the canes, where they are easily harvested. Two other everbearers are 'Heritage' and 'Indian Summer'. The most familiar, traditional variety is 'Latham'.

Rosa rugosa, beach rose. See Deciduous Shrubs.

Vaccinium angustifolium, lowbush blueberry. See Ground Covers.

V. corymbosum, highbush blueberry. Z: all, by variety. Ht: 2'–6' by variety. D.
There are many cultivars of this native species; in making your choice, the only real stipulation is that more than one kind be planted to assure pollination and good fruiting. These plants love acid soil—require it in fact. Their roots are shallow and should be mulched in the fall with a layer of pine needles or other acid mulch.

PERENNIALS

Asparagus officinalis, asparagus. Z: 3–9. Ht: 5'.

This is a long-living perennial that provides delicious young shoots for the table, long associated with signs of early spring. Delicate ferny foliage develops on the stalks that are allowed to mature, as some must be to assure shoots for the next year. Once established, an asparagus plot will grow happily for decades; I once saw one in Connecticut that had been undisturbed for almost thirty-five years.

Chamaemelum nobile (Anthemis nobilis), garden chamomile. Z: 4–9. Ht: 3"–12" by var.
The plant makes a good flowering ground cover; it has tiny daisylike blooms, white with yellow center. The dried flowers are brewed into a tea that is said to soothe frayed nerves and prevent nightmares among other things.

Chrysanthemum x morifolium, chrysanthemum. Z: 4–8. Ht: 12"–36".
The petals are edible and can be shredded into salads or other dishes, or even used whole as a garnish.

Cynara scolymus, artichoke. Z: 8–9. Ht: 4'–5'.
This familiar culinary delight is also a beautiful thistle. It can be grown as an unflowering annual in cold climates, but in the warm zones it will produce enormous magenta flowers the second year. The immature flower heads are the artichokes of the marketplace.

Fragaria vesca, woodland strawberry. Z: 3–8. Ht: 6"–12".
A good ground cover plant, although it needs to be divided every three years or so. The flowers are white with yellow centers appearing in spring and summer and giving way quickly to the wonderful small strawberries that make this plant worth the extra effort in getting them started and keeping them going. The cultivars 'Alpine', 'Everbearing', and 'Perpetual' are said to have come from this species. Some varieties self-sow true.

Helianthus tuberosus, Jerusalem artichoke. Z: 2–9. Ht: 6'–10'.
As ornamentals, these mature into tall yellow sunflowers in the fall. The plant, however, grows from tubers that are delicious. When planting them, space them 18 inches apart in regular garden

soil; they can be invasive, a problem easily remedied by harvesting tubers for the table.

***Hemerocallis* spp.,** daylily. See Perennials. Flower buds can be stir-fried; petals shredded into salads.

***Mentha* spp.,** mint. Z: 4–10 by spp. or var. Ht: ½"–36" by spp. or var.
There are numerous mints; they make wonderful summer teas or add a leaf or two to a cup of hot tea or a tall summer drink. Mint jelly is a natural with lamb and other meats. If the plant has a drawback, it is that if it likes the conditions, it can be invasive. Grow it where this will not be a problem: between the walk and foundation, for example. Flowers, borne above the leaves, are white, purple, or lavender depending on species.

Origanum majorana, sweet marjoram. Z: 6–9. Ht: 2'.
Marjoram has a long history as a flavoring herb, known since ancient times. The leaves are used as a tea, the oil as a medicine, but most commonly it is as a flavoring agent in soups, stews, and other dishes that this herb is known. The flowers are small, white and lavender, and appear in the summer.

O. vulgare, oregano. Z: 3–9. Ht: 2'.
This is the wild oregano, a tough perennial that in hot dry conditions becomes even more peppery. It is dried and used as a strong flavoring herb in chilies, stews, tomato sauces, and so on. Spreading by rhizomes on dry rocky banks, it makes a good aromatic ground cover.

Rheum rhabarbarum, garden rhubarb. Z: 3–9. Ht: to 3'.
The leaves of this plant are truly enormous, and tropical looking. To me they conjure up pictures of a prehistoric rain forest. The greenish flower, really a cluster of flowers, is also an extraordinary curiosity, borne on a single tall hollow stalk from the middle of the clump of huge leaves. A single plant makes an interesting centerpiece among flowering perennials; new plants are easily started by division of the clump, and from pieces of the fleshy root. The stalks are picked when pink and young

and usually stewed into a pudding or pie filling; the leaves are poisonous. Other species of rhubarb have been known to have been used medicinally in China since 3000 B.C.

Rosmarinus officinalis, rosemary. Z: 8–10. Ht: 3″–15″ by var.
This is a very fragrant herb that makes a good ground cover or hedge. It produces blue flowers in spring, and is tolerant of harsh city conditions. In the kitchen, it is used as an herb and is excellent when used sparingly with chicken and other dishes.

Salvia officinalis, common sage. Z: 3. Ht: 12″–24″.
This is a sweet culinary herb that will persist for years once established. It is generally somewhat woody and shrub-like, with grayish green leaves and purple flowers that bloom in summer. It has long been used as a medicinal herb; in fact, its Latin name comes from the Latin word for salvation.

Taraxacum officinale, dandelion. Z: 3. Ht: 12″.
Yes, the lowly dandelion. It certainly deserves a place in my book; it's an undeniable easy-care plant, with a cheerful flower, and for children is even more enchanting when it goes to seed. As an edible ornamental, its leaves are harvested when the plant is young. Age bitters them, as age bitters so many other things. However, there are cultivated varieties of dandelion that have broader, thicker leaves and less bitterness than the wildling.

Thymus spp., thyme. Z: 5. Ht: 1″–12″ by var.
The low-growing thyme species such as *T. serpyllum* and varieties can be walked upon and mowed and in both cases the temporary disturbance will release their wonderful aroma. In the coldest parts of its range, thyme will need some protection during the winter making it less suitable as a ground cover but reasonable in the perennial or rock garden. *T. vulgaris* is the wild thyme of southern Europe and the most aromatic; *T.* x *citriodorus,* lemon-scented thyme, is a good kitchen herb that has a sharp lemon scent. It forms a compact clump in the garden. There are many other thymes to choose from.

ANNUALS

Abelmoschus esculentus, okra. Ht: 4′–6′.
Even if you have no taste for okra in your soup, and many people don't, the hibiscuslike flower which is yellow or yellow with a crimson eye, is lovely.

Beta vulgaris, Swiss chard, spinach beet. Ht: 12″–24″.
Rhubarb chard is a "green" that has brilliant red ribs and stalks and is most attractive. The leaves are harvested about two months after sowing.

Borago officinalis, borage. Ht: 18″–24″.
This drought-tolerant herb is easy to grow and produces pretty star-shaped flowers, 1½ inches across, that are pink as the buds open and become a bright blue. Leaves and flowers are edible and should be used fresh as they lose their flavor when dried. Young leaves can be added to salads, larger leaves can be treated like spinach. Try adding a leaf or two to iced drinks, and as you do think of this translation of an old Italian verse: "When talking of borage this much is clear, / That it warms the heart and it brings good cheer." In the mid-1600s the herbalist John Parkinson praised borage as a cure for sorrows; it has always been considered a plant that assures cheerfulness and because it is now known to stimulate the adrenal gland somewhat there may be some truth in this.

Brassica oleracea, kale. Ht: 6″–24″.
This dark green leafy vegetable likes rich fertile soil and is vulnerable to few pests unless you consider the occasional deer a pest. Ornamental kale, which comes in combinations of red and green and white, grows in a rosette and will remain colorful through the first snowfall. It makes a showy edging plant.

Cicorium intybus, chicory. Ht: 12″, trailing. (Biennial)
The leaves of this plant can be used as a salad green. The roots, dried, roasted and ground, can be a coffee substitute, blanched shoots provide endive, but if you allow chicory to winter over in the garden, it will bloom with blue flowers the following season.

Lactuca sativa, lettuce. Ht: 6″–12″.

Leaf varieties can be very useful and ornamental in cool weather. Red-leaved varieties such as 'Ruby,' 'Red Sails', 'Red Oakleaf', and others are very useful as edging plants.

Matricaria recutita, sweet false chamomile. Ht: 24″.
This is an annual variety of the perennial herb (see above, *Chamaemelum nobile*). It has tiny white and yellow daisylike blooms and makes a good ground cover.

Ocimum basilicum, sweet basil. Ht: 18″–24″.
This is the great pesto herb, and an essential complement to summer's tomatoes fresh from the vegetable garden, if you have one, from the farmer's market otherwise. It is in the mint family, is very easy to grow but can be bothered by some garden pests such as white fly and slugs. Because of recent interest, there are many new varieties—miniatures that form balls, tall ones that have purple leaves, and new flavors that mimic clove, licorice, and cinnamon.

Tetragonia tetragonioides, New Zealand spinach. Ht: 12″.
This green looks and tastes like spinach but is easier to grow, tolerating hotter temperatures.

Tropaeolum majus, garden nasturtium. Trails, spreading about 10′. (Acts as a perennial in zones 9–10.)
The plant's name derives from the Greek *tropaion* (shield), so called because the leaf shape is reminiscent of a kind of shield carried by ancient Greek warriors. As an ornamental, nasturtium is attractive on terraces or in borders; it blooms in late summer producing red flowers. The leaves can be added to salads and the green fruits can be pickled as a kind of caper substitute. There are cultivars available in other flower colors: mahogany, yellow, orange. Some will bloom in spring or earlier in the summer and later into the fall.

T. minus, dwarf nasturtium. Trails to about 12″.
This is a diminutive version of the above; it does not actually trail, but "scrambles" short distances.

BULBS

Allium schoenoprasum, garden chive. Ht: to 16″.

This is the littlest member of the onion family. It produces pretty little purple flowers in the spring and summer and of course delicious leaves that can be chopped into many dishes, from eggs in the morning to salads at night. The plants need moist, rich soil and sun. They are easy to grow but should be divided every three years or so and the soil refertilized.

A. tuberosum, garlic chive. Ht: 18″–24″.

Slightly larger than the garden chive, this plant bears beautiful white globe flower clusters from midsummer into fall. As ornamentals, *Allium* is very attractive in the rock garden.

Crocus sativus, saffron. Ht: 3″–4″.
The flower of this fall-blooming bulb is harvested for its female stigmas which are used in cooking and as a dye. It is grown commercially principally in Spain, and because the bright orange stigmas must be pulled individually, by hand, from each flower, not surprisingly this is one of the most expensive foodstuffs in the world—a pound of Valencia saffron can cost around $1,500. If you grow your own, you can harvest and dry the little threadlike stigmas. To use them, add a few to a little warm water, milk, or broth and allow to steep a few minutes and add to your recipe. This is the basic flavoring in Spanish paella, French bouillabaisse, Italian risotto, and East Indian pilaf.

VINES

Actinidia chinensis, kiwi. See Vines.

Humulus lupulus, hop. Z: 4–9. L: 15′–25′. Perennial.
The common name comes from the old English *hoppan,* meaning "to climb" and indeed this vine will wind clockwise round its support extending about 25 feet. There are male and female plants; while both flower, the female plants will produce the papery cones used in commercial beer-making. In the home garden, harvest the buds and new leaves both of which can be eaten after a light blanching to remove some of the bitterness. A few dried hops can be added to ordinary tea or to a glass of sherry for a healthful aperitif. Hops are thought to stimulate the appetite and aid in digestion.

H. japonicus 'Variegatus', variegated hop. L: 15′–25′. Treated as an annual.
This is the annual hop, a fast-growing vine that makes a good temporary screen on a fence or elsewhere.

Phaseolus vulgaris, scarlet runner bean. L: 6′. Annual.
This climbing vine is a pretty trellis cover; it blooms with beautiful red pea-like flowers and later produces edible snap beans that can be harvested when they are a scant 3 inches long. By picking the beans as they develop, you will not only have a good summer side dish but will also stimulate the vine to flower all season.

Phaseolus cultivars, beans. L: varied. Annual.
In addition to the scarlet runner bean *(P. vulgaris),* there are several other varieties of pole bean, which is a climbing string bean. Their vines have colorful flowers.

Pisum sativum, garden pea. L: varied. Annual.
Many varieties of garden pea have been in cultivation for centuries. Snap peas, the newest entry, are edible-pod peas similar to snow peas, only the pods are crisp, thick, and juicy. All the members of the pea family have pretty flowers white to pink to purple. Varieties include 'Sugar Snap' (the first and still the best, I think), 'Sugar Bon', 'Sugar Pop', 'Sugar Ann', and more. Improvements on the original usually mean earlier or longer production, stringless fruits, and/or changes in the vining habits to create bushy plants.

Vitis labrusca 'Concord', Concord grape. Z: 5–9. L: to 10′ each season. Woody perennial.
A reliable grape especially for the North where it was developed. It is a heavy bearer, good for a very sturdy arbor where it will provide ample shade or to grow over a split rail fence. The fallen fruits will stain tiles or flagstones, perhaps its only drawback, and unless it has plenty of good air circulation, it may be susceptible to fungus and mold, but less so than other grape varieties. Cut back the vine ends in late winter for heavier fruit production.

MISCELLANEOUS

Colocasia esculenta, green taro. See Water Plants.

Eleocharis dulcis, water chestnut. Z: 7–10. Ht: 1′–3′. Perennial.
A water plant that produces an edible corm that is a frequent ingredient in Chinese recipes.

Nasturtium officinale, watercress. Z: 4. Ht: 12″. Perennial.
A water plant that grows happily in the shallows of a running stream, or at least where there is moving water. This plant also thrives where there is a high lime content in the soil. The mature leaves can be picked and added to salads or into little watercress tea sandwiches.

Osmunda cinnamomea, cinnamon fern. See Ferns.

O. claytoniana, interrupted fern. See Ferns.

Opuntia ficus-indica, prickly pear. Z: 8–10. Ht: to 15′.
There are many, many opuntias, some are hardy as far north as Canada. This species is the one most often grown for fruit, although all have ornamental flowers and others have edible fruit. *O. ficus-indica* grows into a huge treelike shrub with masses of flat, spiny pads. Instead of spines, it has bristles that are much more irritating. I find dripping melted wax on the affected skin area, letting it cool, and peeling the wax off, is the best way to remove them.

Zizania aquatica, wild rice. Z: 4. Ht: 3′–10′. Perennial.
This aquatic grass grows in the shallows of streams of moving water.

SUGGESTED READING

There have been literally thousands of books written on various aspects of gardens and gardening, and every gardener has favorites. Those listed here are books that I have found to be consistently helpful. For others, consult the suppliers of garden literature (see Source Guide, pages 287–92).

Brooklyn Botanic Garden. Handbooks in the Plants & Gardens Series. New York: Brooklyn Botanic Garden. See especially, *Garden Structures: A Handbook of Ideas and Construction Plans* (no. 45, 1982); *Natural Gardening Handbook* (no. 77, 1984); *Handbook on Ground Covers and Vines* (no. 86, 1984); *Handbook on Rock Gardening* (no. 91, 1984); *Low-Maintenance Gardening: A Handbook* (no. 100, 1983); and *Water Gardening* (no. 106, 1985).

Brown, Lauren. *Grasses: An Identification Guide*. Boston: Houghton Mifflin, 1979.

Bush-Brown, James and Louise. *America's Garden Book*. Rev. ed. New York: Charles Scribner's Sons, 1980.

Church, Thomas D. *Gardens Are For People*. Reprint. New York: McGraw-Hill, 1983.

Cox, Jeff and Marilyn. *The Perennial Garden*. Emmaus, Pa.: Rodale Press, 1985.

Crockett, James Underwood, and Oliver E. Allen. *Wildflower Gardening*. Alexandria, Va.: Time-Life, 1977.

Diekelmann, John, and Robert Schuster. *Natural Landscaping: Designing with Native Plant Communities*. New York: McGraw-Hill, 1982.

Duffield, Mary Rose, and Warren D. Jones. *Plants for Dry Climates: How to Select, Grow and Enjoy*. Tucson: HP Books, 1981.

Fell, Derek. *Annuals: How to Select, Grow and Enjoy*. Tucson: HP Books, 1986.

Foley, Daniel J. *Ground Covers for Easier Gardening*. New York: Dover Publications, 1961.

Garland, Sarah. *The Complete Book of Herbs & Spices*. New York: Studio/Viking, 1979.

Gessert, Kate Rogers. *The Beautiful Food Garden Encyclopedia of Attractive Food Plants*. New York: Van Nostrand Reinhold, 1983.

Harpur, Pamela, and Frederick McGourty. *Perennials: How to Select, Grow & Enjoy*. Tucson: HP Books, 1985.

Hersey, Jean. *The Woman's Day Book of Wildflowers*. New York: Simon and Schuster, 1976.

Jekyll, Gertrude. *Wood and Garden*. Reprint. Woodbridge, England: Collector's Club, 1981.

Johnson, Hugh, and Paul Miles. *The Pocket Guide to Garden Plants*. New York: Simon and Schuster, 1981.

Kindilien, Dr. Carlin. *Natural Landscaping: An Energy-Saving Alternative*. Lyme, Conn.: Weathervane Books, 1977.

Llewellyn, Roddy. *Beautiful Backyards*. London: Ward Lock, 1985.

Loewer, H. Peter. *Growing and Decorating with Grasses*. New York: Walker and Co., 1977.

Matrin, Lauren. *The Wildflower Meadow Book*. Charlotte, N.C.: Fast & McMillan, 1986.

Niehaus, Theodore F. *A Field Guide to Pacific State Wildflowers*. Boston: Houghton Mifflin, 1976.

Poor, Janet Meakin, ed. *Trees*. Plants that Merit Attention, vol. 1. Portland, Oreg.: Timber Press/The Garden Club of America, 1981.

Reilly, Ann. *Park's Success with Seeds*. Greenwood, S.C.: Geo. W. Park Seed Co., 1978.

Rose, Graham. *The Low-Maintenance Garden*. New York: Studio/Viking, 1983.

Smith, Ken. *Western Home Landscaping*. Tucson: HP Books, 1978.

Smyser, Carol A. *Nature's Design: A Practical Guide to Natural Landscaping*. Emmaus, Pa.: Rodale Press, 1982.

Stevenson, Violet. *The Wild Garden: Making Natural Gardens Using Wild and Native Plants*. New York: Viking Penguin, 1985.

Sunset Western Garden Book. Menlo Park, Calif.: Lane Magazine & Book Co., 1973.

Taylor, Norman. *Taylor's Guide to Ground Covers, Vines & Grasses*. Boston: Houghton Mifflin, 1987.

Wilkinson, Elizabeth, and Margorie Henderson, eds. *The House of Boughs: A Sourcebook of Garden Designs, Structure and Supplies*. New York: Viking Penguin, 1985.

SOURCE GUIDE

PLANTS

When buying through catalogues, select companies located in your area or an area that has climatic conditions similar to yours. Their plants will have a head start on adjusting to your garden. The companies listed below are arranged by state, then alphabetically by company; their specialties are highlighted, but bear in mind that most companies offer other plants as well, and many also sell supplies and books. Some charge a small fee for their catalogue, although in many cases it is deducted from your first order. Write in advance for information, sending a self-addressed stamped envelope.

ARKANSAS

BOSTON MOUNTAIN NURSERIES
Route 2, Box 405-A
Mountainburg, AR 72946
Berry plants, grapevines, fruit trees

CALIFORNIA

CALIFORNIA EPI CENTER
1444 East Taylor Street
P. O. Box 1431
Vista, CA 92083
Orchid cactus, Christmas and Easter cactus, hoyas, succulents

CLYDE ROBIN SEED CO., INC.
25670 Nickel Place
Hayward, CA 94545
Good selection of meadow seeds for various regions around the country

ENDANGERED SPECIES
P. O. Box 1830
Tustin, CA 92680
Shrubs, succulents, bamboo, palms

GREENWOOD NURSERY
P. O. Box 1610
Goleta, CA 93116
Daylilies

HORTICA GARDENS
Don and Pauline Croxton, Owners
3641 Indian Creek Road,
P. O. Box 308
Placerville, CA 95667
Azaleas, Japanese maples, conifers

J. L. HUDSON SEEDSMAN
P. O. Box 1058
Redwood City, CA 94064
Grasses, rare heirloom herbs, flowers, vegetables

NUCCIO'S NURSERIES
3555 Chaney Trail
P.O. Box 6160
Altadena, CA 91001
Camelias, azaleas

ROSES OF YESTERDAY AND TODAY
802 Brown's Valley Road
Watsonville, CA 95076-0398
Antique roses

JIM & IRENE RUSS QUALITY PLANTS
Box 6450A
Igo, CA 96047
Hardy sempervivums, sedums

SHEPHERD'S GARDEN SEEDS
7389 West Zayante Road
Felton, CA 95018
European vegetables, edible flowers

SONOMA HORTICULTURAL NURSERY
3970 Azalea Avenue
Sebastopol, CA 95472
Rhododendrons, azaleas

STEWART ORCHIDS
3376 Foothill Road
P. O. Box 550
Carpinteria, CA 93013
Orchids, plant foods and fertilizers

VAN NESS WATER GARDENS
2460 North Euclid Avenue
Upland, CA 91786-1199
Water plants, grasses, supplies

VIREYA SPECIALTIES NURSERY
2701 Malcolm Avenue
Los Angeles, CA 90064
Warm-climate rhododendrons

COLORADO

COLORADO ALPINES INC.
P. O. Box 2708
Avon, CO 81620
Rocky Mountain wildflowers

CONNECTICUT

CATNIP ACRES HERB FARM
67-NG Christian Street
Oxford, CT 06483-1224
Herbs

COMSTOCK, FERRE & COMPANY
263 Main Street
Wethersfield, CT 06109
Vegetables, flowers, herbs

LOGEE'S GREENHOUSES
55 North Street
Danielson, CT 06239
Herbs, begonias, ferns, houseplants

JOEL W. SPINGARN
P. O. Box 782
Georgetown, CT 06829
Dwarf conifers, Japanese maples, rock garden rhododendrons

VAN ENGELEN INC.
Stillbrook Farm
Maple Street, 307-B
Litchfield, CT 06759
Spring bulbs

WHITE FLOWER FARM
Litchfield, CT 06759
Perennials, heathers, grasses, shrubs

FLORIDA

SALTER TREE FARM
Route 2, Box 1332
Madison, FL 32303
Native shrubs and trees

SLOCUM WATER GARDENS
1101 Cypress Gardens Road
Winter Haven, FL 33880
Water plants

GEORGIA

DAVID SLADE
101 County Line Road
Griffin, GA 30223
Succulents, cacti

H. G. HASTINGS
P. O. Box 4274
Atlanta, GA 30302
Fruit, nut trees, vegetables, old-fashioned favorites, southern varieties

PATRICK'S VINEYARD, ORCHARD NURSERY AND FARM MARKET
P. O. Box 992A
Tifton, GA 31794
Plants for the South

THOMASVILLE NURSERIES
P. O. Box 7
Thomasville, GA 31792
Daylilies, liriopes

IDAHO

HIGH ALTITUDE GARDENS
220 Lewis #8
P. O. Box 4238
Ketchum, ID 83340
Heirloom and gourmet vegetables, wildflowers, native grass, herbs

JACKLIN SEED COMPANY
West 5300 Jacklin Avenue
Post Falls, ID 83854
Wildflowers

NORTHPLAN SEED PRODUCERS
Silver & Gold Brand Seed
P. O. Box 9107
Moscow, ID 83843
Native and wild plants, vegetables

ILLINOIS

KLEHM NURSERY
Route 5, Box 197
South Barrington, IL 60010
European perennials, hosta, peonies, tree peonies, daylilies, iris

McCLURE & ZIMMERMAN, INC.
1422 West Thorndale Avenue
Chicago, IL 60660
Bulbs

MIDWEST WILDFLOWERS
Box 64
Rockton, IL 61072
Wildflower seeds; books

SHADY HILL GARDENS
821 Walnut Street
Batavia, IL 60510
Geraniums

WINDRIFT PRAIRIE SHOP
R. D. 2, N. Daysville Road
Oregon, IL 61061
*Native prairie grasses and forbs
(plants and seeds); prairie publications*

IOWA
DEGIORGI COMPANY, INC.
1409 3rd Street, Box 413
Council Bluffs, IA 51501
*Ornamentals, vegetables, Italian
varieties*

EARL MAY SEED & NURSERY
Co.
205 North Elm
Shenandoah, IA 51603
*Vegetables, flowers; garden sup-
plies*

SEED SAVERS EXCHANGE
RR 3, Box 239
Decorah, IA 52101
"Heritage" heirloom vegetables

SMITH NURSERY CO.
P. O. Box 515
Charles City, IA 50616
Evergreen shrubs

KANSAS
DEMONCHAUX COMPANY, INC.
827 North Kansas
Topeka, KS 66608
*Rare and imported vegetables and
herbs*

SHARP BROTHERS SEED CO.
P. O. Box 140
Healy, KS 67850
Native grasses

LOUISIANA
LOUISIANA NURSERY
Route 7, Box 43
Highway 182 South
Opelousas, LA 70570
*Magnolias, daylilies, Louisiana
iris, unusual plants*

MAINE
CONLEY'S GARDEN CENTER
145 Townsend Avenue
Boothbay Harbor, ME 04538
Wildflowers, ferns

DAYSTAR
R.F.D. 2, Box 250
Litchfield Hallowell Road in
West Gardiner
Litchfield, ME 04350
*Heathers, unusual dwarf shrubs,
trees and conifers, perennials*

JOHNNY'S SELECTED SEEDS
299 Foss Hill Road
Albion, ME 04910
*Short-season vegetable, flower, and
herb seeds; garden supplies and
books*

MARYLAND
KURT BLUEMEL INC.
2740 Greene Lane
Baldwin, MD 21013
*Ornamental grasses, bamboos,
sedges, rushes, ground covers*

CARROLL GARDENS
P. O. Box 310
444 East Main Street
Westminster, MD 21157
*Evergreens, trees, shrubs, roses,
vines, perennials, herbs, ground
covers*

FOXBOROUGH NURSERY
3611 Miller Road
Street, MD 21154
Dwarf evergreens, unusual trees

LILYPONS WATER GARDENS
6800 Lilypons Road
P. O. Box 10
Lilypons, MD 21717-0010
*Water plants and bog plants; sup-
plies for the water garden*

RAYNER BROTHERS, INC.
Mt. Hermon Road
P. O. Box 1617
Salisbury, MD 21801
*Virus-free berry plants, asparagus,
and grapevines, dwarf fruit and ev-
ergreens, brambles*

WICKLEIN'S AQUATIC FARM AND
NURSERY, INC.
1820 Cromwell Bridge Road
Baltimore, MD 21234
Aquatics

MASSACHUSETTS
COUNTRY GARDENS
74 South Road (Route 119)
Pepperell, MA 01463
Unusual perennials

PARADISE WATER GARDENS
14 May Street
Whitman, MA 02382
Ornamental grasses, aquatics

TRANQUIL LAKE NURSERY, INC.
45 River Street
Rehoboth, MA 02769
*Daylilies, Siberian and Japanese
iris*

WYRTTUN WARD
18 Beach Street
Middleboro, MA 02346
Wildflowers, herbs

MICHIGAN
DUTCH MOUNTAIN NURSERY
7984 North 48th Street, Route 1
Augusta, MI 49012
Native trees and shrubs

EMLONG NURSERIES
2671 West Marquette Woods
Road
Stevensville, MI 49127
Fruit trees

FAR NORTH GARDENS
16785 Harrison
Livonia, MI 48154
*Barnhaven primroses and rare
flower seed*

INTERNATIONAL GROWERS
EXCHANGE
P. O. Box 52248
Livonia, MI 48152-0248
*Grasses; rare plants from around
the world*

NEEDLEFAST EVERGREENS
4075 Hansen Road
Ludington, MI 49431
Evergreens, seeds, seedlings

OAKWOOD DAFFODILS
2330 West Bertrand
Niles, MI 49120
Novelty daffodils

REATH'S NURSERY
100 Central Boulevard
Vulcan, MI 49892
Peonies, daffodils

MINNESOTA
BUSSE GARDENS
Route 2, Box 238
Cokato, MN 55321
*Rare perennials; hosta, daylilies,
Siberian iris, peonies*

THE NEW PEONY FARM
Box 18105
St. Paul, MN 55118
Peonies

PRAIRIE RESTORATION, INC.
P. O. Box 327
Princeton, MN 55371
Prairie plants

RICE CREEK GARDENS
1315 66 Avenue, NE
Minneapolis, MN 55432
*Rock garden plants, wildflowers,
and dwarf conifers; garden books*

SHADY OAKS NURSERY
700 19th Avenue, N.E.
Dept. N.G.
Waseca, MN 56093
*Shade-tolerant plants: woodland
wildflowers, ferns, hosta, epimedium, perennials*

MISSOURI
COMANCHE ACRES IRIS GARDENS
Gower, MO 64454
Fancy iris

HERB GATHERING INC.
5742 Kenwood Avenue
Kansas City, MO 64110
*Herb and flower seeds for bouquet
and wreath arrangements; books,
herbal gifts including "Fresh Herbs
to Your Door"*

STARK BROTHERS NURSERIES
Highway 54W
Louisiana, MO 63353
*Fruit trees, nut and shade trees,
shrubs, grapevines and berry
plants; garden supplies*

GILBERT H. WILD & SON, INC.
787 Joplin Street
Sarcoxie, MO 64862-0338
Daylilies, peonies

MONTANA
VALLEY NURSERY
Box 4845
Helena, MT 59604
*Hardy trees and shrubs, new culti-
vars for cold climates*

NEBRASKA
HILDENBRANDT'S IRIS GARDENS
HC 84, Box 4
Lexington, NE 68850
Iris, peonies, poppies, hosta

HORIZON SEEDS, INC.
1600 Cornhusker Highway
P. O. Box 81823
Lincoln, NE 68501
*Native grass seed, selected wild-
flowers*

THE NATIONAL ARBOR DAY
FOUNDATION
100 Arbor Avenue
Nebraska City, NE 68410
Ornamental and fruit trees, shrubs

STOCK SEED FARMS, INC.
R.R. 1, Box 112
Murdock, NE 68003
Prairie wildflowers

NEW
HAMPSHIRE
OAK RIDGE NURSERIES
P. O. Box 182
East Kingston, NH 03827
*Native ferns, wildflowers, bog
plants*

NEW JERSEY

ASGROW
1740 East Oak Road
Vineland, NJ 08360
Vegetable seeds

THE CUMMINS GARDEN
22 Robertsville Road
Marlboro, NJ 07746
Deciduous and evergreen azaleas, dwarf rhododendron and conifers, Kalmias

DUTCH GARDENS INC.
P. O. Box 200, Dept. A58
Adelphia, NJ 07710
Bulbs

QUALITY DUTCH BULBS, INC.
P. O. Box 225, 50 Lake Drive
Hillsdale, NJ 07642
Bulbs for fall planting, spring flowering, bearded iris

THOMPSON & MORGAN
P. O. Box 100
Farmingdale, NJ 07727
Unusual vegetables, ornamental grasses, annuals, perennials

NEW MEXICO

PLANTS OF THE SOUTHWEST
1812 Second Street
Santa Fe, NM 87501
Unusual vegetables—ancient and modern; drought-tolerant southwestern trees, shrubs, and grasses

NEW YORK

AGWAY INC.
P. O. Box 4741
Syracuse, NY 13221
Vegetables, annuals; catalogue through Agway retail stores

BENTLEY SEED COMPANY
P. O. Box 38, Pearl Street
Cambridge, NY 12816
Meadow mixes, grass lawn seed

BOTANIC GARDEN SEED COMPANY
9 Wyckoff Street
Brooklyn, NY 11201
Wildflowers

CARLSON'S GARDENS
Box 305
South Salem, NY 10590
Rhododendrons, azaleas

FLOYD COVE NURSERY
11 Shipyard Lane
Setauket, NY 11733
Daylilies

HARRIS SEEDS HOME GARDEN CATALOGUE
3670 Buffalo Road
Rochester, NY 14626
Perennials (Dusty Miller 'Cirrus')

J. E. MILLER NURSERIES, INC.
5060 West Lake Road
Canandaigua, NY 14424
Fruit trees, berry plants

NEW YORK STATE FRUIT TESTING COOPERATIVE
North Street, P. O. Box 462
Geneva, NY 14456
Hybrid fruit plants for cold climates

ROSLYN NURSERY
Box 69
Roslyn, NY 11576
Rhododendrons, azaleas

SPRAINBROOK NURSERY
448 Underhill Road
Scarsdale, NY 10583
Trees, shrubs, perennials, woodland wildflowers, ferns; no mail order

STOKES SEEDS INC.
Box 548
Buffalo, NY 14240
Vegetables, flowers

VAN BOURGONDIEN BROTHERS
P. O. Box "A"
Babylon, NY 11702
Bulbs, perennials, wildflowers

NORTH CAROLINA

CARDINAL NURSERY
Route 1
State Road, NC 28676
Rhododendrons for rock garden and woodland

GARDENS OF THE BLUE RIDGE
Box 10
Pineola, NC 28662
Native regional trees, shrubs, and wildflowers

HOLBROOK FARM & NURSERY
Route 2, Box 223B
Fletcher, NC 28732
Hardy perennials, native wildflowers, selected trees and shrubs

NICHE GARDENS
Route 1, Box 290
Chapel Hill, NC 27514
Southeastern wildflowers

POWELL'S GARDENS
Route 2, Highway 70
Princeton, NC 27569
Perennials: iris, daylily, hosta; dwarf conifer

OHIO

GARDEN PLACE
6776 Heisley Road
P. O. Box 388
Mentor, OH 44061
Perennials, ground covers, grasses

GLECKLER SEEDMEN
Metamora, Ohio 43540
Unusual vegetables

MELLINGERS, INC.
2310 West South Range Rd.
North Lima, OH 44452
Unusual trees, shrubs, fruits, ornamental grasses

WILLIAM TRICKER, INC.
7125 Tanglewood Drive
Independence, OH 44131
Water lilies, bog plants, aquatic grasses

OREGON

CHEHALEM GARDENS
P. O. Box 693
Newberg, OR 97132
Siberian and spuria iris

COENOSIUM GARDENS
P.O. Box 487
Boung, OR 97009-0487
Dwarf conifers, unusual trees

FOREST FARM
990 Thetherow Road
Williams, OR 97544
Native plants, fruits, trees (conifer, eucalyptus)

GOSSLER FARMS NURSERY
1200 Weaver Road
Springfield, OR 97478-9663
Trees: magnolias, Stewartia, styrax, Hamamelis, carylopsis, and others

GREER GARDENS
1280 Goodpasture Island Road
Eugene, OR 97401
Rhododendrons, azaleas, Japanese maples, rare ornamentals

HALL RHODODENDRONS
1280 Quince Drive
Junction City, OR 97448
Rhododendrons, metal plant tags

JACKSON & PERKINS CO.
P. O. Box 02
Medford, OR 97501
Fruit trees, berry plants, vegetables, shrubs (roses), spring-flowering bulbs

NATURE'S GARDEN
Route 1, Box 488
Beaverton, OR 97007
Wildflowers, ferns, species perennials

NICHOLS GARDEN NURSERY
1192 North Pacific Highway
Albany, OR 97321
Herbs; hard-to-find seeds

OREGON BULB FARMS
14071 NE Arndt RD-C
Aurora, OR 97002
Lilies, bulbs

RUSSELL GRAHAM
4030 Eagle Crest Road, N.W.
Salem, OR 97304
Native plants, specialty bulbs, hardy perennials, ferns, cyclamen

SCHREINER'S GARDENS
3621 Quimby Road
Salem, OR 97303
Iris

SISKIYOU RARE PLANT NURSERY
2825 Cummings Road
Medford, OR 97501-1524
Rare alpines, dwarf plants

PENNSYLVANIA

APPALACHIAN GARDENS
Box 82
Waynesboro, PA 17268
Rare ornamentals: Anemone crinita, new dianthus species, galanthus 'Mighty Atom', gentiana triflora, primula tadedana, sternbergia sicula, and many others

APPALACHIAN WILDFLOWER NURSERY
Route 1, Box 275A
Reedsville, PA 17084
Wildflowers, trees, shrubs

THE BANANA TREE
715 Northampton Street
Easton, PA 18042
Rare tropical plants

W. ATLEE BURPEE SEED CO.
300 Park Avenue
Warminster, PA 18974
Seeds: vegetables, annuals, perennials; bulbs, fruit and berry plants, some fruit and nut trees; full range of garden supplies, tools, fertilizers, books, and more

MICHAEL A. AND JANET KRISTICK
155 Mockingbird Road
Wellsville, PA 17365
Dwarf and unusual conifers, Japanese maples

MUSSER FORESTS INC.
P. O. Box 340
Route 119 North
Indiana, PA 15701
Evergreen and hardwood tree seedlings

O. S. PRIDE NURSERIES
145 Weckerly Road
P. O. Box 1865
Butler, PA 16001
Hollies, azaleas, rhododendrons

STRATHMEYER FORESTS, INC.
255 Zeigler Road
Dover, PA 17315
Trees (in quantity)

TWILLEY SEED CO., INC.
P. O. Box 65
Trevose, PA 19047
*Vegetables, Professional Seed
Series*

VICK'S WILDGARDENS, INC.
Box 115
Gladwyne, PA 19035
Wildflowers, ferns

SOUTH CAROLINA

PARK SEED COMPANY INC.
Highway 254 North
Greenwood, SC 29647-0001
Seeds and plants: bulbs, lilies, vegetables, annuals, shrubs, perennials

WAYSIDE GARDENS
Highway 254, P. O. Box 1
Hodges, SC 29695-0001
Ornamental trees, shrubs, perennials, grasses, bulbs

WOODLANDERS, INC.
1128 Colleton Avenue
Aiken, SC 29801
Rare trees, shrubs, vines, perennials; southeastern natives a specialty

SOUTH DAKOTA

GURNEY SEED & NURSERY CO.
Yankton, SD 57079
Fruits, vegetables, bulbs, trees, shrubs; spring and fall catalogues

TENNESSEE

NATURAL GARDENS
113 Jaspar Lane
Oak Ridge, TN 37830
Well-established plants: wildflowers and perennials

TEXAS

AMERICAN DAYLILIES & PERENNIALS
P. O. Box 7008
The Woodlands, TX 77387
Daylilies, iris

BAMERT SEED COMPANY
Route 3, Box 1120
Muleshoe, TX 79347
Prairie grasses, forbs

LILYPONS
2900 Lilypons Road
P. O. Box 188
Brookshine, TX 77423-0188
Water plants, bog plants, supplies

UTAH

MOUNTAIN VALLEY SEEDS & NURSERY INC.
1798 N 1200 E
Logan, UT 84321
Short-season vegetables, fruits; tree wrap

VERMONT

VERMONT BEAN SEED COMPANY
Garden Lane
Bomoseen, VT 05732
Heirloom hard-to-find vegetables

THE VERMONT WILDFLOWER FARM
Route 7
Charlotte, VT 05445
Wildflower mixes (seeds only)

VIRGINIA

NICHOLL'S GARDENS
4724 Angus Drive
Gainesville, VA 22065
Unusual iris

ANDRE VIETTE FARM AND NURSERY
Route 1, Box 16
Fishersville, VA 22939

WASHINGTON

BEAR CREEK NURSERY
P. O. Box 411
Bear Creek Road
Northport, WA 99157
Hardy fruit and nut trees and shrubs

COLVOS CREEK FARM
Route 2, Box 176
Vashon, WA 98070
Rare trees and shrubs

HUGHES NURSERY
1305 Wynooche West
Montesano, WA 98563
Japanese maples, dwarf conifers

LAMB NURSERIES
East 101 Sharp Avenue
Spokane, WA 99202
Hardy perennials, rock garden plants

REX BULB FARMS
Nethalie Shaver
P. O. Box 774
Port Townsend, WA 98368
Lily bulbs, dahlias, freesia, tulips, iris

WISCONSIN

HAUSER'S SUPERIOR VIEW FARM
Route 1, Box 199
Bayfield, WI 54814
Field-grown perennials and biennials

HIGH MEADOW FARM
3188 Highway P
Mt. Horeb, WI 53572
Wild edible plants; local ecotypes of native wildflowers, grasses, and shrubs; no mail order

LITTLE VALLEY FARM
R.R. 1, Box 287
Richland Center, WI 53581
Woodland, wetland, and prairie plants; books and seed

PRAIRIE NURSERY
P. O. Box 365
32-91 Dyke Avenue
Westfield, WI 53964
Prairie grasses and wildflowers, plants/seeds; garden design service

PRAIRIE RIDGE NURSERY/CRM ECOSYSTEMS
9738 Overland Road
Mt. Horeb, WI 53572
Native seed and plants for woodland, wetland, and prairie; consultation/restoration services

PRAIRIE SEED SOURCE
P. O. Box 83
North Lake, WI 53064
Prairie plants (regional native seeds)

STRAND NURSERY COMPANY
Route 3, Box 187
Osceola, WI 54020
Wildflowers, ferns

WILDLIFE NURSERIES
P. O. Box 2724
Oshkosh, WI 54903
Water plants, wild rice, annuals

WYOMING

ETHERIDGE SEED FARMS
2028 Lane 11
Powell, WY 82435
Grasses

OTHER COUNTRIES

CANADA

ALBERTA NURSERIES & SEEDS LTD.
P. O. Box 20
Bowden, Alberta
Canada TOM OKO
Short-season vegetables, flowers

C. A. CRUIKSHANK, INC.
1015 Mt. Pleasant Road
Toronto M4P 2MI
Ontario, Canada
Herb and perennial seeds, bulbs, hybrid peonies, oriental poppies

WOODLAND NURSERIES
2151 Camilla Road
Mississauga, Ontario
Canada L5A 2K1
Small trees, shrubs, rhododendrons, azaleas; Choice Ornamentals for all Seasons ($3.50 each)

HOLLAND

DUTCH GARDENS, INC.
P. O. Box 30
2160 AA Lisse, Holland
Bulbs

FRANS ROOZEN B.V.
Vogelenzangseweg 49
2114 BB Vogelenzang, Holland
Bulbs

GARDEN HARDWARE, STRUCTURES

If you are ordering something large or heavy—a pool or Rototiller for example—it might be a good idea to buy from a company close to you to keep shipping costs down. Otherwise, location makes little difference, and entries are listed alphabetically. Be sure to send a self-addressed envelope when inquiring about catalogues or a company's stock. In addition to the companies listed here, many of those listed above under Plants also sell supplies and tools.

AMDEGA
Amdega Centre
160 Friendship Road
Cranbury, NJ 08512
Conservatories

BROOKLYN BOTANIC GARDEN
1000 Washington Avenue
Brooklyn, NY 11225
Supplies, gifts, books

BROOKSTONE COMPANY
127 Vose Farm Road
Peterborough, NH 03449
Hard-to-find tools

CHARLEY'S GREENHOUSE SUPPLY
1569 Memorial Highway
Mount Vernon, WA 98273
Gardening and greenhouse supplies

THE CLAPPER COMPANY
1121 Washington Street
West Newton, MA 02165
Garden cart, tools, teak furniture

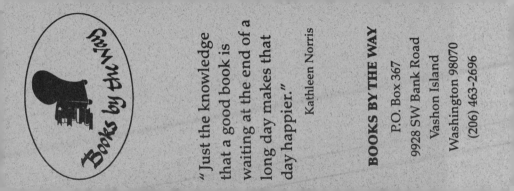

Books by the Way

"Just the knowledge
that a good book is
waiting at the end of a
long day makes that
day happier."

Kathleen Norris

BOOKS BY THE WAY

P.O. Box 367

9928 SW Bank Road

Vashon Island

Washington 98070

(206) 463-2696

J. COLLARD FINE GARDEN ACCESSORIES
P. O. Box 40098
Long Beach, CA 90804-6098

COLONIAL GARDEN PRODUCTS
P. O. Box 371008
El Paso, TX 79937

DALEN PRODUCTS, INC.
11110 Gilbert Drive
Knoxville, TN 37932
Scarecrows, cold frames, garden supplies

DALTON PAVILIONS, INC.
7260-68 Oakley Street
Philadelphia, PA 19111
Gazebos

DAVID KAY GIFTS FOR HOME AND GARDEN
4509 Taylor Lane
Cleveland, OH 44128
Garden cart, tools, accessories, decorative pieces

FULLER BRUSH CATALOG
P. O. Box 1010
Rural Hall, NC 27098-1010
Tools, watering devices, furniture

GARDEN AMERICA CORP.
P. O. Box A
Carson City, NV 89702
Sprinkler systems

GARDEN CONCEPTS COLLECTION
4646 Poplar Avenue, Suite 202
Memphis, TN 38124-1233
Gazebos, bridges, pergolas, arbors, gates, lights, planters, painted wood furniture, trelliswork

GARDENER'S EDEN
100 N. Point Street
San Francisco, CA 94120
Tools, garden accessories

GARDENER'S SUPPLY CO.
128 Intervale Road
Burlington, VT 05401
Garden cart, tools, innovative accessories

HERMITAGE GARDENS
Russell A. Rielle
West of Canastota, NY 13032
Fiberglass garden pools and waterwheels, waterfalls, lights

JANCO GREENHOUSES AND GLASS STRUCTURES
Dept. NG-PR, 9390 Davis Avenue
Laurel, MD 20707
Greenhouses and supplies

JOAN COOK
P. O. Box 21628
Ft. Lauderdale, FL 38335
Planters, outdoor furniture

KINSMAN COMPANY
River Road, Dept. 625
Point Pleasant, PA 18950
Arches and arbor forms, birdhouses, feeders, watering cans, planters

LEHIGH PORTLAND CEMENT COMPANY
718 Hamilton Mall
Allentown, PA 18105
Masonry cements in white and colors

A. M. LEONARD, INC.
6665 Spiker Road
Piqua, OH 45356-0816
Tools, supplies

LILYPONS WATER GARDENS
6800 Lilypons Road
P. O. Box 10
Lilypons, MD 21717-0010
-and-
2900 Lilypons Road
P. O. Box 188
Brookshire, TX 77423-0188
Fiberglass pools, PVC pool liners, pumps, fountains, supplies, books, plants, fancy goldfish and koi

MRS. MACGREGOR'S GARDEN SHOP
4801 1st Street N
Arlington, VA 22203
Tools

MACHIN DESIGNS (USA) INC.
652 Glenbrook Rd.
Stamford, CT 06906
Landscape buildings

THE NATURAL GARDENING CO.
27-C Rutherford Ave.
San Anselmo, CA 94960
Tools and Products

PLOW AND HEARTH
560 Main Street
Madison, VA 22727
Tools, insect catchers, furniture

RAIN BIRD
145 N. Grand Avenue
Glendora, CA 91740
Watering equipment

SMITH & HAWKEN
25 Corte Madera
Mill Valley, CA 94941
Tools, books, garden supplies, furniture

SOUTHEASTERN WOOD PRODUCTS
P. O. Box 113
Griffin, GA 30224
Inexpensive roll fencing

VIXEN HILL GAZEBOS
Main Street
Elverson, PA 19520
Gazebos, video on gazebo assembly ($10)

WALT NICKE COMPANY
Box 443, McLeod Lane
Topsfield, MA 01983
Imported garden tools and specialties

WAVECREST NURSERY AND LANDSCAPING CO.
2509 Lakeshore Drive
Fennville, MI 49804
Supplies, gifts, bird food, rare and unusual trees and shrubs

WOODFORM INC.
9705 N.E. Colfax Street
Portland, OR 97220
"WoodForm" lighting

FURNITURE

ADAM YORK
Unique Merchandise Mart
Building 6
Hanover, PA 17333
Some outdoor furnishings, birdhouses, clothing

AMISH COUNTRY COLLECTION
R. D. 5, Sunset Valley
New Castle, PA 16105
Wood reproduction garden furniture

COUNTRY CASUAL
17317 Germantown Road
Germantown, MD 20874-2999
Wooden garden furniture: Petite Lutyens, Chippendale II, teak swing

THE CRATE & BARREL
P. O. Box 3057
Northbrook, IL 60065

CYPRESS STREET CENTER
350 Cypress Street
Fort Bragg, CA 95437
Redwood furniture

MARION TRAVIS
P. O. Box 292
Statesville, NC 28677
Redwood porch swing

MOULTRIE MANUFACTURING COMPANY
P.O. Drawer 1179
Route 5, Quitman Highway
Moultrie, GA 31768
Wrought iron and other garden furniture, urns, fountains, plaques

WAVE HILL
675 West 252nd Street
Bronx, NY 10471
Lawn chair based on 1918 design by Gerrit Reitveld

WILLSBORO WOOD PRODUCTS
Box 336
Willsboro, NY 12996
Cedar rocking chair

BOOKS, SUPPLIES, SOURCES

ANTIQUE AND RARE FIELD, GARDEN AND FLOWER BOOK CATALOGUE
Elisabeth Woodburn
Booknoll Farm
Hopewell, NJ 08525

BIO-INTEGRAL RESOURCE CENTER
P. O. Box 7414
Berkeley, CA 94707
Information on environmentally sound pest control

CAPABILITY'S BOOKS
Highway 46, Box G13
Deer Park, WI 54007

CAPE COD WORM FARM
30 Center Avenue
Buzzards Bay, MA 02532
Red worms for soil improvements
CKG FARMS
Route 1, Box 176C
Simms, TX 75574
Organic blood and feather meal

DOWN TO EARTH
50 E. 11th St.
Eugene, OR 97402
Bat guano 2-8-1

GARDEN BOOK CLUB
250 West 57th Street
New York, NY 10107

GUANO UNLIMITED COMPOST COMPANY
Box 759
Sparks, MD 21152
Organic fertilizers, especially bat guano, sea bird guano

HEESE COMPANY, INC.
Dept. RG 7, 380 N. Holmes
Idaho Falls, ID 83401
Liquid Compost Plus™ complete natural biological garden fertilization program

HOME GARDENERS VIDEO CATALOG
One Up Productions
P. O. Box 410777
San Francisco, CA 94141
Garden videotapes

HORTUS CATALOG
Timber Press
9999 S. W. Wilshire
Portland, OR 97225
Garden books

Inversand Co.
P. O. Box 45
Clayton, NJ 08312
New Jersey green sand

Kenneth Lynch & Sons, Inc.
Box 488
Wilton, CT 06897
Sculpture; The Book of Garden Ornament

Mother Nature's
Box 1055
Avon, CT 06001
Worm castings

National Coalition Against the Misuse of Pesticides
530 Seventh Street SE
Washington, DC 20003
Membership: $10; advice on nontoxic pesticides

Natural Gardening Research Center
Highway 48, P.O. Box 149
Sunman, IN 47401
Insect/disease/pest controls

Necessary Trading Company
665 Main Street
New Castle, VA 24127
Natural farm and garden supplies, including fertilizers, foliars, and pest/disease controls

Nursery Man Organic Soil
2442 N.W. Market Street
Suite 308
Seattle, WA 98107

Plantjoy
3562 E. 80th Street
Cleveland, OH 44105
Fertilizers, bat guano, castings, and other specialties

Reuter Laboratories, Inc.
8450 Natural Way
Manassas Park, VA 22111
Pesticides, supplies for golf courses, maintenance services, interior plantscapes

Ringer Corporation
9959 Valley View Road
Eden Prairie, MN 55344
Organic supplies, biological insect control

Southern Statuary & Stone
3401 Fifth Avenue
South Birmingham, AL 35222
Sculpture

Timothy Mawson
New Preston, CT 06777
Rare English and antique garden books

STATE SOIL TESTING LABORATORIES

In most cases, laboratories test samples of soil for state residents only. Often, they require that samples be submitted through a Cooperative Extension Service agent. There may be a handling or testing fee. Be sure to send a self-addressed, stamped envelope. If your state is not listed, you can locate a laboratory through a Cooperative Extension agent or garden center.

Soil Testing Laboratory
Auburn University
Department of Botany and Microbiology
Auburn, AL 36849

Plant & Soil Analysis
University of Alaska
Agriculture and Forestry Expt. Stn.
533 East Fireweed
Palmer, AK 99645

Cooperative Extension Service
University of Arizona
Tucson, AZ 85721

University of Arkansas Soil Testing Laboratory
(Submissions through County Extension Service Offices in each Arkansas county seat.)

Soil Testing Laboratory
Colorado State University
Fort Collins, CO 80523

Soil Testing Laboratory
Box U-102
University of Connecticut
2019 Hillside Road
Storrs, CT 06268

Soil Testing Laboratory
College of Agricultural Sciences
University of Delaware
Newark, DE 19717-1303

IFAS Soil Testing Laboratory
Wallace Building #631
University of Florida
Gainesville, FL 32618

Soil Testing and Plant Analysis Laboratory
2400 College Station Road
Athens, GA 30605

Analytic Services Laboratory
Room 68,
College of Agriculture
University of Idaho
Moscow, ID 83843

T. R. Peck, Extension Specialist—Soils
N-121 Turner Hall
1102 S. Goodwin Avenue
Urbana, IL 61801

Plant & Soil Analysis Laboratory
Agronomy Department
Purdue University
West Lafayette, IN 47907

Iowa State University Soil Testing Laboratory
G405 Agronomy
Iowa State University
Ames, IA 50011

Soil Testing Laboratory
University of Kentucky
Division of Regulatory Services
Lexington, KY 40546

LSU Soil Testing Laboratory
Agronomy Department
104 Sturgis Hall
Louisiana State University
Baton Route, LA 70803

Maine Soil Testing Service
25 Deering Hall
University of Maine
Orono, ME 04469

Soil Testing Laboratory
Michigan State University
East Lansing, MI 48824

Soil Testing Laboratory
University of Minnesota
1903 Hendon Avenue
St. Paul, MN 55108

Soil Testing Laboratory
Mississippi Cooperative
Extension Service
P. O. Box 5446
Mississippi State, MS 39762

University of Missouri
Soil Testing Laboratory
27 Mumford Hall
Columbia, MO 65211

Analytical Services Laboratory
Nesmith Hall
University of New Hampshire
Durham, NH 03824

Rutgers Soil Testing Laboratory
Lipman Hall Annex
P. O. Box 231—Cook College
New Brunswick, NJ 08903

Soil, Water, and Plant Testing Laboratory
Agronomy and Horticulture, Dept. 3Q
Box 30003, NMSU
Las Cruces, NM 88003-0003

Cornell Nutrient Analysis Laboratory
804 Bradfield Hall
Cornell University
Ithaca, NY 14853

Agronomic Division
North Carolina Department of Agriculture
Blue Ridge Road Center
Raleigh, NC 27611

Soil Testing Laboratory
Waldron Hall
North Dakota State University
Fargo, ND 58105

Research-Extension Analytical Laboratory
O. A. R. D. C.
Wooster, OH 43210

Soil Testing Laboratory
Oregon State University
Corvallis, OR 97333

Merkle Laboratory
Pennsylvania State University
University Park, PA 16802

Agricultural Service Lab
Clemson University
Cherry Road
Clemson, SC 29634-0391

Soil Testing Laboratory
South Dakota State University
Box 2207-A
Brookings, SD 57007-1096

Plant, Soil, and Water Analysis Laboratory
Utah State University
Logan, UT 84322-4830

University of Vermont
Agricultural Testing Laboratory
Morrill Hall
Burlington, VT 05405

Virginia Tech Soil Testing Laboratory
145 Smyth Hall
Virginia Tech
Blacksburg, VA 24061

West Virginia University Soil Testing Lab
Department of Plant and Soil Science
Morgantown, WV 26506

Soil and Plant Analysis Laboratory
5711 Mineral Point Road
Madison, WI 53705

PHOTOGRAPHY CREDITS

The author gratefully acknowledges permission to use the following photographs: page 4 center, Willard Clay; pages 6 right, 82–83 top, 88, 90, 99 top, 135, 150, 172 bottom right, 205 center, Jerry Harpur; pages 7 bottom, 118 top, 168, 227 bottom right, Judith Bromley; pages 13 bottom left, 46, 47, 48, 49, 219 right center, Ron Lutsko; pages 57 bottom right, 152–153, 182 bottom right, 184, Ann Johnson; pages 58, 137, Richard Rowan; page 77, Michael Selig; page 97 left, Mark Hulla; pages 113, 186 top left, 188 bottom left, 189 bottom right, 199 top, 222 top, 223 bottom, 226 bottom left, 230 bottom left, Lisa Dreishpoon; page 117 top right, William Mills; page 118 center, Judith Bromley; 119, 210 top right, John Neubauer; page 133 bottom right, Linda Yang; page 145, Verena Portman; page 149 left, Harold Druse; page 151 bottom right, Curtice Taylor; page 155, Pam Harper; page 158 bottom center, Michael Dirr; pages 170 right, 171, 195, Dennis Tromberg; pages 180, 181, 191 bottom right, Michael McKinley; page 191 bottom left, Bill Ross; pages 192 top left, 201 bottom right, Hollen Johnson; page 203, Harold Hoffman; pages 225, 229, Kim Steele.